D0081448

DATE DUE			
APR 25 '83	MAR 2 3 '89	OCT 0 7 1998	
MAY 9 '8	APR 1 2 '89	NOV 3 0 1998	
APR 3 '8	MAY 1 1 '90	MAR 2 2 2001	
	OCT 2 '92		
NOV 1 1 '84	NOV 2 3 1993		
JUL 9 '85	APR 0 1 1995		
NOV 8 '86			
DEC 15 '86	OCT 2 5 1996		
MAY 5 '88	DEC 17 1996		
OCT 21 '88	APR 0 4 1998		
DEC 0 8 1995			

MARRIAGE AND FAMILY LIFE

MARRIAGE AND FAMILY LIFE

ERIC GOLANTY

School of New Resources

College of New Rochelle

&

BARBARA B. HARRIS

Foreword by Marvin B. Sussman

University of Delaware

HOUGHTON MIFFLIN COMPANY   Boston

Dallas   Geneva, Illinois   Hopewell, New Jersey   Palo Alto   London

Cover photograph by Ann McQueen.

Chapter-opening photographs:

Chapter 1, Robert B. Goodman/Black Star
Chapter 2, Owen Franken/Stock, Boston
Chapter 3, Susan Lapides
Chapter 4, Chris Morrow/Stock, Boston
Chapter 5, Paul Conklin
Chapter 6, Jeff Albertson/Stock, Boston
Chapter 7, Frank Siteman/Stock, Boston
Chapter 8, Jean-Claude Lejeune
Chapter 9, Paul Conklin
Chapter 10, Susan Lapides
Chapter 11, M. Sullivan/Black Star
Chapter 12, Horst Schafer/Photo Trends
Chapter 13, Frank Siteman/Stock, Boston
Chapter 14, Jean-Claude Lejeune
Chapter 15, Ellis Herwig/Stock, Boston
Chapter 16, Jean-Claude Lejeune
Chapter 17, Anna Kaufman Moon/Stock, Boston

Printed in the U.S.A.

Library of Congress Catalog Card Number: 81-82013

ISBN: 0-395-28721-9

To our loving families.

CONTENTS

FOREWORD

Some twenty years ago, I used to listen regularly over network radio to a marvelous book reviewer. The most important thing I learned from this commentator was that reading should be a joy. In our lifetime we have only so many hours to read, and he viewed his job as providing his listeners with choices of the best books that were available at any given time. To use a metaphor, he sifted the wheat from the chaff, using a reasonable set of criteria for judging the book's quality.

Readability is a major criterion I use in judging a book. If I have to struggle with sentences, paragraphs, or chapters, I feel uneasy and sense that something is amiss: the author has not been able to express the many ideas in a clear and understandable manner. A book in which good English rather than jargon is used is a joy to read. *Marriage and Family Life* is such a book.

A textbook should be based on facts. This means that the author should search for, locate, and use the best available thinking and research. The authors of this book have successfully examined and selected the more relevant investigations in the different subject areas and have presented these materials in a clear and succinct manner. The reader should have no difficulty in understanding the assumptions and conclusions reached by the authors.

A good textbook also treats fairly the material that is presented. Such topics as sex, family planning and abortion, child and spouse abuse, marital relationships, or the family's future evoke strong feelings. It is the author's responsibility to present such topics objectively, enabling the reader to form his or her own opinion. The authors of this volume, sensitive and aware of the range of emotions all of us have about particular family issues and problems, have gone out of their way to be unbiased. This is a solid achievement.

Another criterion of a fine textbook is its coverage. Demographers and institutionally oriented family specialists view families as static units, describing them in terms of their structure, activities, and functions. Other students and writers look at families as interacting systems creating their own dynamic. From this perspective, families are seen as primary groups consisting of persons who possess unique psychological, biological, physiological, and sociological attributes. *Marriage and Family Life* is intended for use in functional courses, yet it has a solid theoretical base. In Chapter 1, the authors present the basic structures of the family and its many activities and functions and discuss how these have changed over time. They then proceed to look at the more dynamic types of relationships, to give us an explanation of our own experience, and to prepare us for future experiences as marital partners, parents, providers, and family representatives in dealings with society and its institutions. The authors selectively use important theoretical concepts, which help the reader to integrate and utilize the information.

Good coverage is shown also by the choice of relevant topics. It is impressive to read a sensitive presentation of love and its meaning, a topic that is often ignored or romanticized in other textbooks. The authors are aware of the importance of working out verbal or written marriage contracts, and this coverage provides the reader with a knowledge of how to form a potentially successful marital relationship based on an informal or formal contract. The emphasis on parenthood is in keeping with the current trend of greater involvement of both parents in the parenting process and is related to the increasing trend for both marriage partners to be gainfully employed. The process of becoming a parent and the considerations given to child spacing, family planning, and activities for successful parenthood add to a comprehensive and meaningful presentation.

The four special topics discussed in Part V—"Separation, Divorce, and Remarriage," "The Changing Status of Women and Men," "Marriage and Family Life in the Later Years," and "Alternative Marital and Family Structures"—are realities that need honest and forthright presentations. Existing demographic data, values and feelings, economic conditions, and perceptions of what is a meaningful life affect the rates of divorce and remarriage, facilitate or impede the development of equitable relationships between men and women, create new requirements for older persons to maintain some form of family life and to use other formal and informal social support networks, and raise questions in the minds of the young as well as the old as to what are appropriate alternatives to legal marriage. The underlying theme is that everyone needs interaction with other persons who can provide emotional support, intimacy, love, and solidarity. In treating these topics, the authors are objective, stating it "as it is" and providing the reader with the information for making judgments as to what is relevant to his or her experience, feelings, and values.

Being practical and useful is another criterion of a good marriage and family textbook. The authors use boxed inserts, well-chosen quotations, illustrations, graphics, their own experiences, oral histories, and clinical data to make explanations more understandable and related to our everyday experience. The hypothetical examples and thought-provoking questions found at the end of each chapter urge the reader to pause and evaluate the chapter's material. The reader should consider all the issues raised by the authors and then determine their personal meaning and usefulness. This textbook provides a base for questioning as well as for confirmation.

The final hallmark of a good textbook is the stimulation it provides: the reader should be moved to take personal responsibility for learning. The reader's task is to try out and examine the fit of the authors' ideas with his or her own; to examine carefully the bases for acceptance or rejection of these ideas; and to assess their roots in empirical knowledge or well-thought-out conceptualizations. *Marriage and Family Life* stimulates readers to clarify their values, evaluate their personal relationships, and think for themselves.

Marvin B. Sussman

Unidel Professor of Human Behavior

University of Delaware

PREFACE

There are two equally important reasons for studying marriage and the family. The first is that almost all of us marry at some point in time and are members of one or more family systems throughout our lives. This very personal interest is coupled with the second reason for studying marriage and the family—the fact that marital and family life interact with, influence, and are influenced by social policy, education, the legal system, religious beliefs, and societal attitudes and behaviors.

Educators and counselors in the marriage and family field are becoming increasingly aware of the benefits of education for partnering and parenting. They recognize that many problems encountered in marital and familial relationships come from unrealistic expectations and unattainable ideals foisted upon individuals by tradition, myth, folklore, and media fantasy. By exposing these myths and exploring alternatives, education can help students develop a set of individually suitable values, beliefs, attitudes, and behaviors that hopefully will help them attain rewarding family lives.

Approach   In this book, we explore marriage and family issues from the standpoint of the individual; we also discuss how situations and interactions within the family are both helped and hampered by society at large. The core of this book is information from relevant research in the fields of psychology, sociology, demography, sexuality, and gerontology written and interpreted for today's college students. Woven into the core material are discussions of how various researchers, educators, and clinicians advise individuals to apply the knowledge gained from the research to their personal lives.

Content and Organization   The book is divided into an Introduction, five thematic parts, and an Appendix on family economics. In the Introduction we present an overview of the American family. We explore the basic structures and changing functions of the family, and the chapter ends with a section on the future of the American family.

In Part I, "Pairing," we explore the nature of love and intimacy, and how people choose partners and develop and deepen love relationships.

In Part II, "Sexual Expression," we discuss sexual values and behavior, as well as the anatomical, physiological, and interpersonal aspects of sexual interaction.

Part III focuses on marriage. In the first two chapters we explore the public side of marriage (religion, legal issues, and social mores) and the private side of marriage (roles and expectations). In a third chapter we explore marital interaction—the family life cycle, communication, resolving conflicts, expressing anger and fighting fair, and family violence.

Part IV is about parenthood. In one chapter we discuss pregnancy and childbirth, as well as infertility and the alternatives to pregnancy —adoption or choosing not to become a parent. Because so many couples are choosing to limit family size, we devote another chapter to the reasons for and methods of family planning. In a third chapter we discuss parenting: traditional and changing parental roles, the effects of children on parents, and the tasks of parenthood.

In Part V, we explore contemporary issues. Topics include separation, divorce, and remarriage; the changing status of women and men; marriage and family life in the later years; and alternative marital and family structures.

Learning Aids   This book is written in a clear and straightforward style and at a level that makes it accessible to students. Boxed supplemental materials which highlight issues in the chapters accompany the text, and each chapter ends with a values-clarification exercise called "Consider This," based on themes developed in the chapter. A glossary containing definitions of important terms is found at the end of the book.

Acknowledgments   We wrote this book because we believe that knowledge and understanding of marital, family, and other intimate relationships can help college students attain the happiness, satisfaction, and fulfillment they seek. We hope that our emphasis is comprehensive, eclectic, and focused on issues of concern to students in the 1980s. We wish to thank the following academic reviewers who read part or all of the manuscript in its various drafts:

- Carole M. Carroll, Middle Tennessee State University

- Robert L. Dunbar, City College of San Francisco
- Carol Rinkleib Ellison, University of California, San Francisco
- Mary Forth, West Hills College
- Richard Jolliff, El Camino College
- William M. Kephart, University of Pennsylvania
- James R. Long, Golden West College
- Willie Melton, Michigan Technological University
- William F. Powers, Suffolk County Community College
- Lynn E. Smith, Ricks College
- Marvin B. Sussman, University of Delaware
- Constance Verdi, Prince George's Community College

We also want to extend very special thanks to Carla Bierbaum, Livingston County Health Department, Howell, Michigan; Nancy Binkin, Family Planning Division, Center for Disease Control, U.S. Public Health Service; Rex Bitner, University of Colorado; Don Hanson, Seattle public schools; Nancy Hanson; Stefan Highsmith; and Evelyn Kawahara for their help and support. And, finally, we wish to thank our students at Sacramento City College and the staff and clients of the Boulder County Women's Resource Center, who shared their experiences with us.

Eric Golanty

Barbara B. Harris

INTRODUCTION

THE STRUCTURES AND FUNCTIONS OF THE MODERN FAMILY

In fact, the one permanent quality about the family is that it always has been in a state of perpetual transformation.

Ms.[1]

1

In the 1970s, questioning the future of the family was all the rage, and many assumed this ancient institution would die. In 1977, for example, sociologist Amitai Etzioni speculated that "if the present rate of increase in divorce and single households continues to accelerate as it did for the last ten years, by mid-1990 not one American family will be left."[2]

Etzioni is not alone in predicting the demise of the modern family. To support the theories that the American family is becoming extinct or that marriage is passé, critics cite evidence such as:

1.   The size of the average American household declined from 3.33 persons in 1960 to 2.78 persons in the late 1970s.[3] Since 1960, with the advent of improved family-planning methods, changing economic conditions, and an increased awareness of world overpopulation, people have been having fewer children.

2.   Forty percent of all marriages end in divorce. The divorce rate has more than doubled over the last two decades (see Figure 1.1), and currently there are well over one million divorces each year.[4] The high divorce rate seems to reflect the greater emphasis on marital satisfaction, the changing divorce laws, and the improvement in women's rights and economic opportunities.

3.   By the late 1970s, there were an estimated two million "unmarried-couple" households.[5] Changes in social values and contraceptive practices have enabled individuals of all ages to experiment with different forms of nonmarital cohabitation. In addition, tax and social security laws, which often favor unmarried persons, provide additional impetus for nonmarital cohabitation.

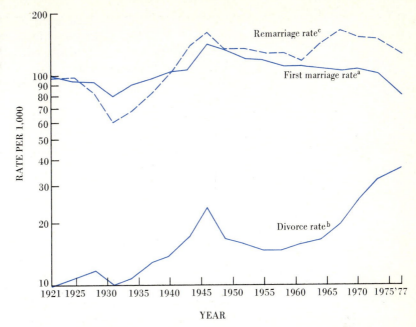

FIGURE 1.1

Rates of first marriage, divorce, and remarriage for women in the United States, 1921–1977.

Source: Paul C. Glick and Arthur J. Norton, "Marrying, Divorcing, and Living Together in the U.S. Today," *Population Bulletin*, 32, No. 5 (1977): 5. Courtesy of the Population Reference Bureau, Inc., Washington, D.C.
[a]First marriages per 1,000 single women 14 to 44 years old
[b]Divorces per 1,000 married women 14 to 44 years old
[c]Remarriages per 1,000 widowed and divorced women 14 to 54 years old

4.   Approximately 23 percent of all U.S. households are one-person households.[6] This figure includes divorced and widowed individuals, as well as the increasing numbers of people who are delaying marriage or choosing to remain unmarried.

5.   It is estimated that approximately 45 percent of all children will live or spend time with a separated, divorced, or widowed parent.[7] Furthermore, the number of children born to unmarried mothers has more than doubled in the past three decades, and juvenile delinquency remains a serious problem.[8]

Although this evidence suggests to some that family life is on the wane, other marriage and family statistics tell us that the family system is still an important part of American society. Ninety-six percent of the Americans surveyed in a recent national poll said that "having a good family life" was a very important goal in their lives.[9] Other research has shown that 95 percent of Americans marry at least once and that two out of three married couples are persons living together in their first marriage.[10] Apparently, most Americans not only marry but also stay married. Moreover, the rate of remarriage after divorce is very high (see Figure 1.1), indicating that many people believe that family life is a genuinely rewarding experience.

Traditionally, marriage and family life have been considered rather simplistically as the interaction of a husband and wife and the production and raising of children. In fact, however, people belong to many different kinds of marital and family relationships. Some of these family structures, such as single-parent families, are very common, but others, such as group marriage, are rare. Apparently, marriage and family life are important to many, but the exact structure of the marital and family relationships people enter into differs according to tradition, economic and social necessities, and psychological needs.

Because establishing a family is likely to be one of the most important decisions of an individual's life, the decision must be made with as much wisdom and care as possible. Although many successfully married couples who have raised happy, healthy children admit that there is probably an element of luck in their success, it is nevertheless true that the more people know about marriage and family life, the more likely it is that they will make wise choices.

In order to help make those choices, in this chapter we examine the modern family—its history, structures, functions, and adaptations to recent social change. This information provides a foundation upon which a person can better assess his or her own needs and requirements for a suitable and satisfying family life style.

WHAT IS THE FAMILY?

Thirty years ago, anthropology professor George Peter Murdock defined the family as "a social group characterized by common residence, economic cooperation, and reproduction. It includes adults of both sexes, at least two of whom maintain a socially approved sexual relationship, and one or more children, [either their] own or adopted, of the sexually cohabiting adults."[11]

Murdock's definition describes the *conjugal*, or *nuclear*, family, which consists of a husband, a wife, and offspring. In most Western societies today, the nuclear family is the principal family unit. Everyone belongs to at least one nuclear family, the family into which he or she is born, called the *family of origin* or *orientation*. If one marries and has children, he or she becomes a member of a second nuclear family, called the *family of procreation*.

Although the nuclear family seems natural to Americans, the family structure of other societies is frequently based upon consanguine relationships. The *consanguine, or extended, family* is either a nuclear family linked by a common ancestry to other kin relations or two or more nuclear families that live together or near each other. Suppose, for example, that there is a family of five brothers. Three of the brothers marry, creating new nuclear families, and these three families and the two single brothers all live near their parents. These individuals and their respective families form an extended family.

To distinguish between conjugal and consanguine relationships, it is helpful to classify your own relatives according to these two forms. Although both conjugal and nuclear can be used to refer to the unit of the husband, wife, and children, the term *conjugal* is defined as the marital unit, the husband-and-wife relation. *Consanguine* means "of the same blood," or biologically connected. Therefore, your spouse and in-laws are conjugal relatives, and your parents, siblings, and parents' relations are consanguine relatives. Children may be classified as either conjugal or consanguine. Technically, they are conjugal relations, since they are products of the conjugal unit, but definitionally they are consanguine or blood relatives, biologically connected to both parents.

Kinship binds nuclear families into extended families.

Harvey Stein

In cultures in which nuclear families are clustered into clans or tribes, the emotional ties among the members of the extended family tend to be strong. In a technological and highly mobile society like ours, however, the contact between members of extended families can be infrequent because the nuclear families live far away from one another; this infrequent contact may weaken the emotional ties among extended family members. One consequence of weakened extended-family ties is that more demands are placed on the nuclear family to satisfy the needs of its members. When your brothers, sisters, aunts, uncles, grandparents, and cousins live in different parts of the country, the members of your nuclear family become dependent on one another for companionship and emotional support.

A major difference between conjugal and consanguine families is that the conjugal family is apparently more fragile than the consanguine family—that is, it is more susceptible to disruption. Divorce, desertion, illness, and death of a spouse seriously disrupt the conjugal relationship. In contrast, individuals belonging to an extended network of kin relations may more easily withstand a variety of stresses. For example, although a widowed individual may experience extreme physical and emotional isolation as a member of a dissolved conjugal relationship, he or she can easily be absorbed into the broader circle of family relationships as a member of a consanguine family. The consanguine family also is better equipped, economically and psychologically, to take care of aged members, a problem in our society that has not yet been resolved satisfactorily. Despite these disadvantages, however, the nuclear family seems to be the relationship most compatible with modern society. Its structure enables people to be independent, mobile, and adaptable to the changing social conditions of a highly technological society.

A VARIETY OF FAMILY STRUCTURES

In the United States, the nuclear family, consisting of husband, wife, and children, captures the most attention. But it is by no means the only family structure existing in this country. There are several other types of families, including the childless family, the single-parent family, the extended family, unmarried heterosexual or homosexual couples living together *(cohabitation)*, and communal families. Each of these is a structure that may meet an individual's social, emotional, and economic needs.

Despite the widespread belief that the traditional nuclear family (a breadwinner father, a housewife mother, and two or more children under eighteen years old) is the dominant family structure in the United States, census data clearly indicate that this is not so. A growing number of households* are made up of other types of family structures. As shown in Figure 1.2, the most significant changes during the 1970s were increases in nonnuclear family households, particularly in the number of single parents and the number of people living alone, and a dramatic decline in the number of households composed of a married couple and their children. Because at least half of all American

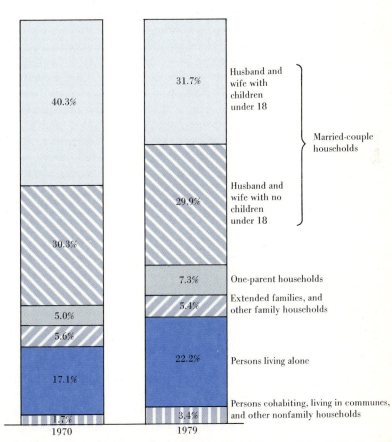

FIGURE 1.2
Changes in composition of American households from 1970 to 1979

Source: U.S. Bureau of the Census, *Current Population Reports*, Series P–20, No. 352, "Household and Family Characteristics: March 1979," Washington, D.C., U.S. Government Printing Office, 1980, Table A, p. 1.

*The terms *household* and *family* are often used interchangeably because a common residence is usually one of the characteristics used to define a family.

married women with children under eighteen work and because expected family size has decreased, the number of families that can be defined as traditionally nuclear actually represents a surprisingly small proportion of American families.

Some people claim that this variety of family structures is evidence of the family's demise. Others argue just the opposite—that the family is as popular as ever and that the variety of family life styles shows that the family is adapting to changes in modern society.

This plurality of family structures has led some sociologists to expand Murdock's definition of the nuclear family. The Maryland Coalition on the Family, for example, suggests that the family is "a unit of two or more persons in a supportive relationship based on such factors as marriage, cohabitation, blood relationships, or legal dependency."[12] This definition encompasses many family structures and further emphasizes the variety of familial relationships existing today.

Although the family is still the predominant social institution, there is no question that it has changed, even during the past decade. Divorce rates are higher than ever, and people are delaying marriage and having fewer children. However, these trends do not necessarily point toward the family's extinction. Rather, they suggest that the institution is adapting to current social and economic conditions. In the following section, we shall discuss how and why the family is changing in terms of the economic, psychological, and social functions it performs.

THE CHANGING FUNCTIONS OF THE AMERICAN FAMILY

Anthropologists and sociologists have determined that in all societies, families have some or all of the following functions: reproduction, socialization of children, sexual regulation, economic support, education, religious training, companionship, protection, and recreation. Depending on a particular culture's social and economic characteristics, these traditional family functions are performed to a greater or lesser degree by a variety of individuals and institutions.

The modern American family carries out the traditional family functions differently from the way the early American family did. Typically, the early American family was a self-contained economic unit which produced and provided for itself. Strong ties existed among the members of extended families, and socialization, religious indoctrination, and educational training were conducted within the home. The family adhered to strict sexual mores and was its own source of protection and entertainment.

But as people began to work outside of the home, their mobility increased, which in turn weakened traditional family ties and placed additional emotional demands on the nuclear family. Moreover, as men began working away from home, women became dependent on them for financial support, and children were no longer regarded as economic assets. Education was emphasized more, social values and norms changed, and the emotional support of the conjugal relationship became more important. As more and more demands were placed on marriage and the family, the marital relationship began to acquire new forms and to change its various functions.

Economic Function

The early American family was an economic unit and all family members cooperated in providing housing, food, clothing, and protection. Although there was a division of labor based on gender, it is important to note that both women and men had productive tasks. Sociologist Gail Fullerton points out that "there was no clear line between a wife's productive functions and her domestic functions. Laundry—a domestic maintenance chore—began with soapmaking—a productive task"[13] (see Box 1.1).

The husband's and wife's skills complemented each other, and their children also contributed to the economic unit. Before and during the early years of the Industrial Revolution, many families depended on their children's labor. In fact, children were considered economic assets, each representing another laborer who could increase the family's economic output.

With the onset of the Industrial Revolution, the American family changed from a producing unit to a consuming unit. Economic activity moved from the household to the factory. The machine offered the individual "a higher standard of living in return for sacrificing his traditional life centered in the home and family."[14]

These changes had a marked effect on American domestic life. The family no longer produced much as an economic unit. With the passage of compulsory-schooling legislation and child-labor laws, children became economic liabilities instead of assets. As the impact of industrialization spread, smaller families became more economically desirable than larger families. It is little wonder that instead of large families (the typical family of 1790 had eight children), a small family with two children is now the norm.

BOX 1.1 Lye Soap

Before washing clothes, the frontier wife first had to perform the arduous task of making lye soap, which this modern-day grandmother recalls:

I remember my grandmother mixing lye with lard. For the lard she used hog crackling (the crisp remains of fat after rendering). The grease and lye would have to be boiled down until the mixture became thick. When it thickened, it was poured into pans and set out for two or three days until it solidified. Then it was cut into bars—ready for use.

Before lye was available in stores, it was made at home from wood ashes. Soft wood was preferable because hard wood had more color and made a darker yellow soap. Ashes were placed in a leach (a wooden tub) and soaked with water. As the water dripped through the ashes, the brown liquid (lye) was caught in a trough or container. The homemade lye then was boiled with the rendered fat until the mixture thickened. Although each step seems simple, the overall process was actually long and tedious.

From the authors' files

Educational Function

Education is another family function that has undergone major change. In the early American family, children were likely to follow in their parents' footsteps, and hence their education was largely vocational. Children were taught how to work on the farm or in the shop, as well as to read, write, and do simple arithmetic.

During the nineteenth century, however, the nation became more aware of the importance of education. Formal education began to replace family-based education. A major justification for free public schools was that the family was finding it more and more difficult to prepare children adequately for productive roles in the increasingly complex American economy, as the following quotation suggests.

Compulsory, free public education was given many justifications, but among the most common was the argument that families—especially immigrant families—simply could not educate their children for a productive role in the growing increasingly complicated American economy. Schools, it was claimed, could do what families were failing or unable to do: teach good work habits, pass on essential skills, form good character, and, in short, Americanize.[15]

The long-term trend in American education can be summed up in one word: more. There now are more schools, more students and teachers,

High school and bachelor's degrees conferred in the United States, 1870–1977 (per 100,000 population)

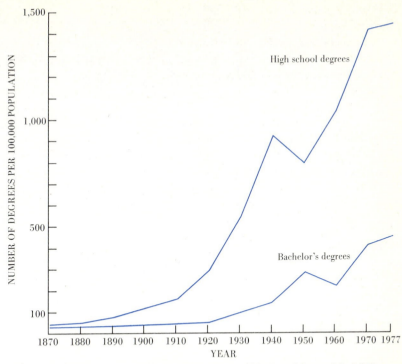

Sources: U.S. Bureau of the Census, *Historical Statistics of the United States, Colonial Times to 1970, Bicentennial Edition*, Part 1, Washington, D.C., U.S. Government Printing Office, 1975; U.S. Bureau of the Census, *Statistical Abstract of the United States: 1979* (100th ed.), Washington, D.C., U.S. Government Printing Office, 1979.

and more days in the school year. In the early 1880s, the average school term was 130 days, but the students actually attended school only about 80 days per year. By the late 1960s, the school year had lengthened to 180 days, and the average number of days attended had increased to 164.[16] Another indication of this trend is the dramatic increase in high school and college degrees granted (see Figure 1.3). Children now start school at an earlier age and leave at a later one. Formal education, both academic and vocational, has long since ceased to be a family function. In fact, it is now legally difficult to justify keeping one's children out of school.

Reproductive and Socialization Functions

The family has retained the biological function of procreation, as well as the responsibility for the support and socialization of children. The

Reproduction and the socialization of children continue to be important family functions.

Arthur Grace/Stock, Boston

family is the first socializing agent that teaches the child language and the society's written and unwritten rules. The family also still provides the emotionally supportive climate in which the child can learn and internalize the values, goals, attitudes, and behaviors of others. Other socializing agents, however—schools, the child's peers, and the mass media—also contribute to this socialization, as this young stepfather describes:

Both Sarah and I are very involved with our careers, and at times, it bothers me that we don't have a lot of extra time to spend with our son. Although I know that David picks up a lot of stuff from his friends and his Cub Scout pack, it doesn't upset me that other people and organizations are influencing him—in fact, it seems natural. But I don't like how television influences him. I'm convinced that as long as you have a loving, supportive family, and you try to be together nights and on the weekends, your kids will turn out O.K. It's the people who never see their kids and don't care who are headed for trouble.

From the authors' files

Regulation of Sexual Relations

All societies regulate sex in some manner, and the most effective regulating institution for sexual relations is the family. The family has traditionally provided the adult members of our society with an approved method for fulfilling affectional and sexual needs. In our society, many people still expect husbands and wives to have sexual relations with only each other, and not before marriage. However, social values and attitudes have changed, and premarital and extramarital relations no longer carry the same stigma of wrongdoing that they once did.

The one exception to this is the *incest taboo*, the strict prohibition against sex relations and marriage between close relatives. Although our society has a strict incest taboo, incest does occur, and the reported incidence of incest in the United States is apparently increasing.[17] Psychologists Blair and Rita Justice suggest that the increase in reported incest is not necessarily due to the more frequent occurrence, but rather to the victims revealing their experiences: "The problem with the taboo against incest is that it has not kept sex in the family from occurring as much as it has kept people from reporting the problem, becoming informed about incest, and taking steps to treat and prevent incest."[18] Justice and Justice indicate that individual, marital, family, and group counseling are helpful in resolving the emotional trauma of incest. It is hoped that future research will uncover the causal factors of incest and offer suggestions for its prevention.

Other Changing Functions

A variety of other traditional functions have been transferred to people and institutions outside the family.

1. Religious training is now provided mainly by institutions outside the family. Family devotionals, usually led by the father, were often held in early America. Later, when communities built churches, attendance became a family activity. But during recent years, church attendance has decreased, and although religion continues to be a vital force in the American way of life, it is centered less and less in the family.

2. Care of the sick, the aged, and the mentally ill is no longer the sole responsibility of the family. Today, this function is carried out mainly by doctors, nurses, medical institutions, and homes for the elderly.

3. The "Code of the West"—the belief that individuals and families have a right to protect themselves—no longer exists. At present, this security function is provided by the various governmental services that offer police protection.

4. The family used to be the center for recreational activities, but now a variety of businesses that cater to Americans' leisure time have taken over this function. And since the 1950s, many people have been spending their free time watching television. Unfortunately, sitting together in front of the TV is not a good substitute for other types of family communication and interaction.

Shared recreational activities promote family communication and interaction.

Horst Schaefer/Photo Trends

Companionship and Emotional Support

In our industrialized society, companionship and emotional support have increased in importance more than any other family function has. The family is the major source of companionship and emotional gratification. Its intimate relations provide support, love, stability, and continuity, as well as contributing to feelings of self-acceptance and self-worth.

In addition to their nuclear families, many people rely on extended families, community ties, and friendship networks for love, support, and recognition (see Box 1.2). Traditional sources of emotional support, however, have diminished in both intensity and longevity. Our increasingly mobile and complex society often produces anonymity, loneliness, and transitory relationships. It has become more difficult to maintain lifelong friendships and to establish community ties. As society becomes more complex, people often experience isolation and alienation. This in turn places an even greater number of emotional demands on family relationships.

The foundation of a nuclear family is the bond between two adults. Unfortunately, marriages often fail because the partners expect total emotional support from each other. But because people have many different needs, expectations, and emotional, educational, and occupational histories, and because their life situations are complex, it is unrealistic to expect one individual to meet all of another's needs. Yet many people continue to search for their "one and only."

Because many people depend heavily on these adult emotional bonds and expect so much from their relationships, they find it difficult to tolerate discontent. As a result, such discontent frequently leads to separation or divorce. Fullerton feels that this may be a result of high expectations:

Because marriage is now more a matter of emotional than economic necessity, we regard as a failure any marriage that is not marked by a high degree of intimacy and emotional commitment. We Americans have concentrated so much emotional need on the conjugal relationship that we have overloaded it. . . . It may be that the American divorce rate is high not because we think so little of marriage but rather because we expect so much of it.[19]

The traditional family did not emphasize emotional gratification as much as families do today. In past generations, marriages often were arranged on the basis of property, social class, or religion; love, if

More and more people are divorced or widowed or are remaining single. When people speak of families and intimate relationships, they usually mean marital relationships or blood ties. But friends often support people as much, if not more, than families do. According to author Jane Howard,

The trouble with the families many of us were born to is not that they are meddlesome ogres but that they are too far away. In emergencies we rush across continents and if need be oceans to their sides, as they do to ours. Maybe we even make a habit of seeing them, once or twice a year, for the sheer pleasure of it. But blood ties seldom dictate our addresses. Our blood kin are often too remote to ease us from our Tuesdays to our Wednesdays. For this we must rely on our families of friends. If our relatives are not, do not wish to be, or for whatever reasons cannot be our friends, then by some complex alchemy we must transform our friends into our relatives.*

The phenomenon of "transforming friends into relatives" suggests to some that, indeed, traditional family life is declining. Others believe, however, that the substitution of friendships for family relationships symbolizes the reorganization of the family into different forms. What do you think?

*Jane Howard, *Families*, New York, Simon & Schuster, 1978, p. 261.

considered at all, was secondary. Today, people seek meaningful and emotionally satisfying relationships, and most would never consider marrying someone they did not love. Although other family functions have been transferred to people and institutions outside the home, the family is still the principal source of companionship, emotional satisfaction, and support.

FORCES THAT CHANGED THE AMERICAN FAMILY

Thus far, we have discussed the structures and the functions of the family. These both affect each other, and if they conflict, one or the other may be forced to change. For example, the family is expected to be responsible for both the care and socialization of its children and for its economic survival. But the responsibility of fulfilling these two functions may be impossible for the single-parent family. Either the parent has to accept responsibility for his or her children and allow other institutions, such as a welfare agency, to provide economic assistance, or the parent must continue to work but delegate child care to centers or to other individuals. The parent might also change the structure of the family by remarrying or living with friends or relatives. Thus, the family either loses some of its functions to outside individuals and institutions, or it changes its structure in order to adapt.

Societal pressures can affect the degree and direction of this change. It is essential that the family's structure and functions be compatible with its role in society. For example, society could help preserve single-parent families by providing inexpensive child care programs which would allow the parent to provide economic support for his or her family. Such programs—along with other options such as extended maternity leave, paternity leave, and more flexible working arrangements—would also help families in which both partners work.

Usually the family, rather than society, has been the institution to change. In the short term, it is easier for a family to adapt to social conditions than it is for society and social attitudes to change. But as the number of families facing change and adjustments grows, public opinion and legislation should encourage society to adapt to and be compatible with a variety of family structures.[20]

In addition to structural and functional changes in the family, social attitudes and values also have changed. One example of attitudinal change is the public's reaction to divorce. Although divorce was once considered a public disgrace, it is no longer highly stigmatized. In fact, the current marriage and divorce laws often are cited as major causes of our society's high divorce rates. It is more probable, however, that these rates reflect the high value placed on marital happiness and satisfaction. (The issue of divorce will be discussed fully in Chapter 14, "Separation, Divorce, and Remarriage.")

Similarly, attitudes toward alternative family styles also have changed. In the past, the stigma of deviancy was attached to communes, single-parent households, group marriages, and homosexual cohabitation or marriage. Recently, there has been more awareness and tolerance of alternative styles. In fact, such television shows as *One Day at a Time* and *Alice* popularize the single-parent family as a viable family structure with its own share of conflicts and successes. It is interesting to note that *The Waltons* and *Little House on the Prairie*, two television examples of traditional families, have historical settings.

Three other social phenomena contributing to changing family patterns are industrialization, the changing status of both women and men, and greater sexual permissiveness.

1. *Industrialization* The preindustrial American family was a self-contained unit which did almost everything for itself. Most families farmed, studied, worshipped, and played together. The family became

more mobile as its members began working outside the home and became dependent on industry for their livelihood. This increase in mobility weakened the nuclear family's ties with the extended family. In addition, the educational, religious, recreational, and socializing functions, which previously had been centered in the family, began to be taken over by other institutions.

2. *The Changing Status of Women and Men*   Chapter 15 is devoted to the changing status of both women and men. Until fairly recently, wives were expected to be subservient to their husbands. Denied the opportunity to work outside of the home, forbidden by law to vote or hold public office, deprived of formal education, and granted almost no legal rights, women traditionally were relegated to second-class citizenship. In some societies, this state of affairs still exists. In the United States, however—mostly because of movements for women's social equality and legal rights—the inequalities between the sexes have begun to disappear. Today, women can vote, and many have achieved economic independence. Career opportunities for women are also expanding.

Changes toward equality have also affected marriage and the family. The decline of the marriage rate during the 1970s may be attributed to the fact that women now have more alternatives to marriage. As mentioned earlier, because economic independence is now available to women, many no longer feel "trapped" in unhappy marriages, and this may have contributed to the rising divorce rate. On the other hand, women's greater financial contributions have economically strengthened marriage and have led to a more flexible division of family responsibilities.

3. *Sexual Permissiveness*   Several factors have contributed to the increase in sexual permissiveness in recent decades (see Chapter 6, "Sexual Values and Behavior"). These factors include the lessening of religious influence, the advent of modern contraceptives, and changing social norms. In the United States, these changing attitudes have been shown by the popularity of sex and marriage manuals such as *Open Marriage*, by Nena and George O'Neill; *The Joy of Sex*, by Alex Comfort; and *Beyond Monogamy*, edited by James and Lynn Smith.

The availability of effective contraception—especially the introduction of the birth control pill in the early 1960s—is one of the principal reasons for the change in sexual behavior. Using contraceptive devices enables people to separate the two main reasons for sexual relations: procreation and recreation. Contraceptives have greatly reduced the fear of pregnancy and permitted the increased emphasis on sexual satisfaction. These changes have influenced sexual and interpersonal relationships, both inside and outside the traditional confines of the marital institution.

CHOICE AND CHANGE: THE FUTURE OF THE AMERICAN FAMILY

Structural and attitudinal changes have increased the possibilities for family life styles. When asked to define the American family, what typically comes to mind is a middle-class, father-headed, mother-at-home-with-the-two-kids family. Although less than half of the U.S. population are members of this type of nuclear family, the mass media, books, schools, families, and politicians constantly proclaim that this is the "ideal family." The conclusion that the family is becoming extinct stems from this narrow definition of the family. The fact that only a small proportion of today's families are classified as some form of nuclear does not mean that the family is dying. It does suggest, however, that the family has many viable structures and that individuals now are able to choose among many workable life styles.

The future of the family will continue to be debated. Those who predict its demise point to high divorce rates and low birth rates. Others feel that these statistics merely reveal the family's perpetual change. Sociologist Jessie Bernard is one of the many who predict an optimistic future for the family.

The future of marriage is, I believe, as assured as any social form can be. There are, in fact, few human relationships with a more assured future. For men and women will continue to want intimacy, they will continue to want the thousand and one ways in which men and women share and reassure one another. They will continue to want to celebrate their mutuality, to experience the mystic unity that once led the church to consider marriage a sacrament. They will therefore, as far into the future as we can project, continue to commit themselves to each other.[21]

In discussing the future of the family, Bernard also explores the alternatives available to the individual.

Not only does marriage have a future, it has many futures. There will be, for example, options that permit different kinds of relationships over time for different stages in life, and options that permit different life styles or living arrangements according to the nature of the relationships. . . . People will be able to tailor their relationships to their circumstances and preferences. The most characteristic aspect of marriage in the future will be precisely the array of options available to different people who want different things from their relationships with one another.[22]

Choice and change aptly describe the family of the future. Change may produce family structures that are efficient and effective, and the individual will have a variety of life styles from which to choose. People are vitally concerned with forming intimate relationships and with being part of a supportive family system. Nevertheless, the structure of the system varies and is determined by many economic, psychological, and situational factors.

SUMMARY

Is the modern American family dying? Many people seem to think so. The divorce rate has been increasing, people are having fewer children, and more and more people are living together as couples without getting legally married. On the other hand, 95 percent of Americans marry at least once, and a high percentage of the formerly married get married again.

Rather than the family's dying, it is more likely that these and other trends indicate dramatic changes in the family's forms and functions. Traditionally, families performed the functions of producing and socializing children, regulating adult sexual behavior, and providing economic and emotional support, recreation, religious indoctrination, education, and protection. An examination of the history of the American family with regard to these functions shows that the family has changed dramatically in the last two hundred years. But the family is not becoming disorganized; rather, it is reorganizing into different forms so as to adapt to current economic and social conditions. As a result, the family's size has shrunk, many of its traditional functions have now been taken over by other institutions, and many of the functions it has retained have been modified.

CONSIDER THIS

Although Tony was alone, he didn't think of himself as lonely. He knew that his move to New York had been a wise decision—at least for his career. But his recent divorce and the distance he had placed between himself and his family and friends had unsettled his life. Tony missed the companionship he'd become accustomed to in his eight-year marriage. One of his reasons for moving to New York was that several of his college friends were in the area, and he hoped to re-establish his old friendships.

Since he had become disillusioned with marriage, Tony avoided any serious involvement with the new women in his life because he believed that marital and family relationships couldn't work for him. He was successful at his job and socialized easily with his coworkers. Tony spent a lot of time with his school friends, Jim and Stan, and their wives, and this companionship met many of his emotional needs.

For many single people in big cities, holiday times can be very lonely, and so Tony was glad that he could spend Thanksgiving with Jim and Stan. Being invited for Thanksgiving made him feel comfortable, and it relieved what he knew was a temporary "holiday loneliness."

Questions
1. Do Tony's friends provide a real family for him?
2. Do you think that good friendships can be as fulfilling as family relationships?
3. How do you define the family?
4. What is your own family structure? Is there any particular family structure that you feel is best suited for you? What factors influenced your answer?
5. What functions does your family perform? Which of the traditional family functions do you feel should be performed by the family and not by other social institutions?
6. What is your prediction for your own family's future?
7. What is your prediction for the future of the family in general?

NOTES

1. *Ms.*, "Who Is the Real Family?" 7 (August 1978): 43.
2. Amitai Etzioni, "The Family: Is It Obsolete?" *Journal of Current Social Issues*, 14 (Winter 1977): 4.
3. U.S. Bureau of the Census, *Current Population Reports*, Series P–20, No. 345, "Households and Families by Type: March 1979 (Advance Report)," Washington, D.C., U.S. Government Printing Office, October 1979, Table 2, p. 3.
4. U.S. Bureau of the Census, *Statistical Abstract of the United States: 1979* (100th ed.), Washington, D.C., U.S. Government Printing Office, 1979, No. 48, p. 40; No. 117, p. 81.

5. Paul C. Glick and Arthur J. Norton, "Marrying, Divorcing, and Living Together in the U.S. Today," *Population Bulletin*, 32, No. 5, Washington, D.C., Population Reference Bureau, 1977, p. 3.

6. U.S. Bureau of the Census, *Current Population Reports*, Series P–20, No. 357, "Households and Families, by Type: March 1980 (Advance Report)," Washington, D.C., U.S. Government Printing Office, 1980, p. 1.

7. Paul C. Glick, "Social Change and the American Family," in National Conference on Social Welfare, *Social Welfare Forum, 1977*, New York, Columbia University Press, 1978, p. 53.

8. Walter F. Mondale, "Introducing a Special Report: The Family in Trouble," *Psychology Today*, 10 (May 1977): 39.

9. Louis Harris, "Factors Considered Important in Life," Louis Harris Survey Release, January 1, 1981, p. 1.

10. Glick and Norton, "Marrying, Divorcing, and Living Together in the U.S. Today," p. 3.

11. George Peter Murdock, *Social Structure*, New York, Macmillan, 1949, p. 1.

12. "Letters from Readers," *Ms.*, 7 (December 1978): 3.

13. Gail Putney Fullerton, *Survival in Marriage*, New York, Holt, Rinehart & Winston, 1972, p. 6.

14. Edward Cornish, "The Future of the Family: Intimacy in an Age of Loneliness," *Futurist*, 13 (February 1979): 45.

15. Kenneth Keniston and the Carnegie Council on Children, *All Our Children*, New York, Harcourt Brace Jovanovich, 1977, p. 15.

16. Abbott L. Ferriss, *Indicators of Trends in American Education*, New York, Russell Sage Foundation, 1969, p. 384.

17. Blair Justice and Rita Justice, *The Broken Taboo*, New York, Human Sciences Press, 1979, p. 260.

18. Ibid.

19. Fullerton, *Survival in Marriage*, p. 51.

20. For a further discussion of the interplay between societal conditions and the structure and functions of the family, see Rodney Stark, *Social Problems*, New York, Random House, 1975, pp. 368–370.

21. Jessie Bernard, *The Future of the Family*, New York, World Publishing, 1972, p. 301.

22. Ibid., p. 302.

SUGGESTED READINGS

Bane, Mary Jo. *Here to Stay: American Families in the Twentieth Century*. New York, Basic Books, 1976. A discussion of the family's future based on an analysis of past and current U.S. population information.

Glick, Paul C., and Arthur J. Norton. "Marrying, Divorcing, and Living Together in the U.S. Today." *Population Bulletin*, 32, No. 5. Population Reference Bureau, Washington D.C., 1977. An examination of the changing U.S. patterns of marriage, divorce, and living arrangements in the mid-1970s.

Knox, David. "Trends in Marriage and the Family—The 1980's." *Family Relations*, April 1980, pp. 145–150. An overview of the latest trends in sex roles, love relationships, mate selection and engagement, marriage and cohabitation, dual-career marriage, sexual behavior and fulfillment, planning, producing, and rearing children, divorce, and gerontology.

Osborn, D. Keith, and Janie Osborn. "Childhood at the Turn of the Century." *Family Coordinator*, January 1978, pp. 27–32. An interesting historical look at child rearing and family life.

Sussman, Marvin B. "The Family Today: Is It an Endangered Species?" *Children Today*, March/April 1978, pp. 32–45. An examination of the strengths and weaknesses of various family structures.

U.S. News and World Report. "The American Family: Bent—But Not Broken." June 16, 1980, pp. 48–61. A special report on the changing American family.

I PAIRING

LOVE

All you need is love.

Song by John Lennon and Paul McCartney

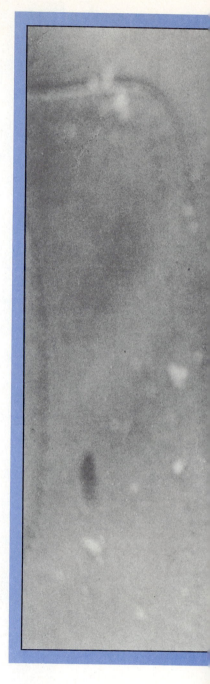

2

Love is the "glue" of marriage and family relationships. This special and familiar feeling leads to the attachment and bonding between marital partners and other pairing intimates, between parents and children, and between members of a closely knit extended family or community. Without love to motivate them to enter into intimate associations, people would behave like "loners" who must fulfill by themselves most of their basic psychological and physiological needs. Such loners would be like *Star Trek's* usually emotionless Mr. Spock, for whom cooperative associations with others are not inspired by an inner need for bonding or the exchange of affection, but merely by the reasoning that many tasks are accomplished more efficiently by joint effort. The mating behavior of our hypothetical loners (as it is for Mr. Spock) would be solely the expression of some periodic biological urge.

But people are not emotionless loners. For most of us, establishing and maintaining intimate relationships is one of life's principal activities. At some time, most people become very concerned about the role of love in their lives and embark on a quest for a "true love" with whom they can "live happily ever after." Even Mr. Spock, who is from a planet where behavior is motivated entirely by logic, occasionally falls in love. He feels affection for others because he is a hybrid creature and has inherited emotions from his human mother.

Love is very important to most of us; virtually everyone wants to have the feelings of closeness, acceptance, understanding, and appreciation that love can bring. A recent survey of over 100,000 people indicated that being in love was one of the primary factors in achieving happiness (see Table 2.1).[1]

But many people are ambivalent about being in love. Perhaps because of a previous unsuccessful love relationship, some people

TABLE 2.1   Reasons People Give for Their Happiness

	Married Women	Married Men	Single Women	Single Men
1.	Being in love	Personal growth	Friends and social life	Friends and social life
2.	Marriage	Being in love	Being in love	Job or primary activity
3.	Partner's happiness	Marriage	Job or primary activity	Being in love
4.	Sex life	Job or primary activity	Recognition, success	Recognition, success
5.	Recognition, success	Partner's happiness	Personal growth	Sex life
6.	Personal growth	Sex life	Sex life	Personal growth
7.	Job or primary activity	Recognition, success	Health	Finances
8.	Friends and social life	Friends and social life	Body and attractiveness	House or apartment
9.	Health	Being a parent	Finances	Body and attractiveness
10.	Being a parent	Finances	House or apartment	Health

Source: Adapted from J. L. Freedman, *Happy People*, New York, Harcourt Brace Jovanovich, 1978, p. 41.

avoid being in love because they fear the potentially unpleasant aspects of love relationships. Lovers sometimes disappoint us, hurt us emotionally (and physically), or capture our attention so completely that we lose our identities and freedom to act. Loving can sometimes be so intense that a person's mind and energies cannot be focused on the other things in life that are both necessary and rewarding. As one pre-law student put it,

I don't want to fall in love. It takes too much effort. Sure I like it, but when I'm in love, I spend too much time with my lover, I can't concentrate, and so my grades go down. That's something I don't want right now.

From the authors' files

To love is also to risk—to risk feeling like a failure when a relationship ends, to risk feeling rejected if a lover terminates a relationship, or to risk feeling guilty if you terminate a relationship.

Everyone wants the feelings of closeness, acceptance, understanding, and appreciation that love can bring.

Paul Conklin

Despite the host of complications inherent in being in love, most people actively seek out and try to maintain lasting love relationships. So great is the need to belong and to share that people risk disappointment and occasional emotional devastation in the hopes of establishing successful love relationships.

No single plan can guide all people to find successful love relationships. But a consideration of the qualities of love may help people better understand the role of love in their lives and may help them achieve their personal goals for love in life.

In this chapter we discuss the nature of love and some aspects of love relationships.

WHAT IS LOVE?

For centuries philosophers and writers have tried to define love, and the fact that today there still is no definition acceptable to everyone testifies to the difficulty of the task. But most people seem to have little trouble recognizing love as it relates to their own experience. A survey of over a thousand college students, for example, found that nearly 90 percent thought they knew what love was.[2] Some knew about love because they had had direct experience with a situation they had recognized as involving love, whereas others knew about it because they identified

with the feelings of love expressed by parents, friends, or fictional lovers in books, in movies, or on television.

One of the reasons that love is so difficult to define is that people apply the term love to almost everything. People say they love baseball, music, beer, dogs, dolls, paintings, ideas, parents, children, sweethearts, spouses, and God. Some people even claim to be in love with love! The *Random House Dictionary of the English Language* lists no fewer than twenty-four meanings for the word love, which tells us immediately that love can have many connotations. When one person says to another, "I just love your new shoes," surely something different is meant than when that same person says to someone else, "I love you very much."

Because love can mean so many different things, it may be impossible to define it precisely. As historian John Moore has noted,

Whatever love is, it has aroused the curiosity of the men and women of Western civilization as has no other subject. Love is something people do or enjoy, something that happens to them, something they fall into. It is something people think about. . . .

But ancients and moderns alike have failed to agree on what love really is. The disagreement is not surprising. Like truth and beauty, love is one of the great intangibles.[3]

Nearly a hundred years ago, author H. T. Finck addressed the problem of defining love with this bit of whimsy:

Love is such a tissue of paradoxes, and exists in such an endless variety of forms and shades, that you may say almost anything about it that you please, and you are likely to be correct.[4]

Although precise definitions of love may not be possible to obtain, most people would agree that the experience of loving has certain qualities, regardless of whom or what is loved. For example:

- Love is an emotion—an internalized feeling about someone or something outside yourself.
- Love involves a positive attitude toward the person, object, or idea that is loved.
- Love involves affection—that is, feelings of warmth and closeness.
- Love involves wanting to interact with whom or what is loved; love does not involve indifference.

For nearly everyone, the most meaningful love experiences are those that involve loving and being loved by other people. Although someone can love a new car, a beautiful painting, or an elegant idea, neither the car, the painting, nor the idea can love the person back. Thus people usually find that the most meaningful love experiences take place within the context of a relationship with another person.

Several scholars and researchers have classified love into various types, each distinguishable by the context in which the loving takes place.[5] Although these classifications differ in detail, they generally identify the following kinds of human loving:

- *parental love*—love that leads to the care, nurture, and protection of infants and other loved ones
- *infant love*—love that bonds infants to their adult caretakers
- *brotherly love*—concern, respect, and caring for other human beings; the kind of love the Bible means by "love thy neighbor"
- *adult pair-bonding love*—love that motivates adults to form affectional pair relationships in which feelings are usually expressed sexually

Parental and infant love are discussed in Chapter 13, "Parenting." In the remainder of this chapter we consider various aspects of adult pair-bonding love.

PASSIONATE LOVE

When you're in love, your light bulb is turned on. Your eyes sparkle, you're energetic, and almost constantly electric with excitement. Whenever you think of your lover or when you're with your lover, the energy is superintense. And when you touch each other, wow!, you can feel bolts of energy flowing back and forth between you.

From the authors' files

Most of us recognize the intense, exciting, consuming, and frequently sexual quality of the love described by this student. This is *passionate*, or *romantic*, *love*—the love glorified in song, story, poem, book, and movie. Passionate love is our culture's ideal of "true love." Nearly all the great love stories are about lovers who are totally committed to each other, who imagine their beloved to be perfect in appearance and deed, who crave physical intimacy, and who would do just about anything—overcome any obstacle—to be together. Passionate love is epitomized by an intense, overwhelming flood of emotion, the feeling of "falling head over heels in love" and finding one's "perfect" partner. So intense is their euphoria that passionate lovers frequently, and sincerely, believe that their love will last forever.

One of the ironies of passionate love is that despite the sincere belief

Passionate love is our culture's ideal of "true love."

Peter Vandermark/Stock, Boston

that theirs is a lasting true love, the lovers' passionate feelings can one day vanish as abruptly as a bursting balloon. Many people use the term *infatuation* to refer to intensely passionate, abruptly ending relationships, in order to distinguish them from the ideal of everlasting "true love." It should be noted, though, that while in the raptures of passion, lovers do not usually refer to their experience as infatuation. It is only in retrospect, when passionate feelings have waned, that such relationships are called infatuations.

One reason that passionate love is fragile is that most people cannot sustain the intensity of a passionate romance. Other aspects of life, such as school, job, family commitments, and personal interests, require attention, and the amount of time spent in passionate fervor must inevitably decrease. And if the relationship is based on little other than the sharing of passion, then the lovers' commitment to it also will diminish.

Another reason that passionate love is fragile is that passionate lovers often idealize their partners. They revel in the partner's good qualities and tend to ignore the bad ones. This is what is meant by the expression "love is blind." Sometimes the loved one's actual personal-

BOX 2.1 Why a Knight in Shining Armor?

Some of our culture's most cherished notions of romantic love stem from the codes of courtly love formulated in the courts and castles of twelfth-century Europe. Those who engaged in and wrote about courtly love were noblewomen, their aspiring lovers—usually knights and noblemen of lesser status—and poet-musicians known as troubadors, who composed songs about love and dramatic or significant love relationships.

Near the end of the twelfth century (about 1185), Andreas Capellanus recorded the rules of courtly love,[*] and several of his principles are also recognizable as themes of modern romantic love. For example, Capellanus wrote that

A true lover does not desire to embrace in love anyone except his beloved.

Every lover turns pale in the presence of his lover.

A new love puts flight to an old one.

He whom the thought of love vexes, eats and sleeps very little.

A true lover considers nothing good except what he thinks will please his beloved.

A lover can never have enough of the solaces of his beloved.

A true lover is constantly and without intermission possessed by the thought of his beloved.[†]

The expression "a knight in shining armor" arose because love was thought to raise a man to a state of ennobled excellence. "Men were believed to be crude and insensitive until love, like a thunderbolt, shook the very marrow of their being; and then they acquired courtesy, a thirst for learning, and gentleness of manner."[‡] A knight "smitten with love's arrow" might worship his beloved from afar, perhaps waiting hours just to get a glimpse of her. With her permission, he might try to win her love by feats of courage and chivalry or by writing songs or poems for her. While doing all this, the suitor did not assume he would be rewarded; instead he longed for some sign of acceptance and the eventual reciprocation of his ardor.

[*]Andreas Capellanus, *The Art of Courtly Love*, New York, Frederick Ungar. 1957.
[†]Ibid., pp. 42–43.
[‡]Bernard I. Murstein, *Love, Sex and Marriage Through the Ages*, New York, Springer, 1974, p. 148.

ity characteristics are not important, as he or she is perceived as the embodiment of a fantasy love—perhaps a "knight in shining armor" (see Box 2.1) or the "girl or boy of my dreams." Consequently, the personal qualities attached to the lover are those of the fantasized person rather than the actual person. In this instance, the lovers' main concern is sharing their passion; little else in the relationship matters. As the partners get to know each other better, however, their true personality characteristics become more and more difficult to overlook, and if the passion is to continue, the desirability of the lover's real-life personality must resemble or exceed that of the ideal.

COMPANIONATE LOVE

Intense, erotic passion receives so much public attention that it is easy to overlook the other qualities of love, which are just as important as passion, if not more so. These qualities include friendship, liking, respect, and the sharing of values and life goals. A thirty-year-old woman says this about her eight-year love relationship:

In the beginning everything was real intense, but now things have quieted down. It's saner. Things may not be as romantic as they once were, but the love we now have is deeper, richer, and more satisfying than before.

From the authors' files

This deeper, lower-key, more steadfast kind of love is called *companionate love*. In contrast to passionate lovers, who are consumed by their

Companionate love involves sharing.

Paul Conklin

desires to express their passionate and usually erotic feelings, companionate lovers devote more time and energy to supporting each other's life goals and sharing common experiences and less time to expressing passionate feelings. Perhaps after many years of marriage, a couple may not even call their affectional feelings "love," because they reserve that term for passion and not for the quiet affection and mutual concern that they feel.

This does not mean that companionate love and passionate love are mutually exclusive. On the contrary, love relationships can contain both passionate and companionate qualities. The degree to which one or the other predominates depends on the dynamics of the couple's relationship.

Charlie and Lynnae have been married for fifteen years, and when you see them you think they're young lovers. They're devoted to each other. They gaze in each other's eyes, they hold hands when they walk down the street, and they're always touching each other. After all these years, the fire is still burning in that romance.

From the authors' files

LOVE AS GIVING AND LOVE AS GETTING

People in love often say that they "need" their lover or that without their lover they would die, implying that love is an entity that satisfies an emotional need in much the same way that food satisfies a physical one. In this sense, love is characterized as something that fills a spiritual void, and a person regards a loved one as a provider of much needed spiritual sustenance.

Psychologist Abraham Maslow has characterized this kind of needy love as *deficiency love* or *D-love*, suggesting that the needs that love satisfies come from deficiencies in one's abilities to fulfill independently some of the basic human needs.[6] Like children, adults often become dependent on loved ones for approval, support, satisfaction, recognition, and companionship. Often an individual loves someone because that person can give or do something that the person cannot get or do alone. This feeling is the principal motivation for many emotional attachments, as many relationships are formed to stave off the alienation and loneliness inherent in our highly mobile, technological society.

In contrast to D-love, Maslow suggests that love has another

dimension, called *being love,* or *B-love.* This kind of love is characterized by selfless, warm caring. It is a nonpossessive love, with few
demands for need fulfillment and personal gratification. This type of
love communicates the sentiment "I care," rather than "I will care for
you if you do (think) such and such." Being love is a giving love, an
unselfish love. It seeks the best for the partner without regard to one's
own welfare. (See Box 2.2 for a discussion of other types of love.)

LOVE AS AN EMOTION

Emotions are intense, internal feelings that motivate behavior. When
people are afraid, they try to seek protection, escape, or even fight off
the fear-producing threat. When people are in love, they try to organize
their lives so that they can interact with their loved ones as much as
possible.

The Two-Component Theory of Emotion

Many studies indicate that emotions are the product of two independent
conditions; this phenomenon is called the *two-component theory of
emotion.*[7] The first condition is a state of physiological arousal, which
usually is characterized by an increase in heart rate, sweaty palms, a
heightened sense of awareness, a flushed feeling, "butterflies in the
stomach," and sometimes accelerated breathing. The second condition
is the labeling of the aroused state as a particular emotion depending
on the environmental situation in which that arousal is experienced. In
other words, people create their emotional experiences according to
how they interpret a particular situation and what their previous
experiences have taught them is appropriate behavior for that situation.

For example, most people are unnerved when someone they do not
know well sits very close to them and gazes into their eyes. Such a
situation frequently produces physiological arousal. How a person
reacts to that situation, however, depends on the circumstances. If you
are on a crowded subway train, the staring of a nearby stranger could
make you afraid and force you to move to another car. On the other
hand, if you are in a romantic, candlelit French restaurant, the intense
gaze and proximity of a new acquaintance might produce positive
affectional feelings.

In these examples, the emotions and their subsequent attitudes and
behaviors are quite different, but each is based on a similar condition
—the physiological arousal produced by another person's nearness and

BOX 2.2   How Do I Love Thee?

Many psychologists have noted that people can love each other in different ways. In their study of love behavior, Thomas and Marcia Lasswell found that there are six basic styles of loving.* The six styles are:

Best-Friends Love. This kind of love is a comfortable intimacy that develops from a sharing of many interests over a long period of time. Best-friends love involves rapport, companionship, and the gradual development of emotional closeness. A best-friends lover is satisfied with his or her present partner and usually does not seek other close relationships.

Pragmatic Love. Pragmatic love is based on a practical assessment of the qualities of the beloved in relation to a predetermined set of desirable attributes. A pragmatic lover feels that his or her partner has a sufficient number of desirable qualities to be considered a good mate.

Game-playing Love. Game-playing love is self-centered love. The major characteristic of game-playing love is manipulation of the partner through strategies designed to keep him or her emotionally off balance. A game-playing lover lacks commitment to the relationship, is reluctant to work through problems, and often has more than one partner.

Possessive Love. This kind of love is characterized by intense dependency and wanting to be possessed by, and to possess, the lover. The possessive lover is continually wary that the partner's affection might be lacking and is often extremely jealous. His or her emotions may alternate between great peaks of excitement and depths of despair.

Unselfish Love. Unselfish love involves unconditional caring and nurturing, giving, and self-sacrifice. An unselfish lover is always forgiving and supportive.

Romantic Love. Romantic lovers are totally captivated by the experience and the idea of being in love. They wish to reveal totally their innermost selves to their partners, and to merge both emotionally and physically with them.

Lasswell and Lasswell believe that partners in love relationships can benefit from knowing their particular loving styles. They have developed a questionnaire to help individuals assess which style, or mixture of styles, of loving predominates in their love relationships.*†

*Thomas E. Lasswell and Marcia E. Lasswell, "I Love You But I'm Not In Love with You," *Journal of Marriage and Family Counseling*, 2 (1976): 211–224.
†Marcia E. Lasswell and Norman M. Lobenz, *Styles of Loving*, New York, Ballantine Books, 1981.

staring. The feelings and actions that follow the arousing situation depend on whether the situation is interpreted as threatening or rewarding.

The Capilano Canyon Experiment   To demonstrate the relationship between a state of physiological arousal and the labeling of the arousal as a particular emotion, researchers interviewed a large group of male tourists after they had crossed one of two bridges over the raging Capilano River in British Columbia,

Canada.[8] One of the bridges was more than two hundred feet above the water and was rickety and unstable. The second bridge was only ten feet above the water and was well built and secure. As these tourists came off the bridges, they were asked by either a male or a female interviewer to help with a school assignment by answering questions pertaining to the scenery.

The experimenters hypothesized that the men on the high, unstable bridge would be more aroused physiologically than the men on the low, sturdy bridge would, and that this state of arousal would lead to the men's feelings of sexual attraction for the female interviewer. This is exactly what happened. The males on the rickety bridge who were interviewed by the female experimenter displayed greater sexual imagery in their responses to the questions than did either the males on the rickety bridge who were interviewed by the male experimenter or the males on the sturdy bridge, whether they were interviewed by the female or the male. The tourists also were given the opportunity to contact their particular interviewer at some future time. Only a few of the men telephoned their male interviewer, and only a few of the men who had crossed the sturdy bridge telephoned their female interviewer. As expected, however, a significant percentage of the men who had crossed the high, unstable bridge telephoned their female interviewer, "just to find out the results of the experiment."

Positive and Negative Emotions

The two-component theory of emotion can be used to explain the feeling of both positive and negative emotions. Although the arousal state may be the same for both emotions, a person identifies the emotion as rewarding or threatening according to an evaluation of the situation and past experiences.

Psychologists Ellen Berscheid and Elaine Walster suggest that the two-component theory helps explain the phenomenon of someone loving a person with whom he or she has negative interactions.[9] They point out that

Stimuli which produce "aesthetic appreciation," "sexual arousal," "gratitude," "rejection," "jealousy," or "total confusion" generally produce states of intense physiological arousal, [and that] these positive *and* negative experiences may all have the potential for deepening an individual's passion for another. What may be important in determining how the individual feels about the person who is apparently generating these intense feelings is how he *labels* his reaction. If the situation is arranged so that it is reasonable for him to attribute this agitated state to "passionate love," he should experience love.[10]

Thus, unpleasant emotions such as fear, rejection, frustration, and anger can stir feelings of love as much as sexual gratification and need satisfaction can. You may hate the graduate school that rejects you, but sometimes you may feel greater love for someone who withholds love or sex.

Labeling Feelings

According to Berscheid and Walster, several factors determine why particular tumultuous feelings are labeled "love." These include:

1. *Childhood Learning*   Children learn from parents and other role models the appropriate labels to attach to emotional arousal in particular situations. By the time they reach adolescence, most young people know when to feel embarrassed, joyful, contemptuous, or loving.

2. *Social Approval*   Sometimes it is not clear how one should feel in a certain situation, and a person may be either confused or feel a mixture of emotions. In such ambiguous circumstances, people tend to give their arousal the label that they think is most socially acceptable. If everyone around you is telling you that your confusion "must be love," it is likely that you eventually will agree with them.

3. *Self-perception*   How people label their aroused states depends on their self-image. People who consider themselves romantic and desirable are likely to label certain feelings "love," whereas people who do not think of themselves as romantic might label the arousal something else.

4. *Expectations*   People who expect love to lead to joy and acceptance are more likely to label their feelings "love," because they wish to increase the amount of pleasure in their lives. Those who believe that love inevitably leads to anguish and despair are less likely to label their feelings "love," because they wish to spare themselves the grief they expect love to bring.

JEALOUSY

Most people have experienced at one time or another at least mild pangs of jealousy. Jealousy can strike when a relationship changes and a partner's needs are no longer met as they once were, or when a person fears that a relationship may become less pleasing to him or her. Family therapist Larry Constantine lists the following elements of jealousy.[11]

Notice that each of Constantine's elements includes the loss of, or the fear of losing, some aspect of a love relationship.

1. Loss of face, status, or ego-enhancement
2. Loss of need gratification, including sexual, intellectual, emotional, and other needs
3. Loss of control over one's partner, over one's own life, and over power in relation to one's partner
4. Loss of predictability and the dependability of one's partner's behavior
5. Loss of privacy, territory, or exclusive access
6. Loss of actual time with one's partner, or reduced contact

Whether jealousy is "good" or "bad" is continually debated. The "jealousy-is-good" side holds that jealousy shows monogamous commitment, whereas the "jealousy-is-bad" side argues that jealousy shows possessiveness and neurotic dependency. Jealousy is probably neither good nor bad in itself but, rather, takes on meaning according to the context in which it is felt. According to Constantine,

Jealousy and jealous behavior are neither intrinsically healthy and good nor unhealthy and bad. Jealousy becomes a problem when it interferes with successful functioning in a chosen lifestyle or relationship. Insofar as it consumes emotional resources exclusively, or antagonizes, alienates, and obfuscates, jealousy will tend to work to the disadvantage of all. Extreme jealousy may be dysfunctional, as may jealousy in response to imagined threats. But where the danger is real, jealousy may indeed be a functional response. Jealousy may be an *early warning signal* that some aspects of the relationship need to be clarified and worked out more thoroughly. Jealousy may serve to draw attention to differences in assumptions and expectations by the partners, to changing assumptions, or the need to change the couple's implicit contract.[12]

Although there is no absolute correlation, there seems to be some relationship between how jealousy affects a couple and how dependent the partners are on each other and whether they feel insecure about the bond between them[13]—or the relative degrees of Maslow's D-love and B-love.[14] When D-love predominates in a relationship, jealousy is more likely to occur, and it may be experienced by the partner as emotionally devastating. On the other hand, jealousy in B-love is less significant, for the partner is more emotionally self-sufficient and is less likely to be devastated by the loss of the beloved. This does not mean that B-love is totally free of jealousy but, rather, that B-lovers are freer to use their jealous feelings to examine aspects of their own personalities and to improve their love relationship.

PEOPLE IN LOVE

Rare is the person who lives out his or her life without experiencing love. Yet, surprisingly, sociologists and psychologists have only recently begun to study Americans' love behavior.

The frequency with which people fall in love was examined in a survey of American college students.[15] The students in the survey reported having had, on the average, six or seven romantic experiences in their lifetimes, only one or two of which they considered "real" love. The other experiences they considered infatuations. But as we already pointed out, infatuation is mostly used to describe previous love affairs that did not work out. If individuals are asked about this when they actually are involved in a love relationship, they are likely to say they are in love, not that they are infatuated. Therefore, it seems reasonable to conclude that the students in this survey had been in love at least a half-dozen times. Also, it is probable that after the survey many students had other experiences of being in love. Although one should not generalize from a college student population to all of society, it is possible that many people have several love experiences in their lives.

Psychologist Zick Rubin and his colleagues have been studying people's love behavior for several years. One of their investigations revealed that women were more likely to instigate the break-up of a love affair and that men were more likely to try to continue the relationship, even to a bitter end.[16] Once the relationship did dissolve, the men tended to suffer more; they felt more unhappy, more lonely, and more depressed than the women did. These findings suggested to Rubin that

Whereas men seem to fall in love more quickly and easily than women, women seem to fall out of love more quickly, and with less difficulty than men, at least in the premarital stages. We found, to our initial surprise, that women were somewhat more likely to be "breaker-uppers" than men were, that they saw more problems in the relationship, and that they were better able to disengage emotionally when a breakup was coming. Men, on the other hand, tended to react to breakups with greater grief and despair. . . .[17]

Thus, it appears that in love relationships at least, men are can be considered FILO—first in and last out—and women can be considered LIFO—last in and first out.

To explain this phenomenon, Rubin suggests that

Women may learn to be more practical and discriminating about love than men for simple economic reasons. In most marriages, the wife's status, income and life chances are far more dependent on the husband's than vice versa. As a result, the woman must be discriminating. She cannot afford to stay in love too long with "the wrong person."[18]

That women tend to exercise more control over their romantic feelings does not mean that they are not romantically inclined, but only that they are more careful and discriminating. A group of men and women were asked to what extent they experienced the following romantic reactions when involved in a love relationship:

- felt like I was floating on a cloud
- felt like I wanted to run, jump, and scream
- had trouble concentrating
- felt giddy and carefree
- had a general feeling of well-being
- was nervous before dates
- had physical sensations: cold hands, butterflies in the stomach, tingling spine, and the like
- had insomnia

The results indicated that the women seemed to be more romantic than the men.[19] Apparently, women want to be sure of many of the major aspects of their love relationships before permitting themselves to fall in love. Once they make the commitment to love, however, they may feel more in love than their male partners do.

IS LOVE ENOUGH?

In our culture most people believe that the inevitable consequence of being in love is marriage, for, as the song says, "love and marriage go together like a horse and carriage." When married couples are asked what motivated them to marry, nearly all reply, "We married because we were in love." The fact that the current divorce rate is approaching 40 percent implies, however, that the loving feelings that lead two people to marry do not necessarily produce a lasting marriage. There are several reasons for this:

1.   People marry for many reasons besides being in love, including financial considerations, the desire to leave home, and the desire for the social prestige accorded by our society to the married.

2.   The love that people feel for each other when they marry can be extremely passionate. But sometimes passion wanes, either disappearing entirely ("burning out") or becoming less important as deeper, more companionate feelings arise. If a couple considers passion the main reason for marrying, then a decline in passionate feelings may signal either that the relationship's goals need to be changed or that the marriage is losing its reason for existing.

3.   One of life's truisms is that few goals are attained without some kind of struggle, and this is also true of marital goals. Yet, millions of people believe (or hope) that by being in love, ordinary obstacles to the fulfillment of life goals either will disappear or will be surmounted easily. If only this romantic myth, perpetuated in so many stories, films, and TV shows, were true. Unfortunately, love does not conquer all, and successful marriages are built on more than love alone. We shall discuss success in marriage more completely in Chapter 10, "Marital Interaction."

SUMMARY

Love is the most important feeling in marital and family relationships. It is the emotional "glue" that links partners and binds parents and children.

Nearly everyone has his or her own idea of what love is, although it is difficult even for scholars to agree on a definition of love. One reason that love is hard to define is that people "love" a great variety of things, not just other people.

Despite this difficulty, most people probably think of love as intense, exciting, consuming, and often sexual passion. This is the kind of love celebrated in song and story, and it is held by our culture to be the ideal or "true" love. It is clear, however, that passionate love can wane and that couples either drift apart or their love takes on the deeper, richer quality of companionate love.

Some psychologists argue that people vary with regard to the degree of dependency they feel in love relationships and that increased feelings of dependency can lead to jealousy.

As an emotion, love can be considered the product of both physiological arousal and the labeling of that arousal as love. Thus, we base our feelings of love on previous learning and on the cues from the environment that it is all right to experience love.

Research indicates that most people fall in love several times in their lives, although they often reserve the term "infatuation" for love relationships that did not work out and that, in hindsight, seem less meaningful.

Research suggests that once involved in a love relationship, women may feel more romantic than men do. However, women seem less inclined to carry on a love relationship and are more likely to be the initiators of a break-up.

Although love is prized in our culture, we must realize that as a foundation for a lasting marriage, love is sometimes not enough.

CONSIDER THIS

As their summer jobs as Forest Service ecologists drew to an end, Cecile and Brad had to face a disruption in their ten-week-old romance, as both were returning to their respective colleges to finish their senior year. One afternoon, on a hike into the backcountry, they talked about their eventual parting.

BRAD: Maybe there's still time for me to transfer.
CECILE: It's really crazy for you to change from Ohio to Oregon. You couldn't transfer enough credits to graduate on time.
BRAD: I want to keep us together. What other way is there?
CECILE: We can write letters and see each other on vacations. And we can get together after graduation.
BRAD: But that's next year. I don't want to wait. Don't you love me?
CECILE: Of course I do.
BRAD: Then why don't you want to be together?
CECILE: It's not that. It's just that we haven't known each other very long. How do we know it will last?

Questions
1. Do you think Brad should try to transfer to Cecile's school?
2. Is there a way for Cecile and Brad to determine whether their love will last?
3. How do you predict Cecile's and Brad's relationship will turn out? Do you think they can remain apart for the school year and then get together after graduation?

4. In your own love relationships, do you tend to fall in love quickly, or does your love grow more gradually?
5. What are the qualities you feel are important in your love relationships?

NOTES

1. Jonathan L. Freedman, *Happy People*, New York, Harcourt Brace Jovanovich, 1978, p. 48.
2. William M. Kephart, "Some Correlates of Romantic Love," *Journal of Marriage and the Family*, 29, no. 3 (August 1967): 471.
3. John C. Moore, *Love in Twelfth-Century France*, Philadelphia, University of Pennsylvania Press, 1972, p. 1.
4. Henry T. Finck, *Romantic Love and Personal Beauty: Their Development, Causal Relations, Historic and National Peculiarities*, New York, Macmillan, 1891.
5. Harry Harlow, *Learning to Love*, New York, Jason Aronson, 1974; Erich Fromm, *The Art of Loving*, New York, Harper & Row, 1956; Theodore D. Kemper, *A Social Interactional Theory of Emotions*, New York, John Wiley, 1978.
6. Abraham Maslow, *Toward a Psychology of Being*. Princeton, N.J., D. Van Nostrand, 1962.
7. Stanley Schachter and Jerome Singer, "Cognitive, Social and Physiological Determinants of Emotional State," *Psychological Review*, 69 (1962): 379–399.
8. P. G. Dutton and A. P. Aron, "Some Evidence for Heightened Sexual Attraction Under Conditions of High Anxiety," *Journal of Personality and Social Psychology*, 30 (1974): 510–517.
9. Ellen Berscheid and Elaine Walster, "A Little Bit About Love," in Ted Huston, ed., *Foundations of Interpersonal Attraction*, New York, Academic Press, 1974, pp. 355–381.
10. Ibid., p. 363.
11. Larry L. Constantine, "Jealousy: Techniques for Intervention," in Gordon Clanton and Lynn G. Smith, eds., *Jealousy*, Englewood Cliffs, N.J., Prentice-Hall, 1977, pp. 190–198.
12. Ibid., p. 191.
13. Ellen Berscheid and Jack Fei, "Romantic Love and Sexual Jealousy," in Clanton and Smith, eds., *Jealousy*, pp. 101–09.
14. Clanton and Smith, eds., *Jealousy*, p. 10.
15. Kephart, "Some Correlates of Romantic Love."

16. Charles T. Hill, Zick Rubin, and Letitia Anne Peplau, "Breakups Before Marriage: The End of 103 Affairs," *Journal of Social Issues*, 32, no. 1 (1976): 147–168.
17. Zick Rubin, "The Love Research," in *Readings in Marriage & Family 78/79*, Guilford, Conn., The Duskin Publishing Group, 1978. pp. 8–9.
18. Ibid.
19. E. J. Kanin, K. D. Davidson, and S. R. Scheck, "A Research Note on Male-Female Differentials in the Experience of Heterosexual Love," *Journal of Sex Research*, 6 (1970): 64–72.

SUGGESTED READINGS

Clanton, Gordon, and Lynn G. Smith. *Jealousy*. Englewood Cliffs, N.J., Prentice-Hall, 1977. A collection of essays covering all aspects of love and jealousy.

Fromm, Erich. *The Art of Loving*. New York, Harper & Row, 1956. A sensitive, eloquent, and philosophical inquiry into the meaning and expression of human love.

Harlow, Harry. *Learning to Love*. San Francisco, Albion, 1971. A discussion of the development of types of love, based largely on the author's work with nonhuman primates.

Schachter, Stanley, and Jerome Singer. "Cognitive, Social and Physiological Determinants of Emotional State." *Psychological Review*, 69 (1962): 379–399. A discussion of the theory that specific emotions are cognitive interpretations of general feelings of arousal.

Walster, Elaine, and William G. Walster. *A New Look at Love*. Reading, Mass., Addison-Wesley, 1978. An introduction to the results from research on love and love relationships.

CREATING INTIMATE RELATIONSHIPS

What men and women seek from love today is no longer a
romantic luxury; it is an essential for emotional survival.
More and more it is the hope of finding in intimate love
something of personal validity, personal relevance, a
confirmation of one's existence.

George Bach and Ronald M. Deutsch[1]

3

In one of her popular songs, Barbra Streisand declares that people who need people are the luckiest people in the world. Why are they lucky? Because, the song says, one day they will find a very special person who will make them feel whole.

The lyrics of that song describe one of the most fundamental human qualities: we all need others with whom we can exchange and share love, affection, closeness, and fun, as well as pursue life goals. Close relationships bring a sense of security—a feeling of belonging. Close relationships also help people avoid the feelings of desperation, anxiety, and rejection that come from feeling lonely and detached.

From infancy, much of a person's life energy is spent maintaining close relationships and developing new ones. Many people's first relationship is with their parents. Simply by being offspring, they obtain love and security. Parent-child relationships do not sustain most people for life, however. In our culture, adults are expected to extend their intimate relationships beyond those with their immediate family by seeking new ones: relationships with peers, teachers, coworkers, employers, lovers, and perhaps a spouse. But these relationships are not established as easily as those with the family are. They have to be cultivated. From the many strangers in the environment, we choose a select few to become close to.

Intimate love relationships are probably the most important kind of close relationship. They are felt the deepest, and they provide a unique sense of attachment and bonding. Intimates are not two separate, independently acting individuals. The mix of their two personalities creates a larger entity, often referred to as a *dyad*, which has qualities not present in the actions of the isolated individuals. A dyad is a relationship of mutual interdependence, and intimates affect each other's behavior, emotions, and attitudes. In addition, the personality of each member is affected by the couple's shared history. Thus, what happened to the dyad in the past has consequences for the present, and what happens now has implications for the future.

Intimate dyads constitute distinct social units within the larger social setting. The partners, through mutual agreement and a shared commitment to their partnership, make their relationship an entity in itself. This gives the partners two sets of relationships with society, those as individuals and those as members of the dyad. The partners' behavior, emotions, and attitudes, therefore, can be affected not only by the social norms and expectations for individuals but also by a different set of norms and expectations for members of dyads.

Virtually everyone wants vibrant, happy, and fulfilling intimate relationships. Yet most people know more about driving a car or playing a sport than they do about making their relationships succeed. In this chapter we discuss some of the major characteristics of intimate dyadic relationships, as we believe that the more partners know about "partnering," the more fulfilling and enjoyable their partnerships will be.

THE QUALITIES OF INTIMATE RELATIONSHIPS

People form intimate relationships to satisfy some of their most basic human needs for love, security, self-esteem, attachment, and the sharing of physical and emotional closeness, as we learn from the people in the following discussion:

GROUP LEADER: What are the qualities of a good intimate relationship?

SUSAN: Respect for each other's individuality.

JAN: Respect for the other person as a person—that person's values and what he or she believes in.

MICHAEL: Sharing.

SUSAN: Being treated as a friend and not as an employee or slave.

MARSHA: Treating the other person the way you would like to be treated.

SAM: Reciprocal support, love, and trust. Honesty.

GROUP LEADER: I think there's one obvious thing you haven't mentioned yet.
SUSAN: Sex!

From the authors' files

Although every person is unique and therefore every dyad is unique, it is nevertheless possible to distinguish certain qualities inherent in virtually every intimate relationship. Among these qualities are intimacy, understanding, and commitment.

Intimacy

Intimacy is a special closeness, which Thomas C. Oden describes as

knowledge of the core of something, an understanding of the inmost parts, that which is indicative of one's deepest nature and marked by close physical, mental, or social association. When I am [intimate with] another, I know that which is ordinarily hidden from public view yet revealed in the closeness and vulnerability of the relationship. When I am aware that someone else is [intimate with me], I know I have been touched in the deepest levels of my consciousness.[2]

The deep knowledge that intimates have of each other comes from their sharing the most important, and often secret, aspects of their personalities—their goals, aspirations, strengths, weaknesses, and physical and sexual selves. The sharing of such private information is called *self-disclosure*.

One of the principal characteristics of intimacy is trust. Intimates feel confident that they can "be themselves" with each other. Intimacy involves freedom to disclose to your partner your innermost feelings, even those you may feel ashamed of. Intimacy allows you to relax many of the defenses you use to prevent others from getting to know too much about you, for you believe that your intimate is completely trustworthy and will neither leave the relationship because you disclose unflattering things about yourself nor use this intimate knowledge to harm you.

Intimacy frequently involves physical closeness. When intimates are together, they usually stay close to each other, touching, holding hands, and if appropriate, making love. Through physical closeness partners are able to feel closer and even more connected.

Understanding

Intimates frequently say that they want their partners to "understand" them. By this they mean that they want their partners to know them as well as, if not better than, they know themselves. Such understanding has three components: behavioral, emotional, and cognitive.

The behavioral aspect of understanding is predictability. In certain circumstances, people who understand their partners may be able to predict how the partner will behave, but being able to predict his or her exact behavior in every situation is probably not possible. People's personalities are complex, and in most circumstances their behavior is affected by many different internal and external factors. Nevertheless, in some situations, your understanding of your partner may enable you to rule out certain behaviors and to expect behavior that is "in character." For example, if your partner is shy, you would not expect him or her to be "the life of the party" at a large gathering.

The emotional aspect of understanding is *empathy*, which is placing yourself in another's frame of reference and feeling the same or similar emotions in a given situation. Empathy enables an individual to experience how a partner is feeling, and this permits the partners to share emotions, such as joy and sadness, and also enhances their communication of support and concern, especially in emotionally difficult situations.

The cognitive aspect of understanding is having the same opinion and view of your partner's personal qualities and characteristics as he or she has. The greater the similarity in the partners' views of each other, the greater is the understanding between them. The understanding in a relationship is also affected by how alike partners' views of the dyad are. The open and honest exchange of information can help partners clarify their perceptions of themselves and their relationship, and this can lead to greater understanding and intimacy.

Commitment

At some point in the development of an intimate relationship, the people involved usually believe that their relationship will continue indefinitely, and they agree to share the responsibility for making their relationship endure. The intent to devote time and energy to maintaining an intimate relationship is *commitment*.

People commit themselves to relationships for many reasons. As partners become accustomed to and comfortable with each other, they

Commitment is devoting time and energy toward maintaining an intimate relationship.

Paul Conklin

find that their partner's behavior is relatively predictable. This minimizes conflict and maximizes the exchange of rewards and pleasures. People also commit themselves to relationships because they believe that they have invested a certain amount of time and energy in the relationship, and it may seem easier to stay with the present partnership than to start a new one. Commitment also offers a way of controlling the partner's behavior, for by committing to the relationship, a person may also agree to conform to the rules of the dyad.

Many of the authorities who have studied and written about love relationships agree that commitment is not simply a promise "to love each other," "to work hard on a relationship," or "to be more concerned with the partner's welfare than with one's own." True commitment requires support of the ongoing process of the relationship. As psychologist Carl Rogers points out:

We each commit ourselves to working together on the changing process of our present relationship, because that relationship is currently enriching our love and our life and we wish it to grow.[3]

Virginia Satir echoes Rogers' sentiments when she states:

Whether or not the initial love between a couple flowers depends on how the two people make the three parts (you, me and us) work. How these three parts work is part of . . . the *process*.[4]

Carl Rogers, Virginia Satir, and other scholars and therapists recognize that all relationships change over time because the people involved continually develop and change as they progress through life. A person's personality never becomes fixed; it continues to change until death. Therefore, commitment cannot be a promise to maintain the status quo. Rather, it is the dedication to reshape and reclarify the relationship's qualities as the partners grow and change.

COMMUNICATION

All human interaction entails communication, the sending and receiving of messages. Through interpersonal communications, people tell each other "the news" in their lives: what is happening, what their plans are, and how they feel about things, situations, and each other. People also depend on communication to help coordinate their behavior with that of others or to persuade others to do something for them.

Sometimes nonverbal communication says it all.

Tom Blau/Photo Trends

Most human communication is the exchange of either spoken or written words. People also communicate through *body language*, gestures and body movements. You can say "I don't know" with a shrug or "I'd like to meet you" with a smile. Nonverbal communication accompanies almost every face-to-face verbal encounter.

Communication theorists such as Gregory Bateson[5] have found that two distinct types of messages can be exchanged in interpersonal communications. The first type of message is the *literal* one. This is the message conveyed by only the words themselves, like headlines or stories in a newspaper: "It's raining"; "I graduated from law school"; "Here's what happened in France yesterday. . . ." Literal messages can be communicated just as easily by a computer as by a human being.

Few interpersonal communications, however, are purely literal, especially those exchanged in close relationships. Besides the literal message, most interpersonal communications carry implicit messages about the reason for the communication, the message's urgency, how the message is to be interpreted, or the nature of the relationship. This is a *metacommunication* or *metamessage* (*meta* is a Greek word meaning "beyond," "additional," or "transcendent"). In some instances, metacommunications are conveyed in the actual words spoken, the most common examples being names and titles denoting superiority or inferiority. In many work situations, a supervisor may call an employee by his or her first name, but the employee may address the supervisor only by his or her surname. This form of communication signifies the balance of power in the relationship. In some languages, different pronouns indicate the nature of the relationship. In French, for example, the words *tu* and *vous* both mean "you." *Tu*, however, is used only when speaking to intimates, children, and pets, whereas *vous* is used to address everyone else.

Much metacommunication is nonverbal. It is revealed through voice quality, the use of space, facial expressions, and body movements (see Figure 3.1). As psychologist Albert Mehrabian points out: "If someone calls you 'honey' in a nasty tone of voice, you are likely to feel disliked; it is also possible to say 'I hate you' in a way that conveys exactly the opposite feeling."[6] People tend to move physically closer to individuals they like (see Box 3.1), and they often lean forward when talking to them. Eye-to-eye contact also communicates metamessages. A glaring stare certainly says one thing and a rapturous gaze another. Touch is also a form of metacommunication. In some situations, touching while speaking is an assertion of power. In other situations, touching might communicate shared concern, and in others it might indicate affection or sexual attraction.

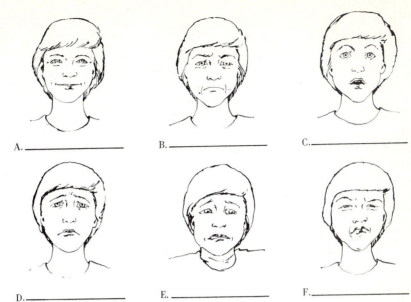

FIGURE 3.1
Individuals communicate much information about their thoughts and feelings through their facial expressions. Can you match these facial expressions to the following feelings? (1) fear, (2) surprise, (3) happiness, (4) anger, (5) disgust, (6) sadness

A. _____ B. _____ C. _____

D. _____ E. _____ F. _____

Most of the time metacommunication occurs unconsciously. The literal message is frequently the focus of the interaction, and the metamessage simply reaffirms the norms of the relationship. There are times, however, when the receiver responds to the metacommunication rather than to the literal one:

Maureen tends not to show her feelings. When we're talking and she gets mad, she continues the conversation as if nothing were wrong, but I know by her actions that she's angry. She gets up, turns around, and walks away. When that happens, I don't hear her actual words, I hear her real message, which is "who needs you?" or "go to hell."

From the authors' files

Psychologists Morton Perlmutter and Elaine Hatfield suggest that responding to metamessages instead of to literal ones helps partners achieve true intimacy:

An intimate moment occurs when the ordinary rules of human interactions are suspended and people begin to talk about their own and their partner's thoughts, feelings, sensations, and acts; these become primary. The literal content of the message—which is usually paramount—is relegated to a position of unimportance.[7]

BOX 3.1   Where Do You Sit?

People generally demonstrate how they feel about a particular person or interaction by how they position themselves with respect to that person. Think about how you position yourself at a table when you are with someone else, and compare your behavior with that reported for other college students.

X X

Side-by-Side Favored above all other seating arrangements for closest intimacy, probably because it permits maximum physical proximity. This arrangement is also frequently used by pairs engaged in some cooperative task.

X

X *Corner Seating* Preferred for casual conversation and the performance of cooperative tasks.

X

Face-to-Face Preferred for almost any kind of direct interaction, including conversing, arguing, cooperating, or competing on a task. This arrangement allows maximum eye contact.

X

X

Distant Seating Preferred for working separately at the same table. This arrangement minimizes any kind of interaction.

X

Source: Robert Sommer, *Personal Space*, Englewood Cliffs, N.J., Prentice-Hall, 1969, pp. 58–73.

Openly responding to metacommunication is a form of self-disclosure. It leads to the sharing of the most deeply felt attitudes and emotions. To do so entails an element of risk, though, for when a metacommunication is exposed and a literal one is ignored, private and potentially unpleasant things are forced out into the open. According to some, this risk taking is essential to the growth of intimacy.[8]

BECOMING INTIMATE: FALLING IN LOVE

We met in the subway, of all places. It wasn't really love at first sight. I just thought to myself when I saw her that she was a very attractive woman and that I wanted to get to know her better. Little did I realize that she was having similar thoughts about me. So, when I finally got up the courage to speak to her, her first words were something like, "I thought you'd never get around to it." After that we went out for a few months, and then we lived together for about a year before we got married.

From the authors' files

This is a familiar scenario for many intimate relationships. Two total strangers become attracted to each other; they devote a period of time to getting to know each other better; and ultimately they commit themselves to some kind of permanent relationship, which frequently includes getting married. Of course, this is not the developmental pattern of every intimate relationship. Some people become intimate only after many months or even years of knowing each other as friends, whereas others fall in love immediately.

For the most part, however, love relationships of some duration progress through three stages: attraction, developing intimacy, and establishing commitment.

Stage 1: Attraction

The first stage of falling in love is attraction, when near or complete strangers are strongly drawn to each other, to the exclusion of virtually everyone else. Very often, attraction is at first one-sided. One day you suddenly notice someone in a class or at a party, and your interest is immediately engaged. You may strike up a conversation or a mutual friend might introduce you, and with luck the person you are attracted to reciprocates your interest. If this does not happen, you might spend days trying to figure out ways to make yourself known to that person and to increase the possibility of interacting with him or her.

The question of what attracts people to each other has received considerable attention from psychologists and sociologists. Their findings indicate that attraction is based on two factors, physical

"I've got you under my skin."

Drawing by Frascino; © 1981 The New Yorker Magazine, Inc.

appearance and inferences about a person's desirability gathered from observations of behavior and determination of that person's values, beliefs, and attitudes.[9] In other words, we appraise a stranger's desirability by how he or she looks, what he or she does, and what he or she thinks and says.

Many studies indicate that physically attractive people are regarded with more favor than their less attractive peers are.[10] People regarded as attractive frequently are considered more responsible for good deeds and less responsible for bad ones; their evaluations usually carry more weight; and people want to interact with them more than with less attractive people. Whatever their standards of physical attraction (remember that "beauty is in the eye of the beholder"), people tend to feel more positively about those they consider attractive.

Psychologists Ted Huston and George Levinger suggest that physical appearance affects attraction in three distinct ways.[11] The first is that physical beauty may be appreciated for aesthetic reasons: pretty people are valued in the same way that good art is. A second reason that physical appearance can promote attraction is that people tend to assume that good-looking people also have good personality characteristics. One study using photographs showed that both males and females rated physically attractive people of both sexes as being more interesting, poised, sociable, kind, strong, and sexually warm than less attractive people.[12] The third reason that physical appearance affects attraction is that people want to associate with physically attractive people in order to increase their own social standing.

Rarely is physical appearance the only factor that attracts people to each other. Because they usually know little about the character of someone to whom they become attracted, they make inferences about that person's desirability—or lack of it—from bits and pieces of information gained by observing the other's behavior, by asking mutual friends about him or her, and by engaging in mutual discussion. Even the most physically attractive person will remain unappealing if he or she does not have what others consider a "good" personality.

Is there any truth to the old saying that opposites attract? Although it certainly applies to electrical charges, it infrequently applies to people. It seems that people become attracted to those whom they perceive to be like themselves, particularly with regard to their attitudes toward life.[13] We tend to be attracted to people who are like us because their similarity makes being together more harmonious and joyful, and it confirms our own feelings of what is correct, thereby enhancing our self-esteem. Moreover, another's similarity increases the probability that he or she will like us in return. This reciprocal liking makes us even more eager to like the other person, for most of us prefer to interact with people who want to interact with us.

Stage 2: Developing Intimacy

Although falling in love sometimes entails passionate interaction with the person to whom someone is physically attracted, most of the time people expect their love relationships to develop beyond attraction to something more—a quality that includes feelings of closeness, positive regard, warmth, and familiarity with the other's innermost thoughts and feelings. This is the quality of *intimacy*.

When two people become attracted to each other, it is highly unlikely that they immediately feel the trust, empathy, and closeness characteristic of intimacy. Most newly formed relationships can be described as "superficial," in that very little knowledge of the person's "true self" has been revealed. As psychologist Sidney Jourard explains: "We conceal and camouflage our true being before others to foster a sense of safety, to protect ourselves against unwanted but expected criticism, hurt or rejection."[14]

Most people are very cautious about sharing their innermost feelings with new-found acquaintances. Therefore, intimacy generally develops gradually over time as potential intimates learn more about their deepest and most private attitudes and emotions.

Apparently, the process of developing intimacy is a progressive, mutual revelation of secrets. Psychologists Irwin Altman and Dalmas

Taylor compare peoples' personalities to onions, having many layers between an outer surface and an inner core.[15] As acquaintances gain more and more knowledge about each other, they penetrate deeper and deeper through the layers of the other's personality, and this establishes their intimacy. Another model compares the development of intimacy to the peeling of an artichoke. Resistances and barriers to sharing information about oneself are like the leaves of the artichoke. As intimacy progresses, intimates peel away the leaves to get to the other's "heart."

One of the main ingredients of intimacy is self-disclosure—what you tell others about yourself (see Box 3.2). When relationships begin, usually very little intimate knowledge is disclosed. People talk about the weather, the stock market, or international politics. They gossip about professors or the host or hostess of a party. And they ask each other the usual leading questions: Where are you from? What do you do? What's your major? People face these questions so often that they become adept at revealing as much as or as little about themselves as feels comfortable. It is when a person begins to talk about personal history, current life problems, hopes and aspirations, and fears and

Intimacy develops through mutual self-disclosure.

Rosalyn Gerstein

personal failures that important information is disclosed—important because to disclose it makes the person feel vulnerable. Most people discuss their deepest feelings only with those special others in whom they have developed considerable trust.

Self-disclosure leads to intimacy in two ways. First, people tend to be affected either positively or negatively by the information that is disclosed. If one makes a positive judgment about someone, he or she will probably continue to interact with that person, expecting future interactions to be equally positive, perhaps even more so. The same logic applies to negative assessments. If one's reaction to what is disclosed is unfavorable, that person is likely to terminate the relationship, or perhaps maintain it at some lesser level of intimacy.

The second way that self-disclosure leads to intimacy is that the *act* of self-disclosure, regardless of the information that is offered, often leads to reciprocal self-disclosure. Sharing important information communicates trust to the other person, and usually that person accepts that trust and becomes more willing to disclose information. In this way intimacy progresses by a cycle of self-disclosure leading to trust, which brings about more self-disclosure, which leads to more trust, and so on.

The timing of self-disclosure apparently is important to the development of intimacy. The disclosure of too much intimate information early in the development of a relationship can create distance between the individuals. One or the other may not feel ready to reciprocate, because he or she may not trust the other to keep the information confidential. Also, if one person discloses a great deal of information early in the relationship, the other person may feel that the "discloser" does this with everyone and therefore is not really demonstrating trust in the listener. In this case, the listener is not likely to reciprocate with disclosure and trust.

The setting in which self-disclosure takes place also affects the development of intimacy. For example, when people are far from home in unfamiliar places, they may freely disclose information to relative strangers. This is sometimes called the "Ft. Lauderdale phenomenon," named after the annual springtime convergence of thousands of young people on Ft. Lauderdale, Florida. People on vacation can meet and, in a short time, disclose all kinds of intimate information, because they know that their relationship is like "two ships passing in the night." They believe that the other individual probably will not have the opportunity to hurt them with whatever information they have learned.

People prefer to disclose important information in private. That is one reason for the stereotype of the romantic, quiet, candlelit supper. Most intimate relationships have difficulty progressing if the partners cannot secure private time to get to know each other.

BOX 3.2 Self-disclosure in College Student Couples

How much personal information do intimate partners reveal to each other? To find out, researcher Zick Rubin and his colleagues asked 231 couples in college—almost all of whom were seeing each other exclusively—how much they shared their personal thoughts, feelings, and expectations about the status of their current relationship, previous sexual relationships, relationships with parents and friends, self-concept and outlook on life, attitudes and interests, and day-to-day activities.*

The researchers found that the highest degree of complete self-disclosure occurred with feelings and attitudes toward parents; classes and work; the couple's sexual relationship; close, same-sex friendships; and general outlook on life. The lowest degree of complete self-disclosure occurred with feelings and attitudes toward the things the individuals were most ashamed of, the partner's faults, and strongest personal fears (see table). Rubin and

his colleagues believe that the couples' high degree of self-disclosure reflects "a historical shift among student couples toward an ethic of openness. Whereas, in previous generations, couples may have kept larger areas of reserve, both during dating and after marriage, the current generation of college students seems to view intimate disclosure as an integral part of a close, opposite-sex relationship."†

The researchers also found that for approximately 55 percent of the couples, the individuals disclosed themselves to an equal extent; that is, neither the woman nor the man disclosed more information. When self-disclosure was unequal, however, the woman, rather than the man, was more apt to disclose her feelings and attitudes. The tendency for women to disclose more than men do may reflect traditional sex-role behavior which expects women to be more emotional and expressive and men to be more unemotional and restrained.

*Zick Rubin et al., "Self-disclosure in Dating Couples: Sex Roles and the Ethic of Openness," *Journal of Marriage and the Family*, 42 (1980): 305–316.
†Ibid., p. 314.

Of course, there are no strict rules governing appropriate self-disclosure. Although some cultural norms suggest the times and settings for sharing intimate information, in each relationship the partners together decide the mode of disclosure most suitable for them.

Stage 3: Establishing Commitment

Most people would agree that the ultimate stage of falling in love is when the two people identify themselves as belonging to a dyadic unit. As family therapist Virginia Satir suggests: "There are three parts to a couple: *you, me,* and *us.* Two people, three parts, each significant, each having a life of its own, and each making the other more possible."[16]

One of the key features of establishing commitment is the degree to

BOX 3.2 (continued)

TABLE Percentages of Members of College Student Couples Who Completely Disclose to Their Partner Their Attitudes Toward and Feelings About Various Topics‡

Topic	Women (%)	Men (%)	Average (%)
Parents	85	72	78
Classes or work	84	70	77
Couple's sexual relationship	74	73	74
Close, same-sex friendships	76	67	72
General outlook on life	68	73	70
Cultural interests	66	73	70
Partner's best-liked qualities	62	71	66
Religious views	66	66	66
Accomplishments	67	58	62
Previous sexual experience with a particular partner	57	57	57
Personal things most proud of	43	56	50
Previous, opposite-sex relationships	48	50	49
Future of current relationship	48	46	47
Political views	33	47	40
Things most ashamed of	38	35	36
Partner's faults	39	33	36
Things most afraid of	39	27	33

‡Ibid., p. 310. Copyright © 1980 by the National Council on Family Relations. Reprinted by permission.

which the partners in an intimate relationship experience *interdependence*.[17] Partners are interdependent when one person's well-being and enjoyment of life is affected by the rewards, disappointments, satisfactions, and joys of the other. Interdependence is the recognition that one's partner's welfare greatly affects one's own.

It is important to distinguish between interdependence and the "anguish of dependency," or the vulnerability associated with the fear of being jilted in a love relationship. At the initial stages of a developing intimacy, it is not uncommon for individuals to feel insecure about their status in the relationship. When the relationship is still in its formative stages, it is only natural for the partners to wonder if the other might suddenly decide to leave the relationship—and the remaining partner heartbroken. By the time the partners have reached a stage of commitment and interdependence, however, that fear disappears (or nearly so), because the partners have agreed to maintain their relationship. In this situation, partners may say they feel dependent, in that one partner's welfare is affected by what happens to the other one. But it is unlikely that they feel vulnerable, for commitment implies that the partners have agreed to try to make their relationship endure. It is assumed that temporary separations will not lead to diminished feelings and, more importantly, that problems will be worked out by negotiation and in a spirit of mutual trust.

The establishment of commitment is also affected by the reactions of the partners' social network. We all have heard the expression, "They make such a good couple." The approval of one's peers often strengthens the partners' view that their relationship has indeed progressed to the stage of the committed dyad. The reactions of parents, whether positive or negative, communicate the same message. If parents approve of their child's dyadic relationship, then such approval will likely reinforce the partners' bond. Parental disapproval, however, may not necessarily weaken this bond. Studies indicate that parental disapproval can initiate the "Romeo and Juliet effect";[18] that is, family pressures intending to disrupt a couple backfire and make the lovers even more committed to each other.

LONELINESS

Some of my friends get the Saturday night crazies—you know, feeling desperate and worried because they're alone *again*. But my worst time is Sunday morning. That's when I feel the loneliest. That's when you're supposed to be with loved ones, not reading the Sunday funnies all by yourself. On those mornings, I feel so lonely and unloved. All I want is a hug.

From the authors' files

Loneliness is a common and pervasive human experience. At some time or another, just about everyone feels the desperation, hopelessness, desolation, emptiness, and "not-belonging" that characterize loneliness.

Loneliness is the result of the emotional isolation caused by not having intimate ties with a spouse or lover, or the social isolation caused by not having close relationships with peers, fellow workers, and friends.[19] Loneliness is not the same as being alone. People who are surrounded by others virtually all day and all night may often feel lonely, whereas individuals who live or work in solitude may feel lonely only infrequently. The distinguishing feature of loneliness is not the quantity of interpersonal interactions, but how closely one's relationships match one's needs and expectations for intimacy.

Because our society accords relatively high status to married (or at least paired) people, single people can feel worthless and lonely, as Suzanne Gordon notes:

We are a couple culture. If you are not in a couple you are missing out on something truly great or potentially truly great. If you are not part of a couple, whether that couple be sanctified by marriage or not, you are a failure. So when are you going to get married, the Jewish-Italian-Polish-Irish-Wasp mother asks her daughter or son. And despite the offspring's terse reminder that mother should tend to her own business, the daughter or son repeats the same question to herself or himself: when am I going to find someone to love?[20]

Unfortunately, marriage is not a guarantee against loneliness. In fact, the severest feeling of loneliness can be felt in marriage, because people often expect marriage to provide abundant love, understanding, communication, and fulfillment. Sometimes, however, intimate relationships are not blissfully fulfilling, and there can be problems, tension, and anger that seem to form a stone wall between the partners. This imbalance between the expectation of intimacy and the reality of emotional separation from a loved one can lead to incredible feelings of despair and isolation.

The emotional isolation caused by the lack of intimate ties with a lover or spouse is not the only reason for loneliness. Ours is a highly mobile society, and this mobility contributes to the prevalence of loneliness.[21] Frequent changes of jobs or residence (the U.S. Postal Service reports that nearly fifty million people move each year and that the average number of lifetime relocations is fourteen) make social networks fragile. People are continually having to say goodby to old friends and having to establish close relationships with new ones. Individuals whose occupations force them to move often may be wary of making close friendships, because they want to avoid the eventual unhappiness of parting.

Another contributor to loneliness is modern mass society, which is based on a variety of impersonal relationships requiring rigid sociological and economic roles—supervisor-employee, doctor-patient, sales-clerk-customer—with no built-in mechanism for establishing intimate relationships. Thus, even though people may interact with others during the course of the day, these interactions are often characterized by indifference, superficial interaction, and expected role behavior. This is the reason for the loneliness felt by some people in big cities. Theoretically, surrounded by thousands of people, urbanites should never be lonely. But loneliness abounds in cities because people feel anonymous—like nothing more than interchangeable parts in the city's intricate machine.

Psychologists Carin Rubinstein, Phillip Shaver, and Letitia Anne Peplau have several suggestions for dealing with and preventing loneliness:[22]

1.   Understand that loneliness has many possible causes—some are social and others are personal—and try to determine the particular causes of your loneliness. Ask yourself if you are to blame or if your loneliness is caused by something in your environment. Be careful not to overemphasize personal factors or to underestimate social conditions.

2.   Ask yourself if the situation causing the loneliness is transitory or if it is likely to be permanent.

3.   Try to make a change, though some social conditions may be more difficult to change than others. For example, it may be more difficult to leave a relationship or a marriage than to find a new job or to transfer to a different school. Also, set new goals for yourself that can be reached in the immediate future, rather than trying to accomplish only long-term tasks.

4.   Avoid thinking negatively about yourself. Telling yourself that you are ugly, stupid, or worthless only leads to social isolation. It is better to like and accept yourself; that often leads to others liking and accepting you.

5.   Try to recognize your own responsibility for your loneliness—are you willing to become intimate with others?

SUMMARY

People need other people with whom they can share love, affection, understanding, and the many joys of life. Although there are many kinds of close relationships, lover or spouse relationships, called dyads, are generally the closest of all.

Intimate relationships have three characteristics. The first is intimacy, which is a deep knowledge of the other formed by the disclosure of closely guarded personal attitudes and feelings. The second is understanding, which allows one partner to predict the other's behavior, to recognize how that partner feels and sees things (empathy), and to view things as he or she does. Intimate relationships also require commitment, the intent to devote energy to maintaining the relationship as it develops.

Close relationships depend on communication, which is the sending and receiving of messages by verbal and nonverbal means. Literal communication is the actual words people exchange. Metacommunication indicates the quality of the message or relationship and is usually conveyed by tone of voice, posture, and facial expressions.

There are three stages in becoming intimate: attraction, when people first choose, from all the strangers in their environment, the most likely candidates for intimacy; self-disclosure, the revelation of secrets and the growth of trust; and the establishment of commitment.

Loneliness is the absence of intimacy caused by not having a lover or spouse or the absence of a network of peers, close friends, and associates. High mobility and strict role relationships contribute to loneliness, but loneliness can be reduced by improving one's self-image or by making changes in those environmental situations that lead to loneliness.

CONSIDER THIS

Joan is a twenty-six-year-old unmarried woman; she works for a county agency. One Friday evening after working late, instead of going directly home to her apartment, she joined some of her coworkers for a TGIF drink at Gino's, the local, after-work "watering hole."

With the group crowded around a couple of small tables, Joan found herself next to Walt, a newcomer to the agency. This was a lucky coincidence for Walt, who had been attracted to Joan for several weeks. Until now their interactions had consisted of nods, smiles, hellos, and how-are-you's when they bumped into each other at work. Walt was interesting, and Joan willingly spent the next two hours engaged in intense conversation with him.

Discovering that they had a lot in common and feeling the excitement of attraction, Joan and Walt decided to continue their conversation at a quiet restaurant. Over a leisurely dinner, their conversation became more personal. Walt told Joan about his previous marriage and why it broke up; Joan told Walt about her recently ended love relationship with Peter. Joan and Walt found being together very easy, and they managed to avoid the usual insincere interpersonal games men and women often play.

Although Joan was having a wonderful time and was feeling very close to Walt, the intensity of it all began to make her uncomfortable. In the back of her mind she thought that it was happening too fast. Joan had always believed that true intimacy cannot develop in just one evening. Despite the warm feelings and all the information they were sharing, Joan knew that she and Walt were still relative strangers and were probably just reacting to not being alone on a Friday night. Even if it were the "real thing," Joan knew that romances between coworkers were risky.

Questions
1. What is your prediction for the future of Joan's and Walt's relationship?
2. Would it be possible for Joan and Walt to establish a committed relationship in one evening?
3. How long do you think it takes to develop intimacy, understanding, and commitment in a relationship? When does trust develop?
4. Do you think Joan was correct to be concerned about getting involved too fast? Do you think she feared commitment? Was her concern about becoming intimate with a coworker valid?
5. Is there any pattern in the development of your close relationships?

NOTES

1. George Bach and Ronald M. Deutsch, *Pairing*, New York, Peter H. Wyden, 1970, p. 15.
2. Thomas C. Oden, *Game Free: A Guide to the Meaning of Intimacy*, New York, Harper & Row, 1974, p. 4.
3. Carl R. Rogers, *Becoming Partners*, New York, Dell Pub., Co., Inc., 1972, p. 201.
4. Virginia Satir, *Peoplemaking*, Palo Alto, Calif., Science & Behavior Books, 1972, p. 127.
5. Gregory Bateson, *Steps to an Ecology of Mind*, New York, Ballantine, 1972.
6. Albert Mehrabian, "Communication Without Words," *Psychology Today* (September 1968): 54.
7. Morton S. Perlmutter and Elaine Hatfield, "Intimacy, Intentional Metacommunication and Second Order Change," *American Journal of Family Therapy*, 8 (1980): 18–23.
8. Rogers, *Becoming Partners*, p. 204.
9. Ted L. Huston and George Levinger, "Interpersonal Attraction and Relationships," *Annual Review of Psychology*, 29 (1978): 115–156.

10. Ellen Berscheid and Elaine Walster, "Physical Attractiveness," *Advances in Experimental Social Psychology,* 7 (1974): 157–215.

11. Ted L. Huston and George Levinger, "Interpersonal Attraction and Relationships."

12. K. K. Dion, Ellen Berscheid, and Elaine Walster, "What Is Beautiful Is Good," *Journal of Personality and Social Psychology,* 24 (1972): 285–290.

13. Zick Rubin, *Liking and Loving,* New York, Holt, Rinehart & Winston, 1973.

14. Sidney Jourard, *The Transparent Self,* New York, Van Nostrand Reinhold, 1971, p. vii.

15. Irwin Altman and Dalmas Taylor, *Social Penetration: The Development of Intimate Relationships,* New York, Holt, Rinehart & Winston, 1973.

16. Virginia Satir, *Peoplemaking,* p. 127.

17. Ted L. Huston and Rodney M. Cate, "Social Exchange in Intimate Relationships," in Mark Cook and Glenn Wilson, eds., *Love and Attraction,* Oxford, England, Pergamon Press, 1979, pp. 263–270.

18. Richard Driscoll, Keith E. Davis, and Milton E. Lipetz, "Parental Interference and Romantic Love: The Romeo and Juliet Effect," *Journal of Personality and Social Psychology,* 24 (1972): 1–10.

19. Robert S. Weiss, *Loneliness: The Experience of Emotional and Social Isolation,* Cambridge, Mass., MIT Press, 1973.

20. Suzanne Gordon, *Lonely in America,* New York, Simon & Schuster, 1976, p. 70.

21. Vance Packard, *A Nation of Strangers,* New York, D. McKay, 1972; Suzanne Gordon, *Lonely in America.*

22. Carin Rubinstein, Phillip Shaver, and Letitia Anne Peplau, "Loneliness," *Human Nature,* February 1979, pp. 58–65.

SUGGESTED READINGS

Adler, Ron, and Neil Towne. *Looking Out/Looking In.* New York, Holt, Rinehart & Winston, 1978. A presentation of the theory and practice of interpersonal communication.

Gordon, Suzanne. *Lonely in America.* New York, Simon & Schuster, 1976. A thorough analysis of the phenomenon of loneliness in the United States.

Huston, Ted L., and George Levinger. "Interpersonal Attraction and Relationships." *Annual Review of Psychology,* 29 (1978): 115–156. A discussion of recent research on the development of interpersonal relationships.

Jourard, Sidney. *The Transparent Self.* New York, Van Nostrand Reinhold, 1971. A thorough presentation of the theory and practice of self-disclosure.

Rogers, Carl. *Becoming Partners*. New York, Dell Pub. Co., Inc., 1972. Case examples are used to present the author's philosophy of creating lasting, committed partnerships.

Rubin, Zick. *Liking and Loving*. New York, Holt, Rinehart & Winston, 1973. An introduction to the study of affiliative and affection-based interpersonal relations.

Satir, Virginia. *Peoplemaking*. Palo Alto, Calif., Science & Behavior Books, 1972. Suggestions for improving communication and developing harmonious relationships.

CHOOSING
A PARTNER

In practice more couples are thrown together by accident than by either the magic of romance or the strategy of intelligence.

Robert O. Blood, Jr.[1]

4

Although many of us assume that love is the reason that we choose a partner or marry, social scientists have shown that there are less romantic factors that affect our choices. Partner selection in our culture is influenced by such factors as age, race, religion, proximity, and social class. Selection of a partner is also determined by social and family pressures and an individual's particular ideals and expectations. Consciously and unconsciously, people screen individuals from a very large pool of potential partners until only those with certain "suitable" characteristics are left. For example, some persons may want mates who are athletic and share an interest in the same sports. Some people prefer outgoing individuals, but others prefer quieter types.

In the United States most people are almost completely free to choose their marital partners. In the past, however, the family or clan determined who married whom, and individuals did not have the freedom to choose their own mates. Even today, in many cultures, arranged marriages are the usual form of mate selection (see Box 4.1).

With the freedom that we enjoy in choosing a partner comes the fear that we will make the wrong decision. As sociologists John Gagnon and Cathy Greenblat explain:

The recognition that the particular individuals who are getting married represent one of a number of possibilities decreases the assurance with which people approach marriage. This is perhaps the most critical change in the mate selection process as it exists in modern industrial and urban societies—that there is now more opportunity for hesitation, ambivalence, deliberation, and personal soul searching. When the choice was made by others, when there was only a limited number of eligibles to choose from, or when people believed that marriages were made in heaven, the question of "correct" choice remained moot. Now it becomes the center of the mate selection process.[2]

We worry that we may never find someone with whom to share our lives, and once we do, we wonder if we have made the right choice.

People often assume that marital discord is caused by having chosen an unsuitable partner. A couple's happiness, however, is affected by much more than the personal characteristics of the partners at the time they marry. Everyone changes and develops with age, and happiness is affected by the experiences shared with a partner and the energy, love, and commitment expressed in close relationships. No single factor or sequence of events can assure the success of any given relationship.

In this chapter, we discuss the motivations and factors that influence the partner selection process. These topics are of obvious interest to those who are contemplating marriage, to those deciding whether or not to remain in existing relationships, and to those contemplating remarriage, because the information to be presented is designed to help an individual examine his or her current paired relationship and clarify expectations regarding future ones. Such information also may help explain the problems that cause relationships to end. These explanations will include theories about trends, not laws or rules. Behavioral scientists have been able to describe some of the factors involved in partner selection, and this information can provide greater insight into the variables and interactive factors that determine who marries whom. In addition, for many people, chance, situational factors, missed opportunities, and coincidence also play a part in the choice of a partner.

MOTIVATIONS FOR MARRIAGE

People marry for many reasons. Some of these are love, companionship, security, status, social pressures, parental pressures, and financial security. People have different reasons or motives for marrying, which depend on individual psychological and social needs. Richard Clayton organizes the different motives for marriage by separating them into "push" and "pull" factors: "The push factors are those that pressure a couple to move more rapidly toward the married state. The pull factors serve as a kind of magnet. They seem to neutralize the fears that many single persons have about married life, such as losing their freedom and being tied down."[3] Clayton discusses three push factors: conformity, legitimation of sex, and love.

BOX 4.1　Arranged Marriages in India

In India, nearly all marriages are arranged by the couple's families. Both caste and religion are extremely important, and intercaste and interreligious marriages are rare. The following is an interview held in 1980 with Indira, a twenty-eight-year-old Indian woman living in the United States. She has spent most of her life in Europe, and both she and her husband have graduate degrees.

QUESTION:　How does mate selection occur in India?

ANSWER:　Arranged marriages are the dominant form. Marriage to someone of one's own choosing involves only a small minority of the population. Those who do choose a marriage partner tend to be more modern, more Westernized—those who have studied abroad. Often it is considered trendy to choose one's partner, since it is so much against the traditional way of marriage. More Westernized Indian individuals date and go out, but the majority abide by the rules set by tradition.

QUESTION:　Was your marriage arranged?

ANSWER:　No, my husband and I met in England where we both were attending school. But it was upsetting for my parents, particularly since I married someone from a lower caste. I was the first in my family to not have an arranged marriage and to marry outside of my caste.

QUESTION:　What role do caste and religion play?

ANSWER:　Indians almost always marry within their religion and caste. Intermarriage is unthinkable—Moslems never marry Hindus. My husband and I returned to India to have a Hindu ceremony. One of my friends had a register [civil] marriage in London, but her family does not recognize the marriage. It is scandalous. It's very important to have a religious ceremony.

QUESTION:　Does your caste change when you intermarry?

ANSWER:　One's caste is established at birth. The four castes are Brahman, Kshatriya, Vaisya, and Sudra—Brahman is the highest. A man's caste is never raised or lowered. Mine was lowered to that of my husband, although if I had been a lower caste and married up, I would not assume the higher caste.

QUESTION:　When are marriages arranged?

ANSWER:　Although it still occurs, arrangements at birth are quite rare. In traditional families, arrangement often occurs at a very young age—ten or twelve. Many of my mother's friends were married when they were nine years old. They remained at home until puberty. They may have never seen their husband before the wedding night. It is so terrible—imagine being thirteen and suddenly being with a complete stranger. It isn't always fixed when you're young. In the cities, parents often begin to look for a partner when you're seventeen or eighteen.

QUESTION:　What procedure do the parents follow in looking for a partner?

ANSWER:　It differs by region. In some parts of India, the girl's parents look for a husband for her, while in other parts the boy's parents look for a wife for their son. Normally they look within their community, but those with contacts and who are more wealthy may look elsewhere. The parents correspond and a meeting is set. Usually the woman is veiled. The families meet and the arrangements are discussed later after a decision has been made.

BOX 4.1   (continued)

QUESTION: Do the parents consider the boy's character or personality along with his caste and religion?

ANSWER: Actually no. They do not see the boy until the families meet, but they do ask around. Is he from a "good" family, doesn't drink or date, good habits, cultural interests? In addition, the boy's family is very important. What is their reputation, do they have any vices, how did they raise their children?

QUESTION: Do the individuals have any say during this time?

ANSWER: Individuals do not have a choice —this is the only system they know. After the meeting, the man has the option to say he doesn't want the girl. But even when it is the girl's parents who initially do the corresponding, she has to abide by their decision. She cannot say no, but the man can.

QUESTION: The system seems unfair to women?

ANSWER: Yes. Indian women are oppressed. They have no choice, and in India they're considered a liability. The parents have to get the girls married. At times, it is very sad. In northern India tbe boy's parents search for a partner. If no one comes around for a woman, she doesn't get married. Her parents do not have the option of selecting a husband for her.

QUESTION: What happens if a couple is unhappily married? Is divorce possible in India?

ANSWER: Divorce is not possible under Hindu law. It can be obtained under civil law, but it's unheard of—it's scandalous, particularly for the woman. More frequently, a man sends his wife away to her parents or leaves her. This is a tremendous disgrace. Often women will kill themselves because they believe it is better to die than to have your family find out that your husband left you. They assume it is your fault—you did not make your husband happy. The burden is on the woman, and out of respect she does everything for the man.

Hindu law doesn't encourage remarriage either—for example, if your husband dies, you are a widow forever. In India, social pressure and tradition force a couple to stay together for life. They accept it. I think the best word in all of this is acceptance—everyone accepts their spouse and their marriage—they don't question it.

QUESTION: What are the advantages of arranged marriages?

ANSWER: It's hard for me to see any. I think the system is oppressive. But my school friends would argue that it places the responsibility for your happiness on your parents. They trust their parents and respect their judgment. The girls feel that their parents are bound to find someone suitable for them. It alleviates the pressures and problems of dating. They feel Western women have a lot of pressure to marry and are looked down on if they do not have a boy friend. Indian women have that pressure removed. They do not have to find someone—someone is chosen for them.

QUESTION: Will the system ever change and allow for more choice?

ANSWER: If it does, it will take a very long time. Women do not have any freedom, and even though men have the freedom to divorce or desert their wives, they don't. It will take a long time for things to change—marriage is so sacred in India.

Source: From the authors' files.

1. *Conformity*   Our society is enamored with marriage. From early childhood on, people are taught the importance of marriage and the family, and they are expected to "conform" by marrying and establishing families of their own.

2. *Legitimation of Sex*   Clayton notes that even though many people engage in nonmarital sexual relations, most will desire, after a period of time, to legitimize their sexual relationships by means of marriage: "Even couples who vehemently disavow any acceptance of societal norms about marriage will usually make some effort to declare their mutual commitment publicly so that their association will not be regarded as totally hedonistic or exploitative."[4]

3. *Love*   People also are taught to consider marriage the expected outcome of a love relationship, a method of translating emotional commitment into a long-term social commitment.

Other push factors include escape from loneliness or an unhappy home situation, the financial pressures felt by a single parent, premarital pregnancy, or the fear that "this may be my only chance."

The pull factors that Clayton discusses are companionship, sharing, and communication:

1. *Companionship*   This is probably the most important aspect of the mate selection decision—the desire to have a regular companion, someone who can be loved and depended on. Companionship brings security and stability to a person's life and helps fulfill most of his or her emotional needs.

2. *Sharing*   Besides someone to meet emotional needs, people want a partner with whom to share ideas, time, and activities. Experiences are usually more meaningful if there is someone with whom to share the highs and the lows.

3. *Communication*   Besides companionship and the sharing of love and activities, people want to communicate intimately with their partners. In intimate relationships, people rarely have to "play games;" they can fully disclose their thoughts and feelings and have their concerns and feelings heard and reciprocated.

Other pull factors that draw individuals to marriage are emotional and financial security, the desire to have children, stability, and status. Clayton feels that pull factors are often overemphasized in our society to the point that people see togetherness and sharing as ideals. Although they are important and attractive factors, companionship and sharing taken to an extreme may become possessive and dominating behavior.

FACTORS INFLUENCING PARTNER SELECTION

In both arranged marriages and mutual-choice marriages, *endogamy* and *exogamy* define each person's pool of eligible partners. Marriage within one's own tribe, race, ethnic group, religion, or social class is called *endogamy*. Examples of endogamous pairings are blacks marrying blacks, whites marrying whites, and Catholics marrying Catholics. Marriage outside one's tribe, race, ethnic group, religion, or social class is called *exogamy*. Interracial and interreligious marriages are examples. In most societies there are laws forbidding incestuous pairings; thus, people must choose a partner who is not a blood relative. In some cultures, marriages between tribe or clan members are also prohibited.

Age

Most people in our society marry within their own age range. There are exceptions, to be sure, but it is more or less expected that first marriages will be between people whose ages are relatively close. Within this range, women traditionally have dated and married slightly older men; in only 15 percent of American marriages are the wives older than their husbands. According to figures compiled by the U.S. government, on the average, husbands are two or three years older than their wives.

The expectations that people will marry within their own age range and that the male will be slightly older than his partner greatly reduce the number of eligible partners for both sexes. For example, if the customary pairing age range is three years, the eligible partners for a twenty-two-year-old man are women between the ages of nineteen and twenty-two. For a twenty-two-year-old woman, only men between twenty-two and twenty-five are likely to be considered suitable partners.

These age differentials are significant to many college students. An eighteen-year-old freshman woman can choose partners from nearly all the students on campus but by the time she is a senior, the number of eligible partners has shrunk to approximately one-fourth of the original number. This situation is reversed for men; a twenty-two-year-old male college senior has about four times the number of potential partners that he had when he was a freshman.

But by the time people reach their thirties, the age differential may not be as important. Men in their mid-thirties, for example, may consider as eligible partners women who are as many as ten years younger than themselves. They also may feel comfortable with slightly older partners. A similar pattern may be true for some older women. Partners several years older or a few years younger may be acceptable for them, as well. Older people may be less strict about age because they realize that it limits the number of potential partners. Also, many people recognize that age is, at best, only an imperfect measure of life experience and that to select a partner solely on the basis of age, without considering personal qualities, may eliminate many possibly compatible partners.

Many are now beginning to question the stereotypical idea that in order for a marriage to be successful, the man must be older than his partner. Relationships between older women and younger men have been the subject of numerous magazine articles, as well as the theme of several movies.

Older women and younger men involved in relationships no longer consider themselves exceptions, as this woman explains:

Bob and I were married when I was thirty-seven and he was twenty-seven. But in the five years since then I'd never questioned the idea that the man *should* be older; I just thought of us as *exceptions*. Then I read an article about single women in their thirties who couldn't find men to go out with. When one was asked if she'd date someone younger, she said, "Oh, no, I couldn't—it would be too embarrassing." I suddenly realized that she wasn't liberated at all—and neither was I! We were still buying the idea that the man should be superior to the woman. Why else should he be older? But does five or ten years make a man smarter? Stronger? Better able to take care of you? When you stop to think about it, it's ridiculous.[5]

Many view the increased tolerance of relationships between older women and younger men as a step forward. As psychotherapist Leah Schaefer states: "The women's movement has given women more freedom in their choice of partners—including the choice of a man who is younger. Any development that frees people from stereotypes and enables them to make choices on the basis of feelings is a healthy development."[6] Men also are feeling freer to choose older partners as well as younger ones.

Americans have tended to marry at a younger age than people in other industrialized societies have. The median age of Americans at first marriage (about 24 for males and 22 for females) is lower than that for the English, French, Norwegians, Swiss, Austrians, and Japanese. The highest median age at first marriage has always been that of the Irish—31.4 for males and 26.5 for females.

As shown in Table 4.1, in the United States the median age at first

TABLE 4.1 Median Age at First Marriage in the United States, 1890–1979

Year	Male	Female
1890	26.1	22.0
1900	25.9	21.9
1910	25.1	21.6
1920	24.6	21.2
1930	24.3	21.3
1940	24.3	21.5
1950	22.8	20.3
1960	22.8	20.3
1970	23.2	20.8
1978	24.2	21.8
1979	24.4	22.1

Source: U.S. Bureau of the Census, *Current Population Reports*, Series P–20, No. 349, "Marital Status and Living Arrangements: March 1979," February 1980, p. 1.

marriage dropped, for both men and women, from the turn of the century until about 1950. During the past three decades, this downward trend leveled off and then reversed itself. Today, the figures for women are about the same as they were in 1890, and those for men are about two years younger. In 1890 the median age at first marriage was 26.1 for men and 22.0 for women; corresponding figures for 1979 were 24.4 for men and 22.1 for women. (College graduates usually marry one or two years later than the average.)

Statistics indicate that the divorce rate for teen-agers is twice that for people in their twenties (see Figure 4.1). The high failure rate for teen-age marriages is attributed to premarital pregnancy, financial and emotional insecurity, less life experience, and the fact that a teen-ager's needs and values may drastically change when that person reaches his or her twenties (see Box 4.2).

Race

Race is clearly an endogamous factor in mate selection: most individuals marry within their own race. Census statistics show that between 1960 and 1970 the number of interracial married couples increased by 108 percent, from 148,000 to 310,000, and the increase between 1970

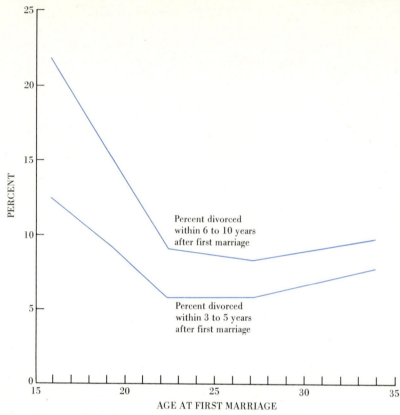

Percent divorced
within 6 to 10 years
after first marriage

Percent divorced
within 3 to 5 years
after first marriage

AGE AT FIRST MARRIAGE

Source: Paul C. Glick and Arthur J. Norton, "Marrying, Divorcing, and Living Together in the U.S. Today," *Population Bulletin*, 32, No. 5 (1977): 16. Courtesy of the Population Reference Bureau, Inc., Washington, D.C.

and 1977 was 36 percent, 310,000 to 421,000.[7] Although the percentage increases seem large, interracial marriages comprise only about three-quarters of 1 percent of the approximately 48 million marriages in the United States. But as sociologist Thomas Monahan suggests, looking at interracial marriages in terms of the numbers of minorities who intermarry produces a different interpretation.

Looked at as a whole, the proportion of all marriages which are of mixed race seems low, being less than 3/4 of 1 percent in any sample year. This is because the marriages of Whites-with-Whites numerically overwhelm the field of data. However, if we ask the more incisive question as to what proportion of the minority marriages are of a mixed nature, then the extent of mixed marriages becomes more impressive.

BOX 4.2 Teen-age Marriages Face Heavy Odds

A number of studies have explored the relationship of age at marriage to marital happiness and the frequency of divorce. Regardless of the criteria used, virtually all of the studies show that early marriages are very likely to be unstable. According to sociologist Marcia Lasswell, who made a survey of the various findings:

Getting married in the teen years is unquestionably the worst time to marry, not only in terms of the stability of the marriage, but in terms of the reported satisfaction which marriage brings to the couple. The divorce rate is correlated with age at marriage and the older the couple is at marriage, the greater likelihood that the marriage will succeed. For men, there is a point of diminishing returns at about age 31 and after age 27 the decline slows down considerably. For women, the divorce rate declines with each year they wait to marry until a gradual leveling off at about age 25.*

Although there is little doubt that very early marriage is associated with marital instability, exactly why this is so is uncertain. Some authorities suggest that those who marry young are too inexperienced and unprepared—both emotionally and economically—for the realities of married life. On the basis of his own intensive investigation, sociologist Gary Lee adds another interesting possibility, that "those who marry young are cognizant of their excellent chances for remarriage in the event of divorce, and are thus less willing to tolerate given levels of dissatisfaction in their current marriages than are those who contract their initial marriages later in life."†

Because our society is "couple conscious," marriage also offers status to many young people. Being married is evidence to a young couple's families and friends, and to society at large, that they are adults capable of making their own decisions. Marriage affords the chance to get away from home, and to some, the glamour of a large, fashionable wedding can be the motivating reason for getting married.

Very little consideration is given to the considerable change in life style that begins immediately after the couple returns from their honeymoon. Because early marriages are so fragile, young people intending to marry would do well to consider carefully their motives and preparation for marriage.

*Marcia Lasswell, "Is There a Best Age to Marry? An Interpretation," *Family Coordinator*, 23 (July 1974): 240.
†Gary Lee, "Age at Marriage and Marital Satisfaction: A Multivariate Analysis with Implications for Marital Stability," *Journal of Marriage and the Family*, 39 (August 1977): 502–503.

The mixed proportion among Negroes becomes several percent, and the Other Races proportion well over 50 percent.[8]

(In Monahan's analysis, "Other Races" include American Indians, Eskimos, Japanese, Chinese, Filipinos, and others.) There are many racial combinations, but generally most attention is focused on black-white marriages, which account for approximately one-quarter of all interracial marriages.

Monahan also points out that the rates of interracial marriages vary from state to state. In his study, the District of Columbia had the largest number of black-white marriages. In regard to other racial combinations, Hawaii and Alaska, both of which have large minority populations, also had remarkably high interracial marriage rates (10.2 percent of all marriages were racially mixed in Alaska, 31.7 percent in Hawaii).[9] A state's rate of racial intermarriage, therefore, should be analyzed in relation to the racial composition of its population.

People reportedly are taking a more tolerant view of interracial marriage than they once did. This seems to be particularly true of younger people and those with a college education. In answer to the question, "Do you approve of marriage between whites and non-whites?" a Gallup Poll found these figures over a ten-year period:[10]

	Approve (%)	Disapprove (%)	No Opinion (%)
1968	20	72	8
1972	29	60	11
1978	36	54	10

The same survey showed that nonwhites were more than twice as likely as whites to approve of interracial marriage (66 percent versus 32 percent). Also, the higher the respondent's educational level, the more likely he or she was to approve of interracial marriage:

	Approve (%)	Disapprove (%)	No Opinion (%)
Grade school	19	70	11
High school	32	57	11
College	53	40	7

Why do people intermarry? Ernest Porterfield's study of black-white intermarriage suggested that:

A majority of interracial dating and marriage is not related to some pathological abnormality or to any crusade against prejudice. . . . Grounds for interracial marriages are usually the same as those for marriage between persons of the same race. . . . [Most] of these couples cited love and compatibility as their primary motives for getting married. . . . Most of them reported that their initial relationships were based on shared interests, ideas, and values.[11]

Although most interracial marriages occur for the same reasons that same-race marriages do, interracial couples sometimes have problems that same-race couples do not have in regard to bigotry, parental relations, housing, job discrimination, and friendship patterns. Some children of interracial marriages are completely accepted by outsiders, whereas others are rebuffed by members of both races and relatives on both sides.[12]

Recent studies indicate that interracial marriages may be more stable than has been popularly believed.[13] For example, in his study of forty black-white couples, Porterfield found that although interracial couples often were alienated from their families and received negative reactions from friends and neighbors, many reported that their marriages were, nonetheless, happy and successful.

A preponderance of the families reported being relatively happy. As far as marital problems are concerned, theirs are no different from those of any other marriage. Quarrels or other family disagreements seldom carry racial overtones.

Most of the parents feel their children will not encounter insurmountable discriminatory problems. They attribute this to the changing nature of race relations in American society. They say that "things are getting better," and that future America will become increasingly free of racial prejudices. A few families, however, do not concur in this opinion.[14]

Interracial marriage is becoming more acceptable.

George Cohen/Stock, Boston

Despite the additional problems an interracial couple may face, these difficulties do not necessarily disrupt the marriage. Perhaps those who marry people of another race have a greater motivation than most people do to make their marriages work.

Religion

The extent of religious endogamy in the United States depends on the particular religion or denomination being considered, and on the individual's commitment to his or her faith. Most studies of interfaith marriage analyze the patterns among the three major religious groups in the United States: Protestants, Catholics, and Jews. All three groups encourage their members to marry within the fold, although there is some variation among the three. The Protestants are the most flexible, the Orthodox Jews are the most rigid, and the Catholics fall between them. Generally, a priest will marry a Catholic and a non-Catholic, but most Orthodox rabbis will not marry a Jew and a non-Jew.

Although the incidence of interfaith marriage in the United States has been increasing, the majority of individuals within these three groups practice religious endogamy. However, it should be kept in

Most individuals practice religious endogamy.

Bill Aron/Jeroboam

mind that statistics on interfaith marriage are difficult to interpret because they usually list a couple's current religious preference rather than their preferences before marriage and, furthermore, do not account for the fact that often one partner converted to the other's religion before or soon after marriage.

As with interracial marriage, public opinion regarding interfaith marriage appears to be growing more tolerant. For example, a 1978 Gallup Poll indicated that less than 15 percent of the respondents were opposed to marriages between Jews and non-Jews or between Protestants and Catholics. The actual breakdown is shown below:[15]

	Approve (%)	Disapprove (%)	No Opinion (%)
Marriage between Jews and non-Jews	69	14	17
Marriage between Catholics and Protestants	73	13	14

It should be noted, however, that although most people say that they approve of interreligious marriages, most people in the three principal religious groups nevertheless continue to marry within their own faith.

A number of sociologists have been studying the characteristics of the intermarried, and their research has revealed that, for instance, Jewish males are much more likely to marry non-Jews than Jewish females are. In marriages between Protestants and Catholics, no parallel tendency has been found. More than one study has indicated that when compared with those who marry within their own faith, persons who intermarry are more likely to have:[16]

- weak religious and familial ties
- a high rate of prior divorce
- a civil rather than a religious ceremony
- parents who also had interfaith marriages
- a high rate of premarital pregnancy
- an urban background

Because Judaism and Catholicism are minority religions in the United States, young people of both faiths are overexposed, statistically speaking, to the larger Protestant group. In certain regions of the country, the proportion of Jews or Catholics is so small that religious exogamy (marrying outside the group) is almost inevitable.

Jews comprise only about 3 percent of the U.S. population. If they adhered to strict religious endogamy, Jewish men and women would exclude themselves from approximately 97 percent of the population of otherwise eligible mates. But in practice, many do not. The Jewish intermarriage rate, although variable—for example, from less than 5 percent in Providence, Rhode Island, to more than 50 percent in Indiana—is unquestionably increasing.[17]

Numerically, the most significant interreligious marriage pattern is that between Protestants and Catholics. There are over fifty million Catholics in the United States; hence, if religious endogamy prevailed, both Catholics and Protestants would be greatly restricted in the partners they could select. However, as with Jewish people, the number of Catholics who intermarry has been increasing, and now approximately one-third of all marriages in the United States involving Catholics contain a non-Catholic partner.

Although the incidence of interreligious marriage is increasing, it is unlikely that religion will disappear as an endogamous factor in partner selection. Many people will continue to feel strongly about marrying someone of the same faith.

Ethnic Group

Throughout its history, the United States has become the adopted homeland for millions of people born in other countries. America's first immigrants were settlers from northwestern Europe. But before this, as sociologist Gerald Leslie points out, there was a forced migration of black slaves:

Little attention is paid, ordinarily, to the fact that the largest migration to America, before 1800, was of [black] slaves. The exact size of this migration will never be known. The number probably falls between 10 and 20 million people. By contrast, the number of migrants from all of Europe during the same period was not over 5 million.[18]

In the nineteenth century, approximately 19 million people immigrated from northwestern Europe—Great Britain, Ireland, Germany, and France. From 1890 to 1930, approximately 22 million people came to the United States from southern and eastern Europe—Italy, Austria-Hungary, and Russia.[19]

Italians are typical of the ethnic groups that began emigrating to the United States in the early twentieth century and that maintain their ethnic traditions and practices. Although the term *Italian* is often used to refer to immigrants from Italy, Sicily, Corsica, and Sardinia, these groups are by no means similar. They speak many different dialects and usually choose to settle among their own *paesani*—kinfolk and friends from their own and neighboring villages.

Italians, like other first-generation immigrants (the first generation refers to the immigrants themselves; the second generation, to their children; and the third generation, to their grandchildren), tend to retain much of the culture and tradition of their homeland. For example, first-generation Italians were forbidden to date non-Italians, and their marriages were often arranged or at least strongly influenced by parents.

As the children and grandchildren of immigrants assimilate into American society, many of the first-generation immigrants' traditions are lost. Although many ethnic groups actively attempt to preserve their cultural heritage, ethnicity is no longer as important a factor in mate selection as it once was. Ethnic endogamy generally is much less prevalent among second- and third-generation ethnic persons than among first-generation immigrants.[20]

Intelligence, Education, and Social Class

Marriage partners tend to have the same range of intelligence. Based on IQ scores, the similarity in intelligence between spouses is approximately the same as that among siblings.

Another similarity between partners is education. Individuals frequently marry someone who has completed a similar level of education.[21] In the past, men usually married women with an equal or lower educational level, and women married men with the same or a higher educational level. One reason for this was that until recently, more men than women had completed college. In addition, because women generally marry men of the same age or older, their spouses are more likely to have achieved higher levels of education before marrying. But now that more women than men are graduating from high school and women are just as likely as men to finish college, it is possible that this pattern will change.

For several decades Americans have tended to marry within their own socioeconomic or social class. Americans typically are identified as belonging to the lower, middle, or upper class. Although concepts and definitions vary, one commonly used definition of social class refers to factors such as occupation, income, and education. According to these criteria, people tend to choose partners within their own social stratum. Researcher Bruce Eckland estimates that between 50 percent and 80 percent of the marriages in the United States are endogamous in reference to social class.[22]

Propinquity

Propinquity means nearness in place, or proximity. For almost fifty years, one of the truisms in sociology has been that people tend to marry those who live nearby. Propinquity obviously is important to partner selection because it influences people's opportunities for interaction. Except for mail-order brides and other kinds of arranged marriages, people generally choose their partners from the group of people they know. In addition to residential proximity, propinquity can also influence people at work, in clubs and organizations, and at favorite restaurants and recreational sites.

The original study of propinquity and mate selection was done by James Bossard in 1932. In transcribing street addresses from five thousand consecutive marriage licenses issued in Philadelphia, Bossard discovered that one-sixth of the couples applying for licenses lived within one block of each other, one-third lived within five blocks, and more than half lived within twenty blocks of each other. As Bossard aptly concluded, "Cupid may have wings, but apparently they are not adapted for long flights."[23] Since Bossard's study, dozens of other studies have verified his findings. Although residential propinquity still is important in today's highly mobile society, it now has a greater influence on partner selection on college campuses, in places of work, and in the neighborhoods that people move to, than in the neighborhoods where people grew up.

Since the number of potential partners increases with the distance from one's residence, why is residential propinquity such a predictable factor in partner selection? The answer is largely dependent on the interplay among propinquity and such factors as religion, social class, and nationality. As many sociologists have asserted, people do not randomly select where they live. Their choice is influenced by occupation, place of work, social class, and sometimes race or cultural background. Thus, when two individuals from the same neighborhood marry, it might be assumed that residential propinquity has fostered another pairing. But such an assumption may not always be valid. Perhaps both individuals are Italians, and they married because of their shared religion, nationality, or social class, all of which are factors determining residential propinquity.

All of the criteria that we have discussed influence partner selection, and their effects have been widely researched. Currently, the relative influence of these various endogamous criteria and their interaction with one another have not been determined.

CHOOSING TO PARTNER

Our discussion so far has dealt with the factors influencing the partner selection process. Inherent in the process of *choosing a partner* is the assumption that one is indeed *choosing to partner or to marry*.

Individual needs, social pressures, family pressures, and career decisions are the principal influences on a person's decision to marry. People may marry for many reasons, such as love, companionship, security, status, and financial support and gain. But they also may decide to stay single for many reasons. Some persons may be too involved with a career to be able to contemplate a partnership, or if they have been single for a period of time, they may not want to exchange a satisfactory and comfortable life style for the unknown outcome of a new relationship. Also, people may want to accomplish other goals, such as finishing college or obtaining a certain job, before they marry.

For these reasons, many people are choosing to remain single longer. Singlehood carries with it its own issues and problems, which are discussed in Chapter 17, "Alternative Marital and Family Structures."

SUMMARY

People marry for a variety of reasons, including love, companionship, conformity, security, status, social pressures, parental pressures, financial security, and the desire to have children. Some of these reasons are "push" factors which pressure a couple toward marriage, whereas others are "pull" factors which attract individuals to marriage.

People may marry because they are in love, but they tend to fall in love with people who live nearby, whom they work with, and who are similar with regard to age, race, religion, ethnic background, intelligence, education, and social class. These variables serve as screening steps in the process of partner selection, and as such, they influence attraction to and interaction with others.

Inherent in this process of choosing a partner is the notion that the individual is choosing to have a partner. There are many factors that influence a person's decision to remain single or to marry. College goals, life-style decisions, and career involvement are some of the factors that may affect an individual's decision to partner or marry.

Dear Diane,

Guess what? Mark asked me to marry him! I should be excited, but I'm having a lot of second thoughts. We love each other a lot, but there seem to be so many reasons why we shouldn't get married.

All along, I knew we didn't have that much in common, and at the time I didn't think it mattered so much. And I guess I wasn't really thinking about any future plans. But now that we've been talking about getting married, all these things have surfaced.

One problem is our ages. At first it wasn't an issue because I thought he was a lot younger and he thought I was older. I still remember his expression when I told him I was twenty-three, and I about died when he said he was thirty-four, was divorced from his wife, and had a thirteen-year-old daughter. His daughter is only ten years younger than I am!

Our age difference doesn't bother me nearly as much as the prospect of instantly becoming the mother of a teen-ager. And I still have a lot of ambition regarding my career. Mark has never liked his job, but he's still there and still complaining. I've always felt that if you weren't happy, you should move on—it seems awful to make compromises like that.

It's funny—I never think of him as an older, divorced man—definitely not high on my parent's list of personality characteristics for a son-in-law. So they're hassling me. But I love him a lot—I'm just not sure that's enough. What should I do?

Love,
Jackie

Questions
1. What advice would you give Jackie?
2. Would your advice to Jackie be different if their ages were reversed and Mark's daughter were an infant?
3. Which of the causes of Jackie's uncertainty—the difference in age, the difference in ambition, or the fact that Mark is divorced and has a teen-age daughter—do you think are most important for her to consider?
4. Is love enough to overcome these obstacles? Do you think they could be happily married?

5. What qualities and characteristics are you looking for in a spouse? Are there some things that you cannot compromise on?

6. To what extent will (or did) your family, friends, career, and living situation influence your decision to marry?

7. How do you know when you have chosen the right partner to marry?

NOTES

1. Robert O. Blood, Jr., *Marriage*, New York, The Free Press, 1969, p. 36.

2. John Gagnon and Cathy Greenblat, *Life Designs: Individual, Marriage, and Families*, Glenview, Ill., Scott, Foresman, 1978, p. 117.

3. Richard Clayton, *The Family, Marriage, and Social Change*, Lexington, Mass., Heath, 1979, p. 363.

4. Ibid.

5. Nancy Oates, "Older Woman/Younger Man," *Woman's Day*, August 7, 1979, p. 68.

6. Ibid., p. 66.

7. U.S. Bureau of the Census, *Current Population Reports: Special Studies*, Series P–23, No. 77, "Perspectives on American Husbands and Wives," December 1978, p. 7.

8. Thomas P. Monahan, "An Overview of Statistics on Interracial Marriage in the United States, with Data on Its Extent from 1963–1970," *Journal of Marriage and the Family*, 38 (May 1976): 225.

9. Ibid., p. 226.

10. Gallup Poll release of November 23, 1978.

11. Ernest Porterfield, *Black and White Mixed Marriages*, Chicago, Nelson-Hall, 1978, pp. 64–65.

12. "People Who Intermarry: Pioneers or Protesters?" *Seattle Urban League Special Report*, Seattle, April 1967.

13. Thomas P. Monahan, "Interracial Marriage and Divorce in Kansas and the Question of Instability in Mixed Marriages," *Journal of Comparative Family Studies*, Spring 1971, pp. 107–120; Thomas P. Monahan, "Are Interracial Marriages Really Less Stable?" *Social Forces*, June 1970, pp. 461–473.

14. Ernest Porterfield, *Black and White Mixed Marriages*, p. 123.

15. Gallup Poll release of November 23, 1978.

16. See, for example, Frank Bean and Linda Aiken, "Intermarriage and Unwanted Fertility in the United States," *Journal of Marriage and the Family*, 38 (February 1976): 61–72.

17. Thomas Monahan, "Some Dimensions of Interreligious Marriages in Indiana," *Social Forces*, December 1973, pp. 195–203; see also the

discussion in Gerald Leslie, *The Family in Social Context*, New York, Oxford University Press, 1979, pp. 403–406.

18. Gerald R. Leslie, *The Family in Social Context*, p. 225.
19. Ibid.
20. See, for example, Frank Mittelbach and Joan Moore, "Ethnic Endogamy—The Case of Mexican Americans," *American Journal of Sociology*, 74 (July 1968): 50–62; Edward Murguia and W. Parker Frisbie, "Trends in Mexican American Intermarriage: Recent Findings in Perspective," *Social Science Quarterly*, 58 (December 1977): 374–389.
21. U.S. Bureau of the Census, *Current Population Reports: Special Studies*, Series P–23, No. 77, "Perspectives on American Husbands and Wives," December 1978, pp. 11–15.
22. Bruce Eckland, "Theories of Mate Selection," *Eugenics Quarterly*, June 1968, p. 78.
23. James Bossard, "Residential Propinquity as a Factor in Marriage Selection," *American Journal of Sociology*, 38 (September 1932): 222.

SUGGESTED READINGS

Davor, Jedlicka. "Sex Inequality, Aging, and Innovation in Preferential Mate Selection." *Family Coordinator*, April 1978, pp. 137–140. An examination of the double age standard which forces most women to remain unmarried after widowhood, whether or not they want to.

Lee, Gary. "Age at Marriage and Marital Satisfaction: A Multivariate Analysis with Implications for Marital Stability." *Journal of Marriage and the Family*, August 1977, pp. 493–504. An investigation of the relationship between age at marriage and marital stability.

Murstein, Bernard. *Who Will Marry Whom?* New York, Springer, 1976. A thorough analysis of research on the factors influencing the choice of a marital partner and the major theories of mate selection.

Porterfield, Ernest. *Black and White Mixed Marriages*. Chicago, Nelson-Hall, 1978. An informative study of intermarriage between blacks and whites.

U.S. Bureau of the Census, *Current Population Reports: Special Studies*, Series P–23, No. 77, "Perspective on American Husbands and Wives." Washington, D.C., U.S. Government Printing Office, December 1979. A report of the demographic and economic characteristics of married couples.

BECOMING PARTNERS

Come up and see me sometime.

Mae West (from the movie Diamond Lil)

5

In the United States, selecting a spouse requires finding and choosing one person from the many people in the population at large. Some people attribute their finding a partner to luck, as the following suggests:

You know, if I really had to analyze how Ann and I got together, I would have to say it was luck. It had been only a couple of months since I ended a very unhappy relationship, and I definitely was not looking for anyone else. Ann and I were assigned to a new project at work and we were really compatible. We had so much in common, and it was so easy to share our feelings and goals. Sometimes I wonder what would have happened if I hadn't been assigned to that particular project—we never would have met.

From the authors' files

Although this man credits his finding a partner to luck, other factors were also at work. As discussed in Chapter 4, "Choosing a Partner," many social factors, such as age, race, religion, education, and propinquity, influence the choice of a partner by defining the pool of potential mates. For the man quoted above, the fact that he and his partner were working together indicates that they might have had similar educational backgrounds and intellectual interests. These factors, along with working together (propinquity) and perhaps other factors he did not mention, served to define the two as potential mates.

After the operation of social factors has established a pool of eligibles, the final selection of a partner is based on more individual characteristics. At first, scholars tried to explain the final selection of a partner by theorizing that for each man there was a particular woman and that a kind of "instinct" guided them to one another. Carl Jung, for example, felt that falling in love was tantamount to being caught by one's "archetype"—a mental image of the "perfect" partner carried in each person's genes. When the person embodying the archetype came along, one was immediately "seized."

Another early theory of mate selection was the psychoanalytic view. Stated simply, this theory assumed that people were guided in their choice of a mate by a "parental image"—a physical and temperamental image of the parent of the opposite sex. Thus, unconsciously, a male would want to pair with someone who resembled his mother, and a female with someone who resembled her father.

Later theorists focused on broad personality traits in an attempt to determine whether "like marries like" *(homogamy)* or whether "opposites attract" *(heterogamy)*. These simplistic theories, however, have been more or less discarded. There is no "archetype," and empirical research has failed to offer convincing evidence that the psychoanalytic concept of "parental image" affects the choice of a mate. Also, the influence of personality factors in mate selection is much more complex than the simple homogamy-heterogamy approach suggests.

Today, mate selection theories and their supporting investigations are sophisticated analyses of factors such as social roles, values, need gratifications, and the various stages of the partner selection process. And though there is still no definitive answer to the question of why one person marries another, several of these current theories provide some insights.

In this chapter we examine some of the mate selection theories that help explain the final selection of a partner. We also discuss the dating system, the process by which potential partners test their compatibility and their suitability as mates.

BASIC THEORIES OF MATE SELECTION

Complementary Needs Theory

One of the first theories of mate selection was Robert Winch's concept of complementary needs. This theory proposed that mate selection is a function of personality need-fulfillment; that is, a person chooses someone who complements his or her personality, thereby gratifying particular personality needs. One example of complements is dominance-deference, which describes the traditional view of marriage roles. Until recently, society required men to be independent and aggressive, and women to be submissive and nurturing—the kinds of relationships portrayed by television's Archie and Edith Bunker. To explain his theory, Winch offers the following hypothetical illustration:

> Let us assume that there is a chap by the name of Jonathan, and that Jonathan's most distinguished characteristic is a need to be dominant in interpersonal relationships. We shall assume further that among his acquaintances are two girls, Jean and Jennifer. Jennifer is like Jonathan in being dominant and in being intolerant of differences in viewpoint, whereas Jean does not have strong convictions and is used to being governed by the judgments and wishes of others. If we are informed that Jonathan is about to marry one of these women, and if on the basis of the information cited above we are asked to guess which one, probably we should agree that Jean would be the more likely choice for Jonathan to make. . . . Thus Jonathan should see Jean as a "truly feminine, tractable, agreeable young lady who knows when and how to help a man," whereas to Jean, Jonathan might well appear as a "vigorous and decisive tower of strength." I should expect further that Jonathan would be repelled by Jennifer and would see her as bossy, unfeminine, and probably shrewish.[1]

The dominance-deference complement does not require that the male always be dominant and the female subordinate. Although it is characteristic of the sex role stereotype and is prevalent in some dyadic relationships, it is entirely possible, and certainly not uncommon, for the female in a dyad to be dominant and the male deferent. Two other examples of complements that Winch postulated are nurturance-succorance and achievement-vicariousness (see Box 5.1).

Although Winch's own research supported his theory of complementary needs, subsequent studies have found that relationships are not so simple. A couple stays together for many reasons besides complementary needs. Moreover, in most relationships neither partner displays one complement all the time. In some situations, even Edith Bunker is dominant and Archie is subordinate.

Role Theory

Role is one of the most commonly used terms in sociology and refers to a set of social expectations and behaviors that are appropriate to a given position or status. These expectations serve as behavioral

BOX 5.1 Theory of Complementary Needs

Robert Winch's complementary needs theory suggests that individuals select partners who complement their personalities. Three examples of complementary needs are dominance-deference, nurturance-succorance, and achievement-vicariousness.

DOMINANCE–DEFERENCE

Dominance – influencing and controlling the behavior of others
Deference – yielding in opinion and judgement to the wishes of another

NURTURANCE–SUCCORANCE

Nurturance – giving sympathy or aid to another
Succorance – being helped, loved, protected, indulged by a sympathetic person

ACHIEVEMENT–VICARIOUSNESS

Achievement – working diligently to accomplish some goal
Vicariousness – obtaining enjoyment and satisfaction from another's achievement

guidelines, reminding the individual of what he or she should and should not do by virtue of being a male, female, employer, spouse, student, and the like. Generally people find that it is more rewarding and easier to fulfill established social roles than it is to "buck the system."

Applied to mate selection, role theory predicts that persons tend to choose partners on the basis of courtship and marital role agreement. Thus, a man who believes that "a woman's place is in the home" probably would not marry a career woman who works at a job fifty to sixty hours a week. Likewise, a woman who prefers a "Marlboro Man" probably would not marry a concert musician.

It is important to note that it is not the roles themselves but the agreement on role playing that is important. A compatible couple would be one in which both partners fulfill the expected or agreed-upon roles, no matter what these roles actually are.

Bernard Murstein points out that roles are situationally and goal determined. Thus, a change in the relationship may also result in changes in the partners' role behavior. Murstein also emphasizes the importance of compatibility between roles and goals:

Since roles are sometimes behavioral means to an end, it is possible that, in some instances, role-similarity may impede the goals of one or both partners. Suppose that both husband and wife desire to essay the role of homemaker and neither wishes to enter the business world. The result is no family income. It is clear, therefore, that what is important is the compatibility of roles with goals, not whether roles are homogamous or complementary.[2]

Like the complementary needs theory, the role theory by itself does not explain all the ramifications of the mate selection process. But because roles are surely important to the partner selection process, many theories of mate selection include the concept of roles.

Value Theory

People tend to form partnerships with those holding similar values. Values refer to ideals, customs, or behavioral patterns about which people have such strong emotional feelings that they think of them as "right" or "wrong," "good" or "bad." People tend to internalize values to such an extent that when their values are attacked, they feel as though they themselves have been attacked. Robert Coombs, who has written extensively on the subject, believes that values are so important that "they are accepted without question and that people interact with individuals who have similar values because this provides them with emotional security."[3]

Coombs also suggests that when a person chooses a partner on the basis of such endogamous factors as race, religion, and social class, the choice is actually based largely on whether or not the partner has similar values. For example, a person may wish to marry someone of the same religion, both because this is an important value in itself and because persons with similar backgrounds will probably also have similar value systems.

Value theory has the advantage of simplicity and also seems to be borne out by common observation. There is evidence that perceived similarity of values is central to the mate selection process; however, it is not yet known exactly which values are most influential in pair formation.

Exchange Theory

Another theory of partner selection is exchange theory. This theory postulates that all social behavior is a kind of "exchange" in which people both give and receive. It suggests that each relationship is an ongoing series of interchanges between two individuals and that people invest in a relationship with the expectation of being rewarded.

What is exchanged may be either material or emotional. For example, John has two tickets to a concert and invites Tim to go. The next week Tim reciprocates by inviting John to dinner. Likewise, a couple who both work may exchange encouragement and approval and have an unspoken agreement to be supportive and understanding of each other's work demands.

According to sociologist Ted Huston, such interaction is goal oriented and can be reduced to a cost-benefit analysis:

Social transactions are regulated by the interactants' desire to derive maximum pleasure and minimum pain from others. . . . More formally, exchange theory suggests that individuals are most attracted to persons who provide the highest ratio of rewards to costs.[4]

When applying exchange theory to partner or mate selection, one should include the two partners' expectations and the resources they bring to the relationship. John Edwards suggests that the following is typical:

One party gives a certain portion of his time and labor for which he receives from the other party a certain amount of appreciation and esteem. . . . The resources exchanged in a social situation need not be of the same kind. What is important is that each party receives in the exchange something he perceives as equivalent to that which is given. There is in any transactional situation, then, the mutually held expectation that reciprocation will occur. One does not incur a cost without the expectation that there will be compensation for it.[5]

Exchange theory can be used to explain how partner selection and relationship interaction operate. It predicts that a relationship begins to deteriorate when one of the partners feels that he or she is contributing more to the relationship than he or she is receiving. Exchange theory also can be used to analyze social behavior and to help develop a more precise model of mate selection.

SEQUENTIAL THEORIES

Each of the preceding theories of mate selection focuses on a particular set of factors, either needs, roles, and values, or the exchange of rewards, gratifications, and satisfactions. It is probable that each of these sets of factors contributes to mate selection. Moreover, it is possible that different sets of factors operate at different stages of partner selection or courtship. Sociologists have termed these stage theories *sequential*, and several of them are worthy of consideration.

Filter Theory

In an attempt to combine value consensus and complementary needs theories, Alan Kerckhoff and Keith Davis hypothesized that certain social attributes and personality relationships operate at different stages of a courtship. They suggested that agreement on values might be paramount at one stage and that need-complementarity might be important at another.

To test this hypothesis, Kerckhoff and Davis surveyed a group of engaged or "seriously attached" couples at both the beginning and the end of the school year. The results of the study indicated that value consensus operates in the early stages of courtship and that need-complementarity occurs later.[6]

The Kerckhoff-Davis theory suggests a sequence of screening or "filtering" factors in the mate selection process. Initially, endogamous factors such as age, religion, and social class determine who interacts with whom. Subsequent interactions are unlikely to progress very far unless there is agreement on values. Later, need-complementarity determines whether or not a permanent pairing will result.

Process Theory

Most theories assume that partner selection is based on endogamous factors, personalities, needs, and roles. A radically different approach, the process approach, deals with the developmental process of the partnership. It proposes that every interpersonal transaction has its own course of events and that each phase of getting closer influences the next. Charles Bolton states that, "in short, the development of love relations is problematic because the product bears the stamp of what goes on between the couple as well as what they are as individuals."[7] This means that a relationship is more than the sum of its parts. Therefore, the process theory is useful because it recognizes that what happens between the individuals is as important as their individual characteristics.

Stimulus-Value-Role Theory

Bernard Murstein has postulated a three-stage sequence of mate selection, called the stimulus-value-role (or SVR) theory.[8] This theory combines an exchange theory and a sequential theory. The SVR theory suggests that in a free-choice, or *open-field*, situation, the selection of a marital partner is a three-stage process, but that in a *closed-field* situation, the first-stage factors are less important and are replaced by interaction factors.

In the following passage, Murstein differentiates between open and closed fields, the two settings in which partner selection occurs:

An "open" field encounter refers to a situation in which the man and woman do not as yet know each other or have only a nodding acquaintance. Examples of such "open field" situations are "mixers," a large school class at the beginning of the semester, and brief contacts in the office. The fact that the field is "open" indicates that either the man or the woman is free to start the relationship or abstain from initiating it, as they wish. The contrary concept is the "closed field" situation in which both the man and woman are forced to relate in some manner by reason of the roles assigned to them by the environmental setting in which they find themselves. Examples of "closed field" situations might be that of students in a small seminar in a college, members of a "Peace Corps" unit, and workers in a political campaign.

This interaction generally enables the individual to become acquainted with the behavior of the "other," which is then evaluated according to the individual's own system of values.[9]

The significance of the difference between open and closed situations is elaborated on in the following discussion of the three stages:

Stimulus Stage In the first stage, a person is drawn to another because of his or her perceptions of the other's physical and social attributes. These initial judgments are influenced by such stimulus factors as attractiveness, poise, dress, personality, and prior knowledge of occupation and reputation.

During this first stage, individuals utilize first impressions to form their opinions of other people, which is particularly important in an open field. Murstein asserts that "the stimulus stage is of crucial importance in the 'open field,' for, if the other person does not possess sufficient stimulus impact to attract the individual, further contact is not sought."[10] Unless there is mutual attraction, a pairing relationship will not materialize. In the open-field situation, the stimulus stage emphasizes people's heavy dependence on first impressions: highly critical observations often may prevent further interaction with very compatible people.

Getting acquainted is the first step in the partner selection process.

Barbara Pfeffer/Black Star

But closed-field situations weaken the influence of first-stage, or "stimulus," factors and maximize interaction factors. For example, if individuals are working together on a political campaign, they will have the opportunity to get to know each other, to observe each other at work, and also to compare each other's values, thus de-emphasizing the importance of physical characteristics or first impressions.

Value Comparison Stage

After mutual attraction, the pairing couple enters the second stage, value comparison. It should be noted that the length of time spent in each stage varies from couple to couple and that the two individuals each may be at different stages at any given time.

The SVR theory holds that the primary focus of the value comparison stage is "information gathering by verbal interaction with the other"[11] and may occur when intimacy begins to develop, as discussed in Chapter 3, "Developing Intimate Relationships." The theory maintains:

> The value comparison stage occurs when the couple has not as yet developed sufficient intimacy to learn and confess the innermost precepts, fears, aspirations, and concerns that each has. Nevertheless, there is much public and private information gleaned about religious orientation, political beliefs, attitudes toward people, parents, friends, interests in sports, the arts, dancing and the like. . . . The couple exhibits increasingly larger areas of what they think and feel. They evaluate their comfortableness, the acceptance of what they reveal, and the effect of their disclosure on their partner's behavior. . . . Self-disclosure among individuals promotes reciprocal self-disclosure, and the relationship may proceed to increasingly deeper levels of personality.[12]

In some cases, a couple may decide to become partners or to marry on the basis of the first two stages—stimulus attraction and value congruence—but for most people it is also necessary to function in compatible roles.

Role Stage

Earlier, we defined roles as sets of social expectations that are appropriate to a given position or status. Therefore, the roles that people adopt are influenced by their own beliefs and idiosyncrasies, by social norms, and by particular situations.

In courtship relationships, individuals have certain expectations of what the ideal mate should be like and of the roles he or she should play. As a relationship progresses, people compare the prospective partner with their ideal. At the same time, they analyze their own behavior and try to determine if it is similar to or compatible with that of the prospective partner. Generally, role behavior is revealed fairly slowly, and it is often difficult to understand. Murstein concludes: "Role compatibility is probably the most complex of all the stages and is probably never completely traversed, since individuals seem to be constantly adding new roles or modifying existing ones."[13]

The SVR theory is one of the most comprehensive mate selection theories because it incorporates many of the single variables—endogamy, values, and roles—and also considers the relationship's time progression.

DATING

Whatever the factors and dynamics of the mate selection process, potential spouses must get to know each other personally in order to develop closeness and to assess their suitability as mates. Perhaps the most common way people do this is through *dating*, otherwise known as *going out*, *seeing each other*, or *getting together*. Many people object to the term *dating* because it sounds formal and old fashioned. However, because it is confusing to use several terms for the same activity, sociologists and psychologists agree (as do we) to use only the term *dating*. Dating refers to the various prearranged social activities between two people, regardless of how they themselves might label these activities.

Modern dating often involves group activities.

Paul Conklin

Generally, there are two kinds of dating, recreational dating and attachment-oriented dating. In *recreational dating*, people casually go out to enjoy each other's company and to have fun; it may or may not include sexual activity. There are no interpersonal commitments implied beyond the date. In *attachment-oriented dating*, people go out in order to look for a lover or spouse, as well as to have fun. Attachment-oriented dating usually has stages. At first it might be recreational, but as the individuals become more committed to the relationship, they usually foresake other dating partners and see each other exclusively. Their relationship is no longer just "for fun"; they perceive it to be "going somewhere."

Besides having fun and finding a potential partner, dating has other functions. It is a remedy for loneliness. Dating interactions can reassure you that you are desirable and acceptable. Sometimes even the fact that you have a date is more important than what happens on the date itself. Dating also helps people refine their social skills, and it enables them to find the best ways to fulfill emotional and sexual needs. For many, the development of social skills and appropriate sexual behavior is difficult. Because modern dating has few rules, lessons often come from embarrassing trial-and-error experiences.

In the United States, dating is now such a familiar social custom that it is hard to imagine that it began only a few generations ago. Until that time, people did not date in order to get to know each other. Because most lived in small communities or in tightly knit ethnically or socially segregated, urban neighborhoods, they usually got to know each other through extensive social exposure and physical proximity (propinquity). From childhood on, they went to church and school with the same people. Their parents and friends knew each other, and they tended to marry "the girl (boy) next door."

By the 1920s the rudiments of our modern dating system came into being. Ever-increasing industrialization, urbanization, physical and social mobility, and public education catapulted people from the familiarity of close social groups into a world of strangers. Women, especially, began to demand more personal freedom (the Nineteenth Amendment to the U.S. Constitution establishing women's right to vote was ratified in 1920). Virtually overnight, the formal propriety of the Victorian era was rejected in favor of the almost carefree behavior of the twenties (see Figure 5.1). In this atmosphere of increased anonymity and the desire to make life choices based on personal needs, dating was started to help potential partners to get to know each other.

The developing technology facilitated dating. First, it contributed to the social conditions that made dating necessary. Second, technology increased most people's leisure time, thus giving dating couples more time to spend together. Third, it provided couples the means by which

FIGURE 5.1

Women's fashions often reflect the social values of the times. In the Victorian era, fashion called for women to be covered from head to toe in layers of clothes and tight-fitting, restraining undergarments. Freedom and gaiety were valued in the 1920s, and flappers dressed accordingly, in short dresses and loose-fitting underwear.

Brown Brothers

they could get to know each other in relative privacy: the automobile, the telephone, and the movies.

Probably from its inception, dating has had a competitive quality. Status is accorded to both those who date frequently and those who date the most desirable partners. The one quality that has always seemed to be in the most demand, at least in initial dating encounters, is physical attractiveness[14] (see Box 5.2).

BOX 5.2   Qualities Most Valued in a Date

Write down the three qualities you most value in a date. Here is how 341 college males and 372 college females in California answered:

Qualities Most Valued by Men	Qualities Most Valued by Women
1. Looks	1. Looks
2. Personality	2. Personality
3. Sex appeal	3. Thoughtfulness, consideration
4. Intelligence	4. Sense of humor
5. Fun, good companionship	5. Honesty
6. Sense of humor	6. Respect
7. Good conversation	7. Good conversation
8. Honesty	8. Intelligence

Source: Adapted from Lloyd Saxton, *The Individual, Marriage, and the Family*, Third Edition, © 1977 by Wadsworth Publishing Company, Inc. Reprinted by permission of Wadsworth Publishing Company, Belmont, Calif. 94002.

In the past (and in some social groups today), men tended to "date down." They preferred to go out with women who were younger, smaller, less intelligent, less educated, and of a lower socioeconomic status than they were. Women, on the other hand, tended to "date up." They wanted partners who were older, taller, more intelligent, and of a higher status than they were. One reason for this *dating differential* was that many men felt threatened by women of equal or greater status and ability. Because men also had to compete socially and economically with other men, they did not want to have to compete with the women they dated. In the past, many women purposely concealed their abilities for fear of frightening off potential suitors. Today, however, fewer women feel the need for such subterfuge.

The competitive nature of dating excludes a number of people from participation. People with less leisure time, less money, and fewer opportunities to meet others are at a disadvantage, compared with those who are more fortunate. Moreover, whatever personal characteristics are deemed desirable, it is certain that not everyone possesses them. Some people are more attractive than others, better athletes than others, smarter than others, and nicer than others.

Besides status and competition, dating has other drawbacks. Parents, for example, may disagree with their children's choices of dating partners and dating activities. Parents also may object if their children cross social, religious, or racial lines, and they may view dating as offering too many opportunities to experiment with drugs and sex.

And unfortunately, in some social groups, dating partners are adversaries. The male is the pursuer and the female is the pursued. He offers attention, flattery, gifts, and he pays for an evening's entertainment in the hopes of being rewarded with sexual favors from her. She, on the other hand, wants to accept all this graciously and to reciprocate but without appearing either too sexually aggressive or too aloof to him. Fortunately, this kind of dating situation is being recognized as counterproductive. How can two people become friends or lovers if their initial encounters are based on a form of ritualized sparring and overt bribery?

Because some people believe that sexual relations are inappropriate before marriage, the question of sex in dating can complicate dating relationships. There is much pressure on both women and men to have some sort of sexual contact with their dating partners, which leads to some of the principal dating questions and concerns: Should I kiss him or her at the end of the date? How many dates does he or she require before sexual intercourse is all right? I genuinely like this person and would like to show him or her some affection, but I'm not ready to have sexual intercourse with him or her. I genuinely like this person and would like to show him or her some affection, but my actions might be taken the wrong way and I might frighten him or her away and embarrass myself. These fears and pressures affect people of all ages, as this forty-five-year-old woman explains:

When I began to go out with men again after my divorce, I would sit in the car and wonder at the end of the evening, should I let him kiss me, say good-night with a handshake, or go to bed with him? It was like being a kid with all those rules all over again.[15]

Unresolved sexual questions can create enormous problems for a dating couple. And because there are so few universally accepted rules governing sexual behavior, at some time individuals must make their sexual intentions clear to their dating partners, or otherwise, sexual issues may disrupt the growth of the friendship.

Dating Anxiety

Recently I met a very attractive man whom I wanted to get to know better. But I just couldn't ask him out. What would he think?

At one time or another, most people have been nervous about dating.

Jon Chase

Intellectually, I know my fear is ridiculous, but emotionally, I guess I'm not ready. I'm too shy.

From the authors' files

At some time or another, just about everyone has been nervous about dating. Beginning a new social relationship is not like applying for a job and being evaluated by grades and a résumé: your success on a date is based on your personality and appearance. You are exposing your *self*, and you want to be liked. But what if your date does not like you? This fear of rejection is called *dating anxiety*. It is estimated that about one-third to one-half of American college students experience dating anxiety,[16] most of them attributing it to their being shy or unassertive. About twice as many men as women are anxious about dating, presumably because men are still expected to be the initiators of dating situations.

There are four general reasons for dating anxiety:[17]

1. *Lack of Social Skills* Some people are unable to meet other people and carry on dating relationships with them because they lack knowledge of and expertise in the rules of social intercourse. It is very much like trying to get people to play tennis with you when you do not know either how to swing a racket or the rules of the game. Your invitations to others to play will be rejected, and eventually your fear of

rejection will prevent you from initiating other games. Once you learn the rules of the game, however, you will become a more accommodating tennis partner and rejections will cease. Fortunately, several self-help methods for overcoming shyness and improving social skills have been developed.[18]

2. *Previous Bad Dating Experiences*   Some people with dating anxiety have adequate social skills, but perhaps because of a bad dating experience of their own or of a friend, they have become fearful about seeking dates.

3. *Low Self-esteem*   Some people are so overly critical of themselves that they assume that potential dating partners will not like them, and hence they are anxious about dating. Frequently, the dating anxiety has nothing to do with a lack of social skills or previous bad experiences. In this case the individual has the necessary social skills but is paralyzed with anxiety caused by a highly negative self-image.

4. *Low Physical Attraction*   Physical attractiveness does affect dating success. Fortunately, standards of attractiveness are highly variable —not every man has to look like Robert Redford or every woman like Jane Fonda to be considered attractive—and people can increase their attractiveness by how they dress and how well they care for their bodies.

Psychologists Bernie Zilbergeld and Carol Rinkleib Ellison point out that "there is no way to avoid being rejected except by never asking for anything."[19] Of course, rejection can hurt and bring disappointment, but most people agree that the consequences of doing nothing are generally worse than the risk of rejection. Besides, not every "no," "I'm sorry," or "I can't" is a personal rejection. People turn down social offers for numerous reasons that have nothing to do with the other person. Perhaps they are already involved with someone else or are just getting over a broken romance. If they do not feel it is proper to share private information with relative strangers, they may decline an invitation without saying why, thus leaving the initiator to wonder, "What's wrong with me?" Some people try to soften their refusals with a brief statement such as "This has nothing to do with you personally; I just don't have the space in my life right now for new acquaintances."

One major difficulty with dating is meeting potential dating partners. Even though people are around us everywhere—in class, in the bank, walking along the street, in the supermarket, and on the bus or subway—for many, striking up a conversation and broaching the subject of a date are very difficult. Aware of these problems among its readers, one major woman's magazine even published thirty-four suggestions on how to meet a man on a bus.[20]

Most dating advisers agree that the best way to meet dating partners is to put yourself where you think eligible, desirable partners are. This may mean going to meetings and lectures that interest you or getting involved in sports activities or interest groups such as drama or political clubs. Group activities are especially good for shy people, for they make it easier to interact with others. Although they are set up to help singles meet, so-called singles bars may not be the best places to meet potential partners because the typical singles bar's atmosphere generally involves too many expectations.

Some people advertise for partners in newspapers, and some enlist the help of computer dating services, which try to match partners according to particular desired qualities. Computer dating services do match people with similar interests, but such meetings do not always lead to successful dates. One reason is that matching similar interests and personality characteristics does not take into account a person's physical appearance and actual personality, nor can a computer predict how a couple will get along.

A recent innovation in technological match making is videodating. Members of a videodating "club" are interviewed on videotape, which is then stored in a tape library. Members then screen taped interviews at their leisure on closed-circuit videoplayback machines and select prospective dates.

A common dating difficulty is, "What do you say after you say hello?" Being introduced to someone at a party is one thing, but actually going out on a date may be quite another. Psychologists Zilbergeld and Ellison suggest that when in doubt, the "minimal approach" is best.[21] In other words, it is wise not to rush into anything. Perhaps the best way to begin a dating relationship is to go out on what is sometimes called a "coffee date." This is a prearranged rendezvous with a set ending time, such as during a lunch hour or the hour before a class begins. The time limit takes away the pressure of having to fill up an extended period of time with a stranger. There also are no sexual pressures, which may be present in an open-ended evening date. The "coffee date" does not have to include food. Walking, jogging, or skating are just as good, as are other activities that you both enjoy.

Keep in mind that dates need not lead to sex, romance, or later commitments, but that they can provide a framework in which people can meet, interact, and become friends.

SUMMARY

Current theories of mate selection recognize that such factors as need gratification, values, social roles, and social exchanges are important to the mate selection process. Furthermore, different sets of factors may operate at different stages of this process. Filter theory suggests that value consensus is important in the early stages of courtship and that need-complementarity occurs later. Process theory proposes that the interaction process is more important than the partners' individual characteristics are.

The stimulus-value-role theory holds that couples go through three stages prior to marriage: (1) the stimulus stage, in which people are attracted to each other's physical and social attributes; (2) the value comparison stage, in which people exchange information and discover similar values; and (3) the role stage, in which people compare their ideals with their partners' actual behavior and beliefs.

Dating is a recent social phenomenon that fosters the development of intimacy and also offers potential marital partners the opportunity to assess their suitability as mates. Individuals with dating anxiety can help themselves by improving their social skills, self-image, and physical appearance, and by avoiding anxiety-producing situations.

CONSIDER THIS

After their jogging workout, Jeff told his best friend Ricardo that he was planning to ask Evelyn to marry him.

RICARDO: Marry! You met her only three weeks ago.

JEFF: Ricardo, it's right. I *know* it is.

RICARDO: Three weeks isn't long enough to know anything. Marge and I dated for two years, and we still weren't sure, even at the altar.

JEFF: We love each other very much, and we have so much in common. She likes jazz and Chinese food. We have the same politics. And most important, each of us wants to be married and settled.

RICARDO: Most of that is surface stuff, which is O.K. for when you're just going out. Marriage takes a lot more. Listen, Evelyn is beautiful, charming, and immensely talented. But I don't see how a ballerina and an aspiring bank executive can make a go at marriage.

JEFF: We've talked about that. Where we're not similar we're complementary. She says that she needs a partner who is down to earth and stable. And I want someone who is creative and spontaneous.

RICARDO: I thought you wanted a stay-at-home wife. Evelyn is exactly the opposite. Who is going to take care of the meals, housework, dog, and kids when she's rehearsing and performing and you're working sixty hours a week at the bank?

Questions   1. Do you think that Jeff and Evelyn are rushing into marriage?
2. Are Ricardo's reservations about Jeff's decision to marry warranted?
3. What features of Jeff's and Evelyn's relationship (values, roles, needs, and the like) suggest that a marriage might work out? What features suggest that a marriage might be risky?
4. What, if anything, would Jeff and Evelyn gain by continuing to go out for six months to a year longer before getting married?
5. Of what importance to you is agreement on values, roles, and need fulfillment in a marital relationship?

NOTES

1. Robert Winch, *Mate Selection*, New York, Harper & Brothers, 1958, p. 97.
2. Bernard Murstein, *Who Will Marry Whom?* New York, Springer, 1976, p. 187.
3. Robert Coombs, "Value Consensus and Partner Satisfaction Among Dating Couples," *Journal of Marriage and the Family*, 28 (May 1966): 166–173.
4. Ted L. Huston, *Foundations of Interpersonal Attraction*, New York, Academic Press, 1974, p. 20.
5. John Edwards, "Familial Behavior as Social Exchange," *Journal of Marriage and the Family*, 31 (August 1969): 519.
6. Alan Kerckhoff and Keith Davis, "Value Consensus and Need-Complementarity in Mate Selection," *American Sociological Review*, 27 (June 1962): 295–303.
7. Charles Bolton, "Mate Selection as the Development of a Relationship," *Marriage and Family Living*, 23 (August 1961): 235–236.
8. Bernard Murstein, *Who Will Marry Whom?* New York, Springer, 1976, pp. 107–133.
9. Ibid., p. 115.
10. Ibid., pp. 116–117.
11. Ibid., p. 123.
12. Ibid., p. 124.
13. Ibid., p. 127.
14. Elaine Walster et al., "Importance of Physical Attractiveness in Dating Behavior," *Journal of Personality and Social Psychology*, 5 (1966): 508–516.
15. Nancy Friday, *My Mother/My Self*, New York, Delacorte Press, 1977, p. 213.

16. Hal Arkowitz et al., "Treatment Strategies for Dating Anxiety in College Men Based on Real-Life Practice," *The Counseling Psychologist*, 7 (1978): 41–46; Philip Zimbardo. *Shyness*, Reading, Mass., Addison-Wesley, 1977.
17. Hal Arkowitz et al., "Treatment Strategies."
18. See, for example, Philip Zimbardo, *Shyness*; Eileen Gambrill and Cheryl Richey, *It's Up to You*, Millbrae, Calif., Les Femmes Publishing, 1976.
19. Bernie Zilbergeld and Carol Rinkleib Ellison, "Social Skills Training as an Adjunct to Sex Therapy," *Journal of Sex and Marital Therapy*, 5 (1979): 340–350.
20. Donna Buys, "How to Meet a Man on a Bus," *Cosmopolitan*, May 1979, 128.
21. Bernie Zilbergeld and Carol Rinkleib Ellison, "Social Skills Training."

SUGGESTED READINGS

Huston, Ted L. *Foundations of Interpersonal Attraction*. New York, Academic Press, 1974. A discussion of the development of intimate relationships.

Murstein, Bernard I. *Who Will Marry Whom?* New York, Springer, 1976. A thorough overview of the major theories of mate selection.

Murstein, Bernard I. "Mate Selection in the 1970s." *Journal of Marriage and the Family*, 42 (1980): 777–790. A review of a decade of research on courtship, dating, and the process of mate selection.

Zilbergeld, Bernie, and Carol R. Ellison. "Social Skills Training as an Adjunct to Sex Therapy." *Journal of Sex and Marital Therapy*, 5 (1979): 340–350. Suggestions for improving social interactions.

Zimbardo, Philip. *Shyness*. Reading, Mass. Addison-Wesley, 1977. The causes of and suggestions for overcoming shyness.

II | SEXUAL EXPRESSION

SEXUAL VALUES AND BEHAVIOR

Sex is the matrix for all kinds of the most lively transactions: embraces and quarrels, seductions and retreats, construction and mischief. It is an aid to happiness and work. It is for fun, pleasure and ecstasy. It binds people together with cords of romance, gratitude and love. And it produces children.

Psychiatrist Eric Berne[1]

At some time in adolescence, most people experience a profound change in their feelings about and attitudes toward their romantic relationships. That is when the innocence of childhood romance—"puppy love"—disappears forever and romantic feelings become inextricably woven with sexual feelings. From then on, sexual matters become part of virtually every intimate relationship.

It is no accident that sexual interest develops in adolescence. The normal process of physical maturation turns children's bodies into those of adult men and women who are capable of being sexually aroused and having sexual intercourse, and who show increasing interest in engaging in sexual activity. Adolescence (and in some cases preadolescence) is also a time when social and cultural factors begin to influence an individual's sexual attitudes and behavior.

Changes in anatomy, feelings, and behavior at adolescence are part of the natural preparation for the reproduction of our species. All living things must reproduce, and sexual activity between men and women leads to the creation of new generations of human beings. Even though reproduction is a responsibility to future generations, most would agree that sexual activity is a pleasant rather than an unpleasant duty. This, too, is an innate feature of sexuality. For if sex were disagreeable, people might resist the biological urges to procreate, and the human species would suffer.

That sex is pleasurable not only encourages reproduction (so much, in fact, that the Earth is rapidly becoming overpopulated with humans) but also makes sex an end in itself. People can engage in sex simply because it feels good regardless of whether or not children are conceived. By using contraception, couples can intentionally separate the procreative aspects of sex from the giving and receiving of sexual pleasure.

Besides reproduction and the exchange of sensual pleasure, sexual activity provides a physical means of emotional expression. Through touching and the physical closeness of sex, people can communicate love, affection, and concern for each other. Sex also communicates acceptance, desirability, and, in some instances, anger and hostility.

In this chapter we discuss various types of sexual relationships: nonmarital, marital, extramarital, and same-sex, or homosexual, relationships.

CHANGING ATTITUDES TOWARD SEXUAL BEHAVIOR

Our culture has traditionally been rather conservative in regard to sexual behavior, with both laws and cultural norms prohibiting nearly all forms of sexual activity except sexual intercourse between legally married, heterosexual adults. The purpose of such restrictions presumably was to preserve the family unit by allowing sexual urges to be expressed only in marriage. These restrictions were aimed at preventing random sexual activity and promoting emotional bonding of the married couple. Confining sex to marriage also removed doubt about the identity of children's parents and helped establish lineage and inheritance rights.

But many of our culture's traditional sexual values, expectations, and behaviors are becoming less restrictive. Unquestionably, our society is much more tolerant of sex than ever before. For example, in the past few years, the public has become increasingly tolerant of the open showing of X-rated films and the existence of resorts and nightclubs where people engage in sex with strangers. And, until recently, television programs in which women ask men for sex, characters have extramarital affairs, or actors or actresses appear nearly nude were totally unacceptable. But today, all of that occurs. Such activities demonstrate that people have grown more tolerant of the public display of sex. One need only observe how much sex is used in advertising to see how tolerant of sex our society has become.

The extent of revolutionary change in individual sexual behavior may not be as evident as the public acceptance of sex. But there have been many remarkable changes. For example, there is an unmistakable trend toward the dissolution of rigid sex roles. Males are no longer expected to be totally unemotional, dominant, and sexually aggressive, and women to be emotional, subordinate, and sexually receptive. Moreover, women are no longer expected to be indifferent to sex. Both

Through touching and physical closeness, people can communicate love, affection, and concern.

Jean-Claude Lejeune

men and women now realize that sex can be satisfying regardless of gender. Because many people view sex as natural and expect it to be pleasurable, many are willing to seek help from specialists and counselors when they have sexual difficulties, rather than pretending everything is all right or assuming that nothing more can be expected.

On the one hand, the easing of rigid restrictions on sexual values and behavior has benefited many, especially women. People can be more honest and open about this important part of life and freer to find their own modes of sexual expression.

On the other hand, more liberal sexual attitudes and behaviors have produced new problems. For example, some people have interpreted "less restrictive" to mean that they must be sexually active to be accepted. They feel obligated to have sex even if they do not want to. This is one reason for the extremely high incidence of unwanted pregnancy among unmarried teen-age women and the alarmingly high rates of gonorrhea and other sexually transmitted (venereal) diseases.

Liberal sexual attitudes sometimes also create performance pressures. Many women and men believe that they must be "perfect" sex partners, capable of engaging in sex often and capable of satisfying their partner in every sexual encounter. But in sexual relations, striving for perfection, an illusory goal, can turn what could be a highly rewarding emotional experience into just another kind of work.[2]

Many sexually active persons do not govern their sexual lives by the traditional rule that sex is permissible only with a marital partner. For them, when, with whom, and the manner of sexual expression all are matters of individual choice. Their sexual behavior is governed by personal values learned from parents and previous life experiences, by personal interpretations of religious and ethical codes, and by an assessment of personal needs for a fulfilling life. This means that many people develop their own sexual values to guide their sexual decision making in relationships (see Box 6.1).

SEX IN NONMARITAL RELATIONSHIPS

Approximately fifty million adults in the United States—one-third of the adult population—are unmarried. This includes people who have never been married, the divorced, and the widowed. Some of these people will choose to remain single or not to remarry, whereas others are waiting to marry or remarry. Other unmarried people are part of living-together arrangements.

Regardless of their marital intent, most unmarried adults have normal sexual needs. Some unmarried people are able to satisfy their emotional and sexual needs in long-term relationships involving deep emotional commitment. For them, sexual expression is similar to sexual expression between married people. But for other unmarried persons, sexual expression can be a problem. Some may not have access to sexual partners, they may feel guilty about having sex outside of marriage, or they may be reluctant to engage in sexual activity when it is not part of a committed relationship. Some divorced or widowed people, after many years of marriage, may not be adept at meeting their

BOX 6.1   Sexual Rights and Responsibilities

Recognizing that many people develop their own guidelines for their sexual lives, Dr. Lester Kirkendall, professor of family life at the University of Oregon, has drafted, and a number of educators and researchers have endorsed, a set of sexual rights and responsibilities. The philosophical basis for these sexual rights and responsibilities rests on the belief that:

Human beings should have the right to express their sexual desires and enter into relationships as they see fit, as long as they do not harm others or interfere with their rights to sexual expression. This new sense of freedom, however, should be accompanied by a sense of ethical responsibility.

The major points of the "Bill of Sexual Rights and Responsibilities" are:

1. *The boundaries of human sexuality need to be expanded.* Sex need not be considered only a means of reproduction; it can be also an expression of intimacy and a source of enjoyment and enrichment. Sexuality can be integrated into a balanced life along with other natural functions.

2. *Developing a sense of equity between the sexes is an essential feature of a sensible morality.* All legal, occupational, economic, and political discrimination against women should be removed, and all traces of sexism should be erased. All individuals, female or male, are entitled to equal consideration as persons.

3. *Repressive taboos should be replaced by a more balanced and objective view of sexuality based on a sensitive awareness of human behavior and needs.* The prohibition of many forms of sexual activity and certain kinds of sexual relationships can impede the full expression of some persons' sexuality. Such activities and relationships should be re-examined according

sexual needs in a world of single people, possibly feeling uncertain about the level of intimacy they wish to express sexually.

Although many unmarried people may be willing to have sexual relations outside the legally sanctioned state of marriage, they may nevertheless feel uncomfortable about having sex outside a committed relationship. They may be able to ignore social, religious, and, in some cases, legal prohibitions against nonmarital sex, but they cannot easily ignore their own personal values. Because sex can be a means of expressing love, affection, and deep emotion, many people are uneasy about sharing themselves with relative strangers:

I don't like casual affairs. I tried it for a while after my divorce, but I didn't like it. I didn't like waking up to somebody I didn't know. Usually the sex wasn't very good either. Two people have to know each other's bodies and souls before lovemaking is good.

From the authors' files

BOX 6.1 (continued)

to their contribution to personal fulfillment and not according to their traditional taboo status.

4. *Each person has both an obligation and a right to be fully informed about the various civic and community aspects of human sexuality.* Although sexuality is usually an individual matter, persons should be open to learning about changes in the social and medical aspects of human sexuality and willing to help others adopt responsible sexual behavior.

5. *Potential parents have both the right and the responsibility to plan the number and the time of birth of their children, taking into account both social needs and their own desires.*

6. *Sexual morality should come from a sense of caring and respect for others; it cannot be legislated.* The only laws necessary to regulate sexuality are those that protect the young and people of any age from abuse. Laws governing certain activities between mature, mutually consenting adults are not desirable.

7. *Physical pleasure has worth as a moral value.* Physical pleasure is not "sinful" or "wicked." Within the context of meaningful human relationships, physical pleasure is ethical as well as conducive to wholesome social relationships.

8. *Individuals are able to respond positively and affirmatively to sexuality throughout life; this must be acknowledged and accepted.* The joys of touching and giving and receiving affection and the satisfaction of intimate body responsiveness are the rights of everyone, no matter how young or how old.

9. *All sexual encounters should incorporate humane and humanistic values.* People's sexual behavior should not hurt or disadvantage others—not their partners and not anyone in the society at large. When questions of doubt or conflict arise, they should be settled by open and honest discussion.

Source: Lester A. Kirkendall, "A New Bill of Sexual Rights and Responsibilities," *Humanist*, January 1976, pp. 7–9.

But not everyone finds casual or recreational sex unfulfilling. Sexuality professor Lewis Diana suggests that most people do not report that uncommitted sex leaves them feeling unfulfilled, disappointed, or depressed, although many, especially women, do feel varying degrees of guilt. According to Diana: "If casual sex involves at least a regard for the person as a person, consideration that is mutual, and sensitivity to the pleasure needs of each, then there is potential for a sense of fulfillment."[3]

Uncommitted sex can be least satisfying when the primary goal is not sexual interaction. People frequently have casual sexual encounters to escape loneliness or to confirm their attractiveness and desirability. Sex itself cannot relieve loneliness or increase self-esteem—that requires genuine close relationships. Therefore, dissatisfaction with casual sex is more apt to be dissatisfaction with one's personal relationships than with the sexual interaction per se.

Whatever the motivation or circumstances, sex outside marriage must be consistent with a person's own value system. Otherwise, the experience is likely to be unsatisfactory and possibly guilt ridden. Many single people are confronted with a "swingles" value system that espouses frequent, uncommitted sex as the key to joy and fulfillment—"if it feels good, do it." Some, however, have difficulty accepting such a *laissez-faire* attitude toward a form of personal expression that for them is extremely meaningful, and it puts them into an uncomfortable, "forced choice" situation: to uphold their values and possibly feel prudish and alienated from their social circle, or to contradict their values and feel immoral and guilty. Many sex educators and counselors agree with Dr. Merle Sondra Kroop that "the potential for suffering is greatest among those indoctrinated into one value system but attempting to live by a conflicting one."[4] Dr. Harvey Caplan's opinion is that:

The "sexual revolution" of the past 15 years has been sorely needed. People do need to see that their sexuality is natural and associated with pleasure as well as reproduction. But we pay a price for our new knowledge. What began as a series of revelations is becoming codified into a series of "shoulds." People are subtly being persuaded to abandon deep-rooted value systems in favor of more "personal freedom."

Sexual expression serves different functions in people's lives, and those functions relate profoundly to personal beliefs and values. Where beliefs are narrow or unrealistic, problems can be created that may require re-evaluation of the beliefs and re-education. But in many cases these beliefs and values serve people well and should not be challenged. Compulsive sexual behavior, reinforced by newer societal expectations, can muddy the issues for a person and even create problems where they wouldn't have existed before.[5]

When unmarried people are making personal sexual decisions, their wisest course often is to trust themselves and to follow their own beliefs.

Attitudes Toward Premarital Sex

In a series of novels published in the late 1960s and early 1970s, Robert Rimmer explored the influences of honesty, consideration, and responsibility in different kinds of traditionally forbidden sexual relationships, such as the marriage of one man and two women, group marriage, and sex among unmarried college students. Rimmer's best-known work, *The Harrad Experiment*, has been read by millions of people, and it is still popular today.

The Harrad Experiment describes life at Harrad College, a fictitious eastern school with a highly unusual curriculum. In addition to the traditional college courses, Harrad students are required to study sex education and the philosophy of sexual responsibility. Moreover, male and female students are paired as dormitory roommates and are permitted to have sexual relations with each other. This book offers a utopian model for sexual relations among young unmarried people that emphasizes open, honest, caring, and responsible sexuality as an alternative to the exploitation, guilt, and unwanted pregnancy that accompany some traditional premarital sexual relationships.

The popularity of *The Harrad Experiment* reflects the change in our society's traditionally restrictive attitude toward sexual relations among young unmarried people. People seem to be adopting a more permissive attitude toward nonmarital sex, which is generally referred to as *premarital sex*. (Some people object to the term premarital sex because it implies that everyone will eventually marry and does not allow for legitimate sexual relationships between adults who may never marry or who have been married but are once again single. Many researchers continue to use the term premarital sex, however, which is why it appears in the discussions to follow.)

In a survey conducted by the National Opinion Research Center in March 1978, respondents were asked their opinion about the wrongness of premarital sex. The results were as follows:[6]

Not wrong at all	38.7%
Wrong only sometimes	20.3
Almost always wrong	11.7
Always wrong	29.3

Analyses of this and other surveys conducted by the same research group between 1972 and 1978 showed a clear trend toward the greater tolerance of premarital sex (see Table 6.1).

Virtually all opinion polls show a marked generation gap in attitudes toward sexual permissiveness. In the 1978 National Opinion Research Center poll, 20.1 percent of the eighteen- to twenty-nine-year-old age group believed premarital sex to be "almost always wrong" or "always wrong." The comparable figure for the thirty to forty-nine age group

TABLE 6.1 Attitudes of Adult Americans Toward Premarital Sex, 1972 to 1978

Opinion	Year				
	1972	1974	1975	1977	1978
Not wrong at all	27.3%	30.7%	32.8%	36.5%	38.7%
Wrong only sometimes	24.3	23.6	24.0	23.0	20.3
Almost always wrong	11.8	12.7	12.3	9.5	11.7
Always wrong	36.6	33.0	30.9	31.0	29.3

Source: Adapted from Norval D. Glenn and Charles N. Weaver, "Attitudes Toward Premarital, Extramarital, and Homosexual Relations in the U.S. in the 1970s," *Journal of Sex Research*, 15, no. 2 (May 1979): 111.

was 42.1 percent, and two-thirds of the over-fifty age group thought premarital sex to be wrong.

Several factors are thought to contribute to this generational gap.[7] First, young people have grown up in a more sexually permissive society than their elders did and hence reflect its changed values and attitudes. Second, older people tend to adhere to the more traditional, restrictive values prevalent when they were young. Being a parent also makes some people less permissive. A young, unmarried woman using contraceptives, when asked how she would feel about *her* daughter getting contraceptives, replied "I'd never allow my daughter to have premarital sex." Another reason for this generational gap in opinion is that young people are the recipients of the pleasures of premarital sex. This makes it more difficult for the young to restrict their own behavior but easier for parents to hold restrictive opinions.

Despite the obvious softening of restrictive attitudes toward premarital sex among young adults, many people still oppose the idea of sex before marriage. As sociologists Norval D. Glenn and Charles N. Weaver point out:

If the 1972–1978 rate of change should continue, more than a fourth of American adults would still have restrictive attitudes [toward premarital sex] in 1990. Premarital sex relations are not yet "generally accepted," nor are they likely to be in the future.[8]

Furthermore, the laws of about half the states still consider premarital coitus, referred to as *fornication*, to be a crime, although there rarely are prosecutions. Many states also have laws prohibiting *statutory rape*, which is sexual relations with an underage person, even with his or her consent.

TABLE 6.2 Relationship of Religious Affiliation to Attitudes Toward Premarital Sex

Religious Affiliation	Percent Permissive*
Protestant	49.3
Catholic	59.6
Jewish	73.1
No religion	90.7

Source: Norval D. Glenn and Charles N. Weaver, "Attitudes Toward Premarital, Extramarital, and Homosexual Relations in the U.S. in the 1970s," *Journal of Sex Research*, 15, no. 2 (May 1979): 113.

Percent permissive refers to the percentage of respondents who gave permissive responses—"wrong only sometimes" and "not wrong at all"—to questions concerning premarital sex.

Religion also exerts a prohibitive influence on premarital sexual attitudes (see Table 6.2). The Roman Catholic church is unequivocally opposed to premarital coitus, an act that it considers a mortal sin and not permissible under any circumstances. Fundamentalist Protestant groups and Orthodox Jews also forbid premarital sex of any kind. Although the mainstream Protestant denominations—Episcopal, Presbyterian, Lutheran, Methodist, and Baptist—and most Jewish sects uphold the tradition that sexual relations should be reserved for marriage, some of their clergy have relatively permissive attitudes. They do not necessarily advocate uninhibited premarital sex, but they do recognize that even religious young people may believe that in certain circumstances premarital sex is acceptable. In the words of one minister:

Well, I'm not sure how much of an issue it is anymore. I mean, I don't refer to it in my sermons. Of course, fornication is a sin—Christians are supposed to know that. But in day-to-day living, things aren't always simple. College students fall in love. And when you're that age, temptations of the flesh are great. Also, birth control is a fact of life. Cohabitation exists in my congregation. I know it, and I know the boys and girls involved. The parents know it, too. Yet they come to church on Sunday, and I can't—I won't—make them feel unwelcome. They seem to be reaching for God, and I think that's very important.

From the authors' files

The Incidence of Premarital Sexual Activity and the Decline of the Double Standard

Reliable data on premarital sexual activity are difficult to obtain because they rely on self-reporting by survey respondents. Some people may underestimate or not report the true extent of their sexual activities, and others may exaggerate them. Moreover, we do not know whether the behavior of those willing to report is representative of the larger group. But we can probably safely assume that the data obtained in most studies represent a close approximation of the actual extent of premarital sexual activity.

Because of the traditional double standard—that premarital sex is permissible for males but not for females—American males have traditionally reported more premarital sexual experience than females have. For example, a 1975 survey of college students in a southern university showed that 73.9 percent of the responding males and 57.1 percent of the responding females had had premarital sexual intercourse.[9] A large-scale national survey conducted in 1979 reported that among nineteen-year-olds, 77.5 percent of the males and 69 percent of the females had had premarital sexual intercourse.[10]

It appears that the double standard is rapidly disappearing. Table 6.3 shows the results of both the interviews and the questionnaire surveys of a large group of married men and women of various ages. The respondents' year of birth ranged from before 1917 to 1954. The survey results showed that 84 percent of the men in the oldest group and 95 percent in the youngest group had had premarital sexual intercourse, an increase of 11 percent in over thirty years. The data for the women, on the other hand, showed an astounding difference between the experiences of the older respondents and those of the

TABLE 6.3   Percent of Married People Reporting Having Had Premarital Sexual Intercourse, by Year of Birth

Year of Birth	Male (%)	Female (%)
Before 1917	84	31
1918–1927	89	36
1928–1937	86	41
1938–1947	92	65
1948–1954	95	81

Source: Morton Hunt, *Sexual Behavior in the 1970s*, Chicago, Playboy Press, 1974, p. 150.

younger respondents. Of the women who were adolescents in the 1930s, 31 percent had had premarital sexual intercourse; of the women who were adolescents in the 1950s and early 1960s, 65 percent had had premarital intercourse; and of the women who were adolescents in the late 1960s and early 1970s, 81 percent had had premarital intercourse.[11]

An analogous increase in the incidence of premarital sex among young women is demonstrated by comparing data from surveys, conducted in 1965, 1970, and 1975, of sexual intercourse among college students. Although the incidence of male experience did not change very much, that of female experience increased dramatically:[12]

	1965	1970	1975
Males	65.1%	65.0%	73.9%
Females	28.7%	37.3%	57.1%

There are several reasons that college students reported a smaller incidence of premarital sexual intercourse than married people did. First, college students are not necessarily representative of the general population. Second, college students usually represent only the eighteen- to twenty-one-year-old age group, whereas the group of married people usually is over twenty-one. Finally, many married people may have abstained from premarital sexual relations with others but may have had premarital sexual intercourse with their intended spouse.

The apparent decline in the double standard indicates that many people no longer consider female chastity important before marriage. For example, surveys of male college students over the past forty years show that respondents have cared less and less whether their marital partners are virgins.[13] When asked to rank in order the importance of eighteen characteristics deemed important in choosing a mate, males over the years have ranked chastity:

- 1939   tenth of eighteen items
- 1956   thirteenth of eighteen items
- 1967   fifteenth of eighteen items
- 1977   seventeenth of eighteen items

In the 1977 survey, only "similar political background" ranked lower than "virginity."

Although attitudes toward permissible sexual behavior vary greatly among the world's societies, all cultures deem acceptable one kind of sexual relationship: marriage. Indeed, one reason for marriage is to give sexual activity a socially sanctioned outlet.

In our culture, the recent liberalization of attitudes toward sex has also affected attitudes toward the nature of sex in marriage. Whereas a few generations ago women were expected to consider sex in marriage a duty that was not supposed to be enjoyed, today it is evident that both American husbands and wives want their sexual relationship to be as pleasurable as possible.

According to survey data, some of the effects of the "revolution" in marital sex are:

1. *An Increase in the Frequency of Marital Coitus*   In the 1930s and 1940s, married couples had intercourse an average of two or three times per week.[14] In the early 1970s, the average frequency of intercourse increased to about three or four times per week.[15] In all surveys, the frequency of marital intercourse was the lowest among the older couples (over fifty-five years old), averaging about once a week. Young married people in all surveys had the highest coital frequencies. A 1979 study, for example, indicated that one-third of the couples under thirty and one-sixth of the couples aged thirty-one to forty had sexual intercourse about five times a week; one-sixth of the under-thirty group engaged in sex about once a day.[16]

All sex researchers and sex educators emphasize that coital-frequency data must be interpreted cautiously and that a particular group's average frequency does not indicate what the "normal" frequency for a specific couple should be. The average frequency of intercourse is simply a statistic for the entire group. It tells us nothing about the wide range of acceptable differences among couples. Some couples have intercourse daily, whereas others are satisfied having intercourse only a few times a year. The best determinant of a couple's frequency of intercourse is their own need for sexual expression, not adherence to some arbitrary definition of "normal" or "average."

2. *An Increase in the Length of Time of Sexual Activity*   In earlier times, when the predominant attitude was that marital sex was something a woman endured to enable her husband to "relieve his sexual tensions," the duration of sexual intercourse was short. Now, however, because the predominant attitude is that sex is supposed to be mutually satisfying for both husband and wife, couples tend to take more time in their sexual activities. In the 1930s and 1940s, couples

tended to spend an average of about five to ten minutes making love.[17] This included a few minutes of kissing and touching sexually sensitive body areas and approximately two minutes of intercourse. These days, couples typically spend twenty to thirty minutes making love. About half that time is spent in kissing and mutual sexual caressing and the other half in having sexual intercourse.[18]

3. *An Increase in the Variety of Sexual Practices* Because modern couples seem to have intercourse more often and to devote more time to their love making than couples in previous generations did, there are more opportunities and motivations to vary sexual activities. Reliance on the standard face-to-face, man-on-top position in sexual intercourse has given way to greater variation in coital positions, including the woman-on-top, vaginal entry from the rear, anal intercourse, and a variety of other positions described by sex manuals. Also, couples tend to engage more in noncoital stimulation, including body massage, prolonged genital stroking, and oral-genital stimulation. Although less common, some couples further diversify their sexual activities by using mechanical aids such as vibrators, dressing in certain clothes to enhance sexual excitement, going together to pornographic films or reading pornographic literature, and having sex in atypical locations such as on a beach, in a wilderness area, or in a "lover's motel" complete with sunken, heart-shaped bathtubs and king-sized water-beds. Sometimes it is not so much the variations themselves that add to the sexual experience as the excitement of experimenting with something new.

4. *An Overall Increase in Sexual Satisfaction* The measured increases over recent generations in the average frequency and duration of marital sex and the increases in the use of, and experimentation with, variations in sexual practices imply an overall increase in sexual satisfaction among married couples. In three separate surveys, a high percentage of couples reported the quality of their marital sexual relationship to be satisfying or pleasurable.[19] (Remarried persons gave the highest percentage of "very good" responses.) Only a very small percentage reported their sex lives to be nonpleasurable or poor.

Difficulties in Marital Sex

The reported increase in marital sexual satisfaction does not mean that married couples have no complaints about their sex lives. For example, one or both partners of some couples may be dissatisfied with the frequency of sexual activity. Distractions such as studies, work, job pressures, children, fatigue, social commitments, and illness may interfere with some people's desires and chances for sexual expression. As many couples have discovered, marriage and the sharing of another's life can demand much time and energy, and it is not surprising that nonromantic duties and responsibilities sometimes interfere with even the best sexual relationships. Some couples have devised rather novel ways to minimize the interference of life demands on their sex lives, as we learn from this mother in a two-worker marriage:

Sometimes we set the alarm for 3 A.M. That way we can make love without being tired or worrying that the kids will pop into the room or the phone will ring. And afterwards we can have a nice, restful sleep before we have to get up for work.

From the authors' files

Another possible solution is to arrange for occasional weekends alone, either at home or on a brief vacation. Although some people claim that such planning takes the spontaneity out of lovemaking, others realize that they will have little time together unless they schedule private time.

Another common complaint regarding marital sex is that one or both partners have lost interest in sex. For various reasons, one or both partners become disinterested in sex, forcing the sexual relationship to deteriorate or to cease. Therapists and counselors refer to the loss of interest in sex as "inhibited sexual desire" (ISD) and note that it can be caused by either sexual or nonsexual reasons.[20] Some of the sexual reasons are:

1. *Underlying Sexual Difficulty* One or both partners may have some serious difficulty engaging in sex, such as the man's inability to get or maintain an erection (impotence) or the woman's experiencing pain during intercourse. Any such problem makes sexual activity unpleasant for either or both partners, and they eventually lose interest in having sex with each other. (Sexual difficulties are discussed in Chapter 7, "Sexual Interaction.")

2. *Failure to Communicate Likes and Dislikes* One partner may find some aspects of marital sex unsatisfying but fail to communicate to his or her spouse either the source of displeasure or how they together might try to improve the situation. Some people believe that suggesting changes is being critical, and they do not want to hurt their spouse's feelings. Most people want satisfying sex, however, and discussing the

problem often helps. But some people have difficulty communicating effectively about sexual matters, and this can hinder sharing likes and dislikes with a partner. Suggestions for improving communication regarding sex are presented in Chapter 7, "Sexual Interaction."

3. *Boredom*   Like anything else in life that becomes routine, sex can become boring if it is always done in the same way and at the same time. As with other activities, the old cliché is true: "Variety is the spice of life." Sex therapists and books, such as Alex Comfort's *The Joy of Sex*,[21] can suggest ways to vary sexual activities.

Some of the nonsexual reasons for inhibited sexual desire are:

1. *Stress, Fatigue, and Depression*   Being emotionally drained by work or other responsibilities or being "low" or "blue" can interfere with sexual desire.

2. *Alcohol and Other Drug Taking*   The heavy use of alcohol or other recreational drugs can sometimes inhibit sexual desire. It may also "turn off" a spouse who does not want to make love to someone who is drunk or on drugs. Some prescription drugs can also inhibit sexual interest.

3. *Pregnancy and Children*   During pregnancy and child raising, the increase in responsibilities and the decrease in private time together can reduce interest in sex. Once a couple realizes that family responsibilities are causing the sexual problem, steps can be taken to return the couple to sexual harmony.

4. *Hostility and Anger*   Unresolved conflicts are a frequent cause of lost sexual interest. Many people find it very difficult to be sexually close to their spouse when angry with him or her. As with other aspects of a marital relationship, the problems causing anger and hostility must be resolved before the sexual relationship can be expected to be satisfying.

5. *Change in Physical Appearance*   Before marriage, most people tend to do whatever they can to make themselves physically attractive to potential mates. But after marriage some people may devote little time and attention to their physical appearance, and consequently, their spouses may come to find them less appealing and lose interest in them sexually.

6. *Physical Illness*   Being sick can produce a loss of interest in sex which is often reversed when the individual is well again.

Many of the difficulties that contribute to the loss of interest in sex can be overcome if the couple wants to improve their sex life and, if necessary, they consult a trained therapist or counselor.

Occupational stress, family problems, and physical illness can sometimes disrupt a couple's sexual life.

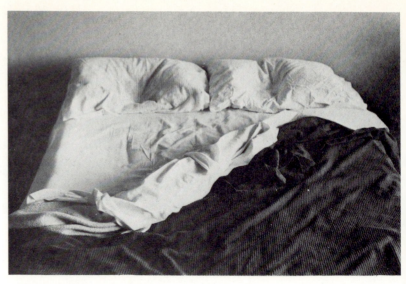

Christopher S. Johnson/Stock, Boston

Because our society has come to value pleasurable sex, many married couples expect their sex always to be satisfying, and anything less is cause for complaint. Life is full of changes, however, and career demands, adjustments to growing older, failure to accomplish certain personal goals, the demands of raising a family, and the responsibilities of caring for elderly parents can sometimes produce a temporary loss of interest in sex. Such ebbs in sexual desire are quite normal and frequently resolve themselves.[22]

For many couples, sex improves with the length of the marriage as intimacy and trust grow, inhibitions are slowly released, the willingness to experiment increases, and each partner gains an intimate knowledge of the other's physical and emotional needs. Even after twenty, thirty, or forty years of marriage, sex can be spontaneous, pleasurable, and highly fulfilling.

EXTRAMARITAL SEXUAL RELATIONSHIPS

One of the traditional ideals of the American marriage is that marital partners have sexual relations exclusively with their mates. Married people are expected to be "faithful" to one another, meaning that they will not have sexual intercourse with other people. In some marriage ceremonies, the partners explicitly vow "to cleave only to one another" or "to foresake all others." Even if such promises are not made verbally, they are nevertheless implicitly understood as part of the marriage contract, because our culture forbids extramarital sex. Sexual intercourse with someone other than the spouse (*adultery*) is a violation of the Seventh Commandment and, in many states, is a crime.

Survey data show that most people disapprove of extramarital sexual relations. The 1977 National Opinion Research Center poll of nearly 4,500 adults indicated that 86 percent of the population thought extramarital sex to be "always wrong" or "almost always wrong."[23] The disapproval rate may decline in the future, as suggested by the finding that about 40 percent of the eighteen- to twenty-nine-year-old age group held more permissive ("wrong only sometimes" or "not wrong at all") attitudes toward extramarital sex.

Marriage promises, custom, religious and secular law, and public attitudes notwithstanding, between 40 percent and 50 percent of the married men and between 12 percent and 24 percent of the married women in the United States admit to having had sexual relations outside their marriage.[24] Nearly all of these extramarital sexual relationships occur without the knowledge and consent of the spouse. This is why extramarital sex is frequently called "cheating," "being unfaithful," "infidelity," "fooling around," and "having an affair." In probably less than 3 percent of the instances of extramarital sex does the spouse know about and consent to it.[25] As yet, there are no commonly used words to describe consensual extramarital relationships, although the spouse's extramarital partner is frequently called a "lover."

The reasons for extramarital sex are many and varied. Sometimes the only purpose of extramarital sexual relationships is to experience physical sexual gratification with a new partner. Such relationships are formed to add variety and excitement to life, regardless of the quality of the marriage's sexual or emotional relationship. Occasionally, extramarital sexual relationships develop because the marital sexual relationship is unsatisfying or nonexistent. Perhaps the spouse is ill or away from home for long periods of time, or perhaps the sexual relationship has declined for other reasons.

Some people have sexual relationships outside their marriage because the emotional relationship with the spouse either has not met premarital expectations or has deteriorated to the point that the partners have difficulty communicating with each other. In these instances, one or both partners may seek emotional support and closeness from others. In some cases, these relationships are rewarding and fulfilling and may last for many years. But sometimes an extramarital relationship can be unsatisfying and exploitative, and can bring considerable guilt and anxiety about being discovered.

Sometimes a person enters an extramarital relationship for other than sexual reasons. Some people want companionship, attention, and the feeling of being attractive, desirable, and understood by another person. These needs can be met by close, nonsexual friendships. Few marriages can meet all the needs of the partners all of the time, particularly if the marriage lasts twenty, thirty, or even fifty years. This is why some people advocate "open marriages" in which each spouse is free to cultivate close relationships in addition to the primary marital one.[26] Whether or not these relationships are sexual depends on a prior agreement by the spouses. The important point is that they do not have to be sexual. It is possible for men and women to enjoy close relationships without having sex.

For those who feel comfortable with the idea of forming close friendships without sexual involvement, marriage and family counselor Marcia Lasswell and writer Norman Lobsenz offer these suggestions:[27]

1. Be certain of your goals for a relationship. To begin a friendship with the "hidden agenda" of having it turn into a romance is not only dishonest but is also likely to be unsuccessful.

2. Do not conceal your marital status from a new friend. This will make clear that your intentions are for friendship and not romance.

3. If the friendship takes on sexual overtones, promptly clear the air with a frank discussion. Such feelings may arise naturally in close relationships, but they do not have to be acted upon.

4. Discuss with your spouse his or her uncomfortable feelings about your friendships with others. Failure to do so may cause hurt or suspicion.

SAME-SEX RELATIONSHIPS

An estimated 5 to 10 percent of the American population maintain sexual and romantic emotional involvements exclusively with members of the same sex. Such men are called *homosexuals* or *gays* and such women, *lesbians*. (The terms homosexual and gay can also apply to women, but lesbian is the most commonly used term.)

Traditionally our culture has strongly forbidden same-sex relationships, asserting that people should have sex only with members of the opposite sex and that same-sex relationships are wrong, illegal, immoral, or indicative of psychological illness. In some other cultures, however, homosexual relationships are, to some degree, condoned.[28] In recent years, gay men and lesbians in the United States have openly voiced their objections to the many negative stereotypes of homosexuals and have pressed for equal social, economic, political, and legal treatment; and it appears that in some communities, particularly the larger cities, attitudes toward same-sex relationships have become more tolerant.

There is such a strong bias in our culture that heterosexuality is natural and homosexuality is unnatural that some people wonder why individuals are homosexual at all. Scientific studies have failed to uncover any genetic, hormonal, or metabolic reasons for homosexual inclinations, and there also is no evidence that homosexuality is a form of mental illness. Indeed, one of the principal messages that homosexuals are trying to communicate to the rest of society is that they are not sick or depraved and that they deserve the same rights and freedoms as everyone else has, including the freedom to express themselves sexually as they wish.

Since homosexuality is neither a biological nor a psychological disorder, the question is not what makes someone homosexual, but rather, what factors determine any person's sexual preference, whether heterosexual, homosexual, or bisexual (attraction for members of either sex). Some people believe that humans are, in fact, inherently bisexual and that any preference for sexual partners of one or the other sex is determined by early learning experiences, just as other forms of sexual behavior are. To support this contention, they point out that surveys show that more than half of the American population has had at least some homosexual experience, often occurring in childhood when sexual experimentation is common, and that many people say they can occasionally be erotically aroused by same-sexed individuals even if they do not act on their feelings by having sex with them.[29]

Homosexual relationships are similar to heterosexual relationships. Some homosexual relationships are fairly casual and do not involve a long-term commitment. Others are similar to marital relationships and are based on the exchange of love, affection, and understanding. The partners in these relationships usually want to have sex only with each other, although some relationships are "open coupled," in which one or both members seek out and engage in sexual activities with partners other than the primary one.[30]

To many homosexuals, issues related to marriage and family life are extremely important. Many believe that society should allow homosexual couples to marry legally and thereby to enjoy the same legal rights and social status that heterosexuals have. Children are also a very important part of many homosexuals' lives. Lesbians and gay men often raise their own children from former marriages or other heterosexual

Gay men and lesbians want the right to express themselves sexually as they wish. Their demands for the same rights and freedoms that heterosexuals have are often voiced at gay rights rallys (see photo on page 149).

Jim Anderson/Stock, Boston

relationships. Others choose to adopt children. Whether or not they see children as part of their family life, homosexuals as well as heterosexuals want the trust, security, and companionship of a long-term, committed relationship that characterizes the ideal of marriage.

SUMMARY

Sexual interest reaches its peak in adolescence as people become capable of having children. Besides procreation, people engage in

Eric Roth/The Picture Cube

sexual activity because it is pleasurable and is a means of emotional expression, especially of love and affection.

Traditionally, our culture has been rather restrictive regarding sex. But in recent years, sexual values and attitudes have changed. The public display of nudity and sex abounds. People expect their private sexual lives to be enriching and mutually satisfying.

Approximately one-third of the adult U.S. population is not married; yet many of these people are sexually active. Polls show that in general, young people favor nonmarital sex, and estimates suggest that a majority of unmarried young adults engage in sexual intercourse. Older people, who grew up in a time when sex before marriage was forbidden and who may now be parents, tend to have more restrictive attitudes toward premarital sex.

Compared with couples of previous generations, modern couples are reporting a greater frequency of sexual intercourse, an increase in the length of time of sexual activity, and an increase in the variety of sexual practices—all of which support the finding that married people now are experiencing more sexual satisfaction than earlier generations did. In the ebb and flow of married life, however, there may be a loss of interest in sex. Frequently this is due to boredom or distractions and, with recognition of the source, it can be overcome.

In the United States, as many as half of married men and one-fourth of married women say that they have had sexual encounters outside their marriages. And about 5 percent to 10 percent of the American population are attracted to and have sexual relations exclusively with members of their own sex.

CONSIDER THIS

Marie is a nineteen-year-old college sophomore who lives on campus but occasionally returns home for a weekend visit with her widowed father. One weekend she invited her boy friend John to come home with her.

"Dad's cool," she told John. But her father became very upset when he came home from work and found John's suitcase and clothes in Marie's bedroom.

"I guess Dad's still into the old double standard," thought Marie.

What a surprise to find that her father was so narrow minded. In the three years since her mother had died, Marie had never objected to her father's sleeping with other women. He was considerate enough to bring home only the nicer ones. And the fact that he didn't keep it a secret or try to hide it made his relationship with Marie more honest.

Perhaps Marie should have written her father first to tell him that she was bringing John for the weekend. It was too late now. The argument was over.

Questions
1. How would you react if Marie were your daughter?
2. If Marie's father had had a son instead of a daughter, do you think he would have reacted in the same way?
3. Should Marie have anticipated her father's reaction? Was there a better way to handle the situation created by bringing John to her father's house?
4. Is it acceptable for Marie's father to believe that nonmarital sex is all right for him but not all right for his daughter?

NOTES

1. Eric Berne, *Sex in Human Loving*, New York, Simon & Shuster, 1970, p. 36.

2. Philip Slater, "Sexual Adequacy in America," *Intellectual Digest*, November 1973, pp. 1–8.

3. Lewis Diana, " 'Casual' vs. 'Committed' Sex," *Medical Aspects of Human Sexuality*, 13, no. 7 (July 1979): 6.

4. Merle Sondra Kroop, "The Sexual 'Rat Race,' " *Medical Aspects of Human Sexuality*, 14, no. 3 (March 1980): 32–47.

5. Harvey Caplan, "Commentary on the Paper by M. S. Kroop," *Medical Aspects of Human Sexuality*, 14, no. 3 (March 1980): 46.

6. Adapted from Norval D. Glenn and Charles N. Weaver, "Attitudes Toward Premarital, Extramarital, and Homosexual Relations in the U.S. in the 1970s," *Journal of Sex Research*, 15, no. 2 (May 1979): 108–118.

7. Ira Reiss and Frank Furstenberg, "Sociology and Human Sexuality," in Harold Lief and Arno Karlen, eds., *Sexual Health Care*, Chicago, American Medical Association, 1980, p. 8.

8. Norval D. Glenn and Charles N. Weaver, *Attitudes*, p. 112.

9. Karl King, Jack O. Balswick, and Ira E. Robinson, "The Continuing Premarital Sexual Revolution Among College Females," *Journal of Marriage and the Family*, August 1977, pp. 455–458.

10. Melvin Zelnick and John F. Kantner, "Sexual Activity, Contraceptive Use and Pregnancy Among Metropolitan-Area Teenagers: 1971–1979," *Family Planning Perspectives*, 12 (1980): 230–237.

11. Morton Hunt, *Sexual Behavior in the 1970s*, Chicago, Playboy Press, 1974, p. 150.

12. Karl King, Jack O. Balswick, and Ira E. Robinson, "The Continuing Premarital Sexual Revolution," p. 456.

13. John W. Hudson, "College Men's Attitudes Regarding Female Chastity," *Medical Aspects of Human Sexuality*, 14, no. 1 (January 1980): 137.

14. Alfred C. Kinsey et al., *Sexual Behavior in the Human Female*, Philadelphia, Saunders, 1953, p. 350.

15. Morton Hunt, *Sexual Behavior in the 1970s*, p. 190.

16. Anthony Pietropinto and Jacqueline Simenauer, *Husbands and Wives*, New York, Times Books, 1979, pp. 91–92.

17. Alfred C. Kinsey et al., *Sexual Behavior in the Human Female*, p. 393.

18. Morton Hunt, *Sexual Behavior in the 1970s*, p. 204; Anthony Pietropinto and Jacqueline Simenauer, *Husbands and Wives*, p. 95.

19. See, for example, Morton Hunt, *Sexual Behavior in the 1970s*, p. 215; Ellen Frank, Carol Anderson, and Debra Rubinstein, "Frequency of Sexual Dysfunction in 'Normal' Couples," *New England Journal of Medicine*, 299, no. 3 (1979): 111–115; Anthony Pietropinto and

Jacqueline Simenauer, *Husbands and Wives*, p. 78.

20. Domeena C. Renshaw, "Sexual Boredom," *Medical Aspects of Human Sexuality*, 13, no. 6 (June 1979): 16–25; Carol Botwin, "Is There Sex After Marriage?" *New York Times Magazine*, September 16, 1979, pp. 108–112.

21. Alex Comfort, *The Joy of Sex*, New York, Simon & Schuster, 1972.

22. Eugene H. Kaplan, "The Normal Ebb and Flow of Marital Sex Relations," *Medical Aspects of Human Sexuality*, 13, no. 5 (May 1979): 87–109.

23. Norval D. Glenn and Charles N. Weaver, *Attitudes*, p. 113.

24. Morton Hunt, *Sexual Behavior in the 1970s*, p. 258; Anthony Pietropinto and Jacqueline Simenauer, *Husbands and Wives*, p. 278.

25. Anthony Pietropinto and Jacqueline Simenauer, *Husbands and Wives*, p. 280.

26. Nena O'Neill and George O'Neill, *Open Marriage*, New York, M. Evans, 1972.

27. Marcia Lasswell and Norman Lobsenz, "Can Men and Women Be Just Friends?" *McCall's*, March 1980, p. 89.

28. Clellan S. Ford and Frank A. Beach, *Patterns of Sexual Behavior*, New York, Harper & Row, 1951.

29. Alfred C. Kinsey, et al., *Sexual Behavior in the Human Female*, p. 459; Morton Hunt, *Sexual Behavior in the 1970s*, p. 315.

30. Alan P. Bell and Martin S. Weinberg, *Homosexualities*. New York, Simon & Schuster, 1978, pp. 129–139.

SUGGESTED READINGS

Botwin, Carol. "Is There Sex After Marriage?" *New York Times Magazine*, September 16, 1979, pp. 108–112. A discussion of the causes and treatments of inhibited sexual desire.

Clayton, Richard R., and Janet L. Bokemeier. "Premarital Sex in the Seventies." *Journal of Marriage and the Family*, 42 (1980): 758–776. A review of the research on both the incidence of and the social and psychological correlates of premarital sexual behavior.

Ford, Clellan S., and Frank A. Beach. *Patterns of Sexual Behavior*. New York, Harper & Row, 1951. A cross-cultural comparison of human sexual behavior.

Hunt, Morton. *Sexual Behavior in the 1970s*. Chicago, Playboy Press, 1974. A thorough survey of sexual behavior in the United States in the early 1970s.

Pietropinto, Anthony, and Jacqueline Simenauer. *Husbands and Wives*. New York, Times Books, 1979. A survey of the sexual behavior of American married couples.

Slater, Philip. "Sexual Adequacy in America." *Intellectual Digest*, November 1973, pp. 1–8. A critique of modern sexual values.

SEXUAL INTERACTION

Sexuality and sexual functioning contribute to human fulfillment, enhance the quality of life, and play an important role throughout the life cycle of the individual.

Herbert A. Otto[1]

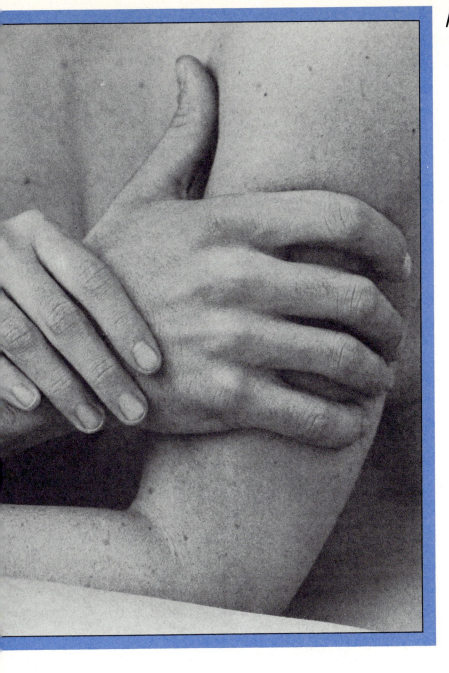

People in love like to be physically close to their partners. They want to touch, kiss, hold hands, hug, and, when appropriate, have sexual relations. Through physical closeness, lovers can exchange the gift of physical pleasure and can also express and affirm their affection for each other. For many individuals, sexual relations are a form of body language that communicates the message "I care."

The desire to be sexual is a normal and natural part of adult life. But the knowledge of how to express sexual feelings is not innate. There is great variation in how people are able to interact sexually, and there is equally great variation in how people prefer to interact sexually. Simply being physically capable of sexual activity is no guarantee that sexual interaction with another person will be harmonious and fulfilling.

Gratifying and joyous sexual interaction is brought about by knowledge of one's own sexual anatomy and the various ways one's mind and body respond during sexual relations, as well as by knowledge of the sexual anatomy and the responsiveness of one's partner. Satisfying sexual interaction also comes from the partners' honest communication about their mutual sexual interaction and their desire to overcome sexual difficulties should they occur.

In this chapter we present some of the fundamentals of human sexual anatomy and response and also discuss sexual communication, sexual difficulties, and sexually transmitted diseases.

FEMALE SEXUAL ANATOMY

The sexual anatomy of the human female consists of several structures located both inside the body and on its outer surface. Although the following description of female anatomy is generally applicable to all women, many sex educators suggest that women learn about themselves directly with the aid of a mirror and a self-help guide or instructor.[2]

Women's internal sex organs include two *ovaries*, almond-shaped structures that lie on either side of the abdominal cavity, and the *Fallopian tubes, uterus,* and *vagina* (see Figure 7.1). These organs make up a specialized tube that extends from the vicinity of each ovary to the outside of the body. The ovaries produce eggs (ova) and sex hormones. Approximately once each month, an egg is released from one of the ovaries. The egg can survive for about two days, and if it is fertilized by a sperm during that time, pregnancy will result.

A Fallopian tube lies adjacent to each ovary. When an egg is released from the ovary, it enters the nearby Fallopian tube, in which fertilization most often occurs. The pair of Fallopian tubes are connected to the uterus, a hollow organ about the size of a small closed

FIGURE 7.1
A front view of the female internal sex organs

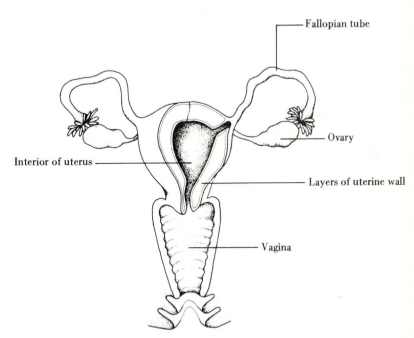

Fallopian tube

Ovary

Interior of uterus

Layers of uterine wall

Vagina

FIGURE 7.2
A side view of the
female internal sex
organs, the urinary
bladder, and the
urethra

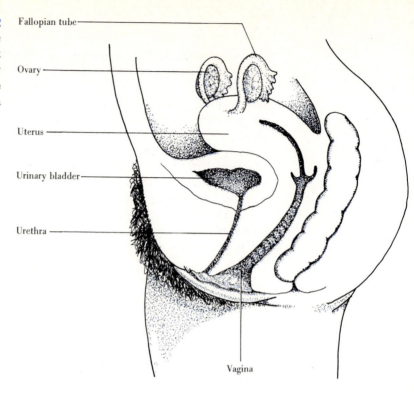

Fallopian tube

Ovary

Uterus

Urinary bladder

Urethra

Vagina

fist. The uterus is situated behind the pelvic bone and bladder (see Figure 7.2). Sperm travel through the uterus to the Fallopian tubes to fertilize the egg. After being fertilized the egg travels down the Fallopian tube into the uterus, where it develops over the next nine months into a baby. If pregnancy does not occur, then each month the inner lining of the uterus is sloughed off, and this is called *menstruation*.

The lower part of the uterus, called the *cervix*, is connected to the *vagina*, which leads to the outside. Normally the vagina is rather narrow, but it can readily widen to accommodate a tampon during menstruation, a penis during intercourse, or the passage of a baby during childbirth. Well-toned pelvic muscles surrounding the vagina can improve a woman's sexual satisfaction and response, as well as her partner's.[3]

Secretions continually emanate from the vaginal walls to help cleanse the vagina and to protect it from yeast and bacterial infections. When a woman becomes sexually excited, the volume of these secretions can increase considerably, and this provides lubrication during sexual intercourse.

A woman's external sexual structures are located in the *vulva*, the region in the lower part of the pelvis and between the legs (see Figure 7.3). The vulva is covered by a small mound of soft tissue, called the *mons*, which is covered by pubic hair. The pattern and thickness of pubic hair varies among women.

A woman's sex organs consist of the vagina, the clitoris, and two pairs of fleshy folds that surround the vagina and the clitoris. The smaller, inner pair of folds are called the *labia minora*, and the larger, outer pair are called the *labia majora*. The *clitoris*, a highly sensitive sex organ, is situated just above the urethra (which is just above the vaginal opening) and is covered by a fold of skin—the *clitoral hood*. When a woman is sexually excited, the clitoris can enlarge somewhat and become hard.

The opening of the *urethra*, which is the opening for the urinary tract, is located in the vaginal region just below the clitoris. Women do

FIGURE 7.3

The vulva, where the female external sexual structures are located

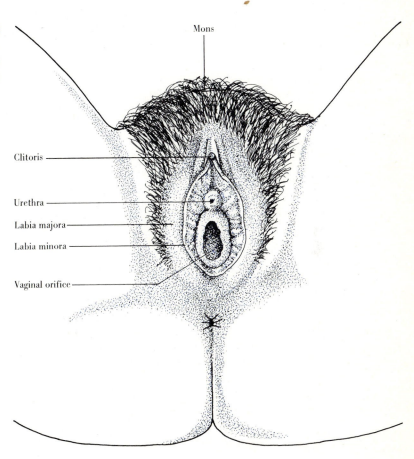

Mons

Clitoris

Urethra

Labia majora

Labia minora

Vaginal orifice

not urinate through the vagina. Because the urethra is only about a half inch long and is located so close to the vagina, it is susceptible to irritation and infection, called *urethritis*. Urethritis is characterized by a burning sensation during urination and usually by a frequent urge to urinate. A common cause of urethritis is extensive sexual intercourse, which can irritate the urethra and sometimes permits bacteria to enter. Urinating immediately after intercourse is one way to help prevent urethritis. Sometimes a bout of urethritis can be cured by drinking a lot of water, but if the pain is severe or blood is present in the urine, a physician should be consulted.

A woman's breasts are a network of milk glands and milk ducts that lead to a single opening in the nipple. There is little variation among women in the amount of milk-producing tissue, which is why a woman's ability to breast-feed an infant is not related to the size of her breasts. The variation in breast size among women is due to the differing amounts of fatty tissue within the breasts.

The breasts are supplied with numerous nerve endings. These nerves are important to the delivery of milk to a nursing baby, and they also make the breasts highly sensitive to touch. Many women find certain forms of tactile stimulation of the breasts to be sexually pleasurable. Sexual arousal, tactile stimulation, and cold temperatures can cause small muscles in the nipples to contract, resulting in the nipples' erection.

MALE SEXUAL ANATOMY

A male's sexual anatomy is structured to produce sperm cells and to deliver them into the female vagina during sexual intercourse. It consists of two *testes*, or *testicles*, the sites of sperm-cell and sex-hormone production, as well as a series of connected *sperm ducts* and the *penis*, the organ of copulation (see Figure 7.4).

The pair of testes are located in a flesh-covered sac—the *scrotum*—which hangs outside the man's body at the lower part of the pelvis. Inside the scrotum, the testes are kept at a temperature a few degrees cooler than the internal body temperature, a condition necessary for the production of reproductively viable sperm. One testis is usually a little lower than the other.

The series of sperm ducts originates in the testes, courses through the pelvis, and terminates in the penis. When a man ejaculates, the sperm are propelled through the sperm ducts and out of the tip of the penis by contractions of both the small muscles that line the ducts and the larger muscles of the pelvis, which also contract during orgasm. As

FIGURE 7.4
The male sexual
anatomy. The testes are
situated outside the
body in the scrotum.

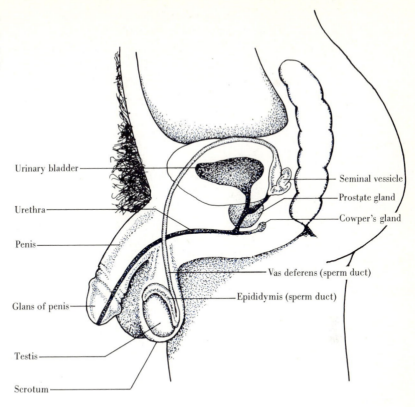

Urinary bladder

Urethra

Penis

Glans of penis

Testis

Scrotum

Seminal vessicle

Prostate gland

Cowper's gland

Vas deferens (sperm duct)

Epididymis (sperm duct)

they make their way out of the body, the sperm mix with *seminal fluid* secreted by the seminal vesicles, prostate gland, and Cowper's glands to form semen. The *semen,* which is the gelatinous, milky fluid emitted at ejaculation, is a mixture of about 300 million sperm cells and about a tablespoonful of seminal fluid. The seminal fluid makes up about 99 percent of the entire volume of semen.

The penis is normally soft, but when a man becomes sexually aroused, its internal tissues fill with blood and the penis enlarges and becomes erect. There is no relationship between the size of the penis, either soft or erect, and a man's general body build. Nor is there any relationship between the size of the penis and a man's ability to give or receive sexual pleasure.

Men are born with a fold of skin, the *foreskin,* covering the end of the penis. For centuries, Jewish and Moslem families have surgically removed the foreskin from male children for religious reasons. In the United States today, this procedure, which is called *circumcision,* is often carried out routinely on newborn males, regardless of religion.

"I love the idea of there being two sexes, don't you?"

Although there is no clear medical indication that circumcision is beneficial, the removal of the foreskin does eliminate the build-up of *smegma,* a white cheesy substance that can accumulate under the foreskin. The belief that circumcision, by exposing the *glans* (the tip of the penis), makes men more easily aroused sexually and less able to delay ejaculation is untrue.[4] For most men, circumcision has no effect on sexual arousal and activity.

SEXUAL AROUSAL AND RESPONSE

In recent years, an enormous amount of scientific information about human sexual response has been accumulated. This information has helped dispel the destructive attitudes that sexuality is immoral, dirty, depraved, and unnatural. These studies provide ample proof that sexual responsiveness is a natural part of being human.

By observing the responses of volunteer human subjects to various conditions of sexual arousal, William Masters and Virginia Johnson showed that regardless of the specific sexual stimulation, be it self-stimulation or sex with another person, the body's physiological response was similar in all people, regardless of gender.[5] Masters and Johnson called this patterned response the "sexual response cycle" (see Figure 7.5). The cycle consists of four phases: (1) the *excitement phase*, during which a person experiences sexual arousal from any source; (2) the *plateau phase*, characterized by more intense sexual arousal; (3) *orgasm*, the release of sexual tension built up in the response cycle's previous phases; and (4) the *resolution phase*, the return to the nonstimulated state. It should be noted that within this sexual response cycle, the extent and duration of individual sexual responses vary, and even the response cycle in the same person varies, for not every sexual encounter is identical.

Excitement Phase

The first phase of the response cycle, the excitement phase, can be initiated by a variety of situations and events. Certain features of another's body, or how he or she dresses or behaves, may trigger a rush of sexual excitement. Night dreams, daydreams, and fantasies also can be sexually stimulating. Most people respond to being touched in particular areas. Some regions of the body—for women, the clitoris, vaginal lips, and breasts; for men, the penis; and for both, the lips, portions of the ear, and the anal region—are highly sensitive to sexual stimulation. In fact, just about anything can be sexually stimulating, and just about everything is. The variety of stimuli that can produce sexual arousal demonstrates that the brain is really the primary sex organ, for it determines what is sexually stimulating. That nearly all reputed *aphrodisiacs*—substances that are supposed to increase sexual

FIGURE 7.5

A generalized representation of the four phases of the sexual response cycle

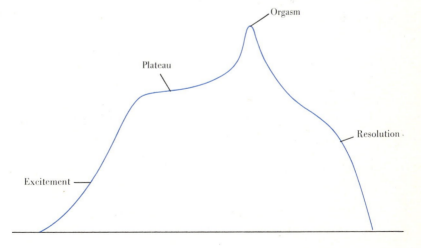

The excitement phase is the first stage of the sexual response cycle.

Paul Fusco/Magnum

desire—are mind-affecting drugs also attests to the brain's primary role in sexual arousal.

The brain not only sets the stage for sexual activity by interpreting situations as sexual, but it also governs the physiological responses that make sex possible. This is why a person who is angry, guilty, anxious, or uncomfortable may not respond to the usual forms of sexual stimulation.

When a person does become sexually aroused, the brain and nervous system prepare the body for sexual activity. Impulses from the brain are transmitted by the spinal nerves to various parts of the body, where they cause physiological changes. These include the tightening of many muscles; the congestion of blood in certain body regions, particularly the pelvis; an increase in heart rate, blood pressure, and respiration; and an increase in feelings of excitement. In the pelvic area, the constriction of certain blood vessels and the dilation of others lead to the accumulation of blood in that region, which causes the most obvious initial physiological responses to sexual arousal: the erection of the penis, the lubrication and enlargement of the vagina, and the swelling of the clitoris.

Plateau Phase

If a person feels comfortable with the idea, and if the time, place, and circumstances are appropriate, the initial phase of sexual excitement can be followed by more intense sexual activity. Increasing the level of sexual arousal and response usually involves kissing and touching the sexually sensitive parts of the body. Kissing may sometimes take the form of so-called French kissing, or deep kissing: the tongue is inserted into the mouth of the kissing partner, and the inner surfaces of the lips and mouth are stimulated. Oral stimulation can also include gently biting the partner's lips and mouth, and sucking and kissing the ear lobes and neck.

Another common type of sexual stimulation is the gentle fondling, kissing, or sucking of the woman's breasts. The breasts usually respond to stimulation by enlarging up to 25 percent in size and becoming firmer, and the nipples frequently become hard and erect.

The most direct form of sexual stimulation is manipulation of the genitalia. The female partner may rub or stroke her partner's penis, scrotum, and entire genital region; and the male partner may explore the entire genital region of his mate, including the vagina, vaginal lips, and especially the clitoris. It is not uncommon, and certainly not unnatural, for sex partners to stimulate orally the genitals of their mates. Oral stimulation of the female genitals is called *cunnilingus*, and oral stimulation of the penis is called *fellatio*. Sometimes sex partners engage in simultaneous oral-genital stimulation, referred to as *soixante-neuf*, or "sixty-nine."

If a couple is going to have sexual intercourse, it usually begins during the response cycle's plateau phase. The most frequently employed coital position is the man-on-top, face-to-face position, sometimes called the "missionary position." Other commonly used positions include the female-above, the on-the-side (lateral) position, and vaginal entry from the rear, which some couples find best during pregnancy. Other variations are coitus while sitting or standing. During coitus, partners may stimulate each other with kisses, manipulation of sexually sensitive regions, and the exchange of vocal signs of pleasure, love, and tenderness.

Orgasm Phase

With continued sexual stimulation, the level of sexual excitement can reach a peak, or climax, and the accumulated physiological sexual tensions built up during the excitement and plateau phases of the response cycle can be released in a pleasurable outburst known as *orgasm, climaxing,* or *coming*. The orgasmic response in both men and women is characterized by rhythmic contractions of the pelvic muscles; tightening of the muscles of the face, hands, and feet; and the feelings of intense pleasure. Most commonly, men ejaculate during orgasm, although it is possible for some males to experience orgasm without ejaculating.[6] Women do not ejaculate at orgasm.

Orgasmic Experience | Orgasmic experiences vary greatly in both sexes. As psychiatry professor Dr. Domeena C. Renshaw points out:

> It is worth noting that for all persons there are big orgasms and little ones, depending on the state of mind (how excited or how relaxed) at the moment of sexual activity. And on some occasions, when persons are too tense or upset or tired, there are none. This is quite natural. Understanding this will provide perspective and prevent needless performance anxiety.[7]

Some women are uncertain whether they experience orgasm. It is not accurate to say that a woman always knows if she has an orgasm. The media have perpetuated the myth that when a woman has an orgasm, bells ring, the earth shakes, lights flash, and she moans and groans. In reality, there are many kinds of orgasmic responses. For example, some orgasms are quiet, and neither partner may be aware that they have occurred (see Box 7.1). Some of the criteria used by sex counselors to help women determine if they have orgasms are (1) the build-up and spreading of waves of sexual feelings from the pelvis to the rest of the body; (2) an awareness of automatic vaginal contractions; and (3) feelings of relaxation and a lack of frustration at the end of the sexual experience.[8]

One of the pervasive myths concerning orgasm is that the ultimate in sexual fulfillment is for both partners to have orgasm simultaneously. In actuality, most couples do not have simultaneous orgasms all the time, nor do they wish to. Sequential orgasms permit partners to experience and appreciate each other's orgasm without being occupied with their own. Striving for the elusive simultaneous orgasm can so distract the partners that neither enjoys sex. Couples may enjoy sex more if they expand their lovemaking to include different orgasmic situations:

1. Either partner may reach orgasm through manual, oral, or other means of stimulation before or after coitus. There is no rule that dictates that orgasm should occur only during intercourse.

2. Sexual activity need not stop simply because one partner reaches orgasm. If a couple chooses, lovemaking can continue until both wish to stop. Even after ejaculation, most men are still capable of intercourse.

BOX 7.1   Should a Man Ask His Sex Partner if She Has Had an Orgasm?

Whether or not a man should ask his sex partner if she has had an orgasm depends on the reason he wants to know, the couple's relationship, and the timing of the question.

In some instances, a man's desire to know about his partner's orgasm is really an attempt to find out how he is performing. It is a way to verify his masculinity and has no bearing on whether or not his partner is enjoying herself. A woman confronted with this motivation may fake an orgasm or lie, simply to avoid offending her partner.

A woman who is asked if she has had an orgasm may interpret the question to mean that she is not a good sex partner. Does it mean that her partner is bored, tired of making love with her, or impatient to finish? Does it mean she is sexually inadequate? The question may make her anxious and bring on unnecessary performance pressures. The goal of sex is mutual pleasure and not just orgasm. Many couples find sex highly satisfying even when there are no orgasms.

It is appropriate, however, for a man to be sincerely interested in whether his partner is deriving satisfaction from their sexual activities together. And, contrary to the popular myth that men are supposed to know if their partners are sexually satisfied, in truth there is no way for a man to be absolutely certain unless his partner tells him.

One way to begin a conversation about sex is to ask if the partner is satisfied with the couple's lovemaking. Or more specific questions can be asked: What can I can do that will give you more sexual pleasure? What orgasmic experience do you derive from our lovemaking?

Certain kinds of communication regarding orgasm can take place during lovemaking by using a signaling system, which can be either verbal or nonverbal.

3.   Neither individual may feel the need for an orgasm during a particular sexual episode. The satisfaction from physically expressing love and affection need not focus on orgasm.

Our society is oriented toward achievement, and unfortunately it has become common to apply measures of success to lovemaking, especially to orgasm. For example, many people believe that success in lovemaking is determined by how frequently the woman partner achieves orgasm during sexual intercourse. By this standard, a "successful male" is someone who can delay ejaculation until his partner has experienced at least one orgasm, and preferably more. The same standard of success applied to women calls for them to have several orgasms in every sexual encounter. Men and women who cannot achieve these standards of performance may be erroneously considered "inadequate" by others or themselves.

With the emphasis on the attainment of orgasm, many of the other pleasurable aspects of sex—touching, kissing, and expressing love and affection—are lost. By focusing on the product of sexual activity, the many different pleasures associated with the process are often over-looked. As Philip Slater points out:

Most sex manuals give the impression that the partners in lovemaking are performing some sort of task; by dint of great cooperative effort and technical skill (primarily the man's), an orgasm (primarily the woman's) is ultimately produced. The bigger the orgasm the more "successful" the task performance. . . . Leisurely pleasure-seeking is brushed aside, as all acts and all thoughts are directed toward the creation of a successful finale.[9]

When people become overly concerned with whether or not they are "succeeding" or "performing well," they can become psychologically detached from the activity and become "spectators" rather than full participants.[10] Rather than abandon themselves completely to the sexual experience, they withdraw their attention and judge their actions by some measure of performance. *Spectatoring,* as this is called, can lead to worry and anxiety, and thoughts of "I wonder how I am doing?" can inhibit sexual enjoyment.

Besides inducing spectatoring and performance anxieties, this emphasis on achieving orgasm tends to limit the definition of sex to sexual intercourse alone. In the words of psychologist Lonnie Garfield Barbach:

Intercourse is only one of a number of ways to give and receive sexual pleasure. Sexual relationships and sexual feelings extend far beyond the act of intercourse. To make intercourse the goal of sex does grave disservice to many enjoyable ways of touching. . . . The term sex includes anything that turns you on and gives you sexual pleasure. It doesn't have to include a partner, but it can. It doesn't have to include orgasm, but that's a possibility. It doesn't have to include any genital touching—it could be just fantasy.[11]

Pleasurable sex comes from learning to appreciate the many sexual sensations from touching and being touched on virtually any body region—face, back, arms, legs, and feet—as well as the genitals and breasts. A total body massage, for example, can be tremendously pleasurable and sensual.

Resolution Phase

With the release of accumulated sexual tension by means of orgasm and without additional sexual stimulation, a person's body usually returns to its prestimulated state. This is referred to as the resolution phase of the response cycle. After ejaculation, most men experience a period of time during which they cannot be sexually stimulated, which is called the *refractory period*. The refractory period can last minutes, hours, or even days, depending on the man and the situation. There is more variation in women's resolution phases than in men's. Some women do not experience a refractory period; they are capable of repeated episodes of sexual arousal and repeated orgasms. Other women may have refractory periods that can last a few seconds to several hours. This is often characterized by the clitoris and external genitalia being too sensitive to be stimulated any further without discomfort.

Many couples would like to continue their sexual activity despite one or the other partner's refractory period. This can be done if the partners recognize the refractory period as a natural part of lovemaking and accept that one or the other may not be interested in or able to continue sexual stimulation after orgasm. Most people, even though they may prefer not to be sexually stimulated any more, nevertheless would like to contribute to their partner's continued sexual stimulation. This can be done through noncoital activities such as touching and oral stimulation.

SEXUAL COMMUNICATION

Even though sex is very important to most love relationships, many couples have difficulty communicating their sexual needs and desires:

It's pretty easy for us to talk about most things in our relationship— except sex. Our sex life is usually O.K., but when it isn't, I don't know how to talk about it.

From the authors' files

Sometimes nonverbal communication in the form of gestures, touches, glances, and certain kinds of dress can tell one partner about the other's current sexual feelings. But communication is always improved if individuals do not assume that they or their partners can read each other's minds. Verbal communication is usually the best way to prevent misunderstanding and hurt feelings.

For some, sexual communication can be difficult because words about sex may seem "dirty," embarrassing, or too analytical. Talking about sex may be difficult also because deeply felt emotions can be hard to convey, and many individuals have been taught that sex is a forbidden topic. Some people may fear that discussing sexual feelings may cause them to be rejected, criticized, or judged harshly. Also, some do not talk about sex because they do not want to risk hurting their partner's feelings.

Although these all are common reasons for not talking about sex with a partner, they nevertheless stand in the way of couples trying to communicate their needs and desires.

If talking about sex is a problem, a couple may find that tension and performance pressures can be relieved by conversing about their sex life in a neutral place (not in the bedroom) and at a neutral time (not while making love). If sex is difficult for you to discuss, it sometimes helps to tell your partner that you feel uncomfortable talking about sex and perhaps why you feel that way. Your partner may have similar feelings, and sharing your difficulty in talking about sex may facilitate communication.

A related way to begin a dialogue about sex in a relationship is to share sexual histories. Partners can recount their experiences with sex education (if any) in their parents' home or in school, where and from whom they learned the most about sex, and how their parents' relationships affected their feelings about love and sex.

Some couples put sex on their communication agenda by talking about articles, novels, or sex manuals. Material can be read individually and then discussed at some appointed time, or partners may read the material together.

Some of the most important issues for sexual communication are contraception, the partners' sexual needs, asking for sex and declining it, and changing habitual sex patterns.

Contraception

Any difficulty in discussing sexual anatomy and sexual functions can be carried over to the discussion of contraceptives. For some, talking about contraception is embarrassing and awkward. Because many contraceptives are used only by the female, many couples feel that contraception is not the male partner's responsibility, even though he may be very interested in and concerned about it. Even if he is concerned, a male might not ask about his partner's contraceptive use, fearing the embarrassment of appearing ignorant or unmanly.

Both partners share the responsibility for contraception because both partners are responsible if an unwanted pregnancy occurs. This fact alone is a reason for talking about contraceptive methods and also about what the couple will do if there is an unwanted pregnancy. Much information and counseling regarding contraception is available. (Contraception is discussed in detail in Chapter 12, "Family Planning.")

Discovering the Partner's Needs

Most partners want to please each other sexually, but they have no way of automatically knowing what their partner likes. Unless the couple establishes some sort of nonverbal signaling system to be used during lovemaking (being fully aware of the risks of misinterpreting nonverbal signals), the best way is to ask.

You can ask yes-or-no questions, such as "Was it good?" or "Do you like this?" But yes-or-no questions can force a partner to give a single-word answer when he or she may have more to say. Also, a question like "Am I doing it right?" may not elicit an honest answer because the partner fears hurting the other's feelings.

There is a similar problem with either-or questions, such as "Do you prefer this or that?" The either-or alternative may not offer the partner the opportunity to explain an answer, or it may force him or her to choose between two alternatives, neither of which really describes his or her actual feelings.

Open-ended questions, such as those listed below, give the partner the opportunity to respond with whatever feelings and information he or she feels comfortable with:

1. What gives you the most pleasure when we make love?
2. What parts of your body do you like to have sexually stimulated, and how?
3. What are your feelings about oral sex?
4. Which coital positions do you like best? Are there any you do not like?

Notice that open-ended questions are straightforward inquiries; they do not suggest an answer, as do yes-no or either-or questions.

Making Requests and Saying "No"

Many people mistakenly assume that their partner automatically knows how to please them. But people have personal preferences about how and where on the body they like to be sexually stimulated. Communicating these preferences gives partners the best chance to please each other.

The more specific a person is about communicating a sexual preference, the less likely the partner is to misunderstand. The best way to communicate verbally a particular preference is to begin most statements with the pronoun "I," as in "I would like . . . ," instead of beginning with the pronoun "you," as in "you should. . . ." "You" statements are often interpreted as accusations, whereas "I" statements are clear expressions of the speaker's thoughts and feelings.

Sometimes one partner asks for sex and his or her request is denied. Some people are surprised to learn that men, as well as women, may not be "in the mood." A myth regarding male sexuality is that men are "sex machines"—always ready to have sex at the slightest hint of a woman's availability.[12] But any person can sometimes be too tired, preoccupied with worries, or uncomfortable with the time and place suggested for sex. He or she may just want to talk or to be close without sex, and therefore may not want to have sex.

The initiator of a request for sex may feel disappointed or even a little rejected if the partner says no. The initiator's feelings can be spared if the partner explains why sex is not desired at that time and emphasizes that the refusal is not a personal rejection. It also helps if the initiator makes clear the reasons he or she desires sex. Sometimes people ask for sex when they really want attention, comfort, or closeness. In this case, partners might be able to reach a compromise that might include holding hands, an attentive discussion, or perhaps gentle touching or a back rub.

A shy or embarrassed partner can be encouraged to disclose his or her preferences with a statement such as, "It would help me a lot to know more about your preferences. Would you be willing to share some of your thoughts with me?"

Not every sexual request requires verbal communication. There are many ways that people can ask their partners for sex. The most common is to employ some kind of suggestive touching, such as snuggling or kissing. One partner can show the other a preferred way of being stimulated by moving the partner's face or hands in a certain way.

Changing Sexual Patterns

Sometimes a person wants to suggest a change in the usual way the couple makes love. The individual may remain silent, however, because he or she does not want to imply to the partner that a desire for a change means that there is something wrong. Psychologist Bernie Zilbergeld suggests that one way to bring up the subject of a change in sexual activities is by saying, "I've been thinking lately that there are some things that might make our sex life more enjoyable for both of us. I'd like to talk to you about it to see if we can make some changes in the usual way we make love."[13]

Once one partner has suggested certain changes, the couple can begin a dialogue about their feelings about possible alternatives, and they can then develop a plan to bring about the agreed-upon changes. Couples should remember that change is often difficult and that patience and support are frequently needed.

SEXUAL DIFFICULTIES

It is not uncommon for people to be occasionally dissatisfied with their sex lives or even be unable to engage in sexual activity. Illness, injury, infection, depression, anger with the sex partner, worry about being an "adequate" lover, or intense stress can limit a person's desire for sex and can alter the body's capability to respond sexually. People can have difficulty becoming sexually aroused; men can have problems getting and maintaining erections; women can have problems producing enough vaginal lubrication to make sex enjoyable; both men and women can reach orgasm so rapidly that it makes sex unsatisfactory; some men and women are unable to experience orgasm; and some people experience painful intercourse. Some of the most common sexual difficulties are discussed below.

Kinds of Sexual Difficulties

Impotence   The inability of a man to get and maintain an erection is called *impotence*. Impotence is sometimes caused by injury or a disease of the nervous system, as well as by the ingestion of too much alcohol, drugs like heroin, or medications to control high blood pressure. However, impotence is most often caused by fear of performing sex poorly (including anxiety about one's ability to have an erection), anger with, or dislike of the sex partner. In most cases, impotence can be overcome by reducing anxiety about getting an erection or reducing tension in the relationship.

Rapid Ejaculation   Clinically, *rapid ejaculation* is defined as the inability to control ejaculation sufficiently to allow both partners to be sexually satisfied. Because how long intercourse should last depends on the needs and desires of the people involved, it is impossible to define "rapid" or "premature" ejaculation quantitatively in terms of so many minutes or seconds. There are several therapeutic techniques that can help a man learn to control ejaculation.

Dyspareunia   *Dyspareunia* is painful sexual intercourse. Although usually considered a woman's problem, men can suffer painful intercourse, too. The major causes of dyspareunia in women are vaginal infections, not producing enough vaginal lubrication during sexual activity (usually the result of not engaging in enough precoital sexual activity to become sexually aroused), and anxiety-produced spasms of the muscles surrounding the vagina, which makes penile penetration difficult and painful. Another source of pain associated with intercourse, which can affect both men and women, is the deep, aching sensation in the female's pelvis or the male's scrotum that sometimes comes after a sexual episode. Normally, the congestion of blood in the pelvic structures is relieved at orgasm, but if orgasm does not occur, the blood remains and causes discomfort or pain.

Difficulty Achieving Orgasm   Some people have difficulty reaching orgasm. This is true for both men and women. For men, the failure to reach orgasm is called *retarded ejaculation,* but it is not a common complaint. But for women, the failure to achieve orgasm is probably the most common sexual complaint. It can be overcome by learning to appreciate one's body, by assuming a positive attitude toward sexual expression, and by learning the ways the body best responds to sexual stimuli and communicating this to one's partner.

Causes of Sexual Difficulties

There are many reasons that people have sexual difficulties (see Table 7.1). Although some problems are the result of physical disabilities, most often sexual difficulties stem from fears, anxieties, and negative attitudes toward sex. According to Dr. Helen Singer Kaplan, sexual difficulties can arise when people:[14]

- avoid or fail to engage in sexual behavior that excites and stimulates both partners.
- fear that they will fail to meet their own or their partner's expectations.

TABLE 7.1   Some Common Sources of Sexual Difficulties

Anxiety	about the possibility of pregnancy
	about the adverse effects of a contraceptive
	about contracting a sexually transmitted disease
	about being discovered and/or punished
Fear	of being unable to please the partner
	of losing control over the body
	of being unable to have an orgasm or to withhold orgasm
Negative Thoughts or Feelings	the thought: "Sex is dirty."
	dislike of or anger at the partner
	unresolved interpersonal conflicts
	general angry feelings or depression

- create mental defenses against erotic pleasure.
- do not communicate openly and without guilt or defensiveness their real feelings, wishes, and responses.

The elimination of sexual difficulties often requires rejecting some learned value, belief, attitude, or behavior that is inhibiting the natural flow of sexual activity. Sometimes, early negative sexual learning experiences must be replaced by more positive experiences. There are a number of self-help books[15] and professional therapeutic procedures (see Box 7.2) that can help people discover and eliminate the reasons for sexual difficulties.

SEXUALLY TRANSMITTED DISEASES

There are several kinds of contagious infections and infestations of the genital and pelvic regions that are passed from person to person through sexual contact. Traditionally, these diseases have been called *venereal diseases,* or VD. However, a concern about the negative connotations of the term VD and an attempt to identify more directly the sources of such diseases have led health professionals to replace the term *venereal disease* with the term *sexually transmitted diseases,* or STD.

BOX 7.2 A Conversation with a Sex Therapist

QUESTION: What is sex therapy?

ANSWER: It's a type of therapy specifically designed to deal with sex problems. There's a problem with calling it only sex therapy, however, because often a sex problem is not simply a sex problem but is part of a larger problem within a relationship.

QUESTION: How do people know if they need a sex therapist?

ANSWER: If someone is not functioning physically as he or she would like to; or if there is a feeling that if sex were better, the relationship would be better. It's sometimes hard to separate out a purely sexual problem from whatever else is going on in a relationship.

QUESTION: How do people locate a reliable sex therapist?

ANSWER: They should be certain to go to someone who has had supervised training in working as a counselor or therapist, such as a psychologist, clinical social worker, or licensed marriage and family counselor, and who has also had special training in sex therapy. Therapists should be asked about their training, if they have the required licenses, if they belong to professional societies, and how long they've been doing therapy.

QUESTION: Is there one approach to sex therapy that is best?

ANSWER: It's probably best to find someone whose therapy involves not only talking about the problem but also who gives assignments to work on at home. To just talk about sex problems is not as helpful as learning new ways of doing sex.

QUESTION: What happens in sex therapy?

ANSWER: It depends. Sometimes the therapist works with couples and sometimes with individuals. Some therapists work with groups of people, all of whom have a similar problem, such as preorgasmic women. In some instances, couples work with a man-and-woman therapy team. At the beginning of therapy, the therapist and clients agree on the nature of the problem and set goals for the therapy. Then the therapist gives the clients assignments to do at home to try to realize the goals of the therapy. In the next session, the therapist and clients discuss what happened at home, and new assignments are given. This continues until the goals of the therapy are reached.

QUESTION: How long does sex therapy usually last?

ANSWER: The time of therapy varies a lot, but the average is about three months. Often sex therapy is just a matter of learning new ways of making love, which may not take much time at all. Other times the relationship may need work. The couple may need to open up new ways of communicating or express long-held angers. That might take several months.

QUESTION: What causes sexual difficulties?

ANSWER: Some people have physical problems from disease, but that's rare. Most of the problems come from the fact that most people learn about sex by trial and error. Unknowingly, they may fall into bad habits, which eventually causes a problem. That's just a learning pattern, and people can easily learn to do sex differently. Another cause of sex problems is performance anxiety. People get caught up in standards of performance that come from who knows where, instead of just enjoying each other. They are concerned with "How am I doing?" rather than just enjoying themselves. Some sex problems are caused by people not

BOX 7.2 (continued)

being comfortable with their bodies or having negative feelings about sex.

QUESTION: How can sex problems be prevented?

ANSWER: If people could learn to communicate so that partners would not emotionally wound each other; if they could learn to ask for changes in their relationships; if they could learn to negotiate issues of disagreement without hurting each other, there would be fewer sex problems. Another way is to teach people how to create sexual pleasure—not just the mechanics of how to do sex, but also how to create intimacy.

Source: From the authors' files.

The reason for this change in classification is not insignificant, for people's negative attitudes toward VD are the principal reason that there is an epidemic of STD today. The total number of reported cases of sexually transmitted diseases exceeds that of all other infectious diseases except the common cold. No one is embarrassed to admit to having a cold, but discovering one has gonorrhea can lead to mortification and even panic. Despite our society's professed openness about sexual matters, many people still consider sexually transmitted diseases "dirty" or "sinful" and taboo topics of discussion. That is why so many people do not seek diagnosis and treatment when they suspect they have STD; they fear being ridiculed and accused of being immoral. And infected people sometimes do not tell their sexual partners of the problem, because they fear being rejected and being considered promiscuous.

Because there are no vaccinations for the bacterial and viral infections that cause the common sexually transmitted diseases, the only way they can be prevented is by people assuming responsibility for eliminating the propagation of these diseases. Sexually active people, particularly those with several sexual partners, should know the first signs of STD and make a commitment to themselves to seek professional diagnosis and immediate treatment should such signs occur. The fact that many infected people show no signs of infection makes it a good idea for sexually active people with more than one partner to have periodic (for example, every six months) examinations for STD, particularly gonorrhea. Many family-planning agencies routinely check for gonorrhea in those clients who are receiving contraceptive services, and most states still require premarital blood tests for syphilis.

Gonorrhea

Gonorrhea also known as "the clap," is responsible for about three million infections in the United States each year. The disease is the result of infection by the bacterium *Neisseria gonorrheae*. Its preference for moist, dark regions of the body means that this organism is also capable of living in nongenital parts of the body, including the throat, the anus and rectum, and the eyes. Therefore, people can transmit gonorrhea by both oral-genital and anal sex, and it can be passed to infants as they pass through the vagina during childbirth. That is why in most states several drops of silver nitrate are put into the eyes of newborn babies; this kills the gonorrhea bacteria and prevents possible blindness. The fact that the organisms live in moist body regions means that they cannot survive on toilet seats, doorknobs, bed sheets, clothes, or towels. They must be passed directly from one body region to another.

One of the reasons that gonorrhea infections are so prevalent is that many infected people have no symptoms to indicate an infection. About 80 percent of all infected women have no symptoms, and about 20 percent of all infected men also have none. When there are symptoms, they usually appear within a week to ten days after contact, and they most frequently include, in men, painful urination and a yellowish discharge, and, in women, painful urination and a vaginal discharge. Both sexes may also experience pain in the groin and abdomen. Men sometimes experience pain in the testes. If there are symptoms or if contact with an infected person is suspected, a simple test for the presence of gonorrhea organisms can be obtained from a public health clinic, a Planned Parenthood clinic, or a physician. If the test confirms the presence of gonorrhea, treatment with antibiotic medicines should eradicate the disease in a few days. But left untreated, the infection can spread into the reproductive organs and cause a painful pelvic infection which can lead to sterility. The body does not build up an immunity to gonorrhea, which means that people are susceptible to reinfection whenever they have contact with infected people.

Syphilis

Syphilis, like gonorrhea, is a bacterial infection, only in this instance the infecting organism is a spiral-shaped bacterium called *Treponema pallidum*, which is often referred to as a *spirochete*. Like the gonorrhea bacteria, spirochetes can be transmitted not only to the genitals but also to the mouth and anus. They can enter the body and blood stream through almost any break anywhere on the skin.

The first noticeable sign of a syphilitic infection is the appearance of an open, painless ulcer or sore, called a *chancre* (pronounced "shanker"), on the infected region. The chancre can appear anytime between the first week and the third month after infection. If the disease is not treated within that time, the chancre will go away by itself, although the person is still infected. Within about six months, the so-called secondary stage of syphilis appears. This is characterized by a skin rash (especially on the palms of the hands and the soles of the feet), the loss of hair, and the appearance of round, flat-topped growths on the moist areas of the body. Should the disease remain untreated, these secondary symptoms also will disappear. The disease then enters a latent stage in which there are no obvious symptoms, but during which the organisms infect many organs of the body, including the heart, brain, and abdominal organs. Infection of the heart can result in early death, and infection of the brain can lead to psychosis and senility.

Syphilis can be successfully treated with a number of medications. As with gonorrhea, the body builds no immunity against these organisms, and so reinfections can occur.

Herpes

Herpes is an infection of the genitals caused by the virus *Herpes simplex*. This virus is similar to that causing cold sores on the mouth, and the genital variety produces similar lesions on the penis, vagina, and the skin of the genital regions: a painful, ulcerated sore that lasts about two or three weeks.

There is no effective treatment for herpes infection. Infected people can minimize the discomfort of the ulcer by not wearing tight clothes and by keeping the area clean. As with cold sores, it is possible to have recurrences of herpes in the same region even if there has been no reinfection, since the viruses remain in the body cells in a dormant condition. Any kind of stress or anxiety, even sunlight or improper nutrition, can bring on a flare-up of herpes. Fortunately, the severity of the symptoms decreases with time.

When herpes sores are present, the disease is highly contagious, and therefore the infected person should abstain from sexual activity until the ulcers clear up.

Pubic Lice

Pubic lice, which are also known as "crabs," are small insects that can inhabit the genital-rectal region. These tiny organisms attach themselves to skin-hairs and feed on blood taken from tiny blood vessels in the skin. Some people are highly sensitive to the bites and may experience intense itching when infected with pubic lice. Itching is often the only symptom of an infestation. Although they are tiny, the lice can be seen. They look like small freckles. Their eggs, which are called "nits," are small white pods, which can be seen attached to the hair shafts. Pubic lice are transmitted by physical contact and also by contact with objects on which the eggs might have been laid, such as towels and bed sheets. Pubic lice can be eradicated by shampooing with a special soap containing a disinfectant.

SUMMARY

Satisfying sexual relationships are based on a knowledge of human sexual anatomy and sexual response. A woman's sexual anatomy consists of both internal and external organs. The internal organs are the ovaries, which produce eggs and sex hormones, and the Fallopian tubes and the uterus, which are necessary for fertilization and pregnancy. The external organs are the vagina, labia minora, labia majora, and clitoris. When a woman becomes sexually excited, vaginal secretions increase to provide lubrication for intercourse, and the clitoris enlarges slightly. A male's sexual anatomy consists of testes, where sperm are produced, sperm ducts, and the penis. When a man becomes sexually excited, the penis fills with blood to become hard and erect.

Sexual response in both sexes can be described in four phases: excitement, plateau, orgasm, and resolution. Our society places much emphasis on orgasm, and this in turn can impose performance pressures on people and reduce their enjoyment of sex.

Satisfying sexual interaction comes from openly discussing sexual matters and not remaining silent, hoping that one partner can read the other's mind. Important areas of sexual communication are contraception, discovering the partner's needs, making requests and declining them, and changing habitual sexual patterns.

Some couples have sexual difficulties, which sometimes reflect problems in their relationships. Most sexual problems can be overcome by improving the relationship, learning new ways of relating sexually, and changing negative attitudes toward sex.

Gonorrhea, syphilis, herpes, and pubic lice are the most common sexually transmitted diseases. All could be virtually eradicated from our population if people sought diagnosis and treatment as soon as they suspected they were infected.

CONSIDER THIS

When the subject of talking about sex first came up in her course on marriage and the family, Susan dismissed it, knowing that she could never talk to Tom about their sex life. They rarely discussed their feelings, and they had never really talked about sex. But she really wanted to make love more often, and she knew she had to talk about it. She had tried on other occasions. However, she just couldn't get the words out. Tonight she had arranged to meet Tom in a restaurant, hoping that it would be easier to talk there than at home.

As she drove to the restaurant, all the questions about what she should say and how he would react went through her mind. How would she begin? Would he be angry? Would he think that she was too aggressive? Why did she feel guilty about asking for this change?

Questions
1. How should Susan start her conversation with Tom?
2. Do you think Susan's concern about her needs and Tom's reactions are valid?
3. What do you think Tom's reaction will be?
4. If Tom does not want to increase their frequency of intercourse, what compromise could they reach?
5. What do you think are the best ways to communicate sexual desires and needs?

NOTES

1. Herbert A. Otto, *The New Sex Education*, Chicago, Follett, 1978, p. xi.
2. Robert Crooks and Karla Baur, *Our Sexuality*, Menlo Park, Calif., Benjamin/Cummings, 1980, pp. 65–66; Boston Women's Health Book Collective, *Our Bodies, Ourselves*, New York, Simon & Schuster, 1976, pp. 26–31.
3. Lonnie Garfield Barbach, *For Yourself*, New York, Anchor/Doubleday, 1975, pp. 54–56; Benjamin Graber and Georgia Kline-Graber, "Vaginal Tone and Orgasm Ability," *Medical Aspects of Human Sexuality*, 14, no. 1 (January 1980): 121; Edwin A. Rudinger, "Relation of Vaginal Tone to Sexual Pleasure," *Medical Aspects of Human Sexuality*, 14, no. 3 (March 1980): 9.

4. William H. Masters and Virginia E. Johnson, *Human Sexual Response,* Boston, Little, Brown, 1966, pp. 189–191.

5. Ibid.

6. Gordon D. Jensen and Mina B. Robbins, "Multiple Orgasms in Men," *Medical Aspects of Human Sexuality,* 11, no. 6 (June 1977): 8.

7. Domeena C. Renshaw, "Women's Uncertainty About Having Orgasm," *Medical Aspects of Human Sexuality,* 13, no. 1 (January 1979): 63.

8. Harvey W. Caplan and Rebecca A. Black, "Unrealistic Sexual Expectations," *Medical Aspects of Human Sexuality,* 9, no. 8 (August 1974): 8–28.

9. Philip E. Slater, "Sexual Adequacy in America," *Intellectual Digest,* November 1973, p. 14.

10. William H. Masters and Virginia E. Johnson, *Human Sexual Inadequacy,* Boston, Little, Brown, 1970, pp. 65–66.

11. Lonnie Garfield Barbach, *For Yourself,* pp. 125–126.

12. Bernie Zilbergeld, "Myth of Men as Sex Machines," *Medical Aspects of Human Sexuality,* 13, no. 4 (April 1979): 77.

13. Bernie Zilbergeld, *Male Sexuality,* Boston, Little, Brown, 1978, p. 178.

14. Helen Singer Kaplan, "No-Nonsense Therapy for Six Sexual Malfunctions," *Psychology Today,* October 1974, pp. 76–87.

15. Lonnie Garfield Barbach, *For Yourself;* Bernie Zilbergeld, *Male Sexuality.*

SUGGESTED READINGS

Barbach, Lonnie G. *For Yourself.* New York, Anchor/Doubleday, 1975. Suggestions for women for improving sexual response and suggestions for couples for achieving satisfying sexual expression.

Crooks, Robert, and Karla Baur. *Our Sexuality.* Menlo Park, Calif., Benjamin/Cummings, 1980. A thorough college text on human sexuality.

DeLora, Joann, Carol Warren, and Carol Rinklieb. *Understanding Sexual Interaction,* 2nd ed. Boston, Houghton Mifflin, 1981. A comprehensive text on human sexuality.

Kaplan, Helen S. "No-Nonsense Therapy for Six Sexual Malfunctions." *Psychology Today,* October 1974, pp. 76–87. A good discussion of the common sexual problems and their treatment.

Zilbergeld, Bernie. *Male Sexuality.* Boston, Little, Brown, 1978. A thorough and insightful analysis of male sexual psychology and function.

III MARRIAGE

THE PUBLIC SIDE OF MARRIAGE: LEGAL AND SOCIAL ISSUES

Like fingerprints, all marriages are different.

George Bernard Shaw

8

Our society is oriented toward marriage. Despite other available life-style alternatives such as singlehood, cohabitation, single parenthood, and group marriage, over 95 percent of Americans marry at some time during their lives. In fact, over half of the population marries before the age of twenty-five (see Figure 8.1).

Just about everyone has experienced being "single in a couple's world." Because our society expects us to marry, the unmarried are often ostracized, and a stigma is frequently attached to remaining single. Some large companies, for example, are reluctant to place unmarried persons in executive positions, because married people are presumed to be more trustworthy and stable than unmarried people are.

In the past, unmarried older women were given the derogatory terms *spinster* or *old maid*. Even today, some very successful professional women are critized for remaining single, as illustrated by the following:

My parents have selective blindness. Even though I'm a very good doctor, they ignore it and focus on the fact that I'm over thirty and not yet married. Sometimes I buy into their prejudice and wonder what's wrong with me. I admit it would be nice to be married, but I believe it will happen soon enough.

From the authors' files

Marriage has both public and private aspects. Publicly, marriage is a social and legal demonstration of the partners' existing commitment.

FIGURE 8.1

Never-married persons
in the United States, by
age and sex, March
1977

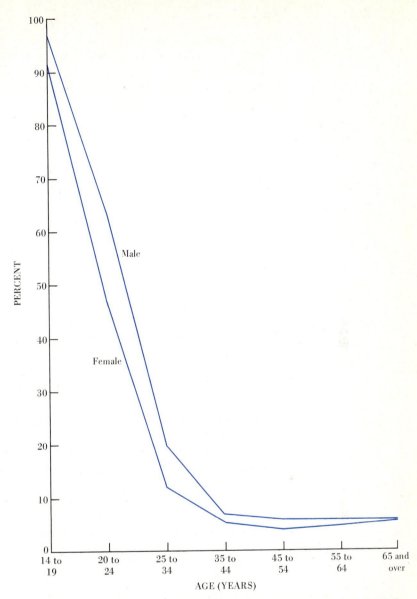

PERCENT

Male

Female

AGE (YEARS)

Source: U.S. Bureau of the Census, *Current Population Reports: Special Studies*, Series P–23, No. 77, "Perspectives on American Husbands and Wives," December 1978, p. 3.

Besides a relationship's public side, there is the very personal, private relationship of the people involved. After marriage, each couple defines or redefines their relationship, and the relationship is affected by the partners' role behaviors and expectations. For some, the act of marrying entails certain duties and roles which are eagerly assumed. Others feel that marriage is an extension of their commitment. Still others find that the combination of the public and private sides of marriage creates problems. If traditional duties and roles do not define how they wish to structure their marriages, these couples may feel that the institution of marriage intrudes into and hinders their private relationships. The following comment by sociologist Arlene Skolnick aptly describes this conflict.

Marriage is an intensely private affair, but it is public as well. "Marriage" seems to lead its own separate existence, quite apart from particular married couples. Indeed many people today experience "marriage" as an alien presence, an unwelcome third party intruding itself into what may be an otherwise delightful relationship.[1]

In this chapter we discuss the public aspects of marriage—religious, legal, and social. The roles and expectations of the private side of marriage are the topics of Chapter 9, "The Private Side of Marriage: Roles and Expectations," and the personal aspects of marital relationships are discussed in Chapter 10, "Marital Interaction."

RELIGION AND MARRIAGE

Traditionally, religion has been an important influence in American marriages. And even today, the majority of Americans are married in religious ceremonies. In every religion, the wedding ceremony, the vows taken by the bride and groom, and the maintenance of religious traditions are highly significant. The Catholic church, for example, considers marriage a sacrament, and all Christian religions believe that marriage is sanctified and ordained by God. In the marriage ceremony, the marital partners take their vows "in the presence of God and these witnesses."

The significance of religion for the married couple's relationship is largely determined by each one's faith and the meaning they give to religious matters. Traditionally, religion and religious education have been important functions of the family. Although religion is no longer completely centered within the family, it is still an important part of many families' lives. Many people grow up as members of a specific faith or denomination, and religious traditions and holidays are part of family life. For example, Christmas and Easter are celebrated as family holidays and gatherings in addition to whatever religious significance they may have.

The majority of Americans are married in religious ceremonies.

Irene Kane/Jeroboam

Some people consider themselves religious even though they do not participate in church or synagogue activities. Each married couple decides how and to what extent their religious involvement will be part of their public and private relationship.

LEGAL ASPECTS OF MARRIAGE

Few people concerned with the marital relationship consider the legal aspects of marriage except when signing the marriage certificate or undergoing divorce proceedings. But when individuals marry, they enter into a legal civil contract that specifies the status, duties, rights, and obligations of married people.

Throughout much of history, marriage was considered a private matter, and arrangements were made between the families of the participants. In industrialized societies, however, the state has taken an increasingly active part in regulating matrimony. There are several reasons for the state's concern with the institution of marriage:

1. The state regulates sexual activity. Traditionally, the state has attempted to limit sexual activity outside marriage and to regulate the acceptable forms of sexual expression. In recent years, however, there has been a trend toward less state interference in people's sexual conduct.

2. The state is concerned with property rights and inheritance. Property rights are redefined when individuals marry, and depending on the particular state, the husband and wife have rights to each other's property and property they acquire jointly during the marriage.

3. The state defines the legitimacy of children. This includes social responsibility for the children, their financial support, name, and inheritance of property.

4. The state attempts to protect individuals from abuse and exploitation. There are, for example, laws against bigamy (being married to two people at the same time), fraud, marriage between individuals who are under age, and child and spouse abuse.

5. The state is concerned with prohibiting marriages between blood relatives. This varies from state to state and may include first cousins, stepparents, stepchildren, and so on.

6. The legality of the marriage contract is guaranteed by contractual requirements and procedures. These requirements specify marriage eligibility, licensing procedures, grounds for divorcing and declaring a marriage invalid, and maintenance of the marital contract once it is made.[2]

Many people are unaware of the law and its complexity, and in the following sections we examine some important aspects of marital law.

The Legal Age of Marriage

In the United States, the legal age for marriage has two classifications: (1) the minimum age for marriage with parental consent and (2) the minimum age for marriage without parental consent. Minimum age requirements vary from state to state. In New York state, for example, the ages are:

	Without Parental Consent	With Parental Consent
Male	18	16
Female	18	14

The legal age of marriage in the United States ranges from thirteen to twenty-one, but the most common age with consent is eighteen for males and sixteen for females, and the age without consent is usually eighteen for both males and females.

In certain circumstances, it is possible for a couple to be married, even though one or both of them are below the minimum age. Various states allow individuals below the age requirement to marry if they have been married before or if the woman is pregnant or is the mother of a child by the husband-to-be.

Some people may question the low minimum age requirements, especially since research has shown that very early marriages are less likely to succeed than are marriages between older partners (see Chapter 4, "Choosing a Partner"). Underage marriages are illegal, but since the courts make no effort to penalize the participants, it could be argued that the age laws are not effective or meaningful. Yet it is doubtful that raising the minimum age requirements would change the situation. Because state laws vary, a couple below the minimum age in their home state can marry in a nearby state that has lower age requirements. If there is a solution to the problem of early marriage, it is increased emphasis on premarital education and counseling, not legal requirements. Gordon Shipman, for example, suggests that young people should be required to have premarital counseling because he believes that this would be more beneficial than raising the minimum age. This is the plan now used in California:

In 1970 California adopted a law which required premarital counseling for any couple applying for a marriage license if either party were under age 18 and the court deemed such counseling necessary. In Los Angeles County the court deemed that all such cases require counseling, and it implemented the law with the cooperation of community agencies under the leadership and direction of the Counseling Services of the Conciliation Court.[3]

Void versus Voidable Marriage

There are two kinds of illegal marriages, void and voidable. *Void marriages* are those that, from the beginning, are never considered legally valid. A marriage between close relatives or a bigamous marriage is always considered void, and in some states, a marriage in which one party is judged insane is also void. Such marriages are illegal and the individuals involved are criminally liable, although prosecutions are rare.

Voidable marriages are those involving some kind of fraud or misrepresentation, and they require a court ruling of annulment to be dissolved. An *annulment decree* cancels a marriage—in regard to property and other rights, it is as though the marriage never existed. Although voidable marriages are entered into fraudulently, they are legal and binding until court action invalidates them.

An example of a voidable marriage is the "shotgun wedding" in which a pregnant woman's father physically coerces the baby's father to marry her. Later, if the threatened man sues for an annulment, the court would probably grant it. If the case is not taken to court, however, the marriage is legitimate. If the man is verbally pressured rather than threatened with physical force, it is doubtful that a court would grant an annulment. Thus, the law is subject to interpretation, and the outcome of a voidable marriage depends on the particular case, its evidence, and the court hearing the case.

Other grounds for voiding a marriage are: (1) if either partner is under age; (2) if either is physically incapable of having intercourse; and (3) if either agrees to the marriage under fraudulent conditions, such as financial misrepresentation, concealment of a previous marriage or divorce, concealment of pregnancy, refusal to have children, or breaking a promise to have a religious ceremony after a civil ceremony.[4]

Consanguinity Laws

State laws prohibiting the marriage of close relatives are called *consanguinity laws*. *Consanguinity* (blood relationship) should not be confused with *incest*, which refers to sexual intercourse between close relatives. The terms are easily confused because the law prohibits both the marriage of close relatives and sexual relations between relatives. Marriage between blood relatives is prohibited because it increases the probability of genetic defects in the couple's children.

Although the specific restrictions differ from state to state, all states prohibit the marriage of mother and son, father and daughter, brother and sister, grandmother and grandson, grandfather and granddaughter, aunt and nephew, and uncle and niece. In addition, more than half the states prohibit marriage to a half brother or half sister and marriage between first cousins. Others also forbid the marriage of second cousins, as well as marriage to a grandniece or grandnephew.

Approximately half the states also have marital restrictions pertaining to *affinity*, a term used to denote a relationship through marriage. For example, many states prohibit marriage between stepparents and stepchildren, between a woman and her husband's father or grandfather, and between a man and his wife's mother or grandmother. These types of marriages are rare, and critics argue that there is little purpose in preventing the marriage of a man to his son's widow or of a woman to her daughter's widower, since no blood relationship exists.

Miscegenation Laws

The term *miscegenation* (from the Latin *miscere*, to mix, and *genus*, race) is commonly used to denote interracial marriage. The United States Supreme Court invalidated state miscegenation laws in 1967, but it is important to note that at one time, more than forty states had laws prohibiting the marriage of whites to nonwhites. In fact, as late as the mid-1960s, miscegenation laws were still in effect in some twenty states.

Licensing

Licensing and recording are important parts of marital regulation. A marriage license has three important functions: (1) the license is written proof that all legal requirements have been met; (2) the completed marriage certificate is legal proof of matrimony (this is often necessary for inheritance, social security, or insurance rights); and (3) the license provides statistical information about marriages.

Marriage licenses are issued by the county marriage-license bureaus. Both residents and nonresidents of the county are eligible to receive a license. Once issued, the license must be used in the state within a certain period of time (usually thirty days). After the ceremony is over and the religious or civil official has signed the marriage license, the license becomes a marriage certificate and is legal evidence that the couple is married.

In a marriage
ceremony, two
individuals declare that
they accept each other
as husband and wife.

Jean-Claude Lejeune

The Physical Examination

Most states require blood tests to ensure that the individuals applying
for a marriage license are free of venereal disease. In some states, even
if syphilis is discovered, the marriage license will still be issued, since
all that is required is that the couple be informed of the presence of the
disease.

There are states and jurisdictions that do not have medical examination requirements: Maryland, Minnesota, Nevada, South Carolina, Washington, and the Virgin Islands. Even in those states requiring a blood test there are legal ways to avoid it. For example, the test may be waived for good cause when the individuals are members of the armed services and have time or distance problems. The blood test can also be avoided by going to a state that has no requirement.

The Waiting Period

Besides the blood test, many states require a waiting period between the time of application and the actual issuance of a marriage license. This waiting period ranges from one to five days.

The purpose of the waiting period is to prevent spur-of-the-moment marriages, although a determined couple can usually find a way to get married quickly. Nevada, for example, has the dubious distinction of requiring neither a blood test nor a waiting period. Consequently, it has established a reputation as a marriage mill or a "Gretna Green" (see Box 8.1).

The Marriage Ceremony

There is very little legal regulation of the marriage ceremony. All that is required is that the two individuals declare in the presence of a church or civil official that they accept each other as husband and wife. This declaration is made also in the presence of witnesses who are required to sign the marriage certificate.

The official may be an ordained member of the clergy or, in most states, an authorized civil official such as a judge, mayor, recorder, justice of the peace, magistrate, and—in some jurisdictions—a notary.

Although various religions have established ceremonies, the states generally make no attempt to regulate the specific form of the ceremony or the actual words spoken by the official.

The Marriage Contract

When two people marry, they enter into a legal agreement, or contract. The *marriage contract*, however, differs in many ways from an ordinary civil contract. A civil contract is a private contract between two parties, whereas the marriage contract includes the state as well. A regular

BOX 8.1 Gretna Green Marriage

The term *Gretna Green* comes from the name of a well-known town in Scotland, just across the border from England. In the days of Queen Victoria, Gretna Green was England's Reno or Las Vegas. Young couples determined to marry despite parental objections went to Gretna Green because the Scottish laws allowed people to marry in a matter of hours. There was no waiting period, a clergyman was not required, and the only stipulation was that the couple had to take their marriage vows in front of two witnesses. Although a twenty-one-day waiting period was established in 1876, the town's reputation has endured, and the term Gretna Green is still used to refer to a marriage-market town.

In the United States, Reno and Las Vegas, Nevada, and Elkton, Maryland, have become symbols of the "quickie" marriage. Because of the various state laws, the attractions of a Gretna Green are obvious—no waiting period, minimal age requirements, no blood test, and often, twenty-four-hour service complete with chapel, flowers, and champagne!

These towns' popularity is noteworthy. Las Vegas, for instance, averages some 70,000 marriages a year. Even Elkton, which now has a waiting period and other requirements, averages around 6,500 marriages a year.

contract is entered into by two parties, regardless of their marital status and blood relationship. A marriage contract, as we have seen, specifically prohibits marriage between individuals who are already married and marriage between blood relatives. Furthermore, a marriage contract cannot be modified or broken by mutual consent. The only way a marriage contract can be terminated is by divorce or death.

Although marriage laws vary from state to state, the marriage contract generally lists contractual obligations regarding domicile, support, property, sex, and child care. These obligations usually reflect traditional marital roles. For example most states' marriage laws specify that (1) the husband is the head of the household; (2) the husband is responsible for family support; (3) the wife is responsible for domestic services; and (4) the wife is responsible for child care.[5]

Some states have other provisions. For example, some specify that the wife's domicile is that of her husband. Thus, if the wife refuses to move with her husband, she may be charged with desertion, which is a ground for divorce.

Few people ever read or are even aware of the binding obligations established by the marital contract. Lenore Weitzman and her colleagues point out that

While its provisions will be enforced by the courts, no state gives the parties the opportunity to read the terms of their marriage contract, nor does any state ask them if they are willing to assume the duties, rights, and obligations it specifies. Nor are the parties allowed to modify the provisions of the contract, or to substitute alternate but mutually acceptable provisions. It is simply assumed that everyone who gets married will want to (or will have to) abide by the state-imposed contract known as legal marriage.[6]

Individual Marriage Contracts

Although many couples want egalitarian relationships, they may find that their efforts are hampered by laws that are outdated and not relevant to current marital needs.

An increasingly popular means of combating this problem is the use of *individual marriage contracts*. Each year many couples draw up their own contracts to clarify the legal and personal issues in their marriages.

In most states, property agreements generally are recognized as legally binding, but stipulations regarding, for example, domestic tasks or obligations generally are not. A state usually does not recognize as legal a contract that stipulates that the husband is not responsible for the support of his wife because the state will have to assume the burden of her support if the contract is not followed.[7] Because state laws vary concerning the legality of personal marriage contracts, it may be necessary to seek legal advice regarding a particular contract or the laws of a specific state.

Although a personal contract may not be enforceable, it can be an important communication device. By drafting their own marriage contract, a couple can specify their needs and expectations with regard to finances, the number and timing of children, birth control, and the sharing of marital roles and household duties. When these provisions are written down on paper, the possibility of misunderstandings decreases. Writing down agreements on child care, household duties, and the importance of a career and other life goals also helps a couple withstand the pressures exerted by family and society to assume traditional husband and wife roles. For some, a written agreement lays the foundation for their relationship and may help the couple break old habits and validate role behaviors and expectations of their own choosing.

The use of written agreements is not new, as this portion of a contract written in 1855 by Lucy Stone and Henry Blackwell demonstrates:

While we acknowledge our mutual affection by publicly assuming the relationship of husband and wife, we deem it a duty to declare that this act on our part implies no sanction of, nor promise of voluntary obedience to, such of the present laws of marriage as refuse to recognize the wife as an independent, rational being, while they confer upon the husband an injurious and unnatural superiority.[8]

Besides specifying an egalitarian relationship, a contract may address a variety of issues. Although individuals may disagree on the topics they wish to include, a contract generally addresses any or all of the following categories: economic issues, children, careers, household responsibilities, sex, expectations of the relationship, relationships with others, vacations, residence, religion, and ownership of property (see Box 8.2).

The popularity of individual marriage contracts is increasing. Some predict that eventually the laws will be changed, and Marvin Sussman, a noted sociologist who has studied contractual arrangements, predicts that within the next ten years, individual marriage contracts "may be *the* form of marriage law."[9] This would allow a couple to establish marriage rights and obligations based on their own needs and life style.

Living-Together Agreements

Contracts for unmarried individuals who are living together also have gained popularity and, in one celebrated lawsuit (the case of *Marvin* v. *Marvin*), considerable publicity. In 1979, Michele Triola was awarded $104,000 for "rehabilitative maintenance" when she sued actor Lee Marvin for half of his earnings and property. The California Supreme Court ruled that unmarried persons could enforce oral agreements and implied contracts based on the length of the relationship, the existence of joint accounts, each partner's expectations, and their method for sharing income and expenses. Many lawyers suggest that unmarried individuals living together draft a "living-together agreement" (LTA) in order to protect each one's property rights. As attorneys Bernard Clair and Anthony Daniele assert:

The advantages of a LTA are manifold—especially if one person takes his or her former lover to court. First of all, the question of just what the couple have agreed on is eliminated. Their promises are on paper, so neither partner has to rely on the ability to convince a judge or jury of his or her version. Second, many courts will recognize only written agreements between unmarried cohabitants; because some states do not feel it is appropriate to provide unmarried persons with the same rights and protection as their married counterparts, implied agreements are rejected. . . . But perhaps the best reason to draft a LTA is the unique opportunity it gives an unmarried couple to foster mutual

BOX 8.2 The Utopian Marriage Contract

In the early 1970s, *Ms.* magazine published an article by Susan Edmiston entitled "How to Write Your Own Marriage Contract" in which the author discussed what she considered the most important parts of a utopian marriage contract:

1. The wife's right to use her maiden name or any other name she chooses.
2. What surname the children will have: husband's, wife's, a hyphenated combination, a neutral name or the name the children choose when they reach a certain age.
3. Birth control: whether or not, what kind and who uses it. (One couple—the wife can't use the Pill—splits the responsibility 50–50. Half the time she uses a diaphragm, the other half he uses a condom.)
4. Whether or not to have children, or to adopt them, and if so how many.
5. How the children will be brought up.
6. Where the couple will live: Will the husband be willing to move if the wife gets a job offer she wants to take? Separate bedrooms? Separate apartments?
7. How child care and housework will be divided: The spouse who earns less should not be penalized for the inequities of the economic world by having to do a greater share.
8. What financial arrangement will the couple embrace? If husband and wife are both wage earners, there are three possibilities:
   a. Husband and wife pool their income, pay expenses and divide any surplus. (This was Leonard and Virginia Woolf's arrangement. At the end of the year, after payment of expenses, they divided the surplus between them, equally so each had what they called a personal "hoard.")
   b. Husband and wife pay share of expenses proportional to their incomes. Each keeps whatever he or she has left.
   c. Husband and wife each pay 50 per cent of expenses. Each keeps what he or she has left. If husband earns significantly more than wife, the couple might consider a) that the disparity is a result of sexist discrimination in employment and there should perhaps be some kind of "home reparations program" to offset this inequity, and b) whether the couple really has an equal partnership if one has greater economic strength, and therefore possibly greater power psychologically, in the relationship.
9. Sexual rights and freedoms: Although any arrangement other than monogamy would clearly be against public policy, in practice some people make arrangements such as having Tuesdays off from one another.
10. The husband might give his consent to abortion in advance.

Source: Reprinted by permission of Julian Bach Literary Agency, Inc. Copyright © 1972 by Majority Enterprises, Inc., currently known as Foundation for Education and Communication, Inc.

understanding and to build a framework on which to base a sturdy and successful relationship.[10]

Thus, for both married and unmarried people, contracts are an important means of establishing understanding and the relationship's goals and expectations.

Deciding on a Married Name

Contrary to popular belief, no state has a law that requires a woman to take her husband's last name. In fact, Hawaii is the only state that has ever had this law, and it was repealed by a statute in 1976. Although this practice is common, adopting the husband's name is a matter of choice, not a legal requirement.

Some women enjoy the tradition of adopting their husband's name, but others prefer to retain their maiden names. Over the years, many women have used their given surnames professionally but have used their husband's names socially.

Today there are many options. A woman can either keep her own last name or take her husband's. The couple can adopt a hyphenated version of their two last names, or they can choose a new name that both of them will use.

Some women feel that they would lose an important part of their identity if they changed their name:

My husband and I didn't have discussions about whether or not I would keep my maiden name after we got married. It just seemed natural. After all, it was *my* name and I didn't want to give it up. My husband was in favor of it even more than I. He said he wouldn't want to change his name so why should I? Some of our friends and family aren't quite sure how to introduce us or address mail to us. Also, we occasionally have to show our marriage license in order to prove that we are a married couple. When we meet new people, I introduce Mike as "my husband Mike Smith" and he says "this is my wife Nancy Robinson." I'm proud of my name and I'm glad I kept it.

From the authors' files

In addition to experiencing family and public resentment, a married woman may also find it difficult to use her maiden name when

voting or obtaining a driver's license. Furthermore, a couple must consider what name their children will use. Again, there are several options. Children can be given the mother's last name, the father's last name, a hyphenated version of the two names, or a new last name. Some couples use the mother's last name for female children and the father's last name for male children.

There are two popular myths regarding common-law marriage. One is that it is never a legal form of marriage, and the other is that if a couple lives together for seven years, they are automatically married. Neither is true.

A common-law marriage is one that is entered into by mutual consent. A valid common-law marriage does not require any written documentation or license. Nor is it necessary for the couple to have blood tests, a ceremony, or witnesses. In order to enter a common-law marriage, the individuals must be of age and legally free, that is, not married to someone else. They must be living together, and both must consider themselves married. Furthermore, they must intend to marry legally at some future date and must be considered married in the "eyes of the community."

Common-law marriage is recognized as legal in the following states and territories:

Alabama	Kansas	Rhode Island
Colorado	Montana	South Carolina
Georgia	Ohio	Texas
Idaho	Oklahoma	Washington, D.C.
Iowa	Pennsylvania	Virgin Islands

Many other states recognize common-law marriages if they are valid in the state where they were established.

Historically, common-law marriage filled both an individual and a societal need. In colonial America, for example, it was frequently impractical and sometimes impossible to have a ceremonial wedding. The settlers often lived far from a religious or civil official. Rather than postpone marriage and "live in sin," common-law unions were often formed.

Many critics feel that common-law marriage has outlived its usefulness and is no longer needed in modern society. They argue that allowing people to marry without being licensed reduces a society's control over specific marital prohibitions and invalidates statistical records, since a nonlicensed marriage is neither reported nor recorded. Of more importance to the partners is the fact that in a common-law marriage there is no marriage license, making it difficult to prove that one is married. Because of this, there have been numerous court cases regarding property rights, inheritance, insurance, and government benefits. As with living-together arrangements, it is advisable for individuals in a common-law marriage to draw up a written contract.

Another important point is that the partners in a common-law marriage have the same rights, duties, and responsibilities as the partners in a "ceremonial" marriage have. Consequently, a common-law marriage may be ended only by death, dissolution, or annulment, and in order to marry again, partners in a common-law marriage must first get divorced.

SOCIAL CUSTOMS OF MARRIAGE—ENGAGEMENT, WEDDING CEREMONY, AND HONEYMOON

When a couple marries, certain social expectations are placed on them. Young married people suddenly acquire adult status and are considered more mature and responsible—consider, for example, the automatic drop in car insurance premiums. Being married also carries with it a certain status in our society, and many social roles abruptly change. Once we marry, we never again have the status of being single. Rather, we become classified as separated, divorced, deserted, or widowed. Marriage symbolizes this transition from unmarried to married, and our society has a variety of customs—engagement, wedding ceremony, and honeymoon—to formalize this change in status and to emphasize its importance.

When a couple publicly announce their intentions to marry, they are "betrothed," or engaged. In the past, promises to marry were considered binding contracts, and the breaking of a promise could lead to a breach-of-promise suit. Generally, women, rather than men, charged breach of promise, since they and their families were more likely to be injured by the breaking of an engagement. If the man broke the engagement, the woman's reputation was damaged, and this reduced her chances for a future marriage. It was even worse if the couple had been sexually intimate, because the woman then became a "fallen woman" if the couple did not marry.

Even today, engagement is important as the declaration of a couple's commitment. The engagement ring has become a traditional symbol of this commitment. About 75 percent of first-time brides and 50 percent of second-time brides receive an engagement ring.[11] More importantly, engagement serves as a period of adjustment for the couple. During this time, they discover and test further their compatibility and their expectations for their future together. Also, many couples see the engagement status as a condition for permissible sexual intercourse.

Although a few couples are getting married in parks, while skydiving, or on roller skates, the majority still have traditional wedding

Jean-Claude Lejeune

ceremonies complete with organ music, white wedding gowns, wedding cakes, and champagne. Since parents generally pay for the wedding, the couple is technically "given a wedding." The ceremony may reaffirm the couple's religious beliefs, and it reinforces the couple's ties to family, friends, and each other.

Another significant marital rite of passage is the honeymoon. The traditional honeymoon is a period of time when the newly married couple can make the transition between the wedding and their new status as husband and wife. Or it may be a period of recuperation, as this woman describes:

I mainly remember how hectic everything was. My husband and I were going to school out of state so we basically had a week to do all the last-minute planning and deal with all the hassles like the organist getting sick and the minister coming late to the rehearsal. After the ceremony, we stayed to visit with all the guests because it had been a long time since we had seen a lot of our friends and relatives. In fact, we were the last to leave. On our way out of town we stopped at a park and collapsed. It had been such a long day. We laughed later when we stopped to get pizza, not exactly your typical honeymoon dinner.

Getting married was a lot of work. We needed our honeymoon just to recover.

From the authors' files

Our society has stereotypes of newlyweds and expectations regarding honeymoon behavior. But our stereotypes leave out a great portion of the population, as Gagnon and Greenblat suggest:

It is difficult to escape our cultural stereotype that marriage necessarily begins when a young couple starts out as a new husband and a new wife living together for the first time alone. Our image excludes older people, remarriages, and marriages that start with children, and the fact of marriage often erases in our minds the relationships the two people may have had previously with each other and with others. As a result, we often use our construct of *the newlyweds* when in fact the two people concerned have little in common with the stereotypical version of being newly wedded.[12]

Although much of the tradition and ritual of the engagement, the wedding ceremony, and the honeymoon have disappeared, all three are still important to the couple's expression of commitment. They symbolize the status change from unmarried to married, and they lay the groundwork for the couple's marital relationship.

SUMMARY

Marriage is an important institution in our society. We are expected to marry, and over 95 percent of us do at some time in our lives. People marry for a variety of reasons, including love, companionship, conformity, legitimation of sex, financial pressures, loneliness, emotional security, the desire to have children, and status.

The institution of marriage has both a public and a private side. The public side includes religious and legal aspects and marital-role expectations.

Religion is an important aspect of marriage. The significance it has for the couple's relationship is determined by each partner's faith and the meaning each attaches to religious matters.

Marriage is also a legal demonstration of a couple's commitment and a civil contract that specifies contractual obligations regarding support, property, sex, domicile, and child care. These contractual obligations allow the states to regulate sexual activity, property rights, inheritance, and who marries whom.

Finally, marriage symbolizes the transition from unmarried to married, and this status change is formalized by such customs as the engagement, the wedding ceremony, and the honeymoon.

CONSIDER THIS

Sarah and Bruce strongly believed that drawing up a personal marriage contract would help them clarify their goals for their upcoming marriage. Their plan was to outline each one's areas of concern and then discuss them. They were excited about working out the details of the contract.

Bruce wanted an egalitarian relationship and a marriage in which both Sarah and he could develop as individuals. He was confident that their ideas regarding household duties, travel, children, and job decisions would match. Bruce was surprised, and somewhat angered, therefore, when Sarah mentioned that she had spoken to a lawyer.

BRUCE: I can't believe you talked to a lawyer. Don't you trust me?

SARAH: It isn't that. I was concerned about the property that Dad left me. I want to be sure that it stays in my family if something happens to me.

BRUCE: You mean if we get divorced.

SARAH: Well, I think we have to be realistic.

BRUCE: If anything ever happens, you know I would never make any claim to that property.

SARAH: I'm sorry. But since my divorce from Doug was so messy, I can't help but feel a little uneasy.

BRUCE: I thought we were writing this contract to define our roles and how we wanted to split things like household responsibilities and child care.

SARAH: We need to discuss financial matters too.

BRUCE: Yes, but we could have worked it out without a lawyer. You're talking about divorce, and we're not even married yet.

Questions
1. Is Bruce justified in being so upset?
2. Do you think Sarah's decision to see a lawyer was necessary? In what circumstances do you think a couple should seek legal advice about personal marriage contracts?
3. What are the advantages and disadvantages of personal marriage contracts?

4. What provisions do you think should be included in a marriage contract?

NOTES

1. Arlene Skolnick, *The Intimate Environment: Exploring Marriage and the Family*, Boston, Little, Brown, 1978, pp. 236–237.
2. Henry A. Bowman, *Marriage for Moderns*, New York, McGraw-Hill, 1970, p. 287.
3. Gordon Shipman, "In My Opinion: The Role of Counseling in the Reform of Marriage and Divorce Procedures," *Family Coordinator*, 26 (October 1977): 403.
4. Ruth Shonle Cavan, "Legal Regulation of Marriage," in Ruth Shonle Cavan, ed., *Marriage and Family in the Modern World Readings*, New York, Thomas Y. Crowell, 1974, p. 237.
5. Lenore Weitzman et al., "Contracts for Intimate Relationships: A Study of Contracts Before, Within, and in Lieu of Legal Marriage," *Alternative Lifestyles*, 1 (August 1978): 307–310.
6. Ibid., pp. 306–307.
7. Ibid., pp. 314–315.
8. Susan Edmiston, "How to Write Your Own Marriage Contract," *Ms.*, Spring 1972, pp. 66–72.
9. Pam Moore, "Marriage Contracts—New Twists on an Old Idea," *Psychology Today*, 9 (August 1975): 29.
10. Bernard E. Clair and Anthony R. Daniele, "Living Together Agreements," *Savvy*, 1 (June 1980): 37.
11. *Wall Street Journal*, July 3, 1980, p. 23.
12. John Gagnon and Cathy Greenblat, *Life Designs: Individual, Marriage, and Families*, Glenview, Ill., Scott, Foresman, 1978, p. 235.

SUGGESTED READINGS

Chesser, Barbara. "Analysis of Wedding Rituals: An Attempt to Make Weddings More Meaningful." *Family Relations*, April 1980, pp. 204–209. An explanation of some of the symbolism of wedding ceremony rituals.

Shipman, Gordon. "In My Opinion: The Role of Counseling in the Reform of Marriage and Divorce Procedures." *Family Coordinator*, 26 (October 1977): 395–407. A discussion of the need for premarital counseling and the advantages of offering it as a service during the marriage registration process.

Skolnick, Arlene. *The Intimate Environment: Exploring Marriage and the Family*. Boston, Little, Brown, 1978. See Chapter 9, "Marriage: Image and Institution," for an excellent discussion of the public and private sides of marriage.

Weitzman, Lenore, et al. "Contracts for Intimate Relationships: A Study of Contracts Before, Within, and in Lieu of Legal Marriage." *Alternative Lifestyles*, 1 (August 1978): 303–377. A detailed report on the traditional marriage contract, alternative intimate contracts, the extent to which intimate contracts support more egalitarian family forms, and the differences between relationships established by contracts and those established by traditional family law.

THE PRIVATE SIDE OF MARRIAGE: ROLES AND EXPECTATIONS

All the world's a stage, and all the men and women merely players.

William Shakespeare[1]

When two people marry each other, their personal lives change in accordance with their expectations regarding marital behavior. These expectations form the foundation of *marital roles*. Roles are the expected behavior for a given position or status, and in most societies, including the United States, certain behaviors are considered socially desirable and acceptable for married persons.

Marital roles regarding support, inheritance, and property rights are dictated by law. The legality of such roles has evolved over the years and is based on the traditional sexual division of labor which separates financial support and home maintenance. Other conventional roles and traditions are perpetuated by societal and family pressures. One example is the custom of a woman changing her last name when she marries. As noted in Chapter 8, this is not a legal requirement, but it has become a social custom. Other common marital role expectations are living in the same residence, sharing material resources, changing sexual expectations and behavior, and changing social relationships. As sociologist Bruce J. Biddle suggests, "to enter into marriage may involve more shifts in roles and treatments than any other act the person may take in his or her lifetime."[2]

One's concept of "correct" marital roles begins to form early in life. A girl or boy learns what being married means by observing parents, aunts and uncles, and other married couples. In addition, individuals are influenced by the mass media, particularly by television. Over the years, such television shows as *Ozzie and Harriet, Father Knows Best, I Love Lucy, The Waltons,* and *Little House on the Prairie* have depicted traditional husband and wife roles. People also learn about pairing from religious training, books, and movies. All of these provide information about and models for intimate behavior.

In this chapter we examine marital roles and expectations, how traditional roles are giving way to more flexible ones, and the advantages and disadvantages of being part of a two-worker family.

THE INFLUENCE OF EXPECTATIONS

Besides the legal and social expectations of the marital role, couples also bring to their marriage private expectations based on their own needs, abilities, habits, and past experiences. Many of us expect that our marital relationships will satisfy almost all of our emotional needs. This is the message of most "family" television programs; it is the implicit agreement in traditional marriage vows "to love and to cherish"; and it is accepted as an important condition of the "ideal relationship." Yet these expectations are often unrealistic. For example, an individual may believe or hope that the marital relationship will solve all of life's problems, provide all that he or she wants, or make up for what he or she felt was missed in growing up or in past relationships.

Accepting a model for a relationship is not necessarily bad. Problems arise, however, when people do not agree on what their needs in a relationship are and, instead, accept models, rules, expectations, and roles that are imposed on them by parents, church, society, friends, and even the intimate partner. Adopting others' established roles and expectations increases the possibility that the person will sooner or later feel angry at having to fulfill a list of expectations that he or she has not freely chosen.

TRADITIONAL MARITAL ROLES

Traditionally, men have had the roles of head of household and breadwinner, and women have had the roles of housekeeper and child raiser. In the past, when the members of a family worked together on a farm or in a family-operated business, the husband and wife shared both economic and domestic tasks. Industrialization, however, separated the domestic and productive functions of the husband and wife. The man no longer worked at home, and his job in the factory focused his attention on his role and success as the economic provider for his family.[3] The man's contributions to the control and daily activities of the household diminished, and his occupation became paramount.

When the husband's role lost its domestic functions and became that of economic provider, the wife's role enveloped nearly all of the domestic tasks. As ready-made goods became more available, the wife's role lost many of its productive functions, such as processing and canning food, making clothes and soap, caring for poultry and livestock, and growing vegetables. The wife's activities concentrated on household maintenance and family care, and she became a domestic administrator.

Although many couples follow conventional marital roles, others try to create more flexible ones. Flexible roles allow couples to choose and design their own marital responsibilities, based on their needs, expertise, and the various tasks that must be done. This is particularly important if both partners work. More and more people are asserting their right to establish their own marital roles based on their own desires and needs. They do not feel that it is necessary to conform to traditional roles unless these roles are best for them.

THE CHALLENGE OF MODERN MARITAL ROLES

The Woman's Role

Today, American married women appear caught in the midst of conflicting values and expectations. If a married woman devotes herself to her husband and their family life, she is classified as "just a housewife," and even if she is satisfied with this role, she may feel guilty that she is not "doing more with her life." The lack of recognition and the repetition of household chores may make a full-time homemaker dissatisfied with her work. Housework is a low-status job in our society, and many people who firmly believe in traditional marital roles fail to recognize that homemaking is an important occupation. Furthermore, society's new emphasis on the importance of careers for both men and women has made many believe that being a homemaker is a secondary, or less important, role. Because homemaking is not recognized as a legitimate occupation, a woman receives no pay or status for doing it. Although some women receive help from their husbands, most still have the primary responsibility for housework, cooking, meal planning, laundry, cleaning, and child care (see Box 9.1).

A married woman who works may become frustrated with the pressures of being both a homemaker and an income provider. A working wife may have to be a "superwoman"—someone who must simultaneously perform all the tasks of worker, mother, wife, and

BOX 9.1   The Technology and Psychology of Housework

Despite technological advances, a full-time homemaker today spends more time on housework than she did in the 1920s. A study of several generations of women indicated that up until the middle of the twentieth century, a homemaker averaged fifty-two hours per week on household tasks. By the 1960s this had crept up to fifty-five hours per week, and since then it has more or less stayed at that level.[*]

Although there now are more labor-saving devices, homemaking standards also have been raised. For example, because we now own more clothes and change them more frequently, today's homemaker spends more time doing laundry than she did in the days when there were no automatic washers and driers. Furthermore, even though less time is spent preparing food, more time is spent shopping and traveling on household errands.

The only women who now spend less time on housework are those who are working full time. This same study found that full-time homemakers spent 8.1 hours per day in family work, compared with 4.8 hours per day for wives employed 30 or more hours per week. This difference, however, did not occur because the employed wives received more help from their families. Husbands spent only 1.6 hours per day on housework, whether or not their wives were working.[†]

Because it is difficult to do two jobs thoroughly, the working wife may be forced to cut corners and do less housework. Also, full-time homemakers may spend more time doing family work because they have higher standards and see family work as their only source of recognition. As Joann Vanek suggests:

> Since the value of household work is not clear, unemployed women feel pressure to spend long hours at it. Time spent in work, rather than the results of the work, serves to express to the homemaker and others that an equal contribution is being made. Women who work in the labor force contribute income to the family and do not feel the same pressure.[‡]

Whatever the reasons, homemaking is a full-time job. And its demands have increased, although its status has not.

[*]Joann Vanek, "Time Spent in Housework," *Scientific American*, 231 (November 1974): 116–120.
[†]Kathryn Waler and Margaret Woods, *Time Use: A Measure of Household Production of Family Goods and Services*, Washington, D.C., Center for the Family of the American Home Economic Association, 1976, p. 41.
[‡]Joann Vanek, "Time Spent in Housework," p. 120.

homemaker, often with little time or energy left for her own desires and needs.

The working wife usually does most of the housework and child raising. For example, studies have shown that although working wives spend less time doing housework than do full-time homemakers, husbands spend the same amount of time on household work, whether or not their wives are employed.[4] This division of labor also applies to child care, particularly when the children are young. Thus, it is not surprising that married working women often feel psychologically and physically drained. In addition, many who combine work and home-making feel that they do neither well.

The demands and pressures of the marital role can take their toll. In her summary of research findings, sociologist Jessie Bernard concluded that marriage imposes more regulations and adjustments on women than on men, that more wives than husbands consider their marriages unhappy and have regretted them, and that more married women than single women suffer mental health disorders such as depression, anxiety, psychological distress, and phobic reactions.[5]

Walter Gove and Jeannette Tudor also report higher rates of mental illness for women than for men, and these researchers believe that the reason for this may be the stresses associated with a married woman's social role. They suggest that a full-time homemaker's stresses may result from the fact that a woman's home and family are typically her only sources of gratification. (A man usually has two roles—those of worker and husband-father. Therefore, if one of his roles is unsatisfactory, he can focus his energies on the other.) Many women are frustrated with the tasks of housekeeping and raising children, as the work is repetitive and often undemanding. In addition, the housewife's role is relatively unstructured and invisible. The housewife is isolated from others, and her work is usually noticed only when it is not done.[6] Gove and Tudor also point out that even when a married woman does work, she is discriminated against in the job market and may feel that her job is secondary in importance to her husband's.

The Man's Role

Today, most married men adopt the traditional role of economic provider. But many also want to be more family oriented, particularly with regard to child care and housework—what Joseph Pleck, program director at the Wellesley College Center for Research on Women, calls *family work*. (Pleck uses the term *family work* in place of *housework* to stress that home care duties are real work—as real as paid work—and that all family members can do it.)

Those men who attempt to balance work and family may feel frustrated by time constraints and work responsibilities. Job demands and schedules may make it nearly impossible for a husband to devote time other than nights and weekends to his family. Also, men who try to participate more fully in family life may be competing with people in the work place who are devoting themselves solely to their careers. Thus, a man who tries to juggle a job and his family life may do so at the expense of one or the other, or both.

In some families, men and women share the housework.

Paul Conklin

As Pleck points out, social science literature uses three different perspectives regarding men's family work. These perspectives form a historical sequence in that each rejects the tenets of the earlier ones.[7]

1.   The *traditional perspective* is the belief that the husband is the sole economic provider of his family and should not be responsible for any substantial amount of housework and parenting. This perspective reflects and accepts the traditional sex-role division of labor and concludes that there is no need for change.

2.   The next view, the *exploitation perspective*, arose in the 1970s and reflects the feminist view that women have been overworked and exploited as a result of the inequality between men and women in the amount of family work each does. Although this view recognizes and emphasizes that men's minimal family participation is wrong, it holds that change is unlikely and pays little attention to possible strategies for change.

3.   The *changing-roles perspective* is more recent. It also recognizes that traditionally men have put little energy into their family role, but it rejects the pessimism of the exploitation view and sees the changing family role of men as a major challenge. Pleck believes that the changing-roles perspective will become more and more important in

the future. Furthermore, he concludes that sex roles will change because of the influence of research on the consequences of changing male roles and family roles, as well as studies of subgroups like single-parent fathers and househusbands.

Like women, men have also had unrealistic demands imposed on them. Although they are still expected to be dominant and successful, the new view of the male role expects men to be open and emotional. They may find themselves attempting to fill contradictory roles, as psychologist Herb Goldberg describes:

Society has placed confusing expectations on the married male, demanding that he be all things to all people: The capable provider, the aggressive competitor, the wise father, the sensitive and gentle lover, the fearless protector, the cool, controlled one under pressure and the emotionally expressive person at home.[8]

It is probable that these rigid definitions of male and female sex roles will continue to break down, and that more and more people will try to establish roles that are better suited to their own personalities. Although more flexible marital role behavior will certainly affect the family, it will not destroy the family as a social institution. As we pointed out in Chapter 1, "The Structure and Functions of the Modern Family," people's needs for family ties remain strong, and individuals are finding different ways to meet those familial needs.

One of these ways is the shared-role marriage, which allows the wife to contribute to the family income and permits the husband to participate in home maintenance and child care. This creates a more balanced relationship in which both partners share the happiness and drudgery of working and family care.

TWO-WORKER FAMILIES

For many couples, a shared-role marriage is an economic necessity. Today more than half of all married American women work outside the home, and for the first time in history, working wives outnumber housewives. Although conforming to traditional marital roles may create conflict and tension for these two-paycheck couples, the working wife nonetheless usually assumes the child-care and housework responsibilities. Though many couples feel that this places an unfair burden on the wife, it is difficult to break the pattern that dictates that the husband must work to support the family, while the wife is responsible for care of the home.

Families in which both spouses work are of two general types, the *dual-worker* household and the *dual-career* household. In most dual-worker families, the wife is not pursuing a career. Rather, she is working to meet financial needs, to put her husband through school, or to earn money for a specific goal—a new car, house, or college education for the children. Rhona and Robert Rapoport have done extensive research on dual-career families, and they explain how a career differs from a job:

The term "dual-career families" was coined to designate a type of family structure in which both heads of household—the husband and the wife—pursue active careers and family lives. "Career" is sometimes used to indicate any sequence of jobs, but in its more precise meaning it designates those types of job sequences that require a high degree of commitment and that have a continuous developmental character.[9]

Thus a career generally requires more energy, dedication, commitment, training, and planning; and persons with careers are expected to have an almost single-minded devotion to their occupation. The women in dual-worker couples, however, typically work before they are married and during the first years of their marriage, leave work when they have children, and then return to work once the children are of school age. Because they do not work continuously, these women are less likely to be hired for salaried and training positions, and they often lose promotional opportunities and seniority. Their interrupted work schedules do not allow them to dedicate themselves to careers. Furthermore, many women take temporary or part-time jobs and do not actively seek or want careers.

Working married women attempt to balance the commitments to their jobs and to their responsibilities at home. In our society, however, both the family and the work place have been structured to accommodate only one wage earner. One example of this is the lack of public day-care centers. This forces one spouse, usually the wife, to remain at home with infant children. Other examples are business, automotive repair, post office, and medical services which are accessible only during the day. This situation forces someone, usually the wife, to do such errands during business hours. This may cause problems if both spouses are expected to meet the demands of a full-time job.

Persons in the labor force may find that they have three jobs—those of spouse, parent, and worker. For women in particular, balancing a job, family, and home requires them to be "superwomen" who do everything well and on time. Some of the problems and benefits for both dual-worker and dual-career families are discussed below. In the following sections, the terms *two-worker* and *two-paycheck* families are used to describe both dual-worker and dual-career families.

Difficulties Faced by Two-Worker Families

Overload The Rapoports discuss the dilemma of "overload" which can occur when couples are pressed for time and must coordinate the responsibilities of career and home life. As one professional woman explains, "I feel I even have to sleep fast."[10]

In conventional families, the wife typically schedules and coordinates cleaning, shopping, cooking, school and extracurricular activities for the children, social arrangements, vacations, and so on. If both partners devote large amounts of time to their work, domestic tasks may become a source of conflict.

There are several ways to deal with the problem of scheduling household activities around work demands. If the couple can afford the cost, they may employ outside help. An alternative is for the husband and wife to redistribute housework and child care more evenly. This usually results in the husband assuming more responsibility for domestic work and family care. The Rapoports also suggest sharing with other families such activities as shopping, child care, and transportation of children.[11]

Career Responsibilities Job demands create additional difficulties for the two-worker family. The two most common are job-related travel and moving. Business travel often causes disruptions in a family's schedule, temporary separations, and additional work for the spouse who remains at home. A job transfer creates even more problems for a family. It requires selling the house; packing; moving; finding a job for the other spouse; finding a new house, schools, doctors, and shopping areas; and establishing new friendships and community ties. Coordination problems are compounded if one or both spouses often work overtime, commute long distances to work, or are frequently required to attend meetings and conferences out of town.

In some marriages, both partners have career goals. Frequently, persons who want to advance in their careers must relocate several times, and a man's family traditionally has moved with him on these job transfers. In dual-career couples, this problem becomes very complicated. The couple has to decide whose career takes priority, whether or not they will take turns on moves, whether they will consider short separations, and what they will do if job opportunities for the spouse are limited in the new location.

In order to accommodate a spouse's job-related relocation, the other spouse may sacrifice a great deal. Generally a couple can foresee this problem early in their careers and discuss how they will handle job relocations fairly. There are several options:

1. The couple may decide that one spouse's career takes priority. This may be because one or the other earns more money or because job openings or locations where one spouse can work are limited.

2. Couples may take turns taking job transfers, regardless of who earns a higher salary or has limited job opportunities.

3. The couple can establish requirements or conditions for relocation. For example, in order for a spouse to take a job transfer, the couple might agree that the job must have a particular salary increase above that which the spouse is currently earning, that the other spouse must be able to find work before the spouse accepts the position, or that job relocations will be accepted only in certain circumstances—if it means a promotion, after the children reach a certain age and agree to the move, and so on.

Because of the problems and conflicts inherent in balancing two careers with a family life, dual-career couples currently represent only a small proportion of dual-worker couples. However, the number of dual-career families will probably increase as career opportunities for women increase; businesses offer part-time work, flexible working hours, and job sharing to both men and women; and child-care facilities expand and improve.

A trend toward an increase in two-career families is evident in data from the College Research Bureau. Their findings indicate that today's college women want smaller families, are more serious about careers, and have more liberal views regarding women's roles in society than college women did ten years ago.[12]

Child Care Another serious problem faced by two-paycheck couples is the lack of adequate child-care facilities. Over the last few decades, the demand for day care has dramatically increased. *Newsweek* magazine's analysis of working mothers found that:

Over-all, 43 percent of married mothers with children under 6 now work outside their home. These mothers have 7 million small children

This dual-career couple is so busy that they meet regularly for lunch to increase their time together.

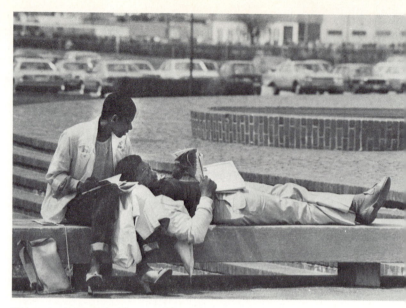

Ellis Herwig/Stock, Boston

to worry about while they earn needed paychecks—and there are precious few places to put them. Counting public, private, and commercial facilities, the United States now has fewer licensed day-care slots available than in 1945: 1.6 million openings. That leaves another 5.4 million kids to be parceled out among babysitters and nursery schools—or left alone.[13]

In many other industrialized countries, day-care facilities are plentiful. Although the need for day care in the United States is evident, Congress has defeated comprehensive day-care bills presented every year since 1970. In 1977, Congress did pass a measure that gives parents tax credits of up to $800 ($400 per child) for child-care costs. (This is only marginally helpful because the estimated actual annual child-care cost averages $2,500.)[14]

The problems of combining careers and families are one reason that many couples are choosing not to have children or are postponing having children, as this woman explains:

It may be a question of my being selfish. I like the lifestyle we have now, and because of the commitment we have to our jobs, I question whether it would be fair to a child.[15]

Benefits of a Two-Worker Marriage

Financial Reward

Although two-job families pay more for child care, transportation, domestic help, and so on, the most tangible benefit for two-paycheck families is the financial reward. This is especially true for couples who do not have children.

In 1980, the Department of Labor compiled statistics on the earnings of both married working couples and families with one wage earner:

New Labor Department figures show that for the 56.3% of married couples in which both husband and wife work, 1979 earnings averaged $496 a week or $25,792 a year. Among couples in which only the husband worked, earnings averaged $322 a week or $16,744 a year. When the wife was the sole earner, earnings averaged $151 a week, or $7,852 a year.[16]

The larger paychecks increase the family's standard of living, allow for more leisure and recreational activities, travel, cars, and so on. They may also make it easier for the husband or wife to change jobs, since one partner's work can provide the family's income while the other is between jobs.

Self-fulfillment

Both men and women can obtain satisfaction and a sense of achievement and recognition from working outside the home. How much happiness and fulfillment is derived from a job depends on the type of work, interaction with coworkers, expectations and goals for the job, and how the work affects one's family life. The combination of a satisfying job and a gratifying family life can be highly rewarding.

But sociological studies have found that the differences in degree of happiness reported by working wives and by full-time homemakers are small. A recent review of studies and national survey data concluded that both outside jobs and full-time homemaking have rewards and drawbacks.[17] Working wives may gain increased independence, income, and feelings of accomplishment but face the stresses of a life style with a diversity of demands. A homemaker, on the other hand, may have a less hectic life style and the personal satisfaction of caring for her family. But she may also be totally responsible for repetitive tasks which may be less fulfilling than other types of work, and she may be more socially isolated.

It appears that a wife's happiness and self-fulfillment are dependent on whether her decision to work agrees with her and her husband's attitudes. For example, several studies have found that the idea that all housewives are unhappy is inaccurate. Many women find full-time homemaking highly satisfying. The most dissatisfied homemakers are married women who want to work but cannot because of family responsibilities, disapproval of husband or family, lack of child care, illness, or limited job opportunities.[18]

Positive and Negative Effects on Children

There is much controversy regarding the effects on children of two working parents. Many of these effects—good or bad—depend on the child-parent relationship, the concern and competence of a hired housekeeper or day-care attendant, the parents' attitudes toward their work, the number and types of activities the parents participate in with the child, and so on.

Some of the advantages of both parents working are that their children observe more parental roles and fewer traditional sex-role stereotypes than the children of nonworking mothers do; they may be able to develop close ties with both parents; and they often become independent, adaptable, and responsible at an early age.[19]

Adequate nonparental day care is a necessity for dual-worker families.

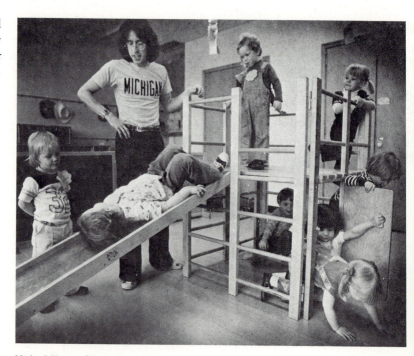

Michael Hayman/Black Star

But a child may have problems if both parents are frequently gone and there is not a capable parent substitute. The parents' attitudes (particularly the mother's) toward working may also affect child rearing. Marian Yarrow and her associates found that whether mothers did or did not work made little difference in child rearing, as long as the woman was doing what she wanted.

When mothers' motivations regarding working are taken into account, the nonworking mothers who are dissatisfied with not working (who want to work but out of a feeling of "duty" do not work) show the greatest problems in child rearing. They describe more difficulties in the area of control, less emotional satisfaction in relationships with children, and less confidence in their functioning as mothers.[20]

TWO-WORKER COUPLES IN THE FUTURE

Critics argue that two-paycheck families will destroy family life, but advocates of two-worker couples applaud their efforts to change conventional marital and sex roles, thus giving spouses more personal freedom. People favoring two-worker households stress that these couples face such institutional and social constraints as inflexible working hours, unequal benefits for part-time workers, and inadequate child-care facilities. They suggest that this type of family may have an impossible task in that it "seeks to combine the luxuries of two full-time, continuous careers and a private nuclear-family household."[21]

Other proponents of two-worker marriages believe that although the combination of two jobs is difficult, it is possible. They emphasize the importance of a couple's agreement on marital roles:

One crucial element seems to be necessary to success: a clear-cut agreement on who should and who will do what. Studies have shown that agreement on marital roles is important for the stability of the marriage. In traditional marriages, the occupants of that world were handed a ready-made set of blueprints. The dual-career couple may have to draw up its own plans, from scratch.[22]

The coordination of two jobs is difficult, and family structures and work institutions—as well as popular ideas about "correct" marital roles—must change to accommodate the needs of two-worker couples. Families in which both spouses work have been forced to examine and

© 1978 Lynn Johnston. Granted permission by Meadowbrook Press, 18318 Minnetonka Blvd., Deephaven, Minn. 55391 from "DO THEY EVER GROW UP?"

possibly redefine traditional marital roles to discover the best way to balance work and household tasks.

SUMMARY

The private side of marriage includes the roles and expectations that each couple uses to structure their marital relationship. Expectations regarding marital behavior form the foundation of marital roles. Some marital roles, such as those regarding support and property rights, are dictated by law, and others are determined by societal and family pressures and have become social customs. In addition, people create their own marital roles based on their particular needs, abilities, habits, and past experiences.

Traditionally, men have taken the head of household and breadwinner roles, and women have had the housekeeping and child-care roles. Some couples, particularly those in which both partners work, are redefining and adapting traditional marital roles to allow for more flexibility and sharing.

There has been a dramatic increase in the number of families in which both spouses work. These couples often have the problems of time demands and pressures in coordinating their jobs and home life. Although they may suffer "overload" and have job-transfer and job-related traveling difficulties, as well as child-care problems, they may also have greater financial rewards, self-fulfillment, and the knowledge that they are sharing both income and home and family care.

CONSIDER THIS

Michael and Frances have been married for five years and have a three-year-old daughter. Frances is an office supervisor, and Michael has just completed his master's degree in English literature. The couple came in for counseling at the end of the school year. Michael doesn't want to teach in the school system in which they live and would like to apply for a position in another district. Frances has been offered a promotion and doesn't want to leave her job. The following conversation is from one of their counseling sessions:

MICHAEL: When I went back to school we agreed that Frances would work until I finished school and found a teaching job. Now she wants to keep working.

FRANCES: Back then I didn't realize that I would enjoy work so much. I like the company, and they've been pleased with me. Now I've built up a lot of experience, and if I move to another company, I will have to start at a lower position, because I don't have as much education as other people doing the same job. I want to keep working, and the promotion is really important to me.

MICHAEL: I prefer that you stay home—I think that's best for Betsy. But I don't want you to be unhappy, and we could surely use the money. I never liked Frances supporting me, but I thought it would be temporary. Our budget was pretty tight so I worked my school schedule around taking care of our daughter, Betsy. She's had everything from Shakespeare to Vonnegut read to her. That was the only way I could get my reading done.

FRANCES: I felt guilty that Michael had to do so much of the housework and take care of Betsy. Now I'm feeling pressured by Michael not to work. It doesn't seem fair that I have to leave my job and have to stay home and be a housewife.

Questions
1. How can Michael and Frances resolve the conflict between their personal desires and marital role expectations? Would it be possible for them to accommodate traditional marital roles in their new situation?
2. What effect do you think Frances's working has had on Betsy?
3. If they became a two-worker couple, what effects would this have on their marriage?
4. Many students get married while they are attending school. What special problems do married couples still in college have?

NOTES

1. William Shakespeare, *As You Like It*.
2. Bruce J. Biddle, *Role Theory: Expectations, Identities, and Behaviors*, New York, Academic Press, 1979, p. 248.
3. For an excellent discussion of economic and domestic tasks and roles, see Gail Putney Fullerton, *Survival in Marriage*, New York, Holt, Rinehart & Winston, 1972, pp. 14–33.
4. Kathryn Walker and Margaret Woods, *Time Use: A Measure of Household Production of Family Goods and Services*, Washington, D.C., Center for the Family of the American Home Economic Association, 1976, p. 41.
5. Jessie Bernard, *The Future of Marriage*, New York, Bantam, 1972.
6. Walter Gove and Jeannette Tudor, "Adult Sex Roles and Mental Illness," *American Journal of Sociology*, 78 (January 1973): 814–815.
7. Joseph H. Pleck, "Men's Family Work: Three Perspectives and Some New Data," *Family Coordinator*, October 1979, pp. 481–488.
8. "Battle of the Sexes: Men Fight Back," *U.S. News and World Report*, December 8, 1980, p. 52.
9. Rhona and Robert N. Rapoport, *Dual-Career Families Re-examined*, London, England, Martin Robertson, 1976, p. 9.
10. *Wall Street Journal*, May 13, 1975, p. 13.
11. Rhona and Robert N. Rapoport, *Dual-Career Families Re-examined*, p. 302.
12. Caryl Rivers, Rosalind Barnett, and Grace Baruch, "He Works/She Works: Does the Marriage Work?" *Working Woman*, 5 (May 1980): 43–44.
13. "The Superwoman Squeeze," *Newsweek*, May 19, 1980, p. 72.

14. Ibid., p. 73.
15. "Two Incomes: No Sure Hedge Against Inflation," *U.S. News and World Report*, July 9, 1979, p. 46.
16. *Wall Street Journal*, March 28, 1980, p. 17.
17. James D. Wright, "Are Working Women Really More Satisfied? Evidence from Several National Surveys," *Journal of Marriage and the Family*, 40 (May 1978): 301–313.
18. Linda Fidell and Jane Prather, unpublished research reported in Carol Tarvis, "Women: Work Isn't Always the Answer," *Psychology Today*, 10 (September 1976): 78; Carol Morgan, "Female and Male Attitudes Toward Life: Implications for Theories of Mental Health, *Sex Roles*, 6, no. 3 (1980): 367–380.
19. Ruth Zambrana, Marsha Hurst, and Rodney Hite, "The Working Mother in Contemporary Perspective: A Review of the Literature," *Pediatrics*, 64 (December 1979): 867.
20. Marian Yarrow et al., "Child-rearing in Families of Working and Nonworking Mothers," in M. E. Lasswell and T. E. Lasswell, eds., *Love, Marriage, Family: A Developmental Approach*, Glenview, Ill., Scott, Foresman, 1973, p. 371.
21. Janet and Larry Hunt, "Dilemmas and Contradictions of Status: The Case of the Dual-Career Family," *Social Problems*, 24 (April 1977): 414.
22. Caryl Rivers, Rosalind Barnett, and Grace Baruch, "He Works/She Works: Does the Marriage Work?" p. 45.

SUGGESTED READINGS

Bird, Caroline. *The Two-Paycheck Marriage*. New York, Simon & Schuster (Pocket Books), 1979. An examination of the impact of two paychecks on marriage, home, money management, and children.

Giele, Janet Zollinger. "Changing Sex Roles and Family Structure." *Social Policy*, January/February 1979, pp. 32–43. A comprehensive look at women's and men's changing roles and the consequent effects on the structure of the family.

Newsweek. "The Superwoman Squeeze." May 19, 1980, pp. 72–79. A timely article on the demands and pressures of the changing female role.

Oakley, Ann. *Woman's Work: The Housewife, Past and Present*. New York, Random House, 1974. An informative investigation of the history and nature of housework.

Pleck, Joseph H., and Jack Sawyer. *Men and Masculinity*. Englewood Cliffs, N.J., Prentice-Hall, 1974. A collection of essays covering all aspects of the changing male role.

MARITAL
INTERACTION

. . . and they lived happily ever after.

Fairy tales

There are two myths about marital interaction. The first myth says, "and they lived happily ever after." This is the myth which holds marriage to be a continuous courtship. The second myth is the picture of the domestic grind; the husband sits behind the paper, the wife moves about in morning disarray; the husband leaves for work, the wife spends the day among dishes, diapers, and dirty little children. Although, as with most myths, no one *really* believes either one of them, they continue to affect the behavior of most people. Perhaps most people faintly hope to live happily ever after, but rather fear dreary domesticity will be their lot.[1]

Neither the "happily ever after," romantic fantasy that marriage is a totally blissful, conflict-free state nor the notion that marriage is always a conflict-filled, "make the best of it" interaction is true. Most marriages tend to fall between these two extremes. Although marriage can sometimes be intensely fulfilling and satisfying, a couple usually also has periods of problems and dissatisfaction. In this chapter we examine making marriage work, the different types of marital interaction, the family life cycle, marital satisfaction, marital conflict, and violence in the family.

MAKING MARRIAGE WORK

Although we may smile or nod in agreement when we hear the refrain "marriage is hard work," many couples often ignore this wise advice.

Marriage does not have a mind of its own. In order to make marriage work, a couple must attend to the relationship, nurture it, and focus their energy on it. The positive aspects of marriage are attained not only by solving marital problems but also by working to make the marital relationship more harmonious and satisfying.

After a couple marries, there are a number of adjustments to living together. For someone who has been living alone, becoming accustomed to living with another person and sharing a routine might be difficult. In the early stages of a relationship, partners determine who sleeps on which side of the bed as well as how they are going to handle their money. Differences in personalities, moods, tastes, and values certainly affect a couple's relationship and, in some instances, may lead to problems and conflict. An example of a difference in life style that may cause problems is when a morning person lives with a night person (see Box 10.1).

When an intimate relationship is flowing smoothly, it can produce a richness of emotional satisfaction unparalleled by any other experience. But when an intimate relationship is not going well, the people involved can be overwhelmed by unhappiness, and they can be angry, depressed, anxious, or distraught, sometimes to the point of being unable to function at work or at school.

It has been suggested that relationships flourish and continue when the partners free themselves of preconceived ideas about themselves and their relationship and let their intimacy grow in its own natural way.[2] Acceptance of the other person—as he or she actually is—is essential to a successful marital relationship.

Unfortunately, most people have expectations and ideas about how their intimate relationships should be and how their spouses ought to act, and they conduct themselves according to how closely their relationships conform to their ideals. If one partner's behavior is inconsistent with the other's ideal, then tensions and angers can arise. If both partners have very different ideas of how their relationship should be and these ideas are not communicated or examined, then the stage is set for failure.

It is better for people to let each other be the person they feel comfortable being, rather than trying to be the "ideal partner." After all, this is the person that one originally found attractive, so why try to change him or her into someone with different personality characteristics? A useful concept to keep in mind is that of "letting go." Love is "letting go"—allowing the partner to develop his or her personality and behavior in ways that he or she deems best. People are not objects that can be manipulated to conform to someone's wishes. Although we may try to influence our partners to behave in certain ways, if such behavior

BOX 10.1 As Different as Night and Day

Are you a "night person"—someone who hates to get up in the morning, whose energy seems to build up as the day progresses, and who by nighttime is "raring to go"? Or are you a "morning person"—someone who likes to get up early, is energetic during the daytime, and in the evening tends to wilt? Many individuals are either "night people" or "morning people." The differences probably arise from differences in circadian (twenty-four-hour) rhythms. Some people, however, favor neither the day nor the night.

To determine whether "nightness" or "morningness" affects marriages, family specialists Bert Adams and Ronald Cromwell asked married couples about the importance of activity rhythms in their lives. The respondents had little difficulty identifying themselves or their spouses as either "night people" or "morning people," or describing how those preferences created either harmony or conflict in their married lives. Shared activities, sexual relationships, and social life were significantly affected by the nightness-morningness dichotomy. According to Adams and Cromwell, "Morning people see themselves as outdoor and physically active types, while night people are described as either quiet homebodies or as party and night-life lovers." Fewer conflicts arise when both partners are either morning or night people.

Morning people: "We enjoy outdoor sports in the sun, which we participate together in very frequently. At night, we relax and/or collapse together."

Night people: "We both like to do things at night, stay up late, etc. Our mornings are not times of great communication. In fact, we've decided if we had to face each other in the morning, our relationship would never survive."

Mismatched couples, on the other hand, repeatedly spoke of being "out of phase" with each other, which resulted in either conflict or compromise: "Differences between us still creates some problems even after 27 years of marriage. . . . I do not try serious discussion with her in the morning and my wife refrains from such in the evening." This sometimes created tension in various activities, including the amount of time the couple had for conversation together: "This mismatch affects my life conversation-wise. We hardly have anything to talk about, or any time to talk."

Other couples understood their problems and have attempted to work out compromises: "For example, Ken will stay up late to help me or for social events. I, in return, will get up early for church, even though I may want to sleep, because of the values and goals we have. Working to balance our differences is important."

Although no absolute conclusions can be drawn, the results of the Adams-Cromwell study, and also common experience, suggest that morning people and night people may have fewer interaction and adjustment problems if they are matched with someone who has a similar morning or night life style.

Source: Substantive material and all quotations used in this box were taken from Bert Adams and Ronald Cromwell, "Morning and Night People in the Family: A Preliminary Statement," *Family Coordinator*, January 1978, pp. 5–13.

is not "natural" for them, they may eventually feel stifled by our expectations and rebel, or even leave the relationship.

Marital unhappiness is often the result of a discrepancy between a person's expectations for his or her marriage and what the relationship actually provides. Expectations also change over time. Thus, some couples' expectations, which were compatible at the beginning of their marriages, may become discrepant over time and with the accumulation of life experiences.

Marital satisfaction is enhanced when a couple is able to discuss their expectations and accommodate each other without sacrificing their own needs. Their acceptance of a marriage's realistic satisfactions, limitations, and changes can be increased by openly discussing marital hopes and conflicts and seeking help when necessary (see Box 10.2).

TYPES OF MARITAL INTERACTION

The relationships of couples who report being happily married vary enormously. In 1965, social scientists John Cuber and Peggy Harroff studied upper middle class persons who had been married more than ten years to the same spouse and who said they had never considered separation or divorce. Cuber and Harroff identified five types of relationships, three of which were classified as utilitarian marriages and two as intrinsic marriages.

Utilitarian Marriages

Utilitarian marriages are described as workable, rational, and satisfying. In these relationships, individuals fulfill security and stability needs. They share similar interests and are often more concerned with their careers and obligations to their children and the community than with deep emotional involvement and close companionship. The emotional bonds of many utilitarian marriages develop slowly, and the partners stay together for practical and moral reasons. It is a marriage of convenience. According to Cuber and Harroff:

By the term Utilitarian Marriage we mean simply any marriage which is established or maintained for purposes other than to express an intimate, highly important *personal* relationship between a man and a

BOX 10.2 Marriage Counseling and Marriage Enrichment Programs

When problems occur in relationships, people generally seek the help of their friends or family. But close friends and relatives may be too emotionally attached to the couple to be able to help or even to listen. Some people seek the help of clergy or family doctors. But more and more couples are utilizing the training and help of professional marriage counselors.

Marriage counseling can help a couple better understand their interaction with each other, identify and resolve communication and other marital problems, clarify their goals for the marriage, and, if necessary, aid them in making changes. If the couple decides to divorce, counseling can also offer support and advice during the dissolution process.

Counseling helps the individual find his or her own answers. The goal of counseling is not to "save the marriage" or to teach a person how to adapt to an unhappy situation. Instead, it focuses on the individual's feelings and needs and helps him or her explore different courses of action.

As Richard Hunt and Edward Rydman aptly conclude:

Now, among professionally trained marriage counselors, there is emerging the position that marriage counseling does not necessarily exist for the purpose of preserving the institution of marriage. It exists for the purpose of aiding individuals in marital conflict to understand their situation, themselves, the underlying reasons for their difficulties, and to carefully examine viable alternatives. . . . Such decisions may sometimes mean divorce and remarriage to other partners. This appears to be a shift in values. If so, it means that people—individuals, men, women, and children—are more important than institutions. *

More and more professionals are focusing on the prevention of marital problems. This preventive concept is applicable to couples who

woman. The absence of continuous and deep empathic feeling and the existence of an atmosphere of limited companionship are natural outcomes, since the purposes for its establishment or maintenance are not primarily sexual and emotional ones. Hence the term utilitarian; the marriage is useful to the mates for reasons outside of personal considerations.[3]

The three types of utilitarian marriages are *conflict-habituated*, *devitalized*, and *passive-congenial*.

Conflict-Habituated Marriage

In the conflict-habituated marriage, there is, obviously, much conflict and tension. The tension is usually controlled, and the couple attempts to conceal their conflict from family and friends, although close family members usually see the couple's fighting as a prominent part of their interaction. The couples themselves acknowledge that "incompatibility is pervasive, that conflict is ever-potential, and that an atmosphere of tension permeates the togetherness."[4]

BOX 10.2 (continued)

are happily married but wish to improve their marital relationship, and it can be an important tool for reducing marital conflict.

Unlike marriage counseling, marriage enrichment programs emphasize the prevention rather than the correction of marital problems. Herbert Otto offers the following definition:

> *Marriage Enrichment Programs* are for couples who have what they perceive to be a fairly well functioning marriage and who wish to make their marriage even more mutually satisfying. The programs are *not* designed for people whose marriage is at a point of crisis, or who are seeking counseling help for marital problems. Marriage enrichment programs are generally concerned with enhancing the couple's communication, emotional life, or sexual relationship, fostering marriage strengths, and developing marriage potential while maintaining a consistent and primary focus on the relationship of the couple.†

Marriage enrichment programs generally consist of small groups of married couples meeting weekly or on weekends. The meetings are run by qualified professionals who may be helped by "team couples," couples who have already been through the enrichment program.

Because the basic goal of marriage enrichment is enhancing the couple's interpersonal relationship, many of the exercises and topics of conversation focus on improving communication. As a result, couples learn ways of improving their interaction and preventing marital discord.

*Richard A. Hunt and Edward J. Rydman, *Creative Marriage*, Boston, Allyn & Bacon, 1979, p. 342.
†Herbert Otto, "Marriage and Family Enrichment Programs in North America," *Family Coordinator*, 24 (April 1975): 137.

Devitalized Marriage
A devitalized marriage is one in which the partners feel that the love and emotional attachment that were once important to their relationship have slowly turned into a companionship that relies on shared interests and routine interaction. Cuber and Harroff believe that this kind of marriage is "exceedingly common." Although the marriage has lost the vitality that it once had in its early years, many people feel that this is the appropriate marital style for couples who have been married for a long time. Although the partners seem to have drifted apart emotionally, they still get along well and explain that there are now "other things in life which are worthy of their attention and energy."[5]

Passive-Congenial Marriage
Although the passive-congenial marriage is similar to the devitalized marriage, individuals in passive-congenial marriages have never experienced the emotional intensity felt by individuals in devitalized marriages. From the start, passive-congenial marriages emphasize

*"In a world gone totally berserk, my dear,
you are an island of sanity."*

Drawing by Mulligan; © 1981 The New Yorker Magazine, Inc.

common interests, need compatibility, and friendship, but not emotional involvement. Cuber and Harroff suggest that individuals decide on
this type of marriage by either default or intention:

Perhaps in most instances they arrive at this way of living and feeling
by drift. There is so little which they have cared about deeply in each
other that a passive relationship is sufficient to express it all. In other
instances the passive-congenial mode is a deliberately intended
arrangement for two people whose interests and creative energies are
directed elsewhere than toward the pairing.[6]

Intrinsic Marriages

The focus of *intrinsic marriages* is on the partners themselves and their
needs and desires. This type of marriage is characterized by emotional

intensity, close sharing, and sexual pleasure. Intrinsic marriages are what many consider the ideal or romantic marital relationship. Indeed, the relationship is the most important thing in the two individuals' lives, and their careers and community obligations may be sacrificed in order to maintain the relationship's intensity. Cuber and Harroff divide intrinsic marriages into vital and total marriages.

Vital Marriage   In a vital marriage, the couple enjoys being together and sharing common interests, and they have a deep emotional bond. Although partners in vital marriages also have tensions and disagreements, they are able to settle their differences quickly and are more willing to compromise than those in conflict-habituated marriages are. The spouse is genuinely the most important part of the other's life, as this man explains:

I've always felt that Linda and I were meant for each other—we seem to "click." There is this incredible closeness that we feel and share. At times it is hard to describe to our friends—they think we're living in a make-believe world. But the romance is still there, our lovemaking is incredible, and I would gladly do anything to keep us together. It's that important to me.

From the authors' files

Total Marriage   A total marriage is even more intense and satisfying than a vital marriage. The partners share even more activities and interests than those in vital marriages do. The couple has a deep emotional bond; yet they are able to maintain their individuality. Although this type of relationship is rare, Cuber and Harroff found that it does exist and can endure. It is interesting that many people in intrinsic marriages attempt to conceal or discount their relationships. They recognize that they are a minority, and they are afraid that their friends would think them odd or immature if they knew the extent of their emotional involvement. Curiously, other couples, for example, those in utilitarian marriages, may be suspicious of those in intrinsic marriages. They may find it difficult to believe that such utopian marital relationships exist, or they may feel that such intensity and commitment cannot last.

Cuber and Harroff emphasize that these five kinds of marriages represent relationships, not personality types, and that their typology describes types of marital interaction, not types of people. Also, a given relationship may have characteristics of more than one of the five types. Furthermore, the five classifications do not show degrees of marital adjustment or happiness. Couples in all five types asserted that they were content, if not happy. Nonetheless, Cuber and Harroff's analysis provides a means of viewing and comparing the different kinds of marital interaction, and it demonstrates that people can be happy in many sorts of relationships.

THE FAMILY LIFE CYCLE

A marriage is a dynamic interaction which is constantly changing, evolving, and adapting to the couple's needs and life style. Even the couple's frustrations and conflicts vary at the different stages of their relationship.

The concept of the family life cycle has been used to describe a couple's interaction during the course of their marriage. It traces family structure and behavior patterns over the years and identifies certain developmental stages. Typically, the family life cycle of couples with children is divided into eight stages:

1. Beginning Families: married couple without children
2. Childbearing Families: oldest child younger than thirty months
3. Families with Preschool Children: oldest child 30 months to 6 years
4. Families with School-age Children: oldest child 6 years to 13 years
5. Families with Teenagers: oldest child 13 years to 20 years
6. Families as Launching Centers: first child gone to last child leaving home
7. Middle-aged Parents: empty nest to retirement
8. Aging Families: retirement to death of first spouse[7]

The family life cycle describes the series of milestones in the life of a relationship. The childless couple in stage 1 is completing educational goals, establishing themselves in careers, and becoming financially established. During this period, they are becoming comfortable with their marital expectations and adjusting to their relationship. For most parents, stage 2 through stage 6 occur when they are in their twenties, thirties, and forties. During these stages, the couple is adjusting to being parents, coordinating requirements as parents with those as spouses and workers, and balancing job demands and increased financial demands. During stage 7, the couple is once again alone, adjusting to health changes, enjoying additional time with each other and for outside activities, and possibly facing problems with becoming reacquainted with each other. Finally, in stage 8, the couple accepts and adapts to retirement, aging, and declining health; takes up new and rewarding activities, enjoys the companionship of children and grandchildren, and prepares for the inevitable death of spouse and self.

For those whose marriages generally follow these stages, it is interesting to learn that a couple spends as much time together without children—stages 1, 7, and 8—as they do with children—stages 2 through 6. One reason for this is that since the turn of the century, the length of time between the birth of a woman's first child and the birth of her last child has decreased, from ten years to about seven years. Today, childbearing usually begins around age twenty-three and ends at thirty, whereas in the early part of the century, it began at age twenty-three but continued until age thirty-three (see Figure 10.1).[8] This shorter span has occurred primarily because women are having fewer children. The average family in 1900 had 3.9 children, but today's average family has only 2.0.[9]

Another reason for the increase in time a couple spends together without children is that people are living longer:

In the twentieth century, an average of nine years (or 25 percent) has been added to married life. The average interval between age at marriage and the death of one spouse, usually the husband, has increased from 35 to 44 years. This fact, plus changes in childbearing patterns, has increased the average empty-nest marital stage from one year to 12 years. . . . Eighty percent of couples will survive to see their last child marry; a generation ago only 50 percent did.[10]

The decrease in the number of childbearing years and the increase in life expectancies for both men and women have added more "couple time" to the family life cycle. The significance of the additional "couple time" in the postparental stages of marriage is discussed in Chapter 16, "Marriage and Family Life in the Later Years."

MARITAL SATISFACTION

Marital satisfaction is difficult to measure. It differs in degree from couple to couple and varies over time for any particular couple. As we stated earlier, a long-term marriage typically goes through a developmental process in which the couple adjusts and adapts to the different experiences they encounter.

Within this developmental process, there are four possible patterns of marital satisfaction: (1) The couple may follow an up-and-down pattern of marital satisfaction. (2) After a happy beginning, the couple's marital satisfaction may steadily diminish. (3) After a period

FIGURE 10.1

Median age of typical mothers in the United States at selected points in the family life cycle, by period of birth and approximate period of first marriage

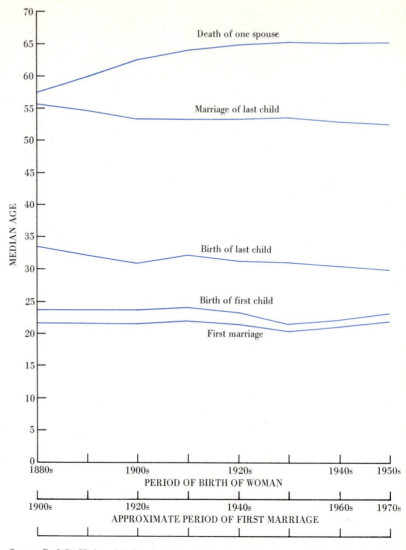

Source: Paul C. Glick and Arthur J. Norton, "Marrying, Divorcing, and Living Together in the U.S. Today," *Population Bulletin*, 32, No. 5 (1977) 21. Courtesy of the Population Reference Bureau, Inc., Washington, D.C.

of maladjustment at the start of their marriage, a couple may become more satisfied as the relationship progresses. (4) The couple may experience no significant change in marital happiness over the years.

Early studies reported that marital satisfaction tended to decline with the passing of time. More recent studies, however, suggest that for most couples in lasting marriages, marital satisfaction resembles a

U-shaped curve.[11] Marital satisfaction seems to be the highest in newlyweds, declines after the first few years and during parenthood, and then, after leveling off, begins to increase in the later years. There are exceptions to this pattern, of course, and more research is needed.[12] It would be interesting, for example, to study the marital satisfaction curves of couples who have been married for a short time, couples who are remarried, couples who are childless, and couples who marry at later ages.

One myth that this research dispels is the notion that people are unhappy when they experience an "empty nest" (the period after the children have left home). On the contrary, they may be very happy during this time: data from six U.S. national surveys indicate that women whose children have left home are happier, enjoy life more, and have greater marital satisfaction than do women whose children are still at home.[13] It appears that the childrearing years are a couple's most difficult and that after the children have left home, marital satisfaction seems to increase. And even though ill health can disrupt the marital equilibrium of an elderly couple, marriage in the later years tends to be highly rewarding and satisfying.

MARITAL CONFLICT

The family life cycle illustrates the rich diversity in a couple's life. Each stage has its happiness and pain. During these stages it requires much energy and conscious effort to maintain a vital and satisfying relationship. Contributing to the difficulty in sustaining a rewarding marriage are several common problems that a couple may face during their years together.

Marital complaints tend to fit into one of the following categories: communication problems, decision-making or marital-power conflicts, sexual dissatisfaction, financial conflicts, in-law problems, and conflicts regarding children.

Communication Problems

Communication—a similar, mutual understanding of a message passed between people—is a fundamental part of any relationship (see Chapter 3, "Developing Intimate Relationships"). Yet poor communication is probably the most common complaint among married couples. Couples often say that "there is no communication between us" or that "we've never really communicated." But it is impossible not to communicate. Silence is communication that may express "relaxation, contentment, fatigue, anxiety, frustration, uncertainty, shyness, avoidance, or thoughtful analysis."[14] One partner may be silent for any of these reasons, and it is easy for the other to make assumptions about what the silence means without ever asking.

In an unhappy marriage, the couple often stops trying to communicate. The lack of communication, however, may be the result of some specific conflict, rather than the cause of it. If you are upset or angry with your partner, you may stop communicating in order to retaliate. Or you may be silent because you want to avoid being psychologically or physically harmed, because you feel hurt, or because you do not know how else to break the exchange of verbal abuse.

Effective communication requires good listening and feedback. We need to make sure that our partners are hearing what we are saying. Feedback allows us to paraphrase what we have heard and to ask clarifying questions. Many couples spend a lot of time not listening to each another and often anticipate what the other will say and respond to it, rather than listening to the message that their partner is really trying to convey. We cannot expect to understand our partner's thoughts and feelings if we are thinking about our answers instead of listening. Often we get into a cycle of complaining and explaining, as Dr. John Schimel describes:

I sometimes quote to a patient the maxim, "Never complain, never explain." The patient may reply "If I never complained or explained, what would I ever talk about?" In some families complaining and explaining constitute the major patterns of exchange. One complains about the other, who then explains why the complaint is unjustified and adds a complaint about the other, who then explains and complains in turn. . . . There is a rhythm of criticism, explanation, and counterattack in such interactions.[15]

Barrie and Charlotte Hopson call these communication patterns "I Hear the Music and My Feet Begin to Tap" conflicts. Once the communication begins, the participants are pulled into patterns of complaining and explaining. An example of this (presented in Box 10.3) shows John and Patricia communicating feelings (text), even though what they say has an underlying meaning (subtext). But they both are so wrapped up in their own thoughts and hurts that they do not really hear either the text or the subtext of the conversation.

In order to break out of this type of communication cycle, it helps to have one person talk without interruption. Before responding, the other person must repeat what he or she has heard. This forces the partners to listen carefully to each other, and it also gives each of them feedback that their messages have been heard. After the feedback process, the other partner then expresses his or her thoughts, and the pattern continues.

Because you have no control over the other person, the best you can do in any communication is to try to express as clearly as possible what you are thinking and feeling. There are two steps to doing this. The first is to be clear in your own mind about how you feel, and the second is to convey those feelings as adeptly and sincerely as possible. The other person's feedback will allow you to judge whether your message has been received and understood correctly. If the message you are trying to convey has not been understood correctly, then either you have not said what you meant accurately or clearly, or the person to whom you are communicating cannot understand your intended meaning because he or she may not be psychologically prepared to accept or even to listen to your point of view. If your partner chooses not to hear you, it is not your fault.

Using I-Messages   Another way to improve communication is to use I-messages instead of You-messages. *You-messages* place the blame on the other person and are likely to elicit a defensive reaction or a justification of the other's behavior. For example, the statement "You spend money recklessly" tells the partner that you think he or she is incompetent. It is a put-down and the partner may react angrily. *I-messages*, however, refer to one's own feelings. Saying "I worry we won't be able to pay the bills when the baby arrives" states your feelings in a nonaccusatory manner. It does not threaten or blame the partner. Instead, it describes the situation and how you feel about it. This helps to open the communication channels and fosters a constructive discussion of the issue.

Decision-Making and Marital-Power Conflicts

There are times in a marriage when one partner influences the behavior of the other. This is called the exercise of marital power.

Julie and Larry, for example, are thinking about moving to a different neighborhood. Julie would like to live in the city so as to be close to work, but Larry would prefer to live in a quiet suburb and commute. If Julie has more power in the relationship than Larry does, then she will be able to influence his decision and they will live in the city. If Larry has more power, then they will live in a suburb.

Since many couples adhere to traditional sex roles, which stress male dominance, they assume that the husband will make the

BOX 10.3   Communication Gone Awry

TEXT: What Is Said	SUBTEXT: What Is Meant
PATRICIA: "God, it's so boring here all day . . . the predictability of washing diapers, feeding children, changing diapers, washing dishes, preparing *your* meal . . ."	He cannot possibly understand the drudgery and sameness of my days. Why should it automatically be me, rather than him, who ends up doing this soul-destroying work?
JOHN: "I realize it must be boring for you, but I try to help as much as I can."	You don't appreciate the sacrifices I am making in my career just because you can't cope with two children like other women seem to manage to do it.
PATRICIA: "Well, it's not enough. You wouldn't do this job. You're out all hours. I could just about manage if you were around here some of the time."	You might think that you are here and help out but, compared to the time that I spend with these children, you do nothing.
JOHN: "Well, I do have to go to work sometimes, you know. I am given a salary for which I'm expected to do something."	You wouldn't be so happy if I didn't earn enough money to provide you with your own car, washing machine, dishwasher and a big house, with no money problems. Yet somehow you expect to have all this without me doing anything. You're just dammed unreasonable.
PATRICIA: "I don't blame you. I wouldn't want to come back to this dump—with a nagging wife and screaming kids."	I do blame you and this whole society for making it so unfair for women. I also feel guilty that I do make so many demands.
JOHN: "Oh, let's not have that routine. You're just never satisfied, no matter what I do. I'm slipping behind in my work as it is."	You don't realize what I am sacrificing for you, you selfish bitch.
PATRICIA: "Oh, so now you're going to try to make me feel guilty for forcing you away from work. Well, if you don't want to be here for your own sake, I don't want you to be here for mine."	I hate you for always making me feel inadequate.
JOHN: "But I *do* want to be here. I like being at home, but you just don't appreciate it. I'm home with you much more than most men are with their wives."	Of course I wouldn't be here so much if you didn't make me feel so goddam guilty. You don't seem to realize what a saint you've got in me.

BOX 10.3   (continued)

TEXT: What Is Said	SUBTEXT: What Is Meant
PATRICIA: "That does it. I hardly ever see you. You come home, pick up the kids and play with them like little dolls and you put them down when you've been entertained enough. You get all the gravy. On weekends it's the same, while you're relaxing reading papers I'm doing the same work as I have to do every other day of the week."	You think you're so generous. I wish you had my life for a week. You would see what it is like: God, I hate you for making me feel like such a bitch.

Source: Quoted from Barrie and Charlotte Hopson, *Intimate Feedback*, pp. 11–13. Copyright © 1974 by Barrie and Charlotte Hopson. Reprinted by permission of Simon & Schuster, a Division of Gulf & Western Corporation.

important family decisions. Consequently, men often have more power in marriages. In addition, if the husband is better educated, older, and has a higher income than his wife, he may have even more power in the relationship, because in our society, people often defer to those who are older and who have more education and a higher occupational and social status.

Studies of marital power have focused on the dominance and power present in family decision making. An important study of family power structures was conducted by Robert Blood and Donald Wolfe. They selected a number of decisions (what kind of car to buy, the husband's choice of jobs, whether the wife should work, and the like) and asked couples whether the husband or the wife—or both—would make the decision.

Their findings revealed that the husband's power increased with his income, education, and occupation. For example, the researchers found that white-collar husbands had more power in family decision making than did blue-collar husbands. They also found that working wives had more power than did nonworking wives, and that a wife's power in family decision making was less when the couple's children were young.

Based on these findings, these researchers formulated the "resource theory" of marital power.[16] This theory proposes that the spouse with the greater resources—education, occupational experience, and social status—wields the greater power and authority in the family.

But a later study by Richard Centers and his colleagues showed that when other areas of decision making—such as clothes buying, entertaining, and home decorating—were added to the ones Blood and

Wolfe used, the husband's power declined.[17] Apparently, a person's power and influence are dependent on the particular decision being made, and the decision-making power shifts back and forth between the husband and the wife. The research on marital power is continuing.

In the early stages of a relationship, a couple usually works out their own balance of power and agrees on a decision-making process. This includes deciding which decisions will be made individually and which will be made jointly. For many couples, the particular areas of power reflect traditional sex roles; that is, the wife decides on such things as the children's clothes, meal planning, and household items, and the husband decides on large family expenditures such as a new car.

There may be a conflict if one partner misuses his or her power or demands more, if there is a crisis such as a spouse becoming sick or suddenly unemployed, or if there is a disagreement about a particular decision. Such situations may change the relationship's balance of power or the satisfaction with the former decision-making process. In such a case, rather than treating it as a win-or-lose situation, the couple can try to negotiate a compromise. Again, open communication is essential to reaching an accord.

Sexual Dissatisfaction

The physical and emotional expressions of love are probably the strongest bonds in an intimate relationship. The desire, love, and fulfillment a person has and conveys to a loved one can be the most satisfying of all personal feelings. And because of the significance and personal nature of physical intimacy, sexual dissatisfaction can be highly frustrating and emotionally damaging.

A couple's sexual satisfaction has high and low periods, just as their general marital satisfaction does. And, of course, the two are related. Often, however, sexual dissatisfaction is seen as the cause of marital dissatisfaction. More often, marital difficulties precede and lead to sexual maladjustment. A couple's intimacy generally is a reflection of their closeness and adjustment.

Many factors can cause sexual dissatisfaction. For example, sexual unhappiness may be a result or a reflection of other marital conflicts. Communication problems, a stressful work situation, financial difficulties, a new baby, and a decrease in the time a couple is able to spend together are only a few of the many factors that may influence sexual needs and desires. Too often, people fail to recognize the pressure of outside situations and focus instead on the tension and ill feelings between them and their partners. A realization that other stresses and conflicts in life can affect one's well-being and happiness can alleviate some of the "pressure to perform" that so often results. Open communication also helps air and resolve such pressure and unhappiness. In sexual matters, as in all others, good communication requires discussion and feedback, not accusations and withdrawal.

Partners are often afraid to reveal their fears regarding their ability to perform sexually and to share with each other what is both pleasurable and dissatisfying about their sexual interaction. Hoping that one's partner will guess one's needs, likes, and desires usually results in feelings of frustration and alienation, since few people are adept at mind reading. If one's sexual needs are not being met, a person can become angry, hurt, and frustrated and may feel rejected and unloved. This can become a vicious cycle in that the more angry and resentful one becomes, the less he or she feels like making love.

Couples can break this kind of cycle by acknowledging their problems, communicating with each other, and, if necessary, being willing to seek outside help. Marriage and sexual counseling are available and can help couples understand and resolve their sexual and marital problems. (Dealing with sexual difficulties is discussed in Chapter 7, "Sexual Interaction.")

Financial Conflicts

Much of a family's communication and decision making centers on money—earning it, spending it, and, sometimes, saving it. For many Americans, however, financial conflict centers on just making ends meet. In 1977, 12 percent of the American population were at or below the government's definition of "poverty," and their concerns were mainly focused on food, shelter, and clothing.[18] But as family income increases, so does the desire to have "bigger and better things," and as a result, debts often increase.

Money problems can place a tremendous strain on a marriage. At times, a couple's money problems may be based on power issues. If the husband is the sole income provider, he may feel that he should also be in charge of how the money is spent. As a result, the wife may feel controlled by and dependent on her husband. But, if the wife works and makes more than her husband does, the husband may feel that his earning power is inadequate and become jealous.

People's values are reflected in how they use and control money. If partners do not have similar ideas about how money should be spent, there may be tensions regarding even small purchases. If one person is thrifty and greatly values money and the other spends money liberally or is careless with it, tensions will almost certainly arise.

A major financial problem in many families is the accumulation of too many debts. Professor Philip Rice explains that there are four reasons why couples go into debt: (1) credit spending, (2) crisis spending, (3) careless or impulsive spending, and (4) compulsive spending.[19]

1. *Credit Spending* The misuse of credit is probably the main reason that couples go into debt. Credit can be extremely helpful in buying a car, home, or major appliance. But because of the availability of "plastic money" and the emphasis of advertising on "buy now, pay later," people often use credit out of habit and run up large bills without weighing the utility of the purchase against time payments and interest charges.

2. *Crisis Spending* Unexpected events can completely undo a couple's budget, and they may be forced to go into debt to meet an emergency. Savings and insurance can be important hedges against illness, fires, accidents, and burglaries. But if a couple is unable to pay for such safeguards, in the event of an emergency, they should carefully consider the available alternatives and compare loans and payments from different institutions.

3. *Careless or Impulsive Spending* Careless or impulsive spending often results in buying inferior goods or items which the family does not need. Budgeting for various expenditures and careful planning can reduce buying on impulse. It may also be wise to carry only a certain amount of cash if one has a tendency to spend what is in his or her pocket.

4. *Compulsive Spending* Compulsive buyers are people who cannot say no. Because they feel that buying gives them power or recognition, they may misuse this power in the marriage and also undermine the couple's financial security.

For couples with different spending habits, a budget may be a marriage saver. Most people think of a budget as a rigid account of every nickel that is spent. A budget, however, may be a very flexible recording of monies coming in and monies being spent. Keeping track of take-home income and expenses allows the couple to see where their money is going and to plan and adjust accordingly. Details on setting up a budget and other financial information can be found in the

Every family member can help plan the family's budget.

Paul Conklin

Appendix, "Family Economics," and in such books as *Sylvia Porter's New Money Book for the 80's*.

In-Law Problems

Most people groan in sympathy when someone mentions an in-law problem, particularly a conflict with a mother-in-law. Yet in-laws and family members can be a tremendous source of support and help to a couple. There can be problems, however, if the couple feels that their in-laws are intruding in their lives, telling them how they should raise their children, or demanding more interaction with the family than the couple feels comfortable with. Families who do not live close to either spouse's parents but feel that they should and would like to have more frequent contact with them may have feelings of guilt.

When a couple marries, they have to establish new kinship relationships and also redefine bondings with their families.

He was stationed at Great Lakes. She was living with the children at her parents' home in Michigan. Their separation was not easy for either of them, and he called home every week to talk with her—just to hear the sound of her voice, he said. One night her voice was heavy with tears and she begged: "Try to find a place near you for the children and me. I can't stand this living with in-laws any more!" Touched and baffled, he replied: "What in-laws are you talking about? You're living with your own folks, aren't you?" Her response was a poignant— "Everybody's in-laws when you're married."[20]

Young married couples more frequently report difficulty with their in-laws than couples who have been married longer do.[21] If a couple has married against their parents' wishes or because of an unplanned pregnancy, their parents may feel freer to criticize or interfere. Also, a young couple may solicit advice or financial help, and this reliance on their families may create additional tensions.

Conflicts Regarding Children

Children often strain a couple's relationship. The responsibilities of being a parent and how this affects people's lives are discussed in Chapter 13, "Parenting."

Parenthood changes a marriage in many ways. Besides the excitement and joy of having a new baby, a couple also may feel the strain of night feedings, added financial responsibility, and different ideas about how the baby should be cared for (what to do when the baby cries, how often to hold or feed it, and the like). During the first months after the baby is brought home, the couple must make adjustments in their work schedules, social activities, sleeping habits, free time, and lovemaking. If the partners are secure in their relationship and have planned for the baby, this time can be tiring but fulfilling. For the unprepared couple or the couple having marital problems, the addition of a new family member may add stress to the relationship.

In recent years, more and more couples are postponing having children or are choosing not to have children. But there can be problems if one partner wants to begin a family but the other wants to wait, or if one partner wants to have children and the other does not.

Contrary to popular opinion, people who have children do not have happier marriages than do people who have chosen not to have children. In an early review of the research studies, Mary Hicks and Marilyn Platt concluded that "perhaps the single most surprising finding to emerge from research is that children tend to detract from, rather than contribute to, marital happiness."[22] Although the differences in happiness reported by parents and childless couples are fairly small, studies consistently show that those who are childless by choice are generally happier than those who have children and those who want children but for some reason cannot have them.[23]

EXPRESSING ANGER AND FIGHTING FAIR

For many, being angry and arguing with a loved one is highly stressful and uncomfortable. Angry words can hurt, and continued conflict can destroy a relationship. And frequently, arguing "only makes things worse."

Yet there are situations in which anger is appropriate. One is when someone is doing something self-destructive, in which case your anger is justified because you do not want the person to suffer or to be hurt. Another situation in which anger is appropriate is when someone is hurting you. You have an obligation to tell your intimates when they hurt you, for presumably they love you and are not hurting you intentionally.

Being angry can also communicate to someone that you care a lot about him or her and that you want to improve your relationship. There are many stresses and tensions in daily living that may produce conflict in the relationship, and not being angry can communicate indifference.

Psychologist George Bach and his colleagues have recognized the importance of anger in healthy intimate relationships and have been

Arguments can hurt.

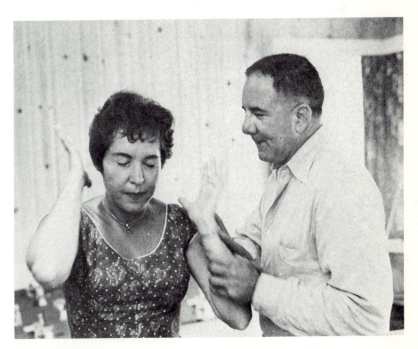

Werner Wolff/Black Star

conducting "fair fighting" clinics for intimates for many years. Bach's experience helped him formulate several suggestions for intimate fighting.

1. Disagreement between intimates is inevitable.
2. Verbal conflicts between intimates help their relationship when they allow partners to be honest with each other and also to release hostile and angry feelings that otherwise would be repressed.
3. Intimates can learn to "fight fair." This includes:
   a. Agreeing on the time, place, and content of fights instead of having them at random times when one or the other person cannot give the issue at hand full attention;
   b. Using "I" statements ("I feel this way when you do that.") rather than accusations and put-downs ("You always do this or that wrong.");
   c. Focusing on the issues at hand instead of dredging up problems from the past; and
   d. Asking for and giving feedback to each other to make sure that the communication is clear and is understood.[24]

It is normal to feel anger occasionally toward an intimate. But rather than feeling guilty or repressing that anger, it is usually better to express it at a suitable time and in an appropriate manner. Such expressions can enhance relationships, as they keep communication channels open and often "clear the air."

VIOLENCE IN THE FAMILY

The ideal family is built on cooperative relationships in which the disagreements, conflicts, and angry feelings that inevitably arise among emotionally close individuals are settled in a spirit of trust, negotiation, and compromise. Unfortunately, however, in many families, violence, psychological abuse, and physical harm are day-to-day fears and frequent occurrences. Spouses—almost always wives—can be coerced, demeaned, and battered; and children can be beaten and subjected to mistreatment of all kinds.

Many people are uncomfortable with the topic of family violence. Our society has long held that family violence is a private matter that should not concern nonfamily members and society at large. When Kitty Genovese, a young New York City woman, was savagely beaten to death by a stranger, many of the people who witnessed the crime said they did not help the screaming victim because they thought that it was a marital argument. Sometimes even the police are hesitant to intervene in family violence, or when they do, as we learn from this woman's experience, they treat it as a "domestic disturbance" rather than as the domestic *violence* that it really is:

Oh sure, the police would come. One would take Jerry in the other room, and the other would sit with me and ask me what I had done to make him so angry and was I sure that I wanted to press charges. They never did anything! And when they would leave, they would pat Jerry on the back, tell him not to do it again, and then tell us to kiss and make up. But as soon as Jerry would hear the car drive off, he would start slugging me again.

From the authors' files

More and more police officers are now being trained in crisis intervention, and many communities now recognize the need for counseling services and women's resource centers, shelters, and *safe houses* (residential facilities for battered women and their children). In addition, judges, lawyers, and social service personnel are becoming more aware of their responsibility to protect the rights of abused family members. There are an increasing number of places to which victims of family violence can turn for help. They do not have to suffer in silence.

Myths about family violence help perpetuate it. Some of the most pervasive myths about wife battering and child abuse are discussed in the following sections.

Wife Battering

Although statistics vary widely, researchers estimate that over 50 percent of marital relationships and living-together arrangements involve some form of psychological or physical abuse.[25] In sociologist Richard Gelles's study of eighty families, 55 percent of the couples had used physical violence on each other. And in those families that had engaged in violent acts, 26 percent of them reported that conjugal violence was a regular occurrence.[26] In a discussion of legislative issues regarding battered women, the U.S. Department of Labor concluded that "available statistics suggest that approximately 40 percent of all American marriages will experience at least one incident of violence, 15 to 20 percent will experience violence periodically, and at least 5 percent will be plagued by chronic wife beating."[27]

Telephone "hotlines" are available to help victims of family violence.

B. Kliewe/Jeroboam

Three common myths about wife battering are:

1. *Marital violence happens only in families of low socioeconomic status and educational level.* Numerous studies have shown, however, that battering occurs at all income, occupational, and educational levels. Wife batterers include doctors, lawyers, police officers, clergymen, and businessmen, as well as nonprofessional workers. One reason for the myth that marital violence is more prevalent in poorer families may be that middle and upper class families are less likely to call the police or to seek help from public agencies.[28]

2. *Women are masochistic and want to be beaten.* Most battered women return to the battering relationship, and this is cited as evidence that women "must want it." They return to their relationships, however, not because they want to be hurt, but for numerous other reasons. Victims of wife battering are frightened, often ashamed, and suffering tremendous emotional strain. Many fear that leaving the husband will only provoke him to more violence. Many women do not leave their abusive husbands because they have no way to financially support themselves and their children. Some women have been told by other family members, police officers, and counselors that they are

responsible for their husband's violence, and they have come to believe it themselves.

Many couples in abusive relationships undergo repeated cycles of violence. In her interviews with battered women, psychologist Lenore Walker found that a battering cycle appears to have three phases.[29] Although both the timing and the intensity vary within each couple and among couples, generally the partners experience an escalation of tension in their relationship (phase 1) before an explosion of violence occurs (phase 2). After the violent eruption, the husband is often repentant, contrite, charming, and loving (phase 3). He promises never to do it again, and the wife, wanting to believe that he really will change, remains in the relationship. The cycle, however, is repeated again and again. Walker found that a batterer typically seeks help only after his wife has left him and he hopes that obtaining help will aid him in getting her back.[30]

3. *Men who beat their wives are abnormal and degenerate.* There is no evidence that wife batterers are actually psychotic, or mentally ill—but they do have a psychological problem. Wife battering generally is a learned behavior, an inappropriate response to stress. Research has shown that men who as children were subjected to or witnessed violence in their families are themselves more likely to be involved in marital violence.[31]

Child Abuse

In American society, using a certain amount of physical force to discipline children is often deemed necessary, as expressed in the saying "spare the rod and spoil the child." Spanking, in particular, is seen as an acceptable means of discipline and control. Yet physical punishment may teach children not only that violence is acceptable but also that it is the only effective way of coping with a crisis.

Tens of thousands of children each year are subjected to serious physical and emotional injury when their parents or caretakers lose control and, in a state of anger, physically harm them. The National Center on Child Abuse and Neglect estimates that currently over 200,000 children a year are physically abused, and between 60,000 and 100,000 children a year are sexually abused.[32] As the center concludes, the number of reported cases is probably just the tip of the iceberg, and "estimates suggest a problem of staggering proportions yet to be revealed."[33]

As with wife battering, there are several myths about child abuse.

Among the most common are that abuse and neglect are problems of the poor, that abusive parents simply do not realize their own strength, and that abusive parents are psychotic.[34]

The facts, however, suggest different conclusions. Children are abused in families of all socioeconomic levels, races, and nationalities. Although minorities and lower income families do account for proportionately larger figures in the statistics, these families are often clients of such public services as welfare agencies, municipal hospitals, and outpatient clinics, and consequently have more contacts with agency professionals.[35] Because their lives are subjected to more professional scrutiny, it is more likely that abusive situations will be discovered and reported.

Parents do not misjudge their own strength. Child abuse is a complex pattern of behaviors, and many factors such as stress, unrealistic expectations, and unwanted pregnancy may contribute to an abusive interaction. And finally, abusive parents are not psychotic, although they do have a serious psychological problem.

The research on child abuse indicates that abusive parents themselves were often abused and maltreated when they were children: "There is one basic premise that is probably most helpful in eliminating attitudes of anger and punitiveness toward abusive and neglectful parents; their parenting behavior is often the product of their own childhood experiences."[36]

Counseling can help a parent deal with his or her own experiences as an abused child, help the individual recognize his or her tendency to react to a crisis with violence, and also learn the different stages of childhood development and what the realistic expectations are for a child of a certain age. In addition, there are telephone "helplines" and "hotlines" available, and these and other community agencies can suggest counseling and help for both children and parents.

SUMMARY

Marriage is neither a "happily ever after," romantic fantasy nor a conflict-filled, domestic grind. Although at times marriage can be intensely fulfilling, at other times a couple can have problems and be dissatisfied. Overall, a marriage can be highly satisfying if a couple focuses their energy on their relationship and works to make it successful.

There are different types of marital interaction. Utilitarian marriages fulfill security and stability needs and are described as workable and rational. Intrinsic marriages are characterized by deep emotional involvement and the sharing of many activities. Every marriage goes through a series of developmental stages over the years, called the family life cycle. For most couples, marital satisfaction is greatest in the early years, declines during the parenting stages, and then begins to increase in the later years.

Over the course of a marriage, couples may face several problems. The most common include communication and decision-making problems, marital-power conflicts, sexual dissatisfaction, financial conflicts, in-law problems, and conflicts regarding children. Each of these can be resolved, and often is helped by more effective communication.

There are times when family members become angry with each other, but it is possible for even the most heated conflicts to be resolved in an atmosphere of trust and common interest. Some persons, however, are unable to control their anger and as a result inflict physical and psychological harm on their spouses or children. Counseling and other forms of assistance can help people express their anger appropriately rather than through violence.

CONSIDER THIS

Cliff and Marcia came directly home from the restaurant where they had had dinner with another couple. Cliff was in a good mood and didn't notice Marcia's silence until she didn't respond to a question.

CLIFF: What's the matter, honey?

MARCIA: Why did you pick up the check tonight? They could have paid their half. Don't you realize we're down to our last twenty again?

CLIFF: I like to treat my friends. So what's the big deal?

MARCIA: You know we don't have a lot of money.

CLIFF: It wasn't that much money. And they do nice things for us.

MARCIA: Now you're making me feel guilty, as though I watch every nickel we spend, but someone has to. You always do it without thinking about the money. It's the same with your Dad.

CLIFF: He's my Dad and I want to help him.

MARCIA: He doesn't need that hundred dollars a month as much as we do.

CLIFF: You can't just ignore your parents, you know.

MARCIA: I think you're more concerned about other people than you are about me and the fact that we're slowly going broke.

Questions   1.   How could this incident have been prevented?
2.   Is Marcia's anger toward how Cliff handles money justified?

3. Which of the two do you think has more power over their financial decisions?
4. Is Marcia fighting fair when she brings up her anger toward her father-in-law?
5. When you have disagreements, how do your conversations with your partner compare with this argument?

NOTES

1. Richard J. Udry, *The Social Context of Marriage*, Philadelphia, Lippincott, 1975, p. 240.
2. Carl R. Rogers, *Becoming Partners*, New York, Dell Pub., Co., Inc., 1972.
3. John F. Cuber and Peggy B. Harroff, *Sex and the Significant Americans*, New York, Penguin, 1965, p. 108.
4. Ibid., p. 45.
5. Ibid., p. 50.
6. Ibid., p. 53.
7. Evelyn Millis Duvall, *Family Development*, Philadelphia, Lippincott, 1971, p. 121.
8. Paul C. Glick and Arthur J. Norton, "Marrying, Divorcing, and Living Together in the U.S. Today," *Population Bulletin*, 32, No. 5, Washington, D.C., Population Reference Bureau (1977): 20.
9. Paul C. Glick and Arthur J. Norton, "Marrying, Divorcing, and Living Together in the U.S. Today"; "A Statistical Portrait of Women in the United States: 1975," *Current Population Reports: Special Studies*, Series P–23, No. 10 (February 1980): 29.
10. James Lieberman, "The Prevention of Marital Problems," in Henry Grunebaum and Jacob Christ, eds., *Contemporary Marriage: Structure, Dynamics, and Therapy*, Boston, Little, Brown, 1976, p. 321.
11. Wesley Burr, "Satisfaction with Various Aspects of Marriage over the Life-Cycle," *Journal of Marriage and the Family*, 32 (February 1970): 29–37; Boyd Rollins and Kenneth Cannon, "Marital Satisfaction over the Family Life Cycle: A Reevaluation," *Journal of Marriage and the Family*, 36 (July 1974): 271–282.
12. There are several methodological problems yet to be worked out. See, for example, Steven Nock, "The Family Life Cycle: Empirical or Conceptual Tool?" *Journal of Marriage and the Family*, 41 (February 1979): 15–26.
13. N. D. Glenn, "Psychological Well-Being in the Postparental Stage: Some Evidence from National Surveys," *Journal of Marriage and the Family*, 37 (February 1975): 105–10.

14. Richard Hunt and Edward Rydman, *Creative Marriage*, Boston, Allyn & Bacon, 1979, p. 27.

15. Interview with John L. Schimel, "Constant Criticism of One's Mate," *Medical Aspects of Human Sexuality*, 14 (May 1980): 76.

16. Robert Blood and Donald Wolfe, *Husbands and Wives: The Dynamics of Married Living*, Glencoe, Ill., Free Press, 1960.

17. Richard Centers, Bertram Raven, and Aroldo Rodriques, "Conjugal Power Structure: A Reexamination," *American Sociological Review*, 37 (April 1972): 264–278.

18. The poverty threshold in 1977 for a nonfarm family of four persons was $6,191. According to the U.S. government, in 1977 there were 24.7 million persons in poverty, 11.6 percent of the total population. U.S. Bureau of the Census, *Current Population Reports*, Series P–60, No. 19, "Characteristics of the Population Below the Poverty Line: 1977," Washington, D.C., U.S. Government Printing Office, 1979, p. 1.

19. F. Philip Rice, *Marriage and Parenthood*, Boston, Allyn & Bacon, 1979, p. 373.

20. Evelyn M. Duvall, "Marriage Makes In-Laws," in Ruth Cavan, ed., *Marriage and Family in the Modern World Readings*, New York, Thomas Y. Crowell, 1974, p. 339.

21. Paul H. Landis, *Making the Most of Marriage*, Englewood Cliffs, N.J., Prentice-Hall, 1975, p. 286.

22. Mary W. Hicks and Marilyn Platt, "Marital Happiness and Stability: A Review of Research in the Sixties," *Journal of Marriage and the Family*, 32 (November 1970): 569.

23. See, for example, Robert Ryder, "Longitudinal Data Relating Marriage Satisfaction and Having a Child," *Journal of Marriage and the Family*, November 1973, pp. 604–607; Susan Bram, "To Have or Have Not: A Social Psychological Study of Voluntarily Childless Couples, Parents-To-Be, and Parents," Ph.D. dissertation, University of Michigan, 1974; Sharon K. Houseknecht, "Childlessness and Marital Adjustment," *Journal of Marriage and the Family*, 41 (May 1979): 259–265.

24. George R. Bach and Peter Wyden, *The Intimate Enemy*, New York, Morrow, 1969; George R. Bach and Ronald M. Deutsch, *Pairing*, New York, Avon, 1970.

25. Lenore E. Walker, *The Battered Woman*, New York, Harper & Row, Pub., 1979, p. ix; Murray A. Straus, "Wife Beating: Causes, Treatments, and Research Needs," in *Battered Women: Issues of Public Policy*, Washington, D.C., U.S. Commission on Civil Rights, January 1978, p. 467.

26. Richard J. Gelles, *The Violent Home*, Beverly Hills, Calif., Sage Publications, Inc., 1972, p. 184.

27. Women's Bureau, U.S. Department of Labor, *Legislative Issues on Battered Women*, February 1978, p. 1.

28. George Miller, "The Battered Family: A Congressional Response," *Change*, 9, (Spring 1980): 11.
29. Lenore E. Walker, *The Battered Woman*, Chap. 3, pp. 55–70.
30. Ibid.
31. Ibid., p. 38.
32. U.S. National Center on Child Abuse and Neglect, *Child Sexual Abuse: Incest, Assault, and Sexual Exploitation*, August 1978, p. 3.
33. U.S. National Center on Child Abuse and Neglect, "An Overview of the Problem," *Child Abuse and Neglect: The Problem and Its Management*, (1975): 9.
34. Ibid., p. 11.
35. Ibid.
36. Ibid., p. 17.

SUGGESTED READINGS

Appleton, William. "Why Marriages Become Dull." *Medical Aspects of Human Sexuality*, March 1980, pp. 73–85. An overview of the causes of marital boredom and suggestions for its resolution.

Hopson, Bernie, and Charlotte Hopson. *Intimate Feedback*, Simon & Schuster, 1975. A collection of communication exercises for improving intimate relationships.

Rice, F. Phillip. *Marriage and Parenthood*. Boston, Allyn & Bacon, 1979. See Part 4, "Marital Relationships," for an extensive discussion of marital interaction and conflict.

Rogers, Carl R. *Becoming Partners*, New York, Dell Pub. Co., Inc., 1972. Case examples are used to present the author's philosophy of creating lasting, committed relationships.

Walker, Lenore E. *The Battered Woman*. New York, Harper & Row, Pub., 1979. An investigation of the myths and realities of wife battering.

IV PARENTHOOD

BECOMING
A PARENT

Be fruitful and multiply and replenish the earth.

Genesis 1:27–28

To most people, becoming a parent means producing biologically related children through sexual intercourse, pregnancy, and childbirth. The father's sperm and the mother's egg carry hereditary information *(genes)* that determines the physical and some behavioral characteristics of their child. When the sperm and egg fuse at fertilization, forming the first cell of the child's body, two human generations become inextricably linked by one of the strongest of human ties—shared heredity.

Not all parents have their own, biologically related children. Some become parents by adoption and others become stepparents by marrying someone who already has a child.

From childhood onward, most people, particularly most women, are taught that having a child is one of the most important achievements in life. Many believe that being a parent is such a special and rewarding part of life that it would be a mistake not to experience it. Therefore, most people never question becoming a parent but simply assume that they will have children, just as their parents did.

People want children for various reasons.[1] A couple may believe that a child is the greatest expression of their love. Others may see having a child as a way to leave a legacy of themselves to the world—a way of achieving some kind of immortality. For some, having children is a way to carry on the family name. Some couples may feel pressured by their families or by societal or religious expectations to have children, and others may hope that having a child will improve their marriage. Being a parent can make some people feel important, needed, proud, or that they are fulfilling their ideas of feminine or masculine roles. And many prospective parents see children as adding fun, excitement, love, and companionship to their lives.

Giving birth to and raising a child is an enormous responsibility for both father and mother, and it often requires major adjustments in their personal lives. It certainly requires a change in the distribution of family resources—time, money, energy, and physical space. It may alter the career plans of one or both parents and change how leisure time is spent; for example, travel may become more difficult. As Joan Ditzion and Dennie Wolf of the Boston Women's Health Book Collective point out,

The decision to parent cannot be taken lightly. As soon as we've decided to become parents through pregnancy, adoption or stepparenting, we find ourselves confronted with new emotional decisions. We want to develop a strong bond with our child and at the same time maintain our partnership, our adult friendships, as well as our other involvements in the outside world. What we discover even before we have a baby is that our lives are thrown off balance once we become parents and we need time to establish a new equilibrium.

The period of parenting is an intense one. Never again will we know such responsibility, such productive and hard work, such potential for isolation in the caretaking role, and such intimacy and close involvement in the growth and development of another human being.[2]

This chapter is about becoming a parent. In it, we examine pregnancy, childbirth, and adoption.

BECOMING PREGNANT

For most couples, becoming parents includes pregnancy—a forty-week period during which a child develops inside the mother's uterus. Every pregnancy begins with *fertilization*, the fusion of a sperm cell from the father and an egg cell (or ovum) from the mother (see Figure 11.1). Fertilization forms the first cell of the child, which, over the next nine months, multiplies into the many billions of specialized cells of a newborn human being (see Figures 11.2 and 11.3).

When a man ejaculates during sexual intercourse, millions of sperm cells are released into the vagina. Propelled by the swimming motion of their long tails, the tadpolelike sperm travel through the uterus and into

FIGURE 11.1
A human sperm and
egg in fertilization.
Many sperm cells
approach the egg, but
only one fertilizes it.

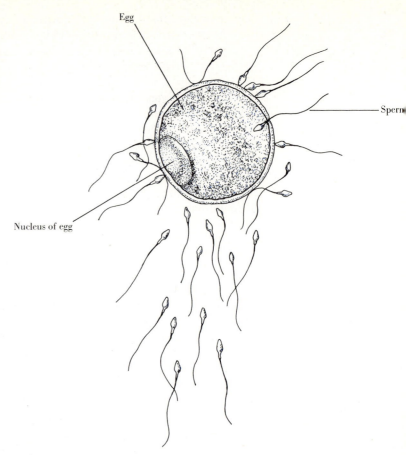

Egg

Sperm

Nucleus of egg

the Fallopian tubes. Approximately once each month an egg is released from one of the woman's ovaries *(ovulation)*, and it may meet the sperm in one of the Fallopian tubes (see Figure 11.4). After one sperm penetrates the egg, the fertilized egg moves to the uterus, where it attaches to the inner lining, and pregnancy begins.

Sperm and Egg Production

Human males and females are capable of reproduction after they become sexually mature during adolescence. From the time of sexual maturity, men normally produce about 150 million sperm cells a day for many years. Women, on the other hand, do not produce eggs daily nor do they usually produce eggs for as long a time as men produce sperm. On becoming sexually mature, women usually produce only one

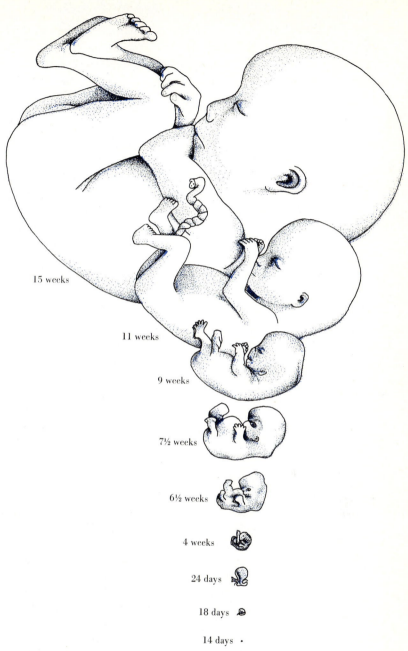

FIGURE 11.2
Some stages in human fetal development

15 weeks

11 weeks

9 weeks

7½ weeks

6½ weeks

4 weeks

24 days

18 days

14 days

egg about once each month, and egg production stops altogether for most women at menopause, which usually occurs between the ages of forty and fifty-five.

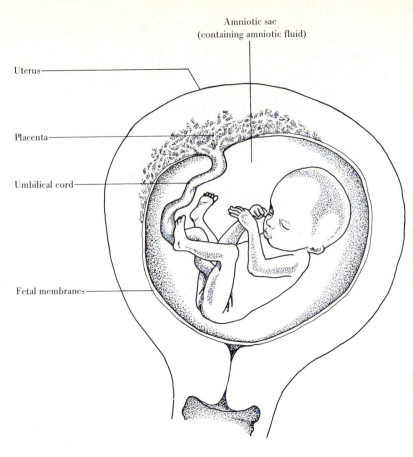

FIGURE 11.3
Fifteen-week-old fetus
in uterus

Amniotic sac
(containing amniotic fluid)

Uterus

Placenta

Umbilical cord

Fetal membranes

The Menstrual Cycle

The almost monthly production of eggs is the basis of a woman's *menstrual cycle*. During each cycle of egg production, a woman's body undergoes several hormone-induced changes that prepare her body for pregnancy should an egg be fertilized. One of these changes is the thickening of the inner lining of the uterus, called the *endometrium*. The thickening of the endometrium enables the uterus to nurture a fertilized egg and support the first stages of pregnancy. Besides the thickening of the endometrium, several small blood vessels in the uterus develop so as to bring maternal nutrients to the developing baby during pregnancy. But if the egg is not fertilized, the thickened endometrium is sloughed off. This produces the loss of about one to several tablespoons of blood and some tissue debris, which leaves the body through the vagina over the course of three to six days. This

FIGURE 11.4

The pathway of sperm
from the vagina to a
Fallopian tube to
fertilize an egg

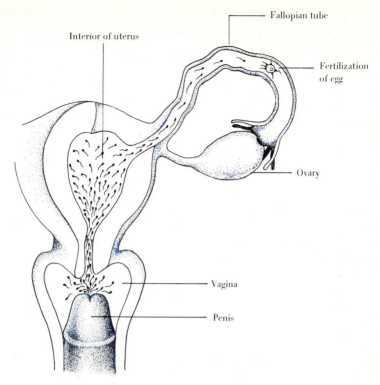

Interior of uterus

Fallopian tube

Fertilization of egg

Ovary

Vagina

Penis

periodic discharge is called *menstruation*, also known as a woman's "period."

The length and regularity of the menstrual cycle varies from woman to woman. Most have menstrual cycles of about twenty-eight days, with cycles of between twenty-four and thirty-five days being the most common. Some women have shorter or longer cycles, or cycles that occur approximately monthly, but with a varied number of days between menstruations.

For some women, menstruation may be unpleasant. Some women experience abdominal pain or "cramps" during their menstrual period. Often, menstrual cramps can be alleviated by taking medications that inhibit the action of *prostaglandins*, hormones that cause the uterus to contract. Another common menstrual difficulty is *amenorrhea*, the cessation of menstrual periods. The most frequent reason that menstrual periods stop is pregnancy, but many other factors can interfere with normal menstruation. These factors include any kind of psychological stress, such as grief, depression, psychic trauma, marital or sexual problems, excess fatigue, and even the fear of pregnancy, as well as nutritional abnormalities—including crash diets or obesity—birth control pills, and disease.

PREGNANCY

The First Signs of Pregnancy

Within two to four weeks after fertilization, the first signs of pregnancy appear. Perhaps the most commonly recognized sign of pregnancy is a missed menstrual period. Other signs of pregnancy are occasional nausea and vomiting, especially on awakening—called "morning sickness"—enlarged and tender breasts, increased fatigue, and increased frequency of urination.

Very often the appearance of some or all the common signs of pregnancy convince a couple that pregnancy has occurred, but actual proof of pregnancy requires confirmation that a fetus is present in the uterus. This information is most often obtained by analyzing a woman's urine for a special hormone called *human chorionic gonadotropin*, or HCG, which is produced only during pregnancy. Doctors or family-planning agencies usually perform pregnancy tests, but women can also administer such tests to themselves with home pregnancy kits. In addition a doctor can feel certain changes in the size, shape, and texture of the uterus, which also suggest that a woman is pregnant.

The Duration of Pregnancy

The duration of the average human pregnancy is 280 days, which is forty weeks, or about nine calendar months. The actual time of a baby's normal development from conception to birth, however, is 266 days. This discrepancy arises because doctors mark the beginning of pregnancy from the first day of menstrual flow of the cycle during which fertilization occurred. Thus, if fertilization took place fourteen days after the beginning of menstruation, then 266 days later the baby would be born. In this case, the duration of pregnancy would total 280 days.

Because it is sometimes not possible to establish the exact day of menstrual flow, the prediction of the day of birth can be wrong. Therefore, some women deliver a week or two earlier than scheduled or a week or two later, not because the length of time of fetal development is erratic, but because the estimation of the day of birth is incorrect.

The duration of pregnancy will be shorter than expected if the baby is born prematurely. Approximately 5 percent of all pregnancies last fewer than thirty-seven weeks.[3]

Ensuring a Healthy Pregnancy

Every child deserves the opportunity to develop a healthy mind and body. A pregnant woman can help ensure a healthy pregnancy for herself and her child by attending to certain health practices:

Obtaining Professional Prenatal Care

The earlier and more regularly a pregnant woman receives professional prenatal care, the fewer problems she will have during pregnancy and childbirth and the more likely she will deliver a healthy baby. Prenatal care can screen for and treat certain diseases of pregnancy (toxemia, diabetes of pregnancy, and various infections), and it can help prepare

Professional prenatal care helps to prepare a mother and her family for the birthing experience.

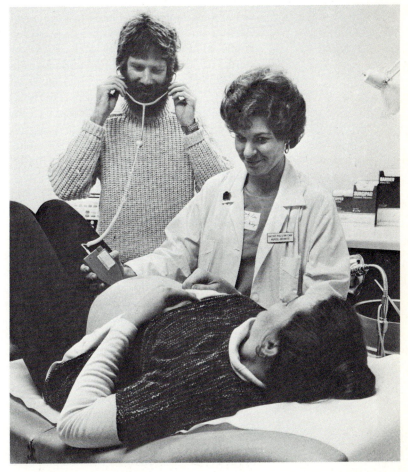

Jean-Claude Lejeune/Stock, Boston

the mother and her family for the birthing experience. It can also screen for some birth defects (see Box 11.1).

Refraining from Smoking and Drinking

Studies show that mothers who smoke cigarettes and drink alcohol may impair the health of their developing babies.[4] It is possible that many nonfood substances have harmful effects on a fetus, which is why pregnant women are advised to refrain from ingesting *any* drugs, even aspirin and caffeine, unless permitted to do so by a physician.

Being Physically Active

During pregnancy, a woman's body takes on unfamiliar proportions and may increase in weight up to 20 percent. This can make her feel lethargic, uncomfortable, unattractive, and clumsy. Coping with the increased size and weight can also produce a few aches and pains in some muscles and joints. By being physically active, a pregnant woman can become more accustomed to the temporary changes in her body, and she can also better prepare herself for the physical demands of childbirth. In addition, physical activity improves blood circulation, which can lessen swelling and varicose veins in the lower legs. Some very athletic women engage in their sports almost to the day of delivery. Pregnant women who are not usually active are often encouraged to undertake an exercise program to maintain correct posture and strengthen abdominal muscles. A pregnant woman's exercise should not be much more strenuous than that before pregnancy. In this matter, as with others pertaining to pregnancy, a physician should be consulted.

Eating a Nutritious Diet

A fetus grows and develops rapidly throughout pregnancy, and during this time, perhaps more than at any other time of life, an ample supply of nutrients is required to ensure proper development. All the baby's nutrients come from the mother via the *placenta,* a special organ that forms in the uterus only during pregnancy to transport both nutrients from the mother to the fetus and waste products from the fetus to the mother. The baby's and mother's blood streams never mix; materials are passed from one blood stream to the other through the placenta. Therefore, a pregnant woman is the major influence on the nutritional status of her baby, and she must be aware of the need to "eat for two"—ensuring that her diet contains adequate nutrients for both herself and her child.

Many women worry about gaining weight during pregnancy. A mother-to-be can expect to gain about twenty-two to twenty-six pounds, much of which comes gradually in the last two-thirds of pregnancy. About seven of these pounds are contributed by the fetus. The enlarged uterus accounts for another two pounds, and the placenta and amniotic fluid each contribute about one pound. About four to eight pounds of

Approximately 3 percent of all newborn infants in the United States have some sort of birth defect—a physical malformation of one (or more) of the body's organs, a disturbance in the way the body functions, mental retardation, or other behavioral abnormalities. Birth defects can be caused by infection with German measles (rubella) during the early weeks of pregnancy, exposure to x-rays and other kinds of radiation, and ingestion during pregnancy of certain kinds of drugs such as synthetic hormones and alcohol. About two thousand kinds of birth defects are caused by abnormalities in the child's genes. Sickle-cell anemia, Tay-Sachs disease, phenylketonuria, Down's syndrome, and cystic fibrosis are examples of inherited birth defects.

The exposure of a woman to certain environmental hazards or a family history of a certain disease may be reason to suspect that a child might be born with a particular birth defect. The mother's age may also be a reason. For example, it is known that the incidence of Down's syndrome, a condition characterized by certain physical deformities and mental retardation, is higher in children born to older mothers than in those born to younger ones. For mothers in their twenties, the incidence of having a Down's child is less than one in two thousand, but over the age of forty, the incidence of Down's syndrome is about one in forty.

It is possible to detect a suspected birth defect early in pregnancy through a test called *amniocentesis*, in which a doctor analyzes a small volume of amniotic fluid, the liquid from the sac that surrounds the developing fetus. This fluid contains some fetal cells, which can be analyzed to determine if any abnormalities exist. At present, about fifty kinds of birth defects can be diagnosed prenatally. Most of the time, the results of amniocentesis show that everything is normal, which, of course, relieves any anxiety the parents may have had. If the results show that an abnormality exists, the parents may choose to have an abortion.

Prenatal diagnosis by amniocentesis can also be used to determine the sex of a fetus, and some parents are using it to choose the sex of their child. Many doctors believe that sex preselection using amniocentesis and abortion is an abuse of the technique.

fluid are added to the maternal system as extra blood volume and extracellular fluid, and the mother-to-be may gain about four pounds of body fat. Figure 11.5 shows the growth of the uterus during pregnancy. Soon after birth a woman begins to lose the body water accumulated during pregnancy, and with exercise and diet control, she can lose all the body fat accumulated during pregnancy and regain muscle tone.

Psychological Changes During Pregnancy

Pregnancy can be a time of intense feelings, not only for the mother-to-be, but also for her husband and others close to her. Both prospective parents may experience enthusiasm, excitement, joy,

FIGURE 11.5

Growth of the uterus
during pregnancy

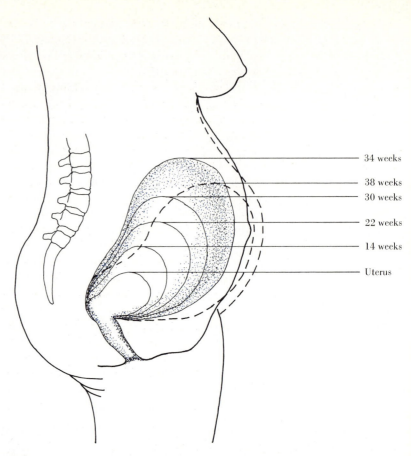

34 weeks

38 weeks

30 weeks

22 weeks

14 weeks

Uterus

anticipation, frustration, irritability, fears about the baby's condition, uncertainties about their suitability as parents, and concern about changing roles and responsibilities in the marriage. At times, one or the other may resent the pregnancy as an intrusion on the couple's usual life style. And that resentment can be followed by guilt for not being enthusiastic about the pregnancy all the time. To recognize that both positive and negative feelings are normal in pregnancy and to accept them with patience and understanding are important to a rewarding pregnancy experience.

Pregnancy can also bring about a change in the desire for sex. During pregnancy, some women have increased desires for love, affection, and sex. Other women lose interest in sex for the entire pregnancy period. Men have similar responses. Some may wish to express their joy over the pregnancy by increased sexual contact. Others may refrain from sexual activity for fear of harming the fetus or for other reasons.

Unless there is some medical problem that would be worsened by sex, sexual intercourse during pregnancy is permissible. Couples can be guided by their sexual feelings and by consultations with their doctor when in doubt.

Several programs and organizations are available to help parents-to-be have a safe and joyous pregnancy and childbirthing experience. These are usually six-to-eight week courses, sometimes called "natural childbirth" or Lamaze classes. Almost all childbirth preparation courses teach the prospective parents the basic biology of pregnancy and childbirth, and they also teach breathing and relaxation exercises to help make the actual delivery of the baby proceed more smoothly and comfortably. While attending the courses, the parents-to-be meet other expectant couples with whom they can share normal anxieties and experiences. The classes also discuss the many choices of childbirth, such as a traditional hospital birth, birth in a homelike setting in a hospital with the father present, or perhaps birth at home.

Studies have shown that childbirth preparation classes have several positive effects.[5] For example, women who participate in childbirth preparation are likely to have less pain and discomfort in childbirth, are likely to require less medication in childbirth, and are likely to have fewer childbirth complications. Moreover, prepared women are more likely to have positive attitudes toward childbirth and parenting. Fathers also benefit from childbirth preparation classes. Husbands who attend classes tend to feel more comfortable about sharing the

Pregnant women attend a childbirth preparation class.

Paul Conklin

childbirth experience with their wives and about helping during childbirth, and they are also more likely to be interested and involved in parenting responsibilities after the baby is born. Overall, childbirth preparation classes (and also educational programs for parents) are highly beneficial, because most people enter parenthood with few parenting skills and many unrealistic expectations about childbirth and parenthood.

CHILDBIRTH

By the end of pregnancy, the fetus is physiologically ready to leave the protection of the mother's body and face the outside world. For the parents, childbirth brings exultation, relief that the nine months of waiting are over, and surprise at the baby's gender and appearance. For onlookers and family members, childbirth elicits wonder, sometimes reverence, and concern for the condition of the mother and baby. No one knows what a new baby feels when being born, but surely the feelings are intense. Frederick Leboyer, a French doctor, has developed a birthing procedure involving dim lighting, soft music, and the delivery of the baby into a bath of warm water to try to minimize the presumed psychic trauma of birth.[6]

A few weeks before the onset of childbirth, or *labor*, the fetus becomes positioned for birth by descending in the uterus. This is known as *lightening*. When this happens the pressure on some of the mother's internal organs is relieved, and she may have less difficulty breathing, standing, or digesting food. In about 95 percent of all births, the fetus is in a head-down position. When not head-down, the fetus may be head-up or lying sideways. In nearly all cases the fetus' legs are tucked up against the abdomen in the "fetal position."

The entire process of labor is usually divided into three stages. The first stage is usually the longest, lasting from eight to twelve hours, and sometimes longer in first-time mothers, but usually only a few hours in experienced mothers. During this stage the mother's cervix dilates to permit the baby to pass out of the uterus. The second stage of labor is the actual emergence of the baby from the mother's body. It can take a few minutes or an hour or two. As the baby emerges, the head and shoulders rotate to make exiting easier (see Figure 11.6). The third stage of labor, the *afterbirth*, is the expulsion of the placenta, which usually takes only a few minutes.

The onset of labor is marked by the appearance of strong, rhythmic, and eventually frequent uterine contractions which provide the expul-

FIGURE 11.6
Childbirth: *a* and *b*, as the fetus begins to emerge from the uterus, its head bends forward, bringing the chin to the upper chest; *c* and *d*, the fetus' head rotates from a sideways position to facing forward; *e*, the head extends upward to permit an easier exit from the vagina; *f*, after emergence of the head, the head rotates back toward the side to facilitate the birth of the shoulders.

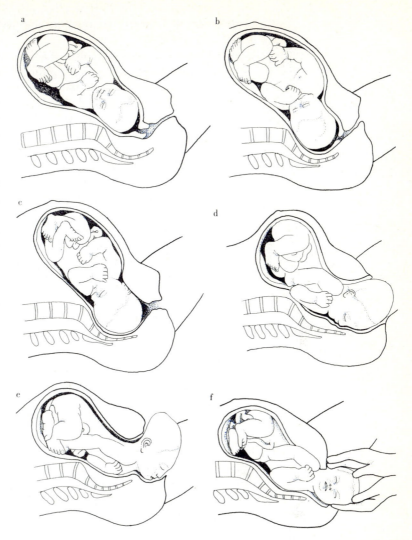

sive force necessary to push the baby out of the mother's body. During the last half of pregnancy, a woman may have intermittent uterine contractions that are not associated with true labor. These are called *Braxton-Hicks contractions*, and they can be distinguished by their occurrence at irregular intervals and their rather short duration. The contractions of true labor usually start as roughly minute-long contractions coming at approximately ten- or twenty-minute intervals. As labor progresses, these regular contractions usually become more intense, frequent, and of longer duration, perhaps up to ninety seconds. By the second stage of labor, the contractions may occur every one and a half to two minutes.

The traditional hospital birth begins with the mother being "prepped" for delivery and perhaps given a tranquilizer, a pain-killing drug, or an injection of an anesthetic drug in the pelvic region to eliminate all pelvic sensations during labor. She spends the first stage of labor in a bed in a maternity ward, but when the baby is about to emerge during the second stage of labor, she is transferred to a delivery room where a doctor and nursing attendants assist with the remainder of the birth. The doctor may perform an *episiotomy*, which is a surgical incision between the vagina and the anus to enlarge the vaginal exit and thereby prevent tears in the vagina and neighboring structures. After the baby is born, mucus and fluid are suctioned from its mouth, and often it is made to cry to encourage it to breathe. The mother usually holds the newborn infant for a few minutes before it is taken to a nursery and the episiotomy is repaired, after which she is taken to a recovery room.

Choosing the Birthing Place

One of the characteristics of the traditional hospital birth is that the families have little control over the procedure. Once the doctor is selected, virtually all decisions about how the birth is carried out are left to the doctor and the hospital's obstetrical assistants. Many families appreciate this, for they trust the doctor and hospital staff to make decisions that they feel unqualified to make. Other families, however, want more control over their birthing experience. For example, they might find a traditional hospital setting too formal and cold for what they feel is a joyous, warm occasion, and consequently they may want to have their baby in an alternative birth center or at home. Because unforeseen medical emergencies can arise during childbirth, many people prefer the alternative birth center—a hospital-based delivery room with a homelike atmosphere—to giving birth at home where no emergency medical help is immediately available.

Besides choosing the birth setting, couples may want to make other decisions about the birth experience (see Table 11.1). They may want the father to be present in the room and to assist the mother:

Marie was in labor for sixteen hours. I was with her in the birthing room for the entire time, coaching her breathing, trying to make her comfortable, and doing whatever I could to give support. Soon after the top of Melissa's head appeared, Marie gave birth to our daughter rather easily. Immediately after she was born, the nurse-midwife handed

TABLE 11.1 Preparing for Childbirth: Factors to Consider

1. Birth setting
   Hospital delivery room; alternative or home-style birth center; childbirth at home
2. Preparation of mother
   Shaving of pubic hair; prebirth enema; episiotomy and intravenous feeding at onset of labor
3. Routine in birth setting
   Can mother walk around? Are visiting hours flexible?
4. Birthing attendants
   Doctor; nurses; midwife
5. Amount, quality, and kind of attention mother and baby receive from birthing attendants
6. Mother's body position during childbirth
7. Conditions for medical intervention
   Induced labor; Cesarean section. Can vaginal delivery be attempted even if previous births were by Cesarean section? Can husband be present during Cesarean section?
8. Procedures for dealing with medical emergencies
9. Will mother and father (if attending the birth) be able to hold the baby immediately after birth?
10. Insurance coverage

Melissa to me. I hugged her gently and put her on Marie's chest. After a while, everyone left the room and the three of us spent the night together.

From the authors' files

Friends, other family members, and even siblings of the newborn child may be present as well. The mother may wish to be alert and in full control of her body and therefore may try to deliver with no anesthesia or other pain relief.

BREAST-FEEDING

Mothers usually can choose whether or not to breast-feed their infants. In the early weeks of pregnancy milk ducts and breast tissue proliferate, and by mid-pregnancy the breasts produce a yellowish fluid, called *colostrum,* which may sometimes leak from the nipples.

A father attending the
birth of his child

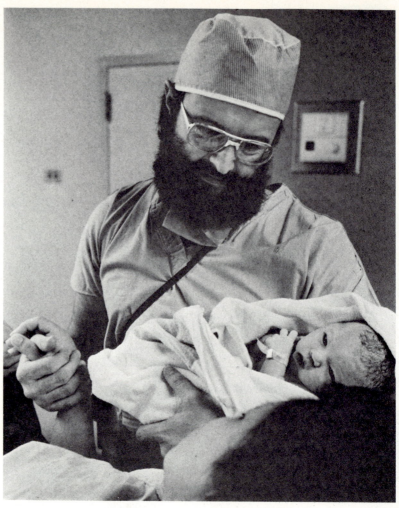

Suzanne Arms/Jeroboam

For the first two days after birth, colostrum is the major nutrient emitted
from the breasts. As the infant nurses, the colostrum is drained from
the breasts, and the milk ducts fill with the mother's milk.

There is little doubt that breast-feeding is superior to bottle-feeding.
The advantages of breast-feeding include:[7]

1. It transfers *immunity* (protection against infections) from the
   mother to the infant, and the breast milk itself and the act of
   nursing stimulate the development of the infant's own immune
   defenses.

Breast-feeding benefits both the infant and the mother.

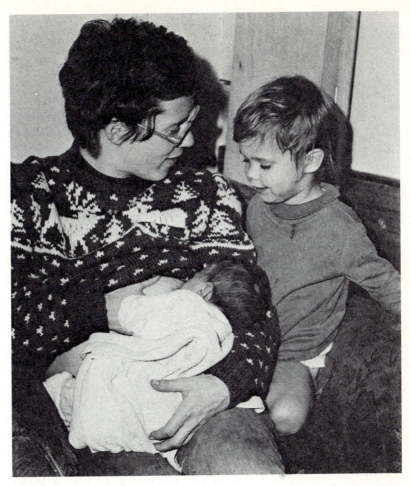

Eric Roth/The Picture Cube

2. Breast milk promotes the development of the infant's digestive system.
3. Breast-fed babies have fewer allergies, less diarrhea, fewer dental problems, and less colic (stomachache).
4. Breast milk is nutritionally balanced for human infants; formulas containing cow's milk are not nutritionally identical to breast milk, although they are nutritionally adequate.
5. Breast-feeding may increase the psychological attachment between mother and infant *(bonding)*, which some believe to be important to the future psychological well-being of both mother and child.

6. The hormones involved in milk production and release contribute to the mother's psychological well-being after childbirth and also help the uterus return rapidly to its normal size.

The many advantages of breast-feeding do not mean that bottle-feeding is bad. There are many healthy, well-adjusted people who were bottle-fed infants. Some women are physically unable to breast-feed their infants. Some mothers choose not to breast-feed because work, family, and other responsibilities make it inconvenient; breast-feeding in public or at work is still not acceptable in many communities or places of employment. Some babies are such vigorous feeders that breast-feeding becomes painful and the mothers must stop. Some women breast-feed their infants for several weeks or months and then gradually substitute bottle-feedings for breast-feedings until the child is completely *weaned*, that is, has stopped nursing altogether. But more important than whether the milk comes from a breast or a bottle is the physical contact and loving the infant receives while being fed.

POSTPARTUM RECOVERY

After the child is born, the mother goes through a several-week period of postpartum recovery called the *puerperium*. During this time, the physiological changes brought about by pregnancy slowly reverse, the vagina and surrounding structures recover from the traumas of labor, and torn tissues and the episiotomy (if one was performed) heal.

For some women, the postpartum period can be difficult. The excitement and changes during the nine months of pregnancy and the physical demands of childbirth can be exceedingly fatiguing. But many women do not have the time to rest sufficiently, as child care and other family duties present themselves soon after childbirth.

I had a difficult labor with my second child—much harder than with the first—so that by the time I got home I was exhausted. To boot, I had bad hemorrhoids, and the stitches from the episiotomy hurt. I could barely walk or go to the bathroom. But I couldn't pamper myself. I had two kids and a husband to take care of.

From the authors' files

The physiological and psychological changes that occur right after birth sometimes are excessive, and some women undergo a period of emotional upheaval and negative feelings, often called *postpartum depression*. Some experts suggest that postpartum emotional problems are caused by the sudden changes in hormone levels that occur at childbirth. Others, though not denying the effect of hormones, emphasize that childbirth is a dramatic life event that brings about many changes: confusion about the new status as a parent; the necessity to heal the body; the responsibility for a new baby; fatigue; and changes in marital and other family relationships.

Postpartum emotional problems tend to abate as the mother's body returns to normal and she becomes accustomed to her new life situation. In the meantime, however, she needs the support of family members and friends. This is why new mothers are encouraged to keep in touch with other new mothers whom they have met in childbirth preparation courses or in the hospital. This is also a time when the father's support and help with family responsibilities are appreciated and, in some cases, are essential to the mother's recovery. Recognizing the benefits of the father's help during the postpartum period, some people suggest the need for paternity leave—the excused absence of fathers from work.

INFERTILITY

Approximately 10 to 15 percent of all American married couples who want to have children have difficulty doing so. These couples are *infertile*, which means that they have not been able to become pregnant after a year of trying without a contraceptive. About half of all infertile couples can eventually have children if the reason for their infertility is discovered and resolved. Permanent infertility is called *sterility*.

Infertility can be caused by many different problems that make successful fertilization improbable or impossible or make a woman unable to complete a normal pregnancy. Some couples, for example, are not successful in becoming pregnant because they are not having intercourse frequently enough during the time of the menstrual cycle when an egg is most likely to be in a Fallopian tube (in most women, about fourteen days before the onset of menstruation). Another cause of infertility is ill health. Gonorrhea, syphilis, certain pelvic infections, diabetes, hepatitis, chronic alcoholism, drug abuse, malnutrition, anxiety, stress, and fatigue can diminish a person's reproductive capabilities. In most of these instances, medical attention or a change in living habits can restore fertility.

Causes of and Cures for Male Infertility

In many cases, infertility is caused by the man's inability to produce or to deliver into the vagina a sufficient number of reproductively capable sperm. Conception is highly improbable unless about twenty million sperm are deposited in the vagina during intercourse. Difficulty in having and maintaining an erection (impotence) or the inability to ejaculate in the vagina are also reasons that males may be infertile. In some cases, hormone therapy can improve sperm production. Erection and ejaculation problems are usually psychological in origin and require behavioral or attitude changes.

If the cause of a man's infertility cannot be resolved, the couple can still have children by means of *artificial insemination*. In this procedure, a doctor introduces a quantity of a man's sperm directly into the upper part of the vagina or the lower part of the uterus. In cases in which the husband produces few but healthy sperm, artificial insemination can improve the probability of conception. If the husband cannot produce sufficient numbers of healthy sperm, the couple can become pregnant through artificial insemination by using the sperm of an anonymous donor. Each year about ten thousand children are conceived by artificial insemination by donor (AID).

Artificial insemination is such an unusual procedure that those who are involved often experience feelings unlike any they have ever had:

When you're at the clinic being inseminated you don't actually comprehend what's going on. You see the syringe and you have to remind yourself, "Gee, there's a baby in there." . . . You're going to go through life knowing you did this, knowing that there's somebody out there who's part of you somehow.[8]

AID recipient

I always wonder how many babies I've produced, but I never ask. After the first time I was [at the clinic], the girl in the lab said, "We've had a success." Wow! I didn't think of myself as the father. At the time you don't think that way. It was just, wow! Later, you'd be sitting down and wondering, "How many times have I been a father?" I wish one day I could see one of them.[9]

Sperm donor

Very special techniques make it possible to freeze sperm. This allows a donor's sperm to be used in artificial insemination months or years after a sample is donated. Several commercial "sperm banks" now operate in the United States. Many of their clients are men who wish to have a *vasectomy*, a method of birth control that permanently sterilizes a man (see Chapter 12, "Family Planning"). Semen specimens are frozen before the vasectomy is performed, and if a man and his wife decide later to have a child, she can be artificially inseminated with his stored semen.

Causes of and Cures for Female Infertility

The causes of infertility in women usually are traced to problems in the transport of sperm from the vagina to the Fallopian tubes, or in the passage of eggs within the tubes or from the tubes to the uterus. Very thick or voluminous mucus produced by the cervix of the uterus or a growth or tumor in the uterus or Fallopian tubes can block the pathway of the sperm. Infections of the female reproductive tract, especially untreated gonorrhea, can cause permanent scarring and blockage of the Fallopian tubes. Sometimes surgery can repair blocked tubes to restore fertility. If not, a woman may still be able to become pregnant through a new and as yet unperfected technique called *in vitro fertilization* (see Box 11.2), which involves surgically obtaining an egg and artificially inseminating it in a special laboratory facility. The fertilized egg is then replaced in the woman's uterus, and a normal pregnancy follows.

Hormone imbalances are another cause of infertility. These can sometimes be remedied by drugs that stimulate hormone production or by direct treatment with hormones. Although such treatments can lead to a successful pregnancy, they also have the tendency to produce multiple pregnancies.

MULTIPLE PREGNANCY

Although women are usually pregnant with only one child at a time, multiple pregnancies with two, three, or as many as six or seven children do occasionally occur. The incidence of twinning in the United States is about one per one hundred births; the incidence of triplet births is about one per ten thousand births. Giving birth to four or more children at one time is extremely rare.

There are two kinds of twins, identical and fraternal. *Identical*, or *monozygotic* (MZ), *twins* occur when one fertilized egg splits in two very early in the pregnancy, and each half develops into a fetus.

BOX 11.2   New Ways to Overcome Infertility

At the moment of her birth in the summer of 1978, Louise Brown became an instant celebrity, not because her parents were famous, but because Louise was the world's first "test tube baby"—the first child to be conceived outside the mother's body. Like millions of other couples, Louise's parents are infertile. The revolutionary medical procedure that helped bring Louise into the world, called *in vitro fertilization,* is only one of several unprecedented ways infertile couples are using, or soon will use, to have children.

In vitro fertilization is a treatment for infertility used when a woman's Fallopian tubes are physically obstructed. The woman can produce eggs, but fertilization cannot take place because the blocked tubes prevent the meeting of egg and sperm. To overcome this problem, a doctor removes eggs from the woman's ovaries and places them in a laboratory dish (the "test tube") where they are bathed with sperm donated by the husband. Fertilization takes place in the dish. Then the fertilized egg is put back into the mother's uterus, where it develops into a baby in the normal way.

Several children conceived in "test tubes" have already been born. And many more test-tube babies are likely to be born as soon as more medical specialists learn the procedure of *in vitro* fertilization. Already, the few specialists who have been successful with this procedure have been deluged with pleas for help from hopeful infertile couples. Recent advances in the surgical repair of obstructed Fallopian tubes may also enable some of these couples to conceive in the normal way, thereby reducing the demand for the "test tube" method.

Although for a few, *in vitro* fertilization raises some ethical dilemmas, most people seem to be enthusiastic rather than worried about it. This is the reason baby Louise's birth was heralded and not deplored. The acceptance of new medical technologies to overcome infertility may allow the application of new and more unusual methods to deal with the problem.

For example, if a woman cannot have a normal pregnancy, a couple can hire a "surrogate" mother to have the child for them. A woman is chosen from a group of consenting candidates to be artificially inseminated with the husband's sperm. The surrogate receives a fee for being pregnant and giving birth to the couple's child.

Another possible way that surrogates may be used is to combine *in vitro* fertilization and surrogate motherhood. The infertile couple donates eggs and sperm, which are brought together in the laboratory to form a fertilized egg. But instead of putting the embryo back into the donor of the egg, it is put inside the surrogate's uterus, where it develops into a child.

Yet another possibility is "prenatal adoption." An egg donated by a surrogate is fertilized *in vitro* with a husband's sperm. The resulting embryo is then put inside his wife's uterus, thus allowing a woman who cannot produce eggs still to experience pregnancy and childbirth.

Couples who overcome their infertility problem with any new procedure are grateful that they can have children. Donors of eggs and sperm and surrogate mothers usually feel very special in that they are helping to give life and also are helping others to fulfill important life goals. As for the children brought into the world by using these unusual techniques, most experts believe that their well-being is not determined by where conception takes place or by who carries the children to term, but by the quality of the love and care received after birth.

BOX 11.2 (continued)

Because *in vitro* fertilization, surrogate motherhood, and prenatal adoption are new, ethical and legal questions concerning them have not yet been settled. For example, one common method of *in vitro* fertilization is fertilization of several eggs at the same time but the implantation of only one of them in a recipient's uterus. The others die. In choosing the surviving embryo, is the doctor exercising unusual power over life and death? With surrogate motherhood, legal questions over right to the child can arise. The woman who bears the child might claim that she is the rightful mother (as some have) and attempt to keep the child. A problem with prenatal adoption arises if the procedure is considered a form of baby buying to circumvent legal adoption. In the years to come, the states will be devising laws to clarify the issues raised by the new procedures for treating infertility.

Because identical twins have exactly the same heredity, they are physically identical and have the same sex. *Fraternal*, or *dizygotic* (DZ), *twins* result when two eggs are fertilized by two sperm. Each fetus, therefore, has a unique heredity, and that is why fraternal twins are not physically identical or always of the same sex. Opposite-sexed fraternal twins, for example, occur as often as same-sexed fraternal twins do.

The frequency of identical twins is about four per one thousand pregnancies and is not dependent on race, maternal age, or heredity. The frequency of fraternal twins, however, varies according to the race and age of the mother and, to a slight degree, on her inheritance. The incidence of fraternal twinning in the American black population (twelve per one thousand pregnancies) is higher than in the white (seven per one thousand pregnancies) or Asian (three per one thousand pregnancies) populations. In all groups, the incidence of fraternal twinning increases with maternal age, mothers between thirty and forty having the highest rate. In all racial groups, the frequency of fraternal twinning is slightly higher among female relatives of a "twinning mother," and a woman with one set of twins is slightly more likely to have another set than a first-time mother is.

ADOPTION

Some couples may not be able to have their own children—or may not wish to—but still want to be parents. The principal alternative for them is adoption. In adoption, all the rights of the natural parents of the adopted child are legally transferred to the adoptive parents, and society recognizes the adoptive parents as the child's own. Even the original birth certificate is destroyed, and a new one is issued in the adopted family's name. Any legal records of the adoption are kept secret, and the courts are usually reluctant to permit access to the records, except in extreme cases.

According to government statistics, approximately 180,000 children are adopted in the United States each year. The majority of these children are placed for adoption by unwed mothers who decide they cannot keep their children. Others are abandoned, neglected, or abused children. In many instances, children are adopted by a stepparent.

About half of all adopted children are adopted by relatives. Of the half that are adopted by strangers, the placement of the child into a suitable family is arranged by either a public or a private adoption agency. Such agencies are staffed by trained social workers whose primary concern is the welfare of the child. Until only recently, many agency staff, wanting to place children in "good homes," excluded nearly all applicants for children except upper class or middle class couples whose life styles were considered "normal." Today, however, although agency personnel still screen prospective families very carefully, they now realize that responsible, loving parents can have a wide range of income levels and life styles. Even some single people are allowed to adopt.

About 10 percent of all nonrelative adoptions are arranged through independent persons such as clergy, doctors, or lawyers. These professionals make all the arrangements between an adopting family and the natural mother. This is a legal service, not to be confused with the so-called black market adoption, in which intermediaries charge adoptive parents enormous sums of money to acquire children.

In many ways, the joys, hardships, loves, and hates of adopting families are the same as those of other families. There is no particular reason that adoption should have any detrimental effect on the closeness of family relationships or on the adjustment of the child into the new family and also into society at large. It is normal for adoptive parents to wonder sometimes about what their child has inherited from his or her natural parents. And it is also normal for the adopted child to wonder about the natural parents, the reasons for the adoption, and the possibility that he or she has inherited a disease. Although these issues can be very important to adopted persons—and in some instances, they go to great lengths to discover the identities of their real parents—the adoptive family need not necessarily be disrupted by issues relating to the adoption.

DECIDING NOT TO BECOME A PARENT

Traditionally, our society has encouraged parenthood by means of social expectations and measures such as tax laws that give deductions for children. Despite such pronatal social values, however, about 5 percent of today's couples choose to remain childless.[10] These couples may view parenthood as an infringement on their career goals or perhaps as an unnecessary or unwanted addition to their intimate partnership. They may have doubts about their psychological or economic abilities to nurture and support children, or they may refrain from parenthood because they know or suspect that their children might inherit a genetic disease.

The incidence of voluntary childlessness may be increasing. In 1978 a survey of American women aged eighteen to thirty-four reported that 11.2 percent did not intend to have children, and among college-educated women this figure was 13.5 percent.[11]

As we pointed out in Chapter 10, "Marital Interaction," couples choosing not to have children are not less satisfied with their marriages than are those who do not have children. On the contrary, research data support the contention that in general, childless marriages are more satisfactory than others. According to research by sociologist Sharon Houseknecht, childless marriages were

significantly more cohesive, which means that spouses did the following things together more frequently: engaged in outside interests; exchanged stimulating ideas; calmly discussed something; and worked on projects. In addition . . . [couples] expressed a stronger desire and determination to continue the marital relationship . . . and also reported a higher degree of happiness. . . . The research findings suggest that marriage can be well-adjusted without children. Childfree couples find other sources of fulfillment to fill the so-called "gap" that many assume would exist without them.[12]

SUMMARY

Most people become parents by having their own biologically related children, although some become parents by adoption. People want children for a variety of social, religious, and personal reasons.

Biological parenthood involves pregnancy, which begins with the fertilization of a woman's egg by a man's sperm. After being fertilized, the egg develops into a baby inside the mother's uterus during the forty weeks of pregnancy.

Men produce sperm cells continually from the time they mature sexually, but women usually produce only one egg during each menstrual cycle until menopause, which generally occurs between the ages of forty and fifty-five.

The first sign of pregnancy is usually a missed menstrual period. A test for the pregnancy hormone, HCG, can confirm a suspected pregnancy. A woman can ensure a healthy pregnancy by obtaining regular professional prenatal care; refraining from smoking cigarettes, drinking alcohol, and taking other drugs; being physically active; and obtaining proper nutrition. Pregnancy can be a time of intense feelings and can change the sexual feelings of both wife and husband.

Childbirth is a three-stage process that can take several hours. Couples can choose whether they want the birth to take place in a traditional hospital setting, an alternative birth center in a hospital, or at home.

After the baby is born, a mother may or may not choose to breast-feed her infant. The decision may depend on whether her responsibilities and duties allow her the time. Postpartum recovery can be a difficult time for some women.

Some couples are infertile, but about half of all infertile couples can eventually have children with the help of medical procedures such as hormone injections, conception counseling, artificial insemination, and *in vitro* fertilization. Sterility is the condition of being permanently infertile.

Multiple births occur in about 1 percent of all pregnancies. Identical twins come from the splitting of a single fertilized egg that develops into two physically identical individuals. Fraternal twins result from the fertilization of two eggs by two sperm. The incidence of fraternal twinning varies according to the mother's age, race, and heredity.

Adoption is the transfer of legal right to a child from the natural birthparents to the adoptive parents. Approximately 180,000 children are adopted in the United States each year. About half of adopted children are adopted by relatives. Adoption need not create unusual family relationships.

About 5 percent of American couples choose not to have children, and their marriages are often more satisfying than marriages with children.

It is always a pleasure for Charles and Andrea to visit their daughter Susan and her husband Ed. Susan and Ed are doing well in their jobs, and they have a lovely home. All they lack is children, as Charles pointed out to them at dinner. On their way home, Charles and Andrea talked about it:

CHARLES: I don't understand why those two don't have kids yet.
ANDREA: They know what they're doing.
CHARLES: I know there's something wrong. I'll bet they can't.
ANDREA: They just don't want to rush into anything.
CHARLES: Five years is hardly rushing.
ANDREA: We waited. You wanted that pay raise, remember?
CHARLES: If they wait too long, they'll never have them.
ANDREA: Not everyone thinks having kids is the most important thing in the world.
CHARLES: You do.
ANDREA: But I'm not Susan. She knows it'll bring a huge change in her life. I respect her for wanting to be sure.
CHARLES: You're never absolutely sure. You just have to have faith in yourself.

Questions
1. What might be some of the reasons that Susan and Ed are waiting to have children?
2. Why is it so important to Charles that Susan and Ed have children soon?
3. Are parents justified in influencing their children's decision to be parents? What forces (parents, religion, and the like) in your life might influence your decision to have children?
4. What are your own reasons for having or not having children?

NOTES

1. Edward Pohlman, *The Psychology of Birth Planning*, Cambridge, Mass., Schenkman, 1969.
2. Boston Women's Health Book Collective, *Ourselves and Our Children*, New York, Random House, 1978, p. 33.
3. D. Frank Kaltreider and Schuyler Kohl, "Epidemiology of Preterm Delivery," *Clinical Obstetrics and Gynecology*, 23 (1980): 17–30.

4. Jonathan E. Fielding and Alfred Yankauer, "The Pregnant Smoker" and "The Pregnant Drinker," *American Journal of Public Health*, 68, no. 9 (1978): 836–838.
5. Rosemary Cogan, "Effects of Childbirth Preparation," *Clinical Obstetrics and Gynecology*, 23 (1980): 1–14.
6. Frederick Leboyer, *Birth Without Violence*, New York, Knopf, 1975.
7. *Medical World News*, "Breastfeeding," February 5, 1979, pp. 62–78.
8. Anne Taylor Fleming, "New Frontiers in Conception," *New York Times Magazine*, July 20, 1980, p. 14.
9. Ibid., p. 21.
10. Jean E. Veevers, "Incidence of Voluntary Childlessness," *Medical Aspects of Human Sexuality*, 13, no. 2 (February 1979): 102.
11. U.S. Bureau of Census, "Fertility of American Women: June 1978," *Current Population Reports*, Series P–20, No. 341 (1979): 24.
12. Sharon K. Houseknecht, "Happiness of Childless Marriages," *Medical Aspects of Human Sexuality*, 13, no. 12 (December 1979): 103.

SUGGESTED READINGS

Boston Women's Health Book Collective. *Our Bodies/Ourselves*. New York, Random House, 1977. Presents a complete, concise discussion of the biology of human reproduction.

DeLora, Joann, Carol Warren, and Carol Rinklieb. *Understanding Sexual Interaction*. Boston, Houghton Mifflin, 1981. Contains excellent information on various aspects of becoming a parent.

Fleming, Anne T. "New Frontiers in Conception." *New York Times Magazine*, July 20, 1980, p. 14. A discussion of the medical, social, legal, and ethical issues regarding the use of new technologies for conceiving embryos and other methods of overcoming infertility.

Leboyer, Frederick. *Birth Without Violence*. New York, Knopf, 1975. The author discusses his methods for nontraumatic childbirth.

FAMILY PLANNING

The strongest principle of growth lies in human choice.

George Eliot[1]

12

Humans have the ability to produce many children. A young couple having regular sexual intercourse without trying to prevent pregnancy is likely to conceive a child within six months.[2] Therefore, if a couple remains healthy and has children throughout their reproductive lifetime (which usually ends with the woman's menopause), they can have more than ten children. Indeed, couples who value large families or who do not believe in family planning for personal or religious reasons often have families of seven or more children.

In early America, a large family was often an economic necessity. Because most families lived on farms, more children meant more help with the farm and household chores. For example, in 1800, the fertility rate for women aged fifteen to forty-four years old—the number of children born each year per one thousand women in that age group— was 278.[3] Since about 1850, however, the fertility rate in the United States has declined steadily (see Figure 12.1), and in recent years the U.S. fertility rate (approximately seventy births per one thousand women aged fifteen to forty-four) has been near an all-time low. And if American women do have the number of children they say they intend to have, the near-future birth rate will remain low. A 1979 survey indicated that among women aged eighteen to thirty-four, 11 percent expected to remain childless and 72 percent expected to have no more than two children. The average number of expected children for the entire group was 2.1 (see Table 12.1).[4]

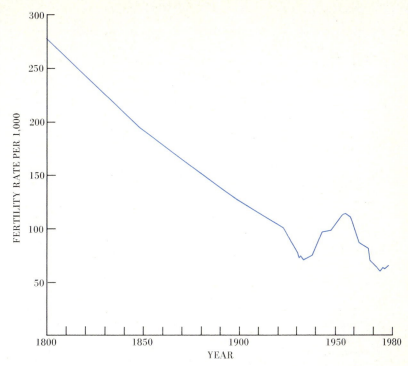

FIGURE 12.1
U.S. fertility rate
(number of births per
one thousand women
aged fifteen to forty-
four years old),
1800–1980

FERTILITY RATE PER 1,000

YEAR

Sources: *Historical Statistics of the United States*, 1975; U.S. National Center for Health Statistics, *Vital Statistics Reports, 1978, 1979, 1980*.

One reason for the low birth rate and small family size is that at no previous time in history could couples exercise the safe, reliable control over the number of children they will have and when their children will be born—or whether they will have children at all—that they can today. Social attitudes now favor family planning, and modern contraceptive methods permit reasonably good control over human reproduction.

In this chapter we discuss the reasons for family planning and the various ways in which family planning can be achieved.

THE REASONS FOR FAMILY PLANNING

Ideally, couples would have children only when they were economically and psychologically ready to provide the best child-rearing environment they could and also when they perceived that they were able to carry out the nearly twenty-year commitment of parenthood. In this

TABLE 12.1 Number of Lifetime Births Expected by U.S. Women, by Current Age, Educational Level, and Marital Status

	Percent of Women Expecting 0, 1, 2, 3, or 4 or More Lifetime Births						Average Number of Lifetime Births Expected
	Total	0	1	2	3	4 or more	
All Women in This Survey	100.0	11.0	13.2	47.5	19.1	9.2	2.1
Age							
18–19	100.0	11.6	10.6	51.3	17.4	9.1	2.1
20–21	100.0	11.7	11.3	50.7	18.5	7.8	2.0
22–24	100.0	11.1	12.9	50.2	18.8	7.0	2.0
25–29	100.0	10.7	14.4	48.2	18.8	7.9	2.0
30–34	100.0	10.9	13.9	42.3	20.4	12.5	2.2
Educational Level							
Not a High School Graduate	100.0	7.9	12.7	38.8	23.3	17.3	2.4
High School Graduate	100.0	10.0	13.6	48.5	19.8	8.1	2.1
1–3 Years of College	100.0	11.8	13.3	49.0	17.7	8.2	2.0
4 Years of College	100.0	16.3	10.5	53.5	14.6	5.1	1.8
5 or More Years of College	100.0	18.3	15.9	50.9	11.7	3.2	1.7
Marital Status							
Currently Married	100.0	5.7	12.5	50.7	21.6	9.5	2.2
Widowed, Divorced, or Separated	100.0	11.6	21.1	38.5	17.2	11.5	2.0
Never Married	100.0	21.9	11.8	44.1	14.6	7.6	1.8

Source: U.S. Bureau of the Census, "Fertility of American Women: June 1979," *Current Population Reports*, Series P–20, No. 358, Washington, D.C., U.S. Government Printing Office, 1980.

way, all children would be wanted and would have the best opportunity to grow up healthy.

For most couples, family-planning decisions take into account several factors, including family economics, the effect of children on family and individual life styles, the effect of childbearing on the woman's life choices, health considerations, and, in some cases, the threat of world overpopulation.

Family Economics

In 1980, the cost of raising a child from birth to age eighteen was estimated by the U.S. Department of Agriculture to be about $70,000 (see Tables 12.2 and 12.3). This sum included such basic items as food, clothes, shelter, medical care, transportation, and education. At a 7 percent annual inflation rate, however, that cost could be expected to double every ten years. A 10 percent inflation rate would drive the cost of eighteen years of child rearing to over $181,000.

In many families, housing accounts for the largest single expenditure. When a couple has children, they often buy a multibedroom house, which can substantially increase their living costs. In general, food is the second largest expenditure in rearing a child, and transportation is the third. If a couple plans to send their children to college, at the approximate current cost of $20,000 for four years, they would have to save over $1,000 per year per child in order to afford it. But if the cost of a college education climbs in proportion to the continuing inflation rate, by the time today's newborn baby is ready for college, the cost could be close to $80,000.

Another economic factor parents often consider is the "lost opportunity costs" for the mother who stays at home to care for the children instead of working. If a mother stays at home until the children are in school, the lost income to the family could amount to well over $100,000.

Individual and Family Life Styles

Having to make physical and emotional "room" for a new child often changes a family's life style. This is true even if the child is not the family's first. Each new family member influences the amount of time family members spend together and changes the nature of their interpersonal relationships.

Family planning allows couples to schedule the births of their children to coincide with their individual and family goals. For example, a couple may decide to have children early in their marriage to give them more free time together when their child-rearing years are over. Or a couple may postpone having children so as to have several years of personal and marital growth beforehand. Couples can also decide on the spacing of the children. Children may be spaced close together so that they can be companions. This also allows the mother to begin and end her childbearing in the shortest length of time. Or the children may be spaced farther apart, which may decrease sibling rivalry and also relieve some of the emotional and physical strain on the mother.

No single childbearing pattern is best for all couples. Success in family life is not related to having a particular number of children in a particular length of time but, rather, to the degree to which parents control their childbearing to suit their wants and needs.[5]

TABLE 12.2   Estimated Annual Cost of Raising an Urban Child[a] from Birth to Age Eighteen (in 1980 Dollars)

Age of Child (Years)	Total	Food at Home[b]	Food Away from Home	Clothing	Housing[c]	Medical Care	Educa-tion	Transpor-tation	All Others[d]
North Central									
Under 1 . .	$3,378	$479	$0	$121	$1,482	$198	$0	$689	$409
1	3,487	588	0	121	1,482	198	0	689	409
2-3	3,255	588	0	197	1,302	198	0	600	370
4-5	3,455	675	113	197	1,302	198	0	600	370
6	3,583	654	113	273	1,235	198	81	600	429
7-9	3,735	806	113	273	1,235	198	81	600	429
10-11. . . .	3,888	959	113	273	1,235	198	81	600	429
12.	4,162	981	135	394	1,280	198	81	645	448
13-15. . . .	4,271	1,090	135	394	1,280	198	81	645	448
16-17. . . .	4,704	1,220	135	546	1,325	198	81	712	487
Total. . .	69,232	15,274	1,714	5,336	23,352	3,564	972	11,382	7,638
Northeast									
Under 1 . .	3,360	567	0	121	1,504	198	0	600	370
1	3,490	697	0	121	1,504	198	0	600	370
2-3	3,400	675	0	212	1,369	198	0	556	390
4-5	3,601	763	113	212	1,369	198	0	556	390
6	3,836	763	135	288	1,347	198	101	556	448
7-9	3,988	915	135	288	1,347	198	101	556	448
10-11. . . .	4,184	1,111	135	288	1,347	198	101	556	448
12.	4,452	1,111	135	424	1,392	198	101	623	468
13-15. . . .	4,583	1,242	135	424	1,392	198	101	623	468
16-17. . . .	4,929	1,373	158	531	1,414	198	101	667	487
Total. . .	73,079	17,453	1,892	5,576	24,962	3,564	1,212	10,586	7,834
South									
Under 1 . .	3,676	523	0	136	1,594	221	0	734	468
1	3,785	632	0	136	1,594	221	0	734	468
2-3	3,550	610	0	212	1,414	221	0	645	448
4-5	3,728	675	113	212	1,414	221	0	645	448
6	3,920	675	135	288	1,347	221	122	645	487
7-9	4,051	806	135	288	1,347	221	122	645	487
10-11. . . .	4,226	981	135	288	1,347	221	122	645	487
12.	4,513	981	158	424	1,392	221	122	689	526
13-15. . . .	4,643	1,111	158	424	1,392	221	122	689	526
16-17. . . .	5,006	1,220	158	546	1,437	221	122	756	546
Total. . .	74,996	15,534	1,984	5,636	25,368	3,978	1,464	12,186	8,846

TABLE 12.2 (cont.)

Age of Child (Years)	Total	Food at Home[b]	Food Away from Home	Clothing	Housing[c]	Medical Care	Educa-tion	Transpor-tation	All Others[d]
West									
Under 1 ..	3,618	523	0	121	1,549	243	0	734	448
1	3,749	654	0	121	1,549	243	0	734	448
2-3	3,557	632	0	197	1,392	243	0	645	448
4-5	3,779	719	135	197	1,392	243	0	645	448
6	4,030	697	158	288	1,369	243	101	667	507
7-9	4,183	850	158	288	1,369	243	101	667	507
10-11....	4,379	1,046	158	288	1,369	243	101	667	507
12.	4,631	1,046	158	409	1,414	243	101	734	526
13-15....	4,740	1,155	158	409	1,414	243	101	734	526
16-17....	5,214	1,307	180	515	1,482	243	101	801	585
Total...	76,655	16,343	2,210	5,424	25,500	4,374	1,212	12,588	9,004

Source: U.S. Department of Agriculture, *Family Economics Review*, Winter, 1981, p. 20.

[a]Child in family of husband and wife and no more than 5 children.

[b]Includes home-produced food and school lunches.

[c]Includes shelter, fuel, utilities, household operations, furnishings, and equipment.

[d]Includes personal care, recreation, reading, and other miscellaneous expenditures.

Postponing Parenthood

Perhaps the greatest changes in family and individual life styles occur with the birth of the first child. This is one reason that many couples are postponing parenthood into their mid-to-late twenties and early thirties (see Figures 12.2a and 12.2b). This gives marital partners the opportunity to establish a strong marriage and to work out patterns of cooperation. It also gives them time to explore and clarify life plans, particularly those regarding children. Postponing parenthood also allows partners the chance to establish careers.

There are some disadvantages to postponing parenthood. For example, a couple may become so accustomed to a childless life style that they cannot decide when, or even if, to have children. It is also possible that a couple can postpone this decision too long and then have difficulty conceiving; the ability to have children declines with age. Another disadvantage to postponing childbearing is the many years that separate the ages of parents and their children. A child of

Age of Child (Years)	Total	Food at Home[b]	Food Away from Home	Clothing	Housing[c]	Medical Care	Education	Transportation	All Others
North Central									
Under 1 ..	$3,191	$436	$0	$106	$1,414	$198	$0	$667	$37(
1	3,300	545	0	106	1,414	198	0	667	37(
2-3	2,943	523	0	167	1,190	176	0	556	33]
4-5	3,120	610	90	167	1,190	176	0	556	33]
6	3,353	610	113	258	1,167	176	81	578	37(
7-9	3,484	741	113	258	1,167	176	81	578	37(
10-11. . . .	3,658	915	113	258	1,167	176	81	578	37(
12.	3,945	915	113	394	1,212	176	81	645	40٩
13-15. . . .	4,054	1,024	113	394	1,212	176	81	645	40٩
16-17. . . .	4,363	1,133	135	485	1,235	198	81	667	42٩
Total. . .	64,571	14,163	1,580	4,974	21,908	3,256	972	10,940	6,77٨
Northeast									
Under 1 ..	3,701	523	0	121	1,594	198	0	778	48٦
1	3,810	632	0	121	1,594	198	0	778	48٦
2-3	3,644	610	0	197	1,459	198	0	712	46٨
4-5	3,866	697	135	197	1,459	198	0	712	46٨
6	4,119	697	158	288	1,437	198	122	712	50٦
7-9	4,250	828	158	288	1,437	198	122	712	50٦
10-11. . . .	4,446	1,024	158	288	1,437	198	122	712	50٦
12.	4,726	1,024	158	440	1,482	198	122	756	54٦
13-15. . . .	4,857	1,155	158	440	1,482	198	122	756	54٦
16-17. . . .	5,297	1,286	180	576	1,527	198	122	823	58٣
Total. . .	78,183	16,059	2,210	5,670	26,628	3,564	1,464	13,346	9,24٢
South									
Under 1 ..	3,832	523	0	136	1,594	221	0	890	46٨
1	3,919	610	0	136	1,594	221	0	890	46٨
2-3	3,553	588	0	212	1,369	221	0	734	42٩
4-5	3,775	675	135	212	1,369	221	0	734	42٩
6	3,904	654	135	288	1,325	221	101	712	46٨
7-9	4,034	784	135	288	1,325	221	101	712	46٨
10-11. . . .	4,209	959	135	288	1,325	221	101	712	46٨
12.	4,533	959	158	440	1,369	221	101	778	50٦
13-15. . . .	4,642	1,068	158	440	1,369	221	101	778	50٦
16-17. . . .	5,063	1,198	180	622	1,392	221	101	823	52٦
Total. . .	75,416	15,142	2,072	5,852	24,874	3,978	1,212	13,746	8,54٦

TABLE 12.3   (cont.)

Age of Child (Years)	Total	Food at Home[b]	Food Away from Home	Clothing	Housing[c]	Medical Care	Education	Transportation	All Others[d]
West									
Under 1 . .	3,958	523	0	121	1,616	243	0	890	565
1	4,067	632	0	121	1,616	243	0	890	565
2-3	3,683	610	0	197	1,392	221	0	756	507
4-5	3,905	697	135	197	1,392	221	0	756	507
6	4,168	675	135	303	1,369	243	122	756	565
7-9	4,321	828	135	303	1,369	243	122	756	565
10-11. . . .	4,495	1,002	135	303	1,369	243	122	756	565
12.	4,821	1,002	158	455	1,414	243	122	823	604
13-15. . . .	4,952	1,133	158	455	1,414	243	122	823	604
16-17. . . .	5,443	1,286	180	531	1,504	243	122	934	643
Total. . .	79,885	15,905	2,072	5,730	25,678	4,286	1,464	14,500	10,250

Source: U.S. Department of Agriculture, *Family Economics Review*, Winter 1981, p. 21.

[a]Child in family of husband and wife and no more than 5 children.

[b]Includes home-produced food and school lunches.

[c]Includes shelter, fuel, utilities, household operations, furnishings, and equipment.

[d]Includes personal care, recreation, reading, and other miscellaneous expenditures.

older parents may have special hardships (see Box 12.1). And older parents whose children also choose to postpone parenthood may not live long enough to become grandparents.

Women's Life Choices

Whatever gains the women's rights movement has made, in our society women still are primarily responsible for child-rearing. Therefore, family-planning decisions tend to affect the lives of women more than the lives of men. For example, more and more women are seeking careers for both personal and economic reasons, but in many instances, the best time for career building overlaps with the childbearing years. With few women having extended families to help care for young children and with few organizations providing child-care facilities for

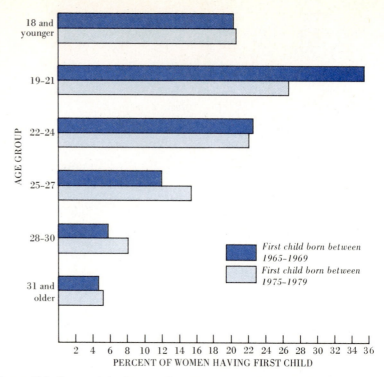

FIGURE 12.2a
A comparison of the percentage of U.S. women in various age groups having their first child in the late 1960s with the percentage of U.S. women in the same age groups having their first child in the late 1970s. The data show that there has been an increase in the percentage of women having their first child later in life.

AGE GROUP

18 and younger
19–21
22–24
25–27
28–30
31 and older

■ First child born between 1965–1969
▫ First child born between 1975–1979

2 4 6 8 10 12 14 16 18 20 22 24 26 28 30 32 34 36
PERCENT OF WOMEN HAVING FIRST CHILD

Source: U.S. Bureau of the Census, "Fertility of American Women: June, 1979," *Current Population Reports*, Series P–20, No. 358, Washington, D.C., U.S. Government Printing Office, 1980.

women employees, deciding when to become a mother can profoundly affect career growth.

Mothers who continue to work, especially those establishing careers, may face a special problem—what psychologists Pamela Daniels and Kathy Weingarten call "overloaded circuits."[6] Trying to combine successfully the duties of attending to children, husband, home, and job can tax a woman's energies to the extreme.

As mothers, these women must continually meet a double test of resilience—in the sphere of being, stretching the boundaries of self to make room for an absolutely dependent someone else in their lives; and in the sphere of doing, expanding their capacity and coping energy to meet the double demands of a double occupation.[7]

Also, women who try to integrate motherhood and working often face a dilemma. On the one hand they want to pursue their careers, and on

FIGURE 12.2b

U.S. fertility rate by age of mother, 1970–1978. In recent years the fertility rate has increased slightly, principally because a large number of women who have postponed until their mid-to-late twenties and early thirties the birth of their first child are now having children.

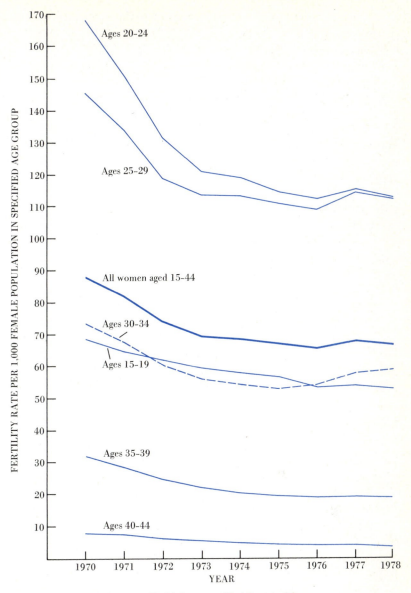

FERTILITY RATE PER 1,000 FEMALE POPULATION IN SPECIFIED AGE GROUP

Ages 20–24

Ages 25–29

All women aged 15–44

Ages 30–34

Ages 15–19

Ages 35–39

Ages 40–44

YEAR

Source: U.S. National Center for Health Statistics, *Vital Statistics Reports*.

the other they do not want to miss the key moments in their children's lives. Wise family planning can help time and space the births of children to coincide with lulls in career development or with periods when spending less time at work is feasible.

BOX 12.1   A Child of Older Parents, *by Merri Rosenberg*

Being the child of older parents isn't all it's cracked up to be. I should know: My parents were in their 40's when I was born, 23 years ago. I am a little perturbed by all the articles extolling the delights of late parenthood, articles written from the perspective of the parents —recent converts to the cause. Implicit in their embrace of postponed parenthood is the assumption the child exists for its parents' pleasure; its birth therefore should be scheduled for maximum convenience. No one seems to have considered the convenience of the child.

Postponed parenthood wasn't born with women's liberation. There are quite a few of us who are offspring of an earlier, "closeted" generation of older parents. Most of us don't consider late parenthood the ideal solution its advocates claim it to be.

Unlike many of the current crop of older parents, our parents came to their decision with much care and some pain. When I was younger, older parenthood conferred a stigma; it was something to be whispered about or hidden— hardly the status symbol it's come to be. Sometimes the decision was dictated by circumstances. One friend's parents lost their youth to Hitler's concentration camps; my own parents suffered the loss of two children before I was born. These are quite different circumstances from those of today's older parents who often choose between a child and another step up the corporate ladder.

Contemporary advocates cite advantages for the child: parents who are financially, emotionally and socially ready to assume the burden of raising a child in our increasingly expensive society; parents who are more mature, patient and tolerant; children who know they are really wanted by their parents, and so on.

No one could have been more wanted that I—my childhood was a continual outpouring of love. I enjoyed European vacations and frequent theater excursions. Yet I felt different from my classmates, whose parents were right in step with society's schedule. That my parents weren't like everybody else's *did* hurt. It mattered that my father couldn't play tennis with me, that my mother's friends weren't my friends' mothers.

These incidents are trivial in retrospect—but try telling that to a child who feels isolated. Nonconformity is appealing to individualistic adults; for a child who wants to be like everybody else, distinction is dreaded. Prospective parents should consider whether they want to impose this condition on a child.

If childhood slights are minor, other concomitants of having older parents are not. The 20's, we're told, should be a decade of exploration, adventure and autonomy. Now, the popular wisdom goes, is the time to establish careers, families, homes, to complete the separation process from one's parents that began in adolescence.

For the children of older parents, the scenario is quite different. Our timetables are compressed. Scarcely are we out of school than we become, in effect, the parents to our parents, by this stage often retired or in poor health. We must do without a decade of freedom before we assume the emotional, physical and, in some cases, financial support of our parents.

Almost before we've left the parental nest we are summoned back and in an uncomfortably reversed role. In college my parents called me to check that I was eating properly and sleeping enough; now I call them with the same questions.

The conventional schedule calls for adults in their late 30's or early 40's to bear the responsibility for elderly parents. I wonder constantly whether, when the time comes for me to make

BOX 12.1   (continued)

more than phone calls, I will have had sufficient life experience to cope. One of my contemporaries must cope with a father who suffered a stroke and a mother who developed severe arthritis—three years after she finished college. Another frets about her father's diabetes and her mother's growing dependency on her.

As a result, those of us who are the offspring of older parents tend to cluster together. Our "normal" peers fail to understand the reality of having older parents. *Their* parents are concerned with paying off mortgages and getting promotions; *our* parents are worried about fixed incomes and illness. Our desire to go home for visits is motivated by a very real concern to give our parents attention and time while they are around to receive it—and sets us further apart from our peers, who go home once or twice a year.

At the heart of our experience as children of older parents is a heightened awareness of time—and the necessity to squeeze as much as possible into the period when our and our parents' lifetimes overlap. In some cases, that impels us to pursue achievement and success with more than usual ambition; others have children perhaps too early so that their parents can be grandparents. We are reluctant to take time-outs or time-offs. We can't afford to waste any of the time we have.

From the perspective of children who have lived through it, older-parenthood chic is not an ideal solution to a difficult problem—how to accommodate career and children—nor should it be. Parenting involves a sacrifice of some sort, unfashionable as that idea may sound; older parenthood only means you pay the piper that much later.

Source: *New York Times*, September 4, 1980, Op-Ed page. © 1980 by The New York Times Company. Reprinted by permission.

Health Considerations

Each year thousands of children are born with inherited diseases, many of which, such as sickle-cell anemia, Tay-Sachs disease, and cystic fibrosis, are very serious. Family planning helps prospective parents who know that a particular disease "runs in the family" to reduce the risk of passing this disease to their children.*

Family planning also helps preserve the health of the mother. Some women have difficult pregnancies and childbirth experiences, or both, and therefore may jeopardize their health if they have large families. Family planning also allows time between births for the mother to recover and regain her strength. Most doctors recommend birth intervals of not less than one year. Family planning can also prevent early pregnancy, which is important because teen-age mothers often

*Genetic counselors are trained professionals who help families determine both the risk of inherited disease and the risk of childbearing.

have more pregnancy-related health problems than mothers in their twenties do.

By ensuring the births of only wanted children, family planning also can promote the mental health of both parents and children. Unwanted children may disrupt family goals and relationships and cause undue mental and emotional strain on family members. Unwanted children may also be more apt to have impaired mental health. Studies of Swedish children born into families that did not want them (those to whom requests for abortion were denied) showed that the unwanted children had significantly more emotional problems, problems with social adjustment, and lower educational levels than did children born into families that wanted them.[8]

World Overpopulation

Some couples keep their families small because they want to take some personal responsibility in limiting the growth of the human population. At the current rate of growth, the world's human population is doubling about every thirty years, which means that by the end of this century it will total almost eight billion. Some people fear that overpopulation will create insatiable demands for food, water, living space, energy, and other resources, and that governments and socioeconomic systems will not be able to cope with these demands. Consequently, some couples are limiting their family to one or two children or are having no children at all.

METHODS OF CONTRACEPTION

Couples wishing to plan the births of their children have a variety of effective contraceptive methods from which to choose. Some of these methods use chemical substances to prevent the production of eggs or to kill sperm, whereas others physically block the union of a viable egg and a sperm. Still others interrupt the early stages of pregnancy. Following is a discussion of the most frequently used contraceptive methods:

Withdrawal

The *withdrawal method* of contraception, also known as *coitus interruptus*, requires the man to withdraw his penis from the vagina at the moment preceding ejaculation. In theory, this prevents the sperm from being deposited in the vagina and subsequently fertilizing an egg.

Although withdrawal has been used as a contraceptive method for centuries, it is not very reliable. Its long popularity has been due more to the lack of better alternatives than to its own effectiveness. There are several reasons for the withdrawal method's failure. One is that great control is needed to accomplish withdrawal, and a man may not remove his penis in time. Another reason for its failure is that there frequently is a slight, unnoticed, sperm-containing emission from the penis before ejaculation. And even if no sperm are deposited in the vagina, pregnancy can still occur if sperm released near the vagina make their way into the vagina or are introduced there inadvertently during body contact after ejaculation.

Rhythm Methods

The *rhythm methods* of contraception are based on the fact that an egg is available to be fertilized for only about two days during a woman's menstrual cycle. This means that intercourse can take place on many days of the menstrual month without the likelihood of conception. Rhythm methods of contraception attempt to determine the times when an egg is present in the female reproductive system, which tells couples when to abstain from intercourse.

The most traditional rhythm method of contraception, called *calendar rhythm,* tries to determine the "safe days"—the days on which conception is unlikely—and the "unsafe days"—the days on which an egg is available for fertilization. This calculation assumes that an egg is available for fertilization approximately fourteen days before the beginning of the next menstrual period, that eggs are fertilizable for only about two days, and that sperm already deposited inside a woman's body remain capable of fertilization for about three days. If a woman's menstrual cycle is regular, it is possible to infer which are the safe and which the unsafe days (see Table 12.4).

Although many couples have used calendar rhythm successfully, it is not a very reliable contraceptive method. Its main drawback is that it is difficult to predict the exact time that an egg is available for fertilization, even in menstrual cycles of regular length, because there is always some variation in how the human body functions. And when the length of a woman's menstrual period varies from month to month, using calendar rhythm to predict the safe days is even more difficult.

To try to improve the reliability of the rhythm method, it is possible to try to determine directly the unsafe days. The *Billing's method,* or

TABLE 12.4 Calculating the Safe and Unsafe Days Using Calendar Rhythm

If Your Shortest Cycle Has Been [no. of days]	Your First Fertile [Unsafe] Day is	If Your Longest Cycle Has Been [no. of days]	Your Last Fertile [Unsafe] Day Is
21*	3rd day	21	10th day
22	4th	22	11th
23	5th	23	12th
24	6th	24	13th
25	7th	25	14th
26	8th	26	15th
27	9th	27	16th
28	10th	28	17th
29	11th	29	18th
30	12th	30	19th
31	13th	31	20th
32	14th	32	21st
33	15th	33	22nd
34	16th	34	23rd
35	17th	35	24th

Source: Robert A. Hatcher, et al., *Contraceptive Technology, 1978–1979*, New York, Irvington Publishers, 1978, p. 95.

*Day 1 = first day of menstrual bleeding.

"natural birth control" ("natural" presumably because it involves no technological devices or chemicals), requires watching for the changes in the color and consistency of cervical mucus that frequently occur when an egg becomes available for fertilization.

Another method of trying to determine directly the unsafe days is the symptothermal method, which monitors the woman's basal body temperature (BBT). The basal body temperature is the body's temperature when it is at rest. A rise of about one degree in the BBT signals the safe days before the onset of the next menstruation (see Figure 12.3). There still is uncertainty, however, about the safe days between the start of menstruation and the rise in BBT.

For some couples, religious or personal factors make rhythm methods the only acceptable means of birth control. With a strong motivation to use one of the rhythm techniques (or two simultaneously) correctly and conscientiously, some of the reasons for the rhythm method's unreliability can be overcome, and it can be used successfully.

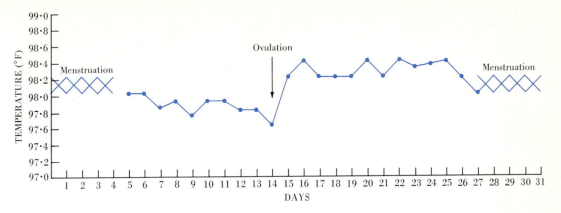

FIGURE 12.3

Changes in basal body temperature (BBT) during the menstrual cycle. The slight rise in BBT after an egg is released from the ovary (ovulation) can be used to help determine the "safe days" for sexual relations.

Oral Contraceptives

The Pill In 1960, the U.S. Food and Drug Administration approved the use of oral contraceptive pills for women. Since that time, the number of women "on the pill" has grown steadily until now approximately ten million women use oral contraceptives. Worldwide, the number of users is currently about fifty million. In the United States oral contraception is the most popular contraceptive method, accounting for nearly 25 percent of total contraceptive use.[9]

Many women take the pill because it is convenient, inexpensive, and has reversible effects. For many, the risks of complications are tolerable (see Box 12.2), and perhaps most important, the pill is nearly 100 percent effective.

The most commonly used oral contraceptives contain a combination of two synthetic hormones similar to the natural female sex hormones, *estrogen* and *progesterone*. A so-called *mini-pill*, which contains only progesterone-like agents, is also available. Compared with the combined-hormone oral contraceptives, the mini-pill is somewhat less effective in preventing pregnancy, but it has fewer side effects and health risks.

The Morning-After Pill Another type of oral contraceptive is the *morning-after pill*. If a woman who has had intercourse believes that she may have become pregnant from that single experience, she can, the next day, obtain this pill,

BOX 12.2   Problems with "The Pill"

Approximately half of the women who use oral contraceptives experience unwanted and unintended side effects from them. Usually, these side effects present little long-term risk to health, and very often they disappear after using the pill for several cycles. The more common of the less serious side effects are nausea, weight gain, breast tenderness, mild headaches, spotty bleeding between periods, decreased menstrual flow, increased frequency of vaginal infections, increased depression, and decreased sex drive. Some other common side effects of the pill are considered by many women to be beneficial. Among these are the decrease and even disappearance of menstrual cramps, fewer menstrual bleeding days, and the absolute regulation of the menstrual cycle.

There is no evidence that fertility is affected by taking the pill, even after many years of use, although some women go several months without having periods after discontinuing the pill, and this may affect their ability to become pregnant soon after discontinuation. There are some data indicating that a small number of former pill users may have an increased risk of spontaneous abortion and stillbirth during their first pregnancy after discontinuing the pill. And there may be a small increase in the number of birth defects in children born to former pill users. [*]

For a small percentage of women, using oral contraceptives presents a severe health risk. Several studies have shown that the risks of developing fatal blood clots and having heart attacks are greater for women who take oral contraceptives than for those who do not. [†] These risks are substantially greater for older pill users who also smoke, and therefore it is recommended that women over thirty-five who use oral contraceptive pills and who also smoke give up one or the other. The chances of developing gallbladder disease, high blood pressure, and stroke also are greater for pill users. Studies to determine the possible relationship between oral contraceptive use and the development of cancer, particularly cancers of the breast, have so far indicated that there is no increase in the incidence of breast cancer among pill users. [‡]

[*]Allan Rosenfeld, "Oral and Intrauterine Contraception," *American Journal of Obstetrics and Gynecology*, 132 (1978): 9–106.

[†]Ibid.

[‡]J. L. Kelsey et al., "Oral Contraceptives and Breast Disease," *American Journal of Epidemiology*, 107, no. 3 (1978): 236–245.

which is nearly 100 percent effective in stopping pregnancy. There are drawbacks to this kind of medication, however. The substances in morning-after pills may cause severe nausea and vomiting. Another possible drawback is that one kind of morning-after pill contains *diethylstilbestrol,* or DES, which may adversely affect the fetus should the contraceptive action fail and the pregnancy continue. Some daughters born to women who were given DES on a long-term basis during pregnancy (to help prevent miscarriages) were found to have developed a rare kind of vaginal cancer later in life. Also, if DES is present in the mother's body in abnormally high amounts during the early stages of fetal development, it may contribute to certain malformations of the fetal sex organs.

Because of the many problems with morning-after pills, many physicians and family-planning clinics are reluctant to prescribe them. Instead, they recommend that a woman who believes she may have become pregnant wait to see if her next menstrual period arrives before taking any action.

The IUD

The *intrauterine device*, or IUD, is a small plastic object that is placed inside the cavity of the uterus to prevent pregnancy (see Figure 12.4). Next to the pill, the IUD is the most effective nonsurgical type of contraception.

There are several kinds of IUDs (see Figure 12.5), including one that is spiral shaped, one that is shaped like a loop, and others in the shape of a seven or a *T* and wrapped with copper to increase their contraceptive potency. Another kind contains a supply of synthetic

FIGURE 12.4
A Copper-7 IUD in place

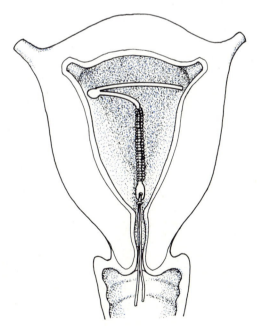

FIGURE 12.5
Several kinds of IUDs

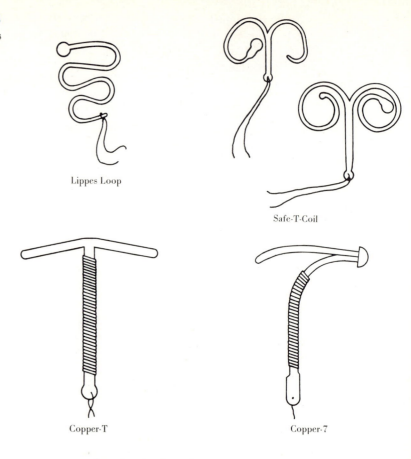

Lippes Loop

Safe-T-Coil

Copper-T

Copper-7

progesterone that is slowly released into the body. The combined effects of the IUD itself and the direct delivery of the synthetic hormone into the uterus make this device as effective as the IUD can be.

The use of the IUD is not without problems. Some women find that they have more severe menstrual cramps and heavier menstrual bleeding than they do when not using the IUD. Sometimes an IUD is inadvertently expelled from the uterus, either during menstruation or after an episode of forceful uterine contractions. This is why many IUDs come with "tails"—strings that hang from the end of the IUD into the vagina. As long as a woman can feel the IUD's tail, she knows it is in place. (It is very rare for a man to feel the IUD's tail during intercourse.) Serious medical problems can arise if the IUD is inserted under nonsterile conditions or if the uterus is damaged upon insertion. The incidence of pelvic infections (called *pelvic inflammatory disease*, or PID) is higher among IUD users than among nonusers.

Barrier Methods of Contraception

There are several highly effective methods of contraception that do not have as great a risk to health as the pill and IUD do. Each of these methods prevents conception by placing a barrier between the sperm and the egg. The principal barrier methods of contraception are the diaphragm, foams and creams, and the condom.

The Diaphragm

The *diaphragm* is a dome-shaped, latex object that is placed in the upper part of the vagina before intercourse takes place. In this position it covers the cervix and therefore prevents the passage of sperm from the vagina to the uterus. The effectiveness of the diaphragm as a physical barrier to sperm is greatly increased by coating the rim and the inside of the diaphragm with a *spermicidal* ("sperm-killing") *cream* (see Figure 12.6). In fact, the effectiveness of the diaphragm may be

FIGURE 12.6
Using a diaphragm

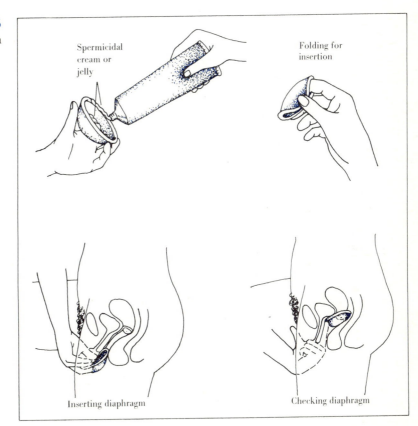

Spermicidal cream or jelly

Folding for insertion

Inserting diaphragm

Checking diaphragm

less the physical barrier than the presence of the spermicide—the diaphragm being an efficient way to place and retain the spermicide where it can act most effectively.

One of the advantages of the diaphragm is that no major side effects or long-term health risks are associated with its use. Perhaps the only reason that a woman might not be able to use a diaphragm is if she were allergic to the latex or the spermicide. A disadvantage of the diaphragm is that it must be inserted each time intercourse takes place, which means its effectiveness is dependent on the couple's motivation to use it correctly and *every time* they have sex. Correct usage includes:

- being sure that the diaphragm is the right size; women are not anatomically identical, and so each must be fit (by a family-planning professional or physician) with a diaphragm that is the right size for her.

- inserting the diaphragm properly and with a liberal amount of spermicide.

- leaving the diaphragm in place for at least six hours after intercourse; early removal increases the risk that some sperm will survive and be able to effect fertilization.

- checking the fit of the diaphragm if there is any change in overall body size (from a gain or loss of weight) or if there has been pelvic surgery or a pregnancy.

Vaginal Foams and Creams

Spermicidal agents alone can also be effective contraceptives, and can be obtained without a doctor's prescription. They come in the form of foams, creams, jellies (like those used with a diaphragm), or vaginal suppositories or tablets that release the spermicidal chemical after being placed in the vagina. (Although often displayed in stores with other feminine hygiene products, spermicidal foams and creams should not be confused with douches, deodorant products or lubricants, none of which are contraceptives.) When using any of these spermicides, it is important that they be placed far back in the vagina so that the spermicide will cover the cervix and prevent sperm from entering the uterus. It is also important to apply additional spermicide *before each act* of intercourse to ensure the greatest possible protection. As with the diaphragm, the spermicides' only complications are related to allergies to the chemicals in them.

The Condom

The *condom*, or "rubber," is a sheath that covers the penis and prevents ejaculated sperm from entering the vagina. Many types of condoms are available, and they can be purchased without a prescription from a pharmacy or through mail-order advertisements found in magazines and newspapers.

To use a condom, one unrolls it over the erect penis, leaving about a half inch of space at the tip to collect the emitted semen. Some condoms are manufactured with a special tip for semen collection. After intercourse, the condom should be held as the penis is withdrawn, to make sure that it does not come off in the vagina. Condoms should be used only once. The contraceptive effectiveness of the condom is greatly increased if it is used in conjunction with one of the vaginal spermicides such as foam.

Besides its use as a contraceptive, condoms are helpful in preventing the transmission of sexually transmitted (venereal) diseases such as gonorrhea, syphilis, and herpes.

Contraceptive Sterilization

Sterility is the condition of being permanently unable to have children. For people who are certain that they do not want children or, as is more often the case, no more children, surgical methods that render a person sterile but that have no effect on his or her ability to engage in or enjoy sex may be the most desirable form of contraception. Indeed, for couples over thirty, "permanent birth control" (sterilization of either the male or the female partner) has become the most frequently chosen method of contraception.[10] Over one million sterilizations are performed in the United States each year—about 60 percent on women. If the current trend holds, nearly 40 percent of today's American couples will choose sterilization rather than any other method of birth control within five years after the birth of their last wanted child; 75 percent will choose sterilization within fifteen years after the birth of their last wanted child.[11]

Female Sterilization

The principal sterilization procedure for women is *tubal ligation*, the cutting and tying of the Fallopian tubes. Tubal ligation is a relatively safe and inexpensive procedure (see Figure 12.7). Most tubal ligations are "Band-Aid" surgeries, so-called because the operation requires that only one or two tiny, inch-long incisions be made. These incisions allow the two Fallopian tubes to be severed and the cut ends tied. The passage of sperm deposited in the vagina is thereby blocked at one end of the cut Fallopian tube, and the passage of the egg is blocked at the other end. Fertilization cannot occur because the paths of the sperm

FIGURE 12.7
Tubal ligation. Each
Fallopian tube is first
cut (shown at left) and
then the ends are tied
(shown at right).

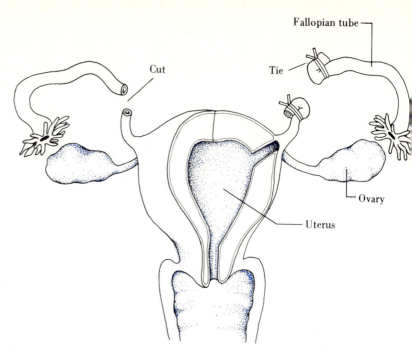

and egg are obstructed. Tubal ligation has no effect on a woman's hormone production, nor does it reduce her desire for, or her ability to have, sex.

Although tubal ligations should be considered permanent, it is possible, in rare instances, for the ends of the tubes to reopen spontaneously and for pregnancy to result. The incidence of pregnancy after tubal ligation is about three per one thousand women. Surgical reversal is also possible, with a success rate of about 70 percent.

Male Sterilization

The sterilization of a man is called a *vasectomy*. This procedure involves cutting and tying each of the two *vas deferens* (the tubes that carry the sperm from the testes to the penis). By cutting each vas, sperm are no longer emitted at ejaculation because their path is blocked (see Figure 12.8).

A vasectomy has no effect on a man's hormone production or his ability to get erections or to have sex. It also has no effect on the organs that produce seminal fluid. Therefore, a man still ejaculates, but the semen no longer contains sperm. And since sperm make up only about 1 percent of the total volume of semen, neither a man nor his sex partner are aware of any change in their sex life.

Some of the major advantages of vasectomy, in addition to its almost

FIGURE 12.8
Vasectomy. Each vas
deferens (sperm duct)
is first cut (shown at
left) and then the ends
are tied (shown at
right).

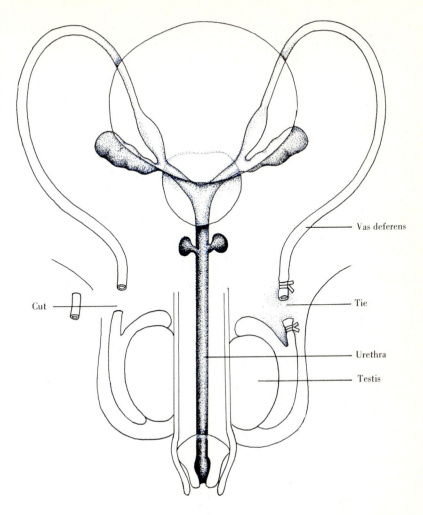

Vas deferens

Cut

Tie

Urethra

Testis

100 percent effectiveness as a contraceptive method (about one couple in one thousand conceives because the cut ends of a vas spontaneously rejoin), are that the procedure is uncomplicated, produces few problems, and is inexpensive. A vasectomy is usually done in a doctor's office with a local anesthetic in about fifteen to thirty minutes. Within a week after the operation, most men return to regular activities, including having sex. The only common complications of vasectomy are that some men experience local soreness and swelling, which go away after a few days.

Although a vasectomy should be considered permanent, it is sometimes possible to reverse the condition by surgically rejoining the cut ends of each vas. The success of vasectomy reversal, as measured by the ability to have children again, is about 50 percent, although some surgeons claim much higher reversal rates.

CHOOSING A CONTRACEPTIVE

None of the currently available contraceptive methods possesses all the qualities of the perfect contraceptive. No one method is simultaneously 100 percent effective, 100 percent free of side effects, 100 percent safe, and 100 percent reversible. Without the availability of a perfect contraceptive, sexually active people who wish to avoid unwanted pregnancy must weigh the benefits and risks of every method and choose the one(s) that best suits them (see Table 12.5).

The most serious risk associated with the use of any contraceptive is the risk to health. Withdrawal, rhythm, the diaphragm, vaginal foams or creams, and the condom are relatively safe methods. Barring surgical complications, female and male sterilization are also low-risk methods. The IUD and the pill, however, present more serious health risks, and their use is occasionally associated with death. For women under thirty, the risk of death from the pill or the IUD is very small (between one and two deaths per hundred thousand women), much smaller than the risk of death from the complications of pregnancy and childbirth (about six deaths per hundred thousand women). For women over thirty, the risk of IUD-related death remains low, but the risk of death for pill users increases with age, especially for women who also smoke cigarettes. Between the ages of thirty and thirty-nine, the risk of death for pill takers who also smoke is five times that for pill takers who do not smoke. After age forty, the risk of death for pill takers who also smoke is over eight times greater than that for pill takers who do not smoke, and it is nearly three times greater than the risk of death from the complications of pregnancy and childbirth.[12]

Another important concern in choosing a contraceptive is its effectiveness. For each contraceptive, one should consider two measures of effectiveness. One is its *theoretical effectiveness*, which reflects how well a contraceptive prevents pregnancy in the most ideal circumstances, in which care is taken to use the method as intended. The other measure, *use effectiveness*, indicates how well a contraceptive actually works. This takes into account improper and careless use. The theoretical effectiveness of the diaphragm is very high, but if the device is left at home while the user is on vacation, its use effectiveness is zero. Thus, the most effective contraceptive method is the one that a couple will use properly. The couple has to understand how the method

TABLE 12.5 A Comparison of Various Contraceptive Methods

Method	How It Works	Effectiveness	Advantages	Disadvantages
Withdrawal	Man withdraws penis from vagina before ejaculation	Moderate if used consistently	Causes no health problems	Requires great control on the part of the male
Rhythm	Intercourse only on a woman's "safe" days	Moderate if used consistently and conscientiously	Causes no health problems; little if any religious objection	Sometimes difficult to predict the "safe" days; may require long periods of abstention from sexual intercourse
The Pill	Prevents the release of eggs from the ovaries	High	Easy to use; does not interfere with sex	May cause unintended physiological effects (weight gain, breast tenderness); may cause serious health problems
IUD	Prevents fertilization, and interferes with first stages of pregnancy	High	Always available; does not interfere with sex	May cause heavy menstrual bleeding and cramps; may increase the chance of pelvic infection
Diaphragm	Blocks sperm from reaching an egg	High if used consistently and correctly	Causes no health problems	Must be used with each incidence of intercourse; must be fit by a health professional
Vaginal Foam and Creams	Kills sperm	High if used consistently and correctly	Causes no health problems; can be obtained without a doctor's prescription	Must be used before each incidence of intercourse; found messy by some couples
Condom	Prevents sperm from entering vagina	High if used consistently and correctly	Causes no health problems; can be obtained without a doctor's prescription; helps prevent the spread of sexually transmitted diseases	May detract from sexual pleasure; may break or tear
Condom and Vaginal Foam Together	Prevents sperm from entering vagina and kills any sperm that accidentally enter	High	Causes no health problems; can be obtained without a doctor's prescription; helps prevent the spread of sexually transmitted diseases	Same as for condom alone and foam alone

TABLE 12.6 Theoretical and Use Effectiveness of Various Contraceptive Methods (Data indicate the number of pregnancies during the first year of use per one hundred nonsterile women initiating a method.)

Method	Theoretical Effectiveness	Use Effectiveness
Tubal Ligation	0.04	0.04
Vasectomy	0.15	0.15
Oral Contraceptive (Combined Pill)	0.34	4–10
Condom + Spermicidal Foam or Cream	less than 1	5
Mini-pill	1–1.5	5–10
IUD	1–3	5
Condom	3	10
Diaphragm	3	17
Spermicidal Foam	3	22
Withdrawal	9	20–25
Rhythm (Calendar)	13	21
None	90	90

Source: Adapted from R. A. Hatcher et al., *Contraceptive Technology 1978–1979*, New York, Irvington Publishers, 1978, p. 20.

works, and they must feel comfortable with its use. A comparison of the theoretical and use effectiveness of the major contraceptive methods is given in Table 12.6.

ABORTION

Abortion is the termination of pregnancy by medical means. Although not recommended as a contraceptive method, many women use abortion as a back-up if methods to prevent pregnancy fail. Since 1973, when the United States Supreme Court legalized abortion in the United States, approximately 5 million have been performed. By 1978 the annual number of abortions in the United States totaled nearly 1.4 million. This number represents about 29 percent of all pregnancies. About one-third of those obtaining abortions are teen-agers, and three-fourths of those obtaining abortions are unmarried.[13]

The most common method of abortion is *vacuum curettage*, which removes the embryo from the uterus by suction. It is used during the first twelve weeks of pregnancy. The procedure can be carried out in a doctor's office, clinic, or hospital, using local anesthesia and costing from $150 to $500. The risk of postoperative complications from abortion is very low. However, the chances of miscarriage in subsequent pregnancies may be as much as two to three times greater after two abortions.[14]

There is no evidence that abortion causes any particular emotional or mental problems. More often, abortion is followed by mixed feelings of relief and sadness.

For many people, the issue of abortion is clouded with uncertainties. With no universally acceptable scientific definition of when life begins, the question of whether abortion can be equated with murder perplexes many. Some opponents of legal abortion believe that its availability encourages irresponsible sexual behavior or haphazard contraceptive use, and some also see abortion as a threat to family life. Even the staunchest proponents of abortion would prefer that it not be necessary, but they argue that abortion is needed as a last resort if contraception fails, if a woman is pregnant because of rape or incest, if the unborn child is genetically defective, or if the woman's life and health are jeopardized by pregnancy or childbirth.

Recent survey data indicate that a large percentage of the American population approves of legal abortion in certain circumstances. Results from a 1980 National Opinion Research Center poll, for example, showed the following approval rates for legal abortion in various circumstances:[15]

1. Ninety percent of those polled approve of legal abortion if the woman's health is seriously endangered by the pregnancy.
2. Eighty-three percent approve of legal abortion if the woman is pregnant because of rape.
3. Eighty-three percent approve of abortion if there is a high probability that the child will have a serious defect.
4. Fifty-two percent approve of legal abortion if the family has a very low income and cannot afford any more children.
5. Forty-eight percent approve of legal abortion if the pregnant woman is not married and does not want to marry the baby's father.
6. Forty-seven percent approve of legal abortion if the woman is married but does not want any more children.
7. Forty-one percent approve of legal abortion for any reason.

THE MALE ROLE IN FAMILY PLANNING

Millions of couples successfully use condoms as their primary method of contraception, and millions more do not use any other form of

Legal abortion is a controversial issue (see also photo on page 327).

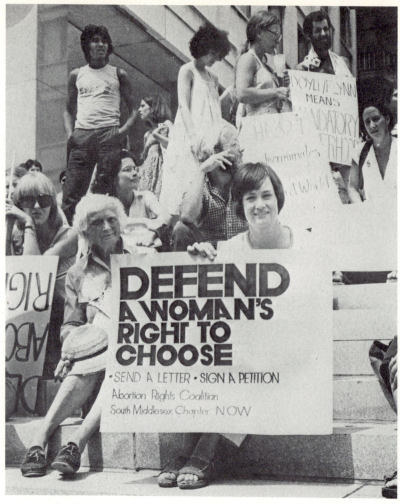

Ellen Shub/The Picture Cube

contraception because the male has had a vasectomy. Yet, men in our culture are stereotyped as having little or no interest in contraception and family planning. There are persistent myths that men only want sex, that men are not concerned about pregnancy and abortion, and that men are sexually irresponsible.

But the truth is that many men feel excluded from the contraceptive decisions that affect them and their partners. They are confronted by the widely held attitude that because it is the female who gets pregnant, it is she who should have the primary responsibility for contraception. This attitude is encouraged by the greater number of contraceptive

Jean-Claude Lejeune/Stock, Boston

methods available for women than for men and also by the activities of family-planning agencies, which traditionally have directed their services to a female clientele. As Tom Clark, a former training director at a Planned Parenthood clinic observed,

With respect to those services related to reproduction, men tend to be regarded with suspicion and hostility. In terms of the whole birth planning process, whether it involves prevention, termination, or pregnancy and parenting, men have at best a poorly defined role and at worst they are ostracized and made to feel like second class citizens.[16]

Men are involved in family planning even if the female is the principal contraceptive user. The male often helps decide on the choice of contraceptive method the couple will use. He may support or interfere with his partner's choice and use of a particular method. And he usually influences whether or not the chosen method is properly used. If an unwanted pregnancy should occur, most men want to help decide what course of action to take.

Thus, the male role in family planning extends beyond the use of a particular contraceptive method to decision making and knowledgeable and responsible use. This means that couples need to discuss their methods of contraception, and such discussions may have an additional benefit: they are conducive to better sex. Not only do they help reduce the fear of unwanted pregnancy, but they also foster more open communication about sexual matters, which in turn can produce a more harmonious sexual relationship.

SUMMARY

At the present time, the United States birth rate is the lowest in history, and it may drop even more in the future as more and more couples utilize available family-planning methods to limit their family size.

Family economics is an important family planning issue. The current costs of raising a child can add up to $70,000. Adjustments for inflation, a nonworking mother's lost income, and a college education can increase that cost to over $200,000.

Family planning also enables couples to time the births of their children to coincide with individual and career goals. This is especially important to women who wish to pursue a career, as the prime childbearing years and the prime career-building years tend to overlap. Family planning is important to those couples who may carry an inherited disease. And some couples limit family size to help ease the burden of world overpopulation.

The most commonly used, reversible contraceptive methods include withdrawal, rhythm, birth control pills, IUDs, diaphragms, vaginal foams and creams, and condoms. Permanent birth control for females (tubal ligation) and males (vasectomy) is the most popular method for people over thirty. All contraceptive methods have advantages and disadvantages. The best contraceptive method for a particular couple is one they are most comfortable with and will use correctly.

Abortion is the termination of a pregnancy by medical means. About 1.4 million abortions are performed in the United States annually.

Currently there is considerable debate about the moral and legal status of abortion.

Many people consider family planning to be solely a woman's issue. But men also are involved in family planning. Men often help decide on the couple's choice of contraceptive method and, in addition, they influence whether or not the chosen method is used responsibly. Occasionally, men take full responsibility for a couple's contraception by the use of condoms or by sterilization.

CONSIDER THIS

John was stunned by the doctor's suggestion that Melanie stop taking birth control pills. Until now he had given little thought to birth control because Melanie had always taken care of it, but now he would have to assume some of the responsibility.

Melanie's reaction to the doctor's suggestion, however, was mixed. She was glad to avoid the possible health risks associated with taking the pill, but she also realized that other contraceptive methods were not as convenient. And though, before, she had resented slightly having to be completely responsible for birth control, now she wasn't sure if she wanted to share that control.

Questions
1. Why would Melanie's doctor have suggested that she stop taking birth control pills?
2. If you were Melanie's doctor, what factors would you suggest that Melanie and John consider when choosing another form of contraception?
3. Because the woman is the one who gets pregnant if contraception fails, should Melanie continue to be the one to have the sole responsibility for birth control?
4. How much influence do you think men should have in contraception decisions?

NOTES

1. George Eliot is the pseudonym for the English novelist Mary Ann Evans (1819–1880), who found it easier to publish her work using a man's name.

2. John MacLeod and Ruth Z. Gold, "The Male Factor in Fertility and Infertility," *Fertility and Sterility*, 4 (1953): 10–33.

3. U.S. Bureau of the Census, *Historical Statistics of the United States*, Part I, Washington, D.C., U.S. Government Printing Office, 1975, p. 49.

4. U.S. Bureau of the Census, "Fertility of American Women: June, 1979," *Current Population Reports*, Series P–20, No. 358, Washington, D.C., U.S. Government Printing Office, 1980.

5. Harold T. Christensen, "Children in the Family: Relationship of Number and Spacing to Marital Success," *Journal of Marriage and the Family*, May 1968, pp. 283–289.

6. Pamela Daniels and Kathy Weingarten, "Postponing Parenthood," *Savvy*, 1 (May 1980): 55–60.

7. Ibid., p. 59.

8. H. Forssman and I. Thuwe, "One Hundred and Twenty Children Born After Application for Therapeutic Abortion Refused," *Acta Psychiatrica Scandinavia*, 42 (1966): 71–78.

9. Kathleen Ford, "Contraceptive Use in the United States, 1973–1976," *Family Planning Perspectives*, 10 (1978): 264–269.

10. Charles F. Westoff and James McCarthy, "Sterilization in the United States," *Family Planning Perspectives*, 11 (1979): 147–152.

11. Ibid.

12. Christopher Tietze, "New Estimates of Mortality Associated with Fertility Control," *Family Planning Perspectives*, 9 (1977): 74–76.

13. Jacqueline Dorroch Forrest, Ellen Sullivan, and Christopher Tietze, "Abortion in the United States, 1977–1978," *Family Planning Perspectives*, 11 (1979): 329–341.

14. David A. Grimes and Willard Cates, Jr., "Complications from Legally Induced Abortion: A Review," *Obstetrics and Gynecological Survey*, 34 (1977): 177–191.

15. Donald Granberg and Beth Wellman Granberg, "Abortion Attitudes, 1965–1980: Trends and Determinants," *Family Planning Perspectives*, 12 (1980): 250–261.

16. Tom Clark, "Institutional and Individual Views of Male Involvement in Family Planning," *Conference Proceedings on the Male Role in Family Planning*, June 6, 1975, San Francisco.

SUGGESTED READINGS

Boston Women's Health Book Collective. *Our Bodies/Ourselves*. New York, Random House, 1979. Contains a discussion of all the common contraceptive methods.

Hatcher, Robert A., and Gary K. Stewart. *Contraceptive Technology, 1981*. New York, Irvington Publishers, 1980. A thorough, somewhat technical report on all contraceptive methods and abortion.

Jaffe, Frederick S., Barbara A. Lindheim, and Philip R. Lee. *Abortion Politics*. New York, McGraw-Hill, 1981. An objective presentation of the public-policy aspects of abortion.

Stewart, Felicia, Felicia Guest, Gary Stewart, and Robert A. Hatcher. *My Body, My Health*. New York, Wiley, 1979. A comprehensive, nontechnical guide to all family-planning methods and aspects of women's sexual and reproductive health.

PARENTING

The thing that impresses me about America is the way parents obey their children.

The Duke of Windsor

13

Parenting requires considerable time and energy for as many as twenty years. Yet many people give less thought to the advantages and disadvantages of becoming a parent than they do to their major in college or a new job. As one mother said, "We knew where babies came from, but we didn't know what they were like."[1] Many people become parents without having any idea of what the demands are and how it will affect their lives.

As sociologist Alice Rossi points out, "We can have ex-spouses and ex-jobs but not ex-children."[2] Parenthood is an irreversible life change—and one for which few people are adequately prepared. Rossi notes that

A doctor facing his first patient in private practice has treated numerous patients under close supervision during internship, but probably a majority of American mothers approach maternity with no previous childcare experience beyond sporadic babysitting, perhaps a course in child psychology, or occasional care of younger siblings.[3]

Few fathers have had even that much experience.

Most parents get their first glimpse of what it is like to be a parent during pregnancy. They begin to comprehend the many facets of the parental role, and their formerly private life together begins to change to accommodate their new family member. But this preparation amounts to only a brief crash course. Parents assume their twenty-four-hour-a-day responsibilities as soon as the baby is born. There is no apprenticeship with parenthood.

In our society, there is a romantic mystique regarding children and parenthood.[4] When confronted with a new baby (or even a photo of a baby), nearly everyone coos and smiles and says, "Oh, how cute!" People are socialized from early childhood to think that babies are soft, cuddly, and beautiful—and therefore desirable. Many people also believe that marriage is incomplete without children, that children add a missing and necessary dimension to life, and that to have children is one's major purpose in life.

As with any myth, the romantic notion of parenthood holds some truth. Babies are cute and cuddly. But they are also helpless, may keep parents awake at night, and are totally dependent on them. And although parenting can be a very fulfilling experience, for some people it is certainly not the only way—nor the best way—to have a satisfying life.

Some parents maintain that parenthood is such a special life event that there is no way to learn about it until you experience it. This does not mean, however, that one cannot benefit from considering the many facets of the parental role before becoming a parent, and that is the focus of this chapter.

THE PARENTAL ROLE

People generally fill several social roles—for example, those of worker, spouse, friend, and citizen—and when they have children, they acquire the additional role of parent. Like other roles, the parental role carries with it a set of expectations that guide a person's behavior. These expectations come from both public and private experiences. Friends, relatives, and various medical, psychological, educational, and religious experts influence a person's conception of his or her role as a parent. But one's own experiences as a child, both positive and negative, have perhaps an even greater influence on parental role expectations. Of course, when a person actually becomes a parent and all the role expectations are put into practice, some may have to be modified to fit the reality of the parental experience.

In our culture, three major themes have dominated the definition of the parental role:

1. The parental role is a "natural" or instinctive aspect of human nature, especially for women.

2. The parental role is best carried out by mothers and that fathers play only a peripheral part.
3. Children's needs always take precedence over adults' needs.

We shall consider these themes in detail.

Is the Parental Role Instinctive?

There may have been a time in human history when parenthood was "natural" in the same way that it seems to be for other animals. Perhaps prehistoric human mothers and fathers instinctively felt the urge to nurture and care for their young, and they may have known instinctively how to raise their offspring.

Many people believe that parenthood is a "natural" or "instinctive" aspect of being human. And although the desire for sexual activity and the ability to produce children through conception, pregnancy, and childbirth are biologically based, it is unclear how nurturing attitudes and knowledge of how to behave as a parent develop. Some researchers propose that within hours after a child is born, the mother, through eye-to-eye contact and touching, becomes emotionally *bonded* to her infant, which leads ultimately to the desire to nurture.[5]

Whatever biological tendency there may be for parenting, it certainly can be overcome. For example, people can choose not to become parents, and some parents harbor mixed or negative feelings about their roles as parents. Early in this century William G. Sumner proposed the rather extreme view that "if procreation had not been put under the domination of great passion, it would have caused to cease by the burdens it entails."[6] Moreover, it is not immediately obvious to many how to behave as parents, as indicated by the hundreds of "how to parent" books that adorn bookstore shelves, the many "advice to parents" articles that appear daily in newspapers and magazines, and courses that profess to teach people how to be effective parents (see Box 13.1).

One reason that humankind has thrived over the centuries is that learning has replaced instinct as a basis for behavior. The ability to learn frees people from rigid, stereotyped behavior and allows them to adapt to physical and social changes. It also fosters culture and technology. In today's modern society, a uniform biologically based parental role would probably fail. Society changes too fast, and parents' duties must also change so as to keep up with their children's needs.

In our society, people develop parental attitudes and learn parental

BOX 13.1   Parent Education: The Search for a Recipe for Child Rearing

Today, parents may have less confidence in their child-raising abilities than they have had at any other time. In societies in which family and tribal systems and social customs do not change from generation to generation, the most workable child-rearing practices are elicited. In our society, however, parents are likely to find it difficult to apply what they learn from their parents or from their own experiences as children to the raising of their own children. Our values and customs change too quickly. This is why millions of parents look to child development experts, hoping to learn the recipe for child rearing.

Parent education, in the form of parents' meetings and magazines for parents, began in the United States in the early 1800s. In the ensuing decades, a massive body of child-rearing information has reached parents through newpaper articles and columns, magazines, books, pamphlets, radio and television programs, study groups, child guidance centers, medical and nursing personnel, lectures, films, seminars, and courses. Throughout the years, the advice for parents has varied according to the time and the expert. For example, the early editions of *Infant Care*, a regularly revised treatise on child rearing, first published by the U.S. government in 1914, counseled that thumb sucking and masturbation were

dangerous impulses that must be curbed. By 1942, however, readers were told that thumb sucking and masturbation were harmless. Early editions also told parents not to coddle a crying infant, lest the child become a spoiled tyrant. Now, however, parents are encouraged to respond to all episodes of crying with warmth and affection.

Two reasons for the differing advice on child rearing are that there is yet no single comprehensive and scientifically valid theory of child development and that social conditions are changing rapidly. The good advice of ten years ago may be today's nonsense. Even with these drawbacks, however, parent education is still beneficial. It teaches parents that parenthood is a skill to be learned and not something that comes "naturally." Also, it is possible that some expert advice gives parents insights that they might otherwise not have had. With such a variety of expert opinions, parents can find the encouragement and advice that best suits them.

Another advantage of parent education is that exposure to the theories and research findings of leading child development scholars may encourage parents to discuss parenthood with each other and with other parents, and in this way gain more confidence in their parenting abilities.

behaviors in conjunction with the learning of their sex roles. As sociologist Jessie Bernard points out:

We define adult sex roles in terms of parenthood and then see to it that girls become the kind of people we say mothers must be and boys the kind of people we say fathers should be.[7]

Traditionally, this has meant that men work outside the home to acquire resources for the family and that women stay at home to attend to the wants and needs of their children. Thus, men usually have attained their social status through work, whereas women have attained theirs through maternity.[8]

A consequence of defining the adult female sex role in terms of motherhood is that the other options for women are viewed as secondary and, in some cases, deviant or pathological. Bernard's analysis indicates that

The institutional structure of our society is based on [the fact that] motherhood is . . . woman's destiny; all else is secondary. Yes, girls should be reared to be attractive sex objects to men. Yes, they should be prepared to support themselves and their children "just in case" or "in a pinch." Yes, let them even become artists, scientists or scholars if they wish. But all that is secondary. Motherhood comes first.[9]

The parental role is only one of the many that parents may fill. Modern parents have many things competing for their time and attention—jobs, hobbies, the marital relationship—as well as children. Some individuals may want to devote much of their energy to the parental role, but others may find that the parental role is too restrictive and that it requires too much personal sacrifice. One's suitability for the parental role may be compared with one's suitability for a particular job.

If we forced every girl to become, say, a librarian or nurse or secretary or what-have-you, we would not be surprised if some performed well and others poorly. Or that some enjoyed their work while others did not. We would recognize that they are all different and that a common career would not be equally congenial to all. We show no such logic in the case of mothers.[10]

To claim the existence of a "maternal instinct," or a paternal one for that matter, seems to do a disservice to everyone and may place a tremendous burden on those to whom the parental role does not come easily.

Mother-Focused Parenthood

For the major part of this century, the primary responsibilities of parenthood have been considered the proper domain of mothers. Supported by interpretations of psychoanalytic theory and observations of children who received little or deficient care when very young, proper child development has been considered by some experts to be based on full-time, continuous, mother-given care in the early stages of life (until about age five).[11] Should a child be "deprived" of maternal care during these formative years, these theories predict that the child will be damaged irreversibly.

One of the effects of the maternal deprivation theory was to justify the rigid sex-role stereotypes of the mother being primarily responsible for child and home care and the father being primarily responsible for financial support and only peripherally responsible for child raising. Since the greatest influence on the child was thought to be proper maternal care, the logical alternative was to idealize the stay-at-home, full-time, self-sacrificing mother and to decry the absent or working mother for depriving her children of needed and irreplaceable love and attention.

That children deprived of love, attention, and proper care do not develop as well as those who receive all of these has never been in dispute, but current assessments of child rearing question the necessity of the mother being the only possible care giver in a child's early years.[12] In many cultures, children are not attended to solely by mothers. Because mothers work, children are raised—without apparent harm—by older siblings, grandparents or other relatives, child-care professionals, or in communal child-care centers. Many studies have shown that the children of working mothers are not any less well adjusted than those of stay-at-home mothers (see Chapter 10, "Marital Interaction"). And having the father or a male father-substitute involved in child care has been shown to be beneficial to child development.[13] In general, the mother-focused view of parenthood is giving way to a more balanced concept, highlighted by the following premises:[14]

1. Mothers should not be solely responsible for all the tasks of child rearing.
2. Both mothers and fathers should be allowed to experience the benefits of parenting.
3. Children benefit when both parents share responsibility for their care.

Mother-focused child care has created a generation of "Super-Moms," women whose daily duties include knowing about all of their children's activities, being responsible for their children's health care (both as nurse and as chauffeur to the doctor's office), going to PTA meetings, and being involved in Camp Fire Girls, Boy Scouts, Little League, dancing lessons, and other child-centered activities. All this

Children benefit when fathers are involved in their care.

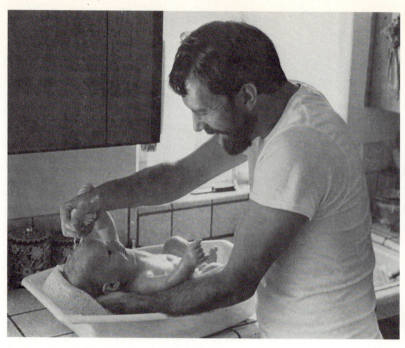

Rosemary Ranck/Black Star

is in addition to their responsibilities as home managers, intimates, companions, and confidantes to their husbands, and, often, wage earners outside the home.

Too much is expected of the maternal role if a woman is supposed to be the "perfect parent" of the "perfect child." A woman who feels totally responsible for her children's welfare and who feels that she must constantly attend to their wants and needs may also feel inadequate and guilty if, for any reason, the children do not meet expectations. Some believe that the key to a rewarding motherhood experience is to lower the expectations for mothers and to call on husbands, friends, family, and society to help with child rearing.[15]

An Alternative: Role-Sharing (Androgynous) Parenthood

Some couples choose to share the responsibilities of child care rather than to divide them according to traditional, stereotypic sex roles. Such role sharing, referred to as *androgynous parenthood*, is characterized by

two parents who share childcare relatively equally; operationally speaking, neither spouse taking more than 60% of the total time devoted to childcare in the family. Androgyny in popular usage refers to the human capacity for members of both sexes to be masculine and feminine in their behaviors—both dominant and submissive, active and passive, tough and tender.[16]

Role-sharing couples give several reasons for dividing the time and effort necessary for child-care duties:[17]

1. The children benefit when their father and mother are equally responsible for their care. Not only do they get to know their father better, but they also learn from both parents.
2. The family benefits both financially and emotionally when both parents work. Not only does this increase family income, but also many working mothers in role-sharing marriages claim to be less bored, to be free of much of the strain of trying to carry out two full-time roles (worker and homemaker), and to be less resentful.
3. Sharing child-care duties frees more time for individual and family leisure.
4. The stresses and responsibilities imposed by traditional sex roles are relieved. The mother does not have to take complete responsibility for the child's development, and the father does not have to take complete responsibility for the family's economic security.

Couples wishing to share equally the responsibilities of child rearing, because of financial or other needs or the desire to create a more egalitarian marriage, may have to overcome certain obstacles. The principal difficulty for androgynous parents seems to be in the realm of work.[18] Role-sharing couples often find that rigid work schedules for both husband and wife often conflict with the demands of child care. Also, few places of work offer child-care facilities or permit parents to bring preschool children to work with them (see Box 13.2). And fathers raised in traditional sex-role families may have to spend additional time and energy learning child-rearing skills.

Couples wishing to share more equitably the responsibilities of parenting say that more flexible working schedules ("flextime"), as well as more and better paying part-time work, would help.[19] Also, parent education courses and parent support groups can help fathers learn

BOX 13.2   Day Care

There is little doubt that children require quality care, but are their parents the only ones who can provide it? During World War II, millions of children were cared for in day-care centers because their fathers were overseas and their mothers had taken jobs to support the war effort. No one suggests that these children, now today's adults, are socially or psychologically inadequate. In many countries, including Sweden, Denmark, the Soviet Union, the People's Republic of China, and Israel, good, professional day care is common, and its recipients seem to be as well adjusted and competent as home-reared children are.

A general standard for quality day care requires that a trained professional be in charge of no more than three or four infants or five or six toddlers, and that while in the day-care center, children receive well-balanced meals, opportunities and equipment for physical exercise and recreation, arrangements for medical and nursing attention, directed learning experiences, and constructive social interactions with other children.

Parents in dual-worker families and single parents are well aware of the need for quality day care. Without it, the demands of parenthood can become burdensome to the point that the joys of parenting are overshadowed by its problems. Some parents need full-time day-care help, whereas others need only part-time help—just a few hours a week to give them time to attend to important matters.

Today, approximately 50 percent of all American women with children under the age of six work, which means that between seven and eight million preschoolers need either full-time or part-time day care. Yet the federal government estimates that there is space in qualified day-care centers for only about 1.6 million preschoolers. Parents who cannot place their children in day-care centers must arrange either for a baby sitter to come to the parents' home or for child care at another person's home (family day care). Despite both these alternatives, finding quality care is often a problem, and having a baby sitter in the home can be expensive.

One alternative is for the parents' employers to provide quality day care for a moderate weekly fee. Besides offering good care at a reasonable cost, employer-sponsored day care would enable the parents to visit their children during the day, and it would reduce transportation costs.

Employers also would benefit from sponsoring day-care centers. The few companies that do offer child-care facilities report a greater ability to attract employees, lower absenteeism, improved employee attitudes toward the company and their work, lower job turnover, favorable publicity, and improved community relations.*

*U.S. Department of Labor, "Childcare Centers Sponsored by Employers and Labor Unions in the United States" (pamphlet issued by the Women's Bureau, 1980).

more about the demands of child care. Whether role sharing will become the dominant form of parenting in the United States remains to be seen.

The parental role is dominated by the belief that "good" parents must give their children top priority, often to the exclusion of other life satisfactions. This role expectation has created the image of the "ideal parent," one who is

a "grownup" before the kids arrive and doesn't go through any unsettling or painful changes after that; [and who] will give selflessly of herself and himself without conflict, ambivalence, or resentment.[20]

Many parents and child development experts do not agree with this model of the "ideal parent."[21] It is unrealistic to believe that people have reached some pinnacle of maturity when they become parents. People grow, develop, and change throughout their lives, and parenthood is one of the most profound developmental experiences. Fulfilling the social expectations of the parental role and interacting with one's own children usually teach people about themselves and offer new perspectives of the world. According to the Group for the Advancement of Psychiatry:

Parenthood is a stage in the life cycle of the individual during which emotional growth and development continue. Though not often emphasized, this is probably the most enduring joy of parenthood. It is an active joy, derived from doing and becoming as opposed to the passive joy of receiving.[22]

Many also criticize the notion that the "ideal parent" must be self-sacrificing. Rather than being totally devoted to their children, parents are being encouraged to attend also to their own needs.[23] Attending to their own needs does not necessarily mean that parents will neglect their children. On the contrary, many believe that children's needs are met more fully when parents' requirements for support, learning, security, leisure, self-esteem, and time alone are met.[24] Rhona Rapoport, Robert N. Rapoport, and Ziona Strelitz, of England's Institute of Family and Environmental Research, believe that

If parents are drawn into the expectation that nothing is enough, nothing is too good, nothing is too great a sacrifice for their children— they are not only likely to surrender their own satisfactions to the altar of child-centered family life, but do damage to the child as well. This does not contradict the opposite danger—that child neglect is harmful.

We assume that parents who are more satisfied people are better influences on their children.[25]

Many parents agree with these experts, as indicated by this mother of four:

I believe that unless I, the parent, feel good about myself and comfortable with myself and my own identity, and have some way of getting myself validated—through work or committee activities or something—my kids become too important to me as extensions of myself. How many parties have we been to where everybody sits around and talks about their kids and what grades they made, and which kids are doing what? I think that as parents, if we begin to sense that we are getting our feelings of identity and goodness about ourselves because our kids are succeeding, we had better take the time to look at ourselves and say, "Now this isn't helping us and it certainly isn't helping our kids." Because sooner or later it puts too heavy a burden on the kids and doesn't free them to be themselves.[26]

By trying to be both fulfilled individuals and good parents, people are more likely to be able to accept the wide range of experiences—both the joys and disappointments—of parenthood, as well as their own imperfections as parents. They will also be better able to view their children as people and not simply as extensions of themselves.

THE EFFECTS OF CHILDREN ON PARENTS

The arrival of a couple's first child probably changes their lives more than any other aspect of their relationship together. The two-person family unit becomes a three-person family unit, and time, attention, and energy are no longer shared exclusively by the marital partners. As one mother said, "Once the baby comes, you're never alone again." The new parents' lives are taken over by their new duties and responsibilities. If a child comes soon after marriage, the couple must make simultaneously the double adjustment of becoming spouses and parents.

The transition from childlessness to parenthood is sometimes so disorienting that it becomes a life crisis, characterized by mothers experiencing a

loss of sleep (especially during the early months), chronic "tiredness" or exhaustion, extensive confinement to home and the resulting curtailment of social contacts, giving up the satisfactions and income of outside employment; additional washing and ironing, guilt at not being a "better" mother, the long hours and seven day (and night) week necessary in caring for an infant; decline in housekeeping standards, worry over physical appearance [that is, increased weight after pregnancy].[27]

New fathers may share some of these feelings and may also complain about the

decline in sexual response of wife, economic pressure resulting from wife's retirement plus additional expenditures necessary for child, interference with social life, worry about a second pregnancy in the near future, and a general disenchantment with the parental role.[28]

Several studies indicate that many couples never fully adjust to the changes incurred by parenthood and that the level of satisfaction in their marriages decreases. In general, childless couples report greater marital happiness than couples with children do (see Chapter 10, "Marital Interaction").

Despite the difficulties of being parents, most parents say they are glad they had children and would do it again if they had their lives to live over.[29] Apparently, the costs of parenthood, many of which were discussed in Chapter 12, "Family Planning," are balanced, and perhaps exceeded, by the rewards.

A large-scale study of American mothers revealed that the arrival of the first child has many effects on the family[30] (see Table 13.1). In general, the mothers reported the experience of parenthood to be mostly positive, even though having children sometimes prevented them from having the freedom to work, to acquire more education, to have time to themselves, to travel, to socialize as much as they wanted, or to engage in recreational activities.

The study also found that the arrival of a new child could change significantly the husband-wife relationship. For example, for some, becoming parents shifted husbands and wives toward more traditional sex-role behavior: men became more concerned with being providers, and women focused their energies on being homemakers. The study also showed a slight trend toward a greater separation of friendship spheres—husbands and wives having fewer friends in common and more friends of their own.

Although parenthood may separate spouses' interests and activities, it often brings the couple closer together emotionally. About 70 percent of the women in the study reported that their marriages had become closer because the child gave the spouses a common task, something

TABLE 13.1   The Ten Most Common Answers of First-Time Mothers to the
Question, "How Is a Woman's Life Changed by Having Children?"

1. It gives life fulfillment, a goal, meaning, and enrichment.
2. You feel more adult, more mature; you become a woman.
3. You have more responsibility.
4. You feel needed, useful.
5. It brings happiness, joy, fun.
6. It ties you down; you can't act impulsively; you can't do specific things.
7. You lose your individuality; your life is not your own.
8. You become a better person.
9. It is a growth experience.
10. It gives a sense of achievement, creativity.

Source: Adapted from L. W. Hoffman, "Effects of the First Child on the Woman's Role," in W. B.
Miller and L. F. Newman, eds., *The First Child and Family Formation*, Chapel Hill, N. C.,
Population Center of the University of North Carolina, 1978, pp. 340–367.

they could do together. Parenthood also enabled them to share the joys
of watching their child grow and perform developmental tasks, such as
taking the first step or speaking the first word. Couples also felt closer
because they saw the child as a part of themselves; as some said, "a
product of our love."

Having one's first child is a major life event, bringing with it the
need for many adjustments in one's life style. In this regard, the
transition to parenthood can be viewed as a crisis. But it is a crisis that
leads to a new stage in a person's personal development, rather than a
crisis from which the person returns to life as it was before. Thus, along
with the first child comes the difficult task of giving up many of the
perspectives and values of the preparental stage of life and finding new
sources of life satisfactions and purposes. While the adjustments in
activities, relationships, and perspectives are being made, a couple
may experience considerable strain—it often is uncomfortable to
change life patterns—but it appears that most people's transition to
parenthood is a positive and rewarding life experience.

THE TASKS OF PARENTHOOD

All the tasks of parenthood focus on one particular end result: to rear
children to be competent and healthy adults. This means that parents
must provide an environment that both fulfills their children's biologi-

cal and psychological needs and influences their development so that they learn what is considered socially acceptable behavior. Ellen Peck and William Granzig, the authors of *The Parent Test,* give this brief sketch of a few parental tasks:

Children require lots of physical care when young, and lots of psychological nurturing when young *and* older. Children are like foreign visitors to a country where we, the adults, are experienced natives, and we must act as their interpreters, explaining the language and customs of this less-than-logical land that we have brought them into. Having a child means not only changing diapers and teaching to walk, but explaining love and social justice, war and crime and energy policy, racism and sexism, algebra and why Erlichman went to jail but Nixon didn't, and why you can't stay out till 11 P.M. even if everybody else can.[31]

Most child development experts organize the various tasks of parenthood into five categories:

1. *Providing for Children's Physical Needs* All children require adequate nutrition, shelter, medical care, and safe surroundings to promote physical well-being.

2. *Fostering Emotional Well-Being and Normal Personality Development* Children need to feel loved, wanted, and valued, which gives them a sense of belonging and self-esteem. This helps them to become independent and interdependent individuals.

3. *Encouraging Optimum Intellectual Development* Children are born with the ability to learn many kinds of intellectual skills. The child's physical and emotional environments greatly influence the degree to which intellectual and creative potentials are realized.

4. *Teaching Moral Values* Children need to learn society's "rules" —what is considered right and wrong—and to master the self-discipline needed to behave responsibly toward others.

5. *Fostering Development of Acceptable Social Relations* Children develop concepts of money, success, work, and future plans. They also learn about social relations with the opposite sex and formulate their own opinions about the parental role.

Parents influence the development of their children in several ways. By providing love, affection, and care, parents help their children to feel secure and worthy. By providing a stimulating environment—one with a variety of challenges for a developing mind—parents foster intellectual development. By rewarding and punishing their children's behavior and by acting as models of proper behavior, parents encourage their children's moral and social development.

The Benefits of Loving Care

Within the first year of life, nearly all babies form deep emotional attachments to a few special adults. These adults are the people who feed, cuddle, talk to, and play with the infant. They are the ones to whom the child turns when distressed, hungry, or playful. They are the people most likely to be able to soothe the baby. And their absence increases the child's anxiety, whereas their presence reduces the child's fear of unfamiliar situations. Because in our society mothers are often the primary caretakers in a child's first year of life, the child's first deep emotional attachment is usually to her, although the first attachment can also be to the father or to another adult caretaker.

Attachment develops through a process of mutual interaction between a baby and the caretakers. Infants do such things as cry, smile, gaze intently, and vocalize, which elicit caretaking behavior from adults. Those who respond to a baby's behaviors attain a prominent position of trust and favor, which certainly is infant love. Often, the adult caretakers develop their own deep attachment to the child (parental love), but this may not always happen.

After about the age of two, children develop the capacity for symbolic thought, and a form of child-parent love, different from infant attachment, emerges. This *symbolic* love is based on the child's assessment of his or her parents' love. Thus, children who did not see one of their parents in infancy (because of war separation, for example) can nevertheless love that parent if they believe that he or she loves and values them.

Infant attachment seems to form the basis of feelings of security in a child's early years, and the parents' continued loving and valuing leads to greater feelings of security and to the development of feelings of self-worth.

The Benefits of Environmental Stimulation

Most child psychologists believe that children's intellectual and social development is enhanced in an environment that presents a wide variety of stimuli that attract a child's attention. This belief is based on observations of institutionalized children whose basic physical needs are cared for but who have little opportunity to explore their environ-

Children's intellectual development is enhanced by a stimulating environment.

Jean-Claude Lejeune

ment, play with interesting toys and games, or interact frequently with adults. These children generally are not alert; they acquire language more slowly; and their intellectual and social development is retarded.

But the intellectual and social capabilities of children exposed to varied and stimulating environments tend to develop more quickly. One representative study showed, for example, that children who frequently receive emotional and verbal responses from parents or other adult caretakers, who have appropriate play materials, and who have a variety of stimuli develop more of their mental abilities.[32] In addition, a stimulating environment presented with love and care can be a major factor in the development of self-worth and self-confidence.

The Socialization of Children

The socialization of children is their acquisition of the behaviors, beliefs, ethical standards, and attitudes valued by their families and society. Socialization teaches a young person how to control aggressive feelings, how to be generous and helpful, how to get along in society, and the consequences of not getting along. Children are also socialized to adopt the attitudes and behaviors considered appropriate for members of their sex (sex roles). One of the traditional purposes of sex-role socialization is to promote marriage and childbearing, and hence to perpetuate the family and society.

Parents are usually the most influential agents of socialization. They train their children by rewarding appropriate behavior and by punishing inappropriate behavior. This teaches children not only the rules for proper behavior in specific situations but also the more general moral principles guiding all actions. Another way parents influence socialization is through modeling. Children learn many behaviors simply by imitating their parents, and they also learn by identifying with their parents. Through identification, children adopt their parents' values, feelings, and actions, usually without any conscious motivation or direct instruction by parents.

Sex-Role Socialization Most behavioral differences between males and females appear to be a product of *sex-role socialization,* a complex process involving the child's learning about the kinds of attitudes and behaviors that are expected of members of his or her sex. Sex-role socialization begins with the *sex typing* of newborn infants—the labeling of them as males or females. And sex typing leads to the development of *gender identity,* the awareness of being either a male or a female.[33] When a child is born, almost the first thing that is noticed is the child's biological sex. Once an infant is labeled a girl or a boy, she or he is thereafter treated by caretaking adults and others as a member of that gender (for example, pink is considered the appropriate color for girls and blue the appropriate color for boys). Having been sex typed at birth, the infant eventually incorporates into her or his self-image the awareness of being a female or a male. By the age of about five years, the gender identity is fixed for life.

How a child comes to express femaleness or maleness depends on the interrelationship of what is learned and, to a limited extent, on sex hormones.[34] By far the greatest contribution to the development of sex roles is learning. Children learn early in life which attitudes and behaviors are supposed to be appropriate for the members of the two sexes. By the age of three, most children can cite a long list of behaviors that are characteristic of one gender but not the other.

Exactly which attitudes and behaviors are deemed appropriate for the sexes depends on the particular culture. The specifics of sex-role behavior often differ from society to society and from time to time in any given society. For example, in some agrarian societies, only the men carry out the agricultural duties that sustain the family, whereas in other agrarian societies only the women do the planting and harvesting.

The traditional stereotype of maleness in American society calls for

 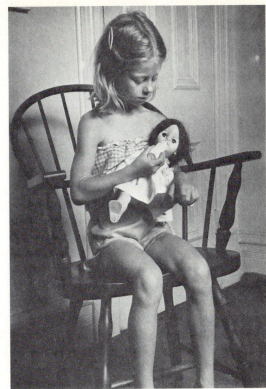

Sex-role socialization begins early in childhood.

Photo at left by James T. Coit/Jeroboam; photo at right by Jean-Claude Lejeune.

men to compete for economic resources and to share what they acquire with mates and children. Men are also expected to defend themselves, their families, and their society with acts of physical violence. To fulfill these expectations and other duties of their sex role, men are expected to be more aggressive, logical, brave, independent, and unemotional than women are.

The traditional American stereotype of the sex roles for women restricts them to domestic duties. The cultural expectation is that women are supposed to marry, see to the physical, emotional, and sexual needs of their husbands, and care for the home and children. To fulfill this role, women are expected to be more emotional, passive, and dependent than men are.

As we mention elsewhere in this book (particularly in Chapter 15, "The Changing Status of Women and Men"), the traditional sex-role stereotype for American women and men is unrealistic and occasionally destructive and oppressive. In response, women in increasing numbers are entering the labor force, and some spouses are sharing the responsibilities of family care. Women are becoming more assertive about their needs and wants, and men are becoming freer to express their feelings and display emotion.

NONPARENTAL INFLUENCES ON CHILD DEVELOPMENT

Although parents are the major influence on their children's development, other factors and individuals also are important. For example, each child is born with particular inherited characteristics. The degree to which these inherited, or biologically derived, characteristics can be modified by the environment has still not been determined.

Children are also affected by other family members, especially siblings. About 80 percent of all American children have siblings, and what they learn from their brothers and sisters can range from cooperation and empathy to competition and domination. The effects of siblings on a child depend primarily on birth order (see Table 13.2) and sex, and the influence of siblings is probably the most prominent when the child is between two and ten years of age.[35] Grandparents and other

---

TABLE 13.2   Some Effects of Birth Order on Child Development

---

First-born Children Are:

- more likely to identify with parents and to adopt parental rather than peer values
- more strongly motivated toward achievement
- more affiliative and dependent on others for support
- more conforming to authority and to social pressures
- more conscientious
- more prone to feelings of guilt
- more concerned with cooperation and responsibility
- more inclined to enter occupations requiring parent-surrogate role (teacher, nurse)
- more likely to achieve eminence in their profession

Later-born Children Are:

- more likely to suffer feelings of inadequacy
- more realistic in self-evaluation
- less cautious in behavior
- more likely to acquire more social skills and therefore greater popularity
- better able to accommodate the needs and wishes of others
- more likely to emulate older siblings

Source: Adapted from Paul H. Mussen, John J. Conger, and Jerome Kagan, *Child Development and Personality* (5th ed.), New York, Harper & Row, Pub., 1979, pp. 370–372.

members of the extended family can also affect the child's development.

Because American families do not live in total isolation from the rest of society, a child's development is influenced by many factors outside the family. Children learn from their playmates, their playmates' parents, and their schoolteachers. Many children are also influenced by religious education. And there is no doubt that children are affected by what they see and hear in the media, particularly television.

Nearly every child lives in a house with a television set. And just as they model themselves after their parents and other adults in their lives, children also model themselves after characters on the television screen. Children are highly susceptible to what they see on television; and violent programs can increase the likelihood of aggressive behavior, whereas programming that emphasizes sharing, helpfulness, and sympathy can increase altruistic and cooperative behavior.[36] Children also learn sex-role behavior on television.[37] Besides the other child-rearing tasks, monitoring the content of their children's television viewing has become one of parents' major tasks.

SUMMARY

Parenthood is one of the most demanding life experiences but is one for which few people are adequately prepared. People are socialized from childhood to think that children are desirable and that parenthood is both a means of personal fulfillment and a family and social duty. Yet rarely do prospective parents comprehend the full implications of being a parent.

The parental role is dominated by the notions that parenthood is instinctive, that the mother is the only proper caretaker, and that parents should devote all their attention and resources to their children. There is little to suggest that nurturing attitudes or child-rearing methods are instinctive in humans. Neither are mothers the only ones who can give proper child care. Fathers and other adults can also successfully care for children. A few parents share child-rearing duties so as to involve the father equally in the children's lives and to free the mother from total responsibility for home care and child rearing, as well as to free the father from total responsibility for the economic support of his family. Many child development experts and parents disagree with the premise that parents need to be totally self-sacrificing. They claim that children, as well as parents, benefit when parents devote time and energy to their own personal needs.

The entry of children into a family radically changes a couple's life style and relationship. Children compete for attention, they take up time and family resources, and they curtail their parents' individual freedom. Nevertheless, most parents would have children again if they had their lives to live over.

Parental tasks include satisfying the children's physical and emotional needs and providing an environment that promotes intellectual development, instills moral values, and teaches acceptable social behavior. Parents do all this by giving loving care and offering a varied and stimulating environment that engages the child's curiosity. Children learn ethics and acceptable social behavior (socialization) by being either rewarded or punished for their behavior and by imitating their parents. Sex-role behavior is based on a child's knowledge of his or her gender (gender identity) and the attitudes and behaviors considered appropriate for members of that sex.

Parents, siblings, grandparents, other family members, peers, peers' parents, teachers, and the media (particularly television) all influence the child's development.

CONSIDER THIS

Linda was at the end of her rope. Since marrying Stan a year ago, she'd been trying everything to make a real family life for her new husband and his three children.

But no matter what she did, it just wasn't good enough. The children wouldn't accept her as their new mother. John, the oldest at fifteen, ignored her completely. Margo, aged thirteen, was at least polite, but their relationship was strained. Only Susannah, who was eight, was warm, although cautious. And the children were always between her and Stan. They seemed to get all of his attention, and sometimes he harshly criticized Linda's attempts to discipline them.

Linda was accustomed to doing things well, and so she was upset to be failing as a stepmother. What was worse, because she was thirty-four years old and had not been married before, she considered this her only chance to experience motherhood and family life. But now, a year later, instead of the love and warmth she had expected, she felt like an outcast and resented her new family.

Questions
1. What are some of the reasons that Linda is having so much trouble fulfilling her expectations as a stepparent?
2. What would you advise Linda to do to improve her relationship with Stan's children?

3. How can the natural parent help the stepparent adjust to the parental role?
4. How do you feel about the possibility of becoming a stepparent?
5. How does the role of stepparent differ from that of natural parent?

NOTES

1. E. E. LeMasters, "Parenthood as Crisis," *Marriage and Family Living*, 19 (1957): 353.
2. Alice Rossi, "Transition to Parenthood," *Journal of Marriage and the Family*, 30 (February 1968): 26.
3. Ibid., p. 29.
4. E. E. LeMasters, *Parents in Modern America* (rev. ed.), Homewood, Ill., Dorsey Press, 1974, pp. 18–32; Arlene Skolnick, *The Intimate Environment*, Boston, Little, Brown, 1977, pp. 291–294.
5. Roberto Sosa, "Maternal-Infant Interaction During the Immediate Postpartum Period," *Year Book of Pediatrics*, Chicago, Year Book Medical Publishers, 1978, pp. 451–465.
6. William G. Sumner, *Folkways*, Lexington, Mass., Ginn, 1906, p. 310.
7. Jessie Bernard, *The Future of Motherhood*, New York, Dial Press, 1974, p. 25.
8. Alice Rossi, "Transition to Parenthood."
9. Jessie Bernard, *The Future of Motherhood*, p. 25.
10. Ibid., p. 31.
11. John Bowlby, *Attachment and Loss*, London, Hogarth Press, 1973.
12. Rhona Rapoport, Robert N. Rapoport, and Ziona Strelitz, *Fathers, Mothers and Society*, New York, Basic Books, 1977.
13. Michael E. Lamb, *The Role of the Father in Child Development*, New York, John Wiley, 1976.
14. John DeFrain, quoted in Rhona Rapoport, Robert N. Rapoport, and Ziona Strelitz, *Fathers, Mothers and Society*, p. 57.
15. Boston Women's Health Book Collective, *Ourselves and Our Children*, New York, Random House, 1978.
16. John DeFrain, "Androgynous Parents Tell Who They Are and What They Need," *Family Coordinator*, April 1979, p. 237.
17. Linda Haas, "Role Sharing Couples: A Study in Egalitarian Marriages," *Family Relations*, 29 (1980): 289–296.
18. John DeFrain, "Androgynous Parents."
19. Ibid.
20. Boston Women's Health Book Collective, *Ourselves and Our Children*, pp. 4–5.

21. Jerome Kagan, "The Psychological Requirements for Human Development," in N. B. Talbot, *Raising Children in Modern America: Problems and Prospective Solutions*, Boston, Little, Brown, 1976.

22. Group for the Advancement of Psychiatry, *Joys and Sorrows of Parenthood*, New York, Scribner's, 1973, p. 15.

23. Rhona Rapoport, Robert N. Rapoport, and Ziona Strelitz, *Fathers, Mothers and Society*; Boston Women's Health Book Collective, *Ourselves and Our Children*.

24. Boston Women's Health Book Collective, *Ourselves and Our Children*, p. 5.

25. Rhona Rapoport, Robert N. Rapoport, and Ziona Strelitz, *Fathers, Mothers and Society*, p. 26.

26. Boston Women's Health Book Collective, *Ourselves and Our Children*, p. 5.

27. E. E. LeMasters, "Parenthood as Crisis," p. 354.

28. Ibid.

29. Robert O. Blood and Donald M. Wolfe, *Husbands and Wives*, Glencoe, Ill., Free Press, 1960, pp. 138–141; Angus Campbell, Philip E. Converse, and Willard L. Rodgers, *The Quality of American Life*, New York, Russell Sage Foundation, 1976.

30. Lois Hoffman, "Effects of the First Child on Woman's Role," in W. B. Miller and L. F. Newman, eds., *The First Child and Family Formation*, Chapel Hill, N.C., Population Center of the University of North Carolina, 1978, pp. 340–367.

31. Ellen Peck and William Granzig, *The Parent Test*, New York, Putnam & Sons, 1978, p. 18.

32. R. H. Bradley and B. M. Caldwell, "The Relation of Infants' Home Environment to Mental Test Performance at Fifty-four Months: A Follow-up Study," *Child Development*, 47 (1976): 1172–1174.

33. J. L. Hampson and J. G. Hampson, "The Ontogenesis of Sexual Behavior in Man," in W. C. Young, ed., *Sex and Internal Secretions* (3rd ed.), Baltimore, Williams & Wilkins, 1961; John Money and Anke A. Ehrhardt, *Man and Woman, Boy and Girl*, Baltimore, The Johns Hopkins University Press, 1972.

34. Anke A. Ehrhardt and Heino F. L. Meyer-Bahlburg, "Effects of Prenatal Sex Hormones on Gender-Related Behavior," *Science*, 211 (1981): 1312–1318; Robert T. Rubin, June M. Reinisch, and Roger F. Haskett, "Postnatal Gonadal Steroid Effects on Human Behavior," *Science*, 211 (1981): 1318–1324.

35. Paul H. Mussen, John J. Conger, and Jerome Kagan, *Child Development and Personality* (5th ed.), New York, Harper & Row, Pub., 1979.

36. David Elkind and Irving Weiner, *Development of the Child*, New York, John Wiley, 1978, pp. 284–287.

37. Paul E. McGhee and Terry Frueh, "Television and the Learning of Sex Role Stereotypes," *Sex Roles*, 6 (1980): 179–187.

SUGGESTED READINGS

Bernard, Jesse. *The Future of Motherhood*. New York, Dial Press, 1974. A discussion of the traditional maternal role and suggestions for its change.

Boston Women's Health Book Collection. *Ourselves and Our Children*. New York, Random House, 1978. An examination of all aspects of becoming and being a parent.

LeMasters, E. E. *Parents in Modern America*. Homewood, Ill., Dorsey Press, 1977. A study of the many dimensions of parental responsibility.

Peck, Ellen, and William Granzig. *The Parent Test*. New York, Putnam & Sons, 1978. Suggestions on how to determine one's suitability for parenting.

Rapoport, Rhona, Robert N. Rapoport, and Ziona Strelitz. *Fathers, Mothers, and Society*. New York, Basic Books, 1977. A thorough examination of parental roles and suggestions for sharing parental responsibilities.

V

CONTEMPORARY CONCERNS

SEPARATION, DIVORCE, AND REMARRIAGE

Divorcees are people who have not achieved a good marriage—they are also people who would not settle for a bad one.

Paul Bohannan[1]

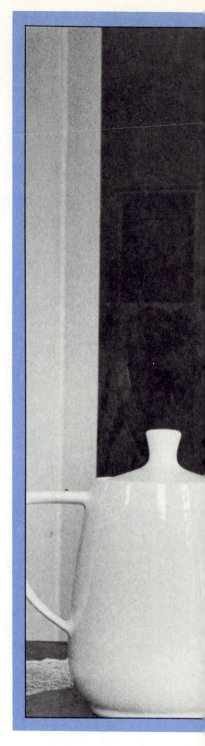

14

Divorce is the legal termination of marriage. Besides the change in legal status, divorce is a major change in an individual's life. It redefines relationships with the former spouse and one's children, relatives, and circle of friends. It may require a change in living arrangements and employment, and the emotional turmoil may affect a person's energy level, concentration, and feelings of self-worth.

In our society, divorce is often equated with failure. Many people believe that bad marriages break up but that good marriages stay together. Yet intact marriages are not always happy marriages. Stresses and conflict are part of nearly every marriage, and depending on the two individuals and their personal situation, marital problems may or may not eventually lead to divorce.

For some, divorce is not an acceptable way to deal with a troubled marriage. Some people's personal or religious convictions may forbid divorce, or they may see divorce as an admission of failure. Others may find the emotional or financial costs of divorce too high. When divorce is not an alternative, couples may simply resign themselves to their situation, perhaps by lowering their expectations for marital happiness or by devoting themselves to their work, children, or other activities.

The United States has one of the world's highest divorce rates. And even though many American marriages end in separation or divorce, people are stunned, angered, and surprised when it happens to them. Separation and divorce are emotionally wrenching events, and many people are unprepared for the emotional upheaval, physical exhaustion, and, at times, financial strain and illness that occur with a change in marital status (see Box 14.1).

BOX 14.1   Divorce as a Stressful Life Change

Almost all life changes, both positive and negative, cause stress. Psychiatrists Thomas Holmes and Richard Rahe devised the "Social Readjustment Rating Scale" (SRRS) to help quantify the degree of stress associated with various major life events. The SRRS ranks life changes according to Life Change Units (LCU) which have values from zero to one hundred. The life changes that require the most readjustment carry the highest LCU values (see table).

According to Holmes's and Rahe's research, the death of a spouse is the most stressful life event (earning 100 LCU). Divorce is the second most stressful life event (73 LCU), and marital separation is third (65 LCU). This means that as a single life event, divorce and separation are extremely difficult to adjust to. Furthermore, when a person divorces, there are other life changes which add to the total number of LCU. For example, a divorced person's financial state usually changes (38 LCU), living conditions change (25 LCU), residence chang-es (20 LCU), social activities change (18 LCU), and sleeping habits change (16 LCU).

Even in an amicable divorce, a person can easily accumulate over 150 LCU in a short period of time. Research with the SRRS has shown that the accumulation of more than 150 LCU in one year carries with it the high probability that a person will experience a negative health change within that year or soon thereafter. Apparently, the demands of dealing with accumulated stresses deplete an individual's physical resources, which in turn may result in illness or other forms of physical harm such as accidents, infectious diseases, the worsening of a previous illness, injuries, and so on. There is probably no way to avoid accumulating a large number of LCU when divorcing, but divorcing individuals can guard their health if they are aware of the degree of stress that the divorce and the life changes related to the divorce are causing.

TABLE   Social Readjustment Rating Scale

Rank	Life Event	Mean Value
1	Death of spouse	100
2	Divorce	73
3	Marital separation	65
4	Jail term	63
5	Death of close family member	63
6	Personal injury or illness	53
7	Marriage	50
8	Fired at work	47
9	Marital reconciliation	45
10	Retirement	45
11	Change in health of family member	44
12	Pregnancy	40
13	Sex difficulties	39

BOX 14.1   (Continued)

Rank	Life Event	Mean Value
14	Gain of new family member	39
15	Business adjustment	39
16	Change in financial state	38
17	Death of close friend	37
18	Change to different line of work	36
19	Change in number of arguments with spouse	35
20	Mortgage over $10,000	31
21	Foreclosure of mortgage or loan	30
22	Change in responsibilities at work	29
23	Son or daughter leaving home	29
24	Trouble with in-laws	29
25	Outstanding personal achievement	28
26	Wife begin or stop work	26
27	Begin or end school	26
28	Change in living conditions	25
29	Revision of personal habits	24
30	Trouble with boss	23
31	Change in work hours or conditions	20
32	Change in residence	20
33	Change in schools	20
34	Change in recreation	19
35	Change in church activities	19
36	Change in social activities	18
37	Mortgage or loan less than $10,000	17
38	Change in sleeping habits	16
39	Change in number of family get-togethers	15
40	Change in eating habits	15
41	Vacation	13
42	Christmas	12
43	Minor violations of the law	11

Source: Table reprinted with permission from *Journal of Psychosomatic Research*, Vol. 11 (1967), Thomas H. Holmes and R. H. Rahe, "The Social Readjustment Rating Scale," copyright © 1967, Pergammon Press, Ltd. Other information in box from same source, pages 213–218.

In this chapter we examine the current divorce statistics, characteristics of divorced people, a brief history of divorce, legal changes in divorce laws, the emotional and economic impact of divorce, children and divorce, divorce mediation, separation and desertion, and remarriage.

THE DIVORCE RATE

Until the Civil War, divorce was a rare phenomenon, and the problem was not considered important enough to warrant the collection of national statistics. The U.S. Census Bureau did not publish its first divorce tabulations until 1867. The total number of divorces reported in that year was 9,937. One hundred years later, in 1967, the number had increased to over one-half million, and the number of divorces exceeded the one-million mark in 1975.[2]

It is difficult to obtain accurate national divorce statistics because each state has different methods of record keeping, and only about half the states report their divorce records to the federal government. In addition, the popularly cited divorce rates are often misleading (see Box 14.2). All divorce calculations, however, indicate that the divorce rate in the United States has been steadily increasing (see Figure 14.1).

Demographic Characteristics Associated with a Higher Divorce Rate

Although people's individual reasons for divorce vary widely, the likelihood of divorce tends to be higher in groups having certain demographic characteristics. These factors do not cause divorce but, rather, indicate the group characteristics that have been shown to be associated with higher rates of divorce.

1. *People who marry when they are young generally have higher divorce rates than those who marry when they are older.* As we saw in Chapter 4, "Choosing a Partner," the divorce rate for teen-age marriages is twice that for marriages of persons in their twenties.

2. *Marriages that end in divorce are generally of short duration.* The most probable time of separation is the one- to two-year period immediately following marriage, and the longer a marriage lasts the less likely it is that there will be a divorce. For example, for marriages of two years or less duration, approximately 1 couple in 275 gets divorced. After thirty years of marriage, however, only 1 couple out of 625 gets divorced.[3]

Because couples who separate may not apply for a divorce immediately and because legal procedures are lengthy, "the average elapsed time from the wedding until the issuance of the divorce decree is about seven years—giving rise to the expression 'seven-year itch.' "[4]

3. *For white males, the probability of divorce is higher for those with a low socioeconomic status.* Thus, the divorce rate decreases as educational level, occupational status, and income increase. This pattern is different for white women and blacks, particularly with regard to levels

BOX 14.2   What Do Divorce Rates Really Measure?

Periodically, the media report alarming statistics on the rapidly increasing divorce rate in the United States. The divorce rate most often cited compares the number of divorces in a year with the number of marriages in that year. Currently, this figure is approaching one divorce for every two marriages. But this measure of the divorce rate is misleading because it compares two different populations—the population of single people who are marrying in a given year and the population of already married individuals who married that year or in previous years, and who are now divorcing.

Another commonly used divorce statistic is the *crude rate of divorce*, which calculates the number of divorces for each 1,000 persons. It is also misleading because it includes children and people who have chosen not to marry. To remedy these measurement problems, *demographers* (persons who study the characteristics of human populations) use a *redefined divorce rate*. This measures the number of divorces each year per 1,000 married women, which permits calculation of the percentage of all existing marriages terminated by divorce that year. At the end of the 1970s, this rate was 21.9 per 1,000 married women (see Figure 14.1), which means that in 1978 approximately 2.2 percent of all the marriages in the United States ended in divorce.

The redefined divorce rate; the *age-specific divorce rate*, which measures the rates of divorce per 1,000 married women in various age categories; and the *standardized divorce rate*, which is based on the age-specific rate, give a clearer and more accurate picture of divorce trends. In addition, statistical methods allow demographers to use the divorce rate for a particular year to predict the proportion of all marriages that will be terminated by divorce. The current prediction is that 40 percent of all marriages will end in divorce.*

*For an excellent critique of divorce rates see J. Lynn England and Phillip R. Kunz, "The Application of Age-Specific Rates to Divorce," *Journal of Marriage and the Family*, 37 (February 1975): 40–46.

---

of income. For white women, the proportion of those divorced is higher for those at higher income levels. For black men, the relationship between income and divorce is U-shaped, with just as large a proportion of divorced men at higher income levels as at lower income levels, but a smaller proportion at middle income levels.[5]

4.   *Blacks generally have higher divorce rates than whites do, although there is much regional variation.*   The higher black divorce rates occur at all levels of education, occupation, and income. However, the differences in divorce rates for blacks and whites are greater at the higher educational and income levels than they are at the lower levels.[6]

5.   *In the United States, the divorce rates tend to increase as one moves from east to west.*   Vital statistics gathered over many decades reveal that the New England and the Middle Atlantic states have the lowest rates, the Midwest has intermediate rates, and the Pacific Coast has the highest divorce rates.[7]

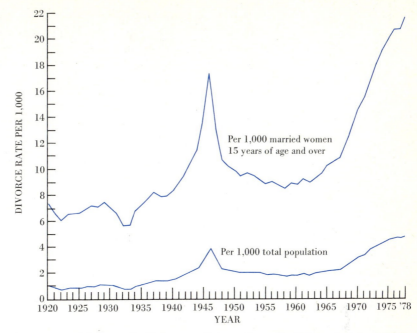

FIGURE 14.1
Divorce rates in the United States, 1920–1978

Source: National Center for Health Statistics, "Advance Report Final Divorce Statistics, 1978," *Monthly Vital Statistics Report*, 29, No. 4 (July 31, 1980): 1.

Not all of the reasons for this pattern have been identified, but the differences in the ethnic, racial, and religious composition of these areas may affect their divorce rates. The low rates found in the Northeast, for example, could be attributed to the high percentage of Catholics in the population. In addition, the western states have always been viewed as "frontier areas" and consequently are generally less conformist than the eastern and midwestern sections of the country are.

6. *Divorced persons who remarry have a higher divorce rate than do those marrying for the first time.*[8] In general, the divorce rate for remarried individuals is one and one-half times greater than that for first-time married people.

Societal Factors Contributing to a Higher Divorce Rate

There are several societal variables that have contributed to the rising divorce rate in the United States:

1. *Changing Family Functions* As discussed in Chapter 1, "The Structure and Functions of the Modern Family," the functions of the

family have changed, and many have been taken over by other societal institutions. As a result, more and more emphasis is placed on partners' emotional fulfillment, and consequently, there are fewer functional or practical reasons to keep a marriage intact.

2. *Increasing Numbers of Teen-age Marriages* Because families no longer have the control over mate selection that they once had, marriages based on romantic love are more or less taken for granted, and youthful marriages are quite common. Teen-age marriages have a high divorce rate, and this in turn has increased the United States' overall divorce rate.

3. *More Jobs for Women* With the entrance of large numbers of women into the labor force, an important barrier to divorce has been removed. Today, women are able to be economically independent, and this has released them from financially secure but unhappy marriages.

4. *Decline in Moral and Religious Sanctions* Although the Catholic church still does not condone divorce, most Protestant and Jewish denominations are now more tolerant of divorce. In addition, the stigma attached to divorce has largely disappeared, and there now is less pressure on a couple to keep an unhappy marriage together.

5. *Acceptance of Other Family Life Styles* In the past, there was a great deal of social pressure on people to marry. Today, however, there is recognition and acceptance of being single and having other life styles. It is no longer assumed that marriage is for everyone.

A BRIEF HISTORY OF DIVORCE

Until the latter part of the Middle Ages, divorce was considered a private matter and was generally available only to the husband. Among the ancient Greeks and Hebrews, for example, a husband could divorce his wife for almost any reason, whereas the wife usually had no grounds available to her.

With the advent of Christianity, the church became responsible for divorce regulation. Marriage came to be regarded as a sacrament and was dissoluble only through death. The church did grant annulments, however, which declared that a marriage never existed. The church also recognized that in certain conditions marriage could be intolerable, and therefore it also granted a form of *limited divorce*—a divorce from bed and board. A limited divorce was authorized only for grave and serious reasons—"cruelty which doth threaten life and health"—

and though it permitted the partners to live apart, it did not allow them to remarry.

The Protestant Reformation transferred marriage and divorce regulation from the church to the state. The Protestant reformers allowed divorce and remarriage, but the grounds for divorce had to be serious charges such as adultery, cruelty, and desertion. Divorce was granted to the innocent spouse as a relief from the wrongdoing of the guilty spouse.

In the United States, most state legislatures came to adopt the traditional principles that divorce could be granted for only grave and serious reasons and that one party, and one party only, could be "guilty." Assigning guilt, in the legal sense, created the fault system of divorce.

The Fault System of Divorce

The fault system of divorce is an adversary approach to divorce. Thus the plaintiff—the spouse who is supposedly innocent—brings charges against the defendant—the spouse who is supposedly guilty.

The defendant is notified of the hearing, but generally he or she does not attend. Since the defendent is not in court to oppose the charges, the court assumes that he or she is guilty, and the divorce is granted. Occasionally, a divorce suit is contested, but approximately 90 percent of divorce fault cases are not.

If the defendant proves that he or she is innocent or if the court finds that both spouses are guilty, the divorce may not be granted. When a divorce is granted, it is used as a legal punishment against the "guilty" spouse. It is somewhat ironic that the punishment of divorce is often exactly what the guilty party wants. If both parties are found guilty, the couple is punished by being denied a divorce.

The main criticism of the fault system of divorce is that it is hypocritical. In most cases, the spouses have more or less agreed beforehand which of them will be the plaintiff, what the grounds will be, and that the spouse who is the defendant will not contest the divorce suit. For couples who mutually agree that their marital relationship should end, the fault system requires them to agree on the grounds for divorce and then to testify in court that one of them has been "wronged." Furthermore, the "guilty" party frequently is punished with an unfair financial arrangement. The conflict and tension of making the spouses adversaries in the legal system only increase the emotional trauma of a divorce. Proponents of the no-fault system, which will be discussed later in this chapter, stress that eliminating the fault system helps to decrease some of the legal trauma of divorce.

Grounds for Divorce   It is difficult to appreciate the complexity and diversity of divorce laws in the United States until one checks the statutes of the individual states. Since marriage and divorce laws are under state jurisdiction, divorce laws vary from state to state. Several states have a single ground such as "irretrievable breakdown," but just as many have a dozen or more grounds. Altogether, there are nearly fifty legal grounds in the various states and territories, some of which are presented in Box 14.3. Despite the wide array of available grounds in the United States, most of them are seldom used. Contrary to public opinion and the media, adultery is probably used in less than 1 percent of all divorce suits. In fault cases, most divorces are granted for cruelty (mental or physical), desertion, and economic nonsupport.

Contested Divorce   Although most divorce cases are uncontested, occasionally one of the spouses does not agree to the divorce, and a legal and emotional battle ensues. Contested divorces are usually long, hostile, and bitter legal struggles. There are several reasons that a divorce may not be granted in fault divorce suits.

1. *Recrimination*   By definition, *recrimination* is a countercharge or an accusation in return, and a divorce may be denied if both spouses are guilty of marital fault. Therefore, if one partner admits his or her guilt but can prove the other partner's guilt, the divorce will not be granted. For example, a wife accuses her husband of desertion, and he is unable to disprove the accusation. But if he in turn accuses his wife of mental cruelty and the court accepts his proof, the wife's request for a divorce may be denied.

2. *Collusion*   According to fault procedures, the principle of *collusion* means that the spouses have cooperated in getting their divorce. Since our legal system stipulates that a divorce suit must be a legal contest, each spouse is expected to pursue his or her own interests, and if the court discovers collusion, the divorce will be denied. There are three forms of collusion:

a.   The couple may submit false evidence of an offense that was not actually committed.

b.   An offense may be committed by one of the parties for the sole purpose of having grounds for divorce. For example, a husband may desert his wife and refuse to come home, thus providing evidence for a desertion charge.

c.   A legitimate defense may be suppressed by the defendant. For example, a woman may charge her husband on the ground of cruelty, but her husband does not appear in court to explain that his anger and abuse were provoked by her affair with another man.

BOX 14.3 Grounds for Divorce

Before the enactment of no-fault divorce statutes, there were a variety of grounds for divorce, many of which are listed below:

- Abandonment
- Adultery
- Attempt to corrupt son or to prostitute daughter
- Bigamy
- Consanguinity
- Conviction of a felony
- Cruel and inhuman treatment
- Desertion
- Deviant sexual conduct
- Drug addition
- Fraud
- Habitual drunkenness
- Refusal by wife to move with husband to another state
- Seven years' absence, absent party not being heard from

- Idiocy
- Impotence
- Imprisonment
- Incapability of procreation at time of marriage
- Incest
- Incompatibility
- Incurable physical incapacity
- Infection of spouse with communicable venereal disease
- Insanity
- Irretrievable breakdown of marriage
- Mental cruelty
- Mental incapacity at time of marriage
- Nonsupport
- Vagrancy by husband
- Voluntary separation
- Wife being pregnant by another man at time of marriage without knowledge of husband

The adversary nature of fault divorce forces a couple who both want to end their marriage to resort to collusive practices. Consequently, many fault divorces are collusive in nature, but collusive practices seldom come to light in the courtroom and are rarely used as grounds to contest a divorce.

3. *Connivance* Connivance is related to collusion and is usually found in adultery cases. It occurs when one partner consents to or encourages the partner's act of a marital offense. For example, a husband arranges for a man to seduce his wife and for pictures to be taken. He then submits this as proof of infidelity and petitions for divorce. This type of arrangement was common in the past in states that had adultery as the only ground for divorce.

4. *Condonation* If one spouse has committed a marital offense, the court will grant the innocent spouse a divorce. However, the innocent spouse is entitled to a divorce only if he or she has not forgiven the wrongdoing. Since forgiveness is difficult to define, *condonation* is usually assumed if the individuals are still living together or if they engaged in sex relations after the marital offense was committed.

Therefore, in fault-divorce cases, the court routinely asks, "When did you last have sex relations with your spouse?" and if it concludes that condonation has occurred, the divorce will not be granted.

In recent years a number of states have eliminated the defenses of recrimination, collusion, connivance, and condonation. Because of the increase in no-fault provisions, the use of these divorce defenses has decreased.

The No-Fault System of Divorce

A no-fault divorce system is based on the principle of marital breakdown. It allows a couple to dissolve their marriage for reasons of "irreconcilable differences" or "irretrievable breakdown." The adversary nature of divorce is removed, and neither spouse is found "guilty" or "innocent." Since both individuals recognize and agree that the marriage should be dissolved, neither spouse is forced to accept total responsibility for the dissolution of their marriage.

In 1970, California became the first state to institute a no-fault divorce law. Since then, forty-six other states, the District of Columbia, and Puerto Rico have adopted no-fault provisions or have added no-fault grounds to their existing divorce grounds.[9]

The concept of no-fault divorce has radically changed divorce law. Researchers Lenore Weitzman and Ruth Dixon, who have extensively studied the effects of no-fault divorce in California, found that four elements of traditional divorce law have changed as a result of no-fault grounds:

1. The no-fault system of divorce has eliminated the concept of fault, and filing for divorce no longer requires evidence of misconduct.

2. It has eliminated the adversary process of divorce and has reduced some of the legal trauma that surrounds fault-based divorce.

3. Under the no-fault system, the financial aspects of divorce are based on ability to pay, equality, and financial need rather than on determination of fault or sex-role divisions.

4. The traditional responsibilities of a husband and wife have been redefined more equitably. Because the no-fault system is based on the idea that both partners have contributed to the marriage, the court attempts to distribute, equitably and fairly, the couple's assets. In addition, both spouses may become responsible for their children's support after the divorce. As Weitzman and Dixon point out, however, this may place heavier burdens on the wives than on the husbands because "the laws may be instituting equality in a society in which

women are not fully prepared (and/or permitted) to assume equal responsibility for their own and their children's support after the divorce."[10] Yet many states do recognize that there may be a need to support a wife who faces a transition into the work force or is unable to become self-supporting.

After the adoption of the no-fault system in California, its divorce rates increased, and critics of liberal divorce laws argued that couples were divorcing for trivial reasons and that the new laws were encouraging the breakdown of marriages. Research by Weitzman and Dixon discovered, however, that although the California divorce rate increased after the enactment of no-fault divorce provisions, "a careful analysis of the components of this increase reveals that the adoption of the no-fault law did not by itself lead to any real acceleration in the rate of marital dissolution in California."[11] Rather, the increases were attributed to divorces being postponed until the new law took effect, people staying in California to divorce rather than going to Nevada to divorce, and the new law's shortened residence requirements and waiting periods from filing to final decree. Weitzman and Dixon concluded that the California divorce rate has grown steadily under both the fault and the no-fault legal system.[12]

The no-fault divorce system is a major step in reducing the conflict and collusive practices that were and are so evident under the fault system. It eliminates the accusations of real, imagined, or fabricated wrongdoing and attempts to treat a couple's decision to dissolve their marriage in a respectful and straightforward fashion.

DIMENSIONS OF DIVORCE

Divorce is a complex event, and the confusion is heightened because several things may be occurring simultaneously. Sociologist Paul Bohannan suggests that there are at least six different experiences of divorce:

1. Emotional divorce, which centers around the problems of the deteriorating marriage
2. Legal divorce, based on grounds
3. Economic divorce, which deals with money and property
4. Co-parental divorce, which deals with custody, single-parent homes, and visitation
5. The community divorce, surrounding the change of friends and community that every divorcee experiences

6. The psychic divorce, with the problem of regaining individual autonomy[13]

These six forms of divorce may vary in order and intensity, but most divorced individuals have experienced all six. And feelings of anger, confusion, and loneliness may be present during each phase of the divorce:

Divorce is an institution that nobody enters without great trepidation. In the emotional divorce, people are likely to feel hurt and angry. In the legal divorce, people often feel bewildered—they have lost control, and events sweep them along. In the economic divorce, the reassignment of property and the division of money (there is *never* enough) may make them feel cheated. In the parental divorce, they worry about what is going to happen to the children; they feel guilty for what they have done. With the community divorce, they may get angry with their friends and perhaps suffer despair because there seems to be no fidelity in friendship. In the psychic divorce, in which they have to become autonomous again, they are probably afraid and are certainly lonely.[14]

Bohannan adds that the resolution of any or all of these types of divorce may also lead to feelings of satisfaction. An individual may feel a sense of accomplishment—doing something that he or she felt had to be done but that was very difficult to do.

Since many people in our society still frown on divorce, divorce is often described as a very negative experience, something to be avoided. Although the trauma and anguish of the divorce process itself may be devastating, divorce is also a new beginning, particularly for the person who has been unhappy and dissatisfied with his or her marriage.

The Emotional Impact of Divorce

Divorce is often an emotionally exhausting event filled with confusion, guilt, anger, sadness, and a sense of loss. At times, there may also be feelings of relief. A divorced person is often not sure how he or she should behave socially, and friends do not know whether to offer congratulations or sympathy.

Until recently, there was nothing for the divorced person that resembled the established support and mourning process that help the widowed person deal with the loss of his or her spouse. Now many churches and organizations sponsor support groups and single-parent groups for the divorced, and many books are available that offer advice on dealing with the problems and emotions of the divorced.

People deal with the stress and adjustments of a divorce differently. Some withdraw, others attempt to maintain (at least to others) a sense of strength and calm, and still others feel—and look—emotionally devastated. Frequently, however, people undergo a sequence of coping responses, which psychologist Kenneth Kressel divides into four stages:

1. An initial *period of denial* during which the individual refuses to face the possibility that the marriage may be dying, or engages in behaviors which suggest a strong unconscious wish that the marriage still be intact.
2. A *period of mourning* involving withdrawal from social contacts and intense feelings of personal failure and confusion.
3. A *period of anger*, involving feelings of betrayal, and hostility directed at the spouse and perhaps members of the opposite sex generally.
4. A gradual *period of readjustment* during which the person begins to start planning realistically and (ideally) gains psychological insight into him/herself and the dynamics of the relationship with the former spouse.[15]

In addition, separated and divorced persons often suffer periods of extreme loneliness, which include a desire for companionship, love, and intimacy. Feelings for the former spouse may continue, and often these alternate between positive feelings and negative feelings. Robert Weiss found that these feelings of attachment to the former spouse were common and that they contributed to the emotional problems of divorce.[16] Divorced persons should remember that such feelings are normal and, as with any aspect of the divorce process, should feel comfortable seeking professional help if stresses and conflict mount.

Researchers Graham Spanier and Robert Casto found that individuals who separate and divorce have to make two separate but overlapping adjustments:

First is the adjustment to the dissolution of the marriage. This includes dealing with the legal process, working out a property settlement, and working out custody arrangements if children are involved. It also includes informing and otherwise dealing with persons in one's social network, such as family, friends, and business acquaintances. It involves coping with the emotional effects of the dissolution including feelings about the (former) spouse, such as love, hate, bitterness, guilt,

Divorce can be
emotionally
devastating.

Paul Fortin

anger, envy, concern, and attachment; feelings about the marriage,
such as regret, disappointment, bitterness, sadness, and failure; and
more general feelings such as failure, depression, euphoria, relief,
guilt, lowered self-esteem, and lowered self-confidence.[17]

Spanier and Casto stated that the second adjustment, creating a new
life style, is important to one's overall feelings of well-being and may
be even more difficult than coping with the dissolution of the marriage:

The second adjustment is to the process of setting up a new lifestyle,
such as finding a new residence, living on less (or occasionally more)
money, getting a job, or applying for welfare. If children are involved,
it includes adjusting to single parenthood if one has custody, or
adjusting to limited visits with the children if one does not. It also
usually includes finding new friends and establishing new heterosexual
relationships. Finally, the separated and divorced must adjust to
feelings such as fear, frustration, loneliness, or inadequacy, as well as
possible feelings of freedom, happiness, and heightened self-esteem if
their adjustment is to be successful.[18]

Bohannan agrees that the "psychic divorce"—the adjustment to a
new life style and to being autonomous—is probably the most difficult
part of divorce. This is particularly true for the person who has been

married for some time and has trouble becoming an independent person again, rather than being a part of a couple or family.[19]

The Economic Impact of Divorce

One of the most stressful parts of divorce is the division of property and the awards of alimony and child support. Because the partners are often hurt and angry and because money and resources are seen as means of control and power, economic settlements often are made with much bitterness.

The effect of divorce on income is one adjustment in which there are significant sex differences. Women usually undergo a dramatic decrease in economic status when they separate or divorce. This is especially true in families in which the husbands were the sole breadwinners. Stan Albrecht found, for example, that 66 percent of the women in his sample reported that their incomes following divorce were significantly lower than before the divorce. The figure for males was 19 percent.[20]

Some of the reasons for this drastic change in economic status include the greater prevalence of divorce among lower income families, low and irregular alimony and child support payments, little public assistance aid, fewer job opportunities for female heads of household, and lower wages for working women than for working men.[21]

Child Support and Alimony

Legally, the father is financially responsible for the care of his children, whether or not he has custody of them. All states have child support provisions which continue until the child is of age (usually eighteen) or is married, but the court may relieve a father of total support responsibilities in special circumstances that make it impossible for him to work or otherwise pay support.

In the past, *alimony* (support money paid to a former spouse by the other during legal proceedings and/or after a legal separation or divorce) was granted as support for the wife who obtained a "bed-and-board" divorce:

Thus in its origins, alimony was paid by a man to support a woman who was still his wife, although she had won the right to live separately and to be exempted from her marital duties. Such an award was not as unfair to the husband as it might seem, for under English common law, the husband came into control at marriage of any property his wife owned, and had the income or rents from that property at his disposal.[22]

Later, when the laws changed to allow women to acquire and hold property, the original bases for support were removed, although alimony continued to be a punitive award.

With the increase in no-fault provisions, alimony is no longer solely a punishment for marital fault. Although alimony statutes vary from state to state, more and more states consider the following factors in awarding alimony: length of marriage, wife's income and earning potential; wife's age; and husband's ability to pay.

Generally, if the woman is found at fault in the divorce, alimony is not awarded. Also, alimony payments stop once a woman remarries. In 1979, the U.S. Supreme Court ruled that state laws that stipulated that only husbands could pay alimony were unconstitutional. Alimony may be awarded to a husband, but it is usually for financial reasons rather than as a punitive award. In practice, alimony awards to husbands are extremely rare.

A recent concept is that of "rehabilitative alimony" for the wife:

This is short-term alimony, where the husband pays his former wife a monthly stipend for a limited period, generally two years, or even a lump sum. The idea is for the ex-wife to take advantage of the alimony period to return to school, take a brushup course, or to launch a career—with the expectation that in time she will be able to support herself. . . . Sometimes the alimony is geared to a specific income goal—until the wife is earning, say $10,000 a year—without any time limit. In other cases, the alimony may be open-ended, and the settlement is returned to the court for adjustment if necessary.[23]

Although the husband's remarriage does not relieve him of his alimony obligations, some courts lower alimony payments when the husband remarries, since the support of two families is usually a heavy financial burden. It should be noted, however, that most divorce suits do not entail alimony, and for those that do, the alimony awards are generally low.[24]

Children and Divorce

A divorce legally severs the marital relationship, but many psychological and familial ties remain. Parents may divorce each other, but they do not divorce their children, nor do they usually eliminate the emotional tie of their parenting relationship.

A common belief was that couples should "stay together for the sake of the children" because the emotional damage of divorce to children was irreparable. More recently, attitudes have shifted to the opposite extreme—that children are very resilient and are better off living in a happy, single-parent home than in a conflict-filled, two-parent family.

But researchers Judith Wallerstein and Joan Kelly point out that neither an unhappy family life nor a divorce contributes to a child's well-being. In their study, even children who knew that their parents were unhappy said that they preferred the unhappy marriage to the divorce.[25]

There is no doubt that divorce is a very traumatic experience for children. Children, like their parents, may experience a variety of emotions during and after divorce. Some feel frightened, angry, and alone; others may fear abandonment and believe that the divorce is somehow their fault; still others are confused and feel conflicting loyalties toward both their mother and their father.

Wallerstein and Kelly also found that the first few years following the decision to divorce were often the most frightening and overwhelming for the children:

For children and adolescents, the separation and its aftermath was the most stressful period of their lives. The family rupture evoked an acute sense of shock, intense fears, and grieving which the children found overwhelming. Over one half of the entire group were distraught, with a sense that their lives had been completely disrupted. Less than 10 percent of the children were relieved by their parents' decision to divorce despite the high incidence of exposure to physical violence during the marriage.[26]

This and other research emphasize the importance of the relationship between parents and children after the divorce. The love, involvement, and support of both parents can maintain continuity in the child's life and reduce feelings of rejection and anxiety.

It is also helpful to tell children about the divorce before it happens and the reasons why the parents are divorcing. This, and preparing them for the changes in life style that will likely occur, help alleviate some of the confusion and fear surrounding divorce.

Child Custody A couple who amicably work out a divorce settlement according to no-fault provisions may nevertheless engage in a legal battle over the custody of their children. Until the mid-1800s, fathers generally were awarded custody because children were considered economic assets. Later changes in social values led to custody being awarded to mothers, who were considered to be the better-qualified parent. Today, in most cases, custody continues to be awarded to the mother because it is considered to be "in the best interests of the child."

Children benefit from
open discussions of
divorce.

Peter Vandermark/Stock, Boston

Recently, more and more parents have been exploring *joint custody agreements*, in which both parents share equal legal rights and responsibilities for the care of their children. The advantages of joint custody are that neither parent is burdened with the complete responsibility for the children; one parent is not forced to be a "weekend," or visiting, parent who is often isolated from his or her children and is allowed to visit only under very structured conditions; children benefit from having a close relationship with both parents; and children are not caught in the middle of a bitter court confrontation.

On the other hand, joint custody may result in time-scheduling problems, disagreements over methods of child raising, difficulties for the child moving back and forth between his or her parents' homes and life styles, and tensions and conflicts between the two parents. Yet, if the divorced parents are motivated to work cooperatively according to a joint custody decision, the children may be happier than in a sole custody arrangement, as Professor Judith Greif points out:

Another belief about joint custody is that children end up being pawns in parental battles, and that this produces a situation of divided loyalties. Quite to the contrary, children often seem "used" in sole custody arrangements because of the inherently unequal distribution of power between the parents. Noncustodial parents have to negotiate or "beg" for more time with the child; sole custodial parents withhold visitation if a support payment is late. In joint custody arrangements, however, parental power and decision-making are equally divided, so there is less need to use children to barter for more.[27]

Joint custody agreements can be very successful if the parents are able to separate marital issues from parental issues, if both are committed to making the arrangement work, if both are flexible in sharing responsibilities, and if both are able to agree to and carry out the rules of the arrangement.[28]

The living arrangements and financial decisions of joint custody agreements vary widely. Depending on where the parents live, the child often lives with one parent for a specified period of time (for example, a week, two weeks, or six months) and then lives with the other. Although it may be confusing for a child to have two homes, joint custody attempts to enable the child to maintain close relationships with both parents. Another arrangement, which is rare and can be very expensive, is for the children to live in one residence and for the parents to alternate living there with their children.

DIVORCE MEDIATION

Many divorcing couples who wish to reach an amicable divorce agreement may find financial, property, child custody, and other issues too complicated or emotionally charged to settle themselves. Yet they may be wary of being represented by separate attorneys. A lawyer's main concern is his or her client's best interests, and in many divorce cases the legal adversary system further aggravates the conflict and tensions in reaching a divorce settlement. Individuals, lawyers, and the courts all have expressed dissatisfaction with the adversarial approach to deciding divorce settlements, and increasingly, lawyers, social workers, marriage counselors, psychologists, and other professionals are exploring and seeking training in *divorce mediation*.[29]

In divorce mediation, an impartial third party helps the couple negotiate a mutually agreeable divorce settlement. Working with a mediator, the divorcing individuals learn their legal rights, clarify their financial needs, and then cooperate in reaching a fair economic settlement. According to O. J. Coogler, director of the Family Mediation Association, "The major goal of mediation in family disputes is to help the disputing couple to become rational and responsible enough to cooperate toward making compromises acceptable to both."[30] This may be very beneficial for a couple who wants to reach a

Divorce mediation can help a couple deal with the complex and emotionally charged issues of divorce.

Judith Sedwick/The Picture Cube

compromise but find they cannot do it without the help of an objective third party. For couples negotiating a joint custody arrangement, the divorce mediation process can set a precedent for future cooperative interaction regarding their children. More importantly, it allows the partners to look toward the future knowing that their divorce was settled fairly and in a dignified and respectful manner.

Divorce mediation may not be suitable for every divorce. In some instances, a compromise may be impossible. For those wanting no future interaction with the spouse, the mediation process may prolong feelings of anger and guilt.

SEPARATION AND DESERTION

Divorce is not the only form of marriage dissolution. Marriages are also terminated by death, annulment, separation, and desertion.

A separation may be temporary or permanent. Often marriage partners require time apart from each other to work out their differences, and a temporary separation may allow them to resolve their conflict. For others—those who wish to avoid divorce because of religious reasons, who do not desire to remarry, or who do not wish to go through the legal and emotional struggle of divorce—separation may become permanent.

One of the most prevalent types of marital separation is desertion. Technically, either spouse may desert, but the number of deserting wives is negligible compared with the number of deserting husbands.

Husbands desert for many different reasons, including marital and financial strains and feelings of unhappiness, rejection, and inadequacy. Desertion has often been called the "poor man's divorce," since it is more common in the lower socioeconomic levels. Financial support by the husband is frequently sporadic, and because they are not legally separated or divorced, deserted wives cannot petition the court for alimony. In some cases the wife has no choice but to apply for public assistance. Some husbands, in fact, feel pressured to leave. The reason for this is that in many states, a family cannot receive public aid if the father is present, a legality that may encourage him to leave until he finds employment. According to Lillian Snyder:

An unemployed father is faced with a devastating decision: Should he stay home and try to fulfill his role as father when there is no food on the table? or Should he leave home so that his wife can apply for public assistance? Unable to cope with this dilemma, many men turn to booze, drugs, or burglary. Others develop ulcers, heart trouble, mental breakdowns, or, through negligence sustain an injury on the job. These men are frequently blamed for the family split.[31]

The husband who deserts may be plagued with feelings of remorse, frustration, and guilt, and a loss of self-respect. Likewise, the wife may be embarrassed, hurt, and angry, and often overwhelmed with financial worries and welfare problems. And many deserted wives, for years, are never sure whether they are permanently separated or widowed.

REMARRIAGE

Approximately four out of five divorced persons remarry (83 percent of all divorced men and 75 percent of all divorced women).[32] The increasing numbers of individuals who divorce and marry a second time have popularized the phrase *serial polygamy*, which is defined as the practice of marrying, divorcing, and marrying again.

Many people who have divorced are very willing to marry again, and fairly quickly. According to census data, approximately one-half of those whose first marriages have ended in divorce remarry within three years. The remainder of those who remarry do so at successively longer periods of time.[33]

Divorced persons are much more likely to marry than are widowed persons. Approximately 50 percent of all widowed persons remarry, as compared with 80 percent of all divorced persons.[34] As Hugh Carter and Paul Glick discovered, the difference is not simply due to the fact that widowed persons are, on the average, older than divorced persons. Instead, it is probably related to the fact that many people divorce in order to marry someone else.[35]

Although persons who remarry, as compared to those who are marrying for the first time, usually are older and more mature, have more marital experience, and have a strong desire to "make this marriage work," they may encounter new problems. Children from one or both of the former marriages may create a totally new network of kinship ties and interactions. The husband may still be paying alimony or child support, and this may strain the couple's finances. In one study, persons reported that financial difficulties were the major problem in their second marriages.[36]

Approximately 59 percent of second marriages end in divorce, compared with the 37 percent of first marriages.[37] Since remarried individuals have experienced divorce once, they are more likely to divorce again if their new relationships are unsatisfactory. Nevertheless, the 40 percent who remain married the second time often have a deeper commitment to being married, and this, in addition to their support and love for their spouses, generally results in very rewarding and successful marriages.

SUMMARY

Divorce legally terminates a marriage, and the process may be emotionally exhausting. It is a major change in an individual's life and affects his or her relationships with others.

In the United States, the divorce rate continues to increase and is highest in the early years of marriage, for people who marry at a young age, for blacks, and for remarried persons. Divorce rates also vary geographically.

Contributing to the increase in divorce are the changes in family functions, the increasing numbers of teen-age marriages, the additional job opportunities for women, the decline in moral and religious sanctions, and the acceptance of other family life styles.

Although most states now have, or are including, no-fault grounds for divorce, in the past, divorce was granted only on the basis of fault. This resulted in an adversary approach to divorce which required that one spouse be found "innocent" and the other "guilty." The no-fault system of divorce has attempted to eliminate some of the legal confusion and trauma of divorce.

Besides the legal issues of divorce, a couple also must deal with their emotional divorce, economic divorce, coparental divorce, community divorce, and psychic divorce. All of these are stressful and may produce various problems and conflicts. Divorce mediation—a process in which a third party helps a couple reach a fair divorce settlement—may help a couple deal with the complex and emotionally charged issues of divorce.

Marriages are also dissolved by death, annulment, separation, and desertion. Separated and deserted persons may have tremendous financial burdens, and because support from their spouses often is sporadic, they may be forced to apply for public assistance.

Approximately 80 percent of all divorced individuals remarry. Some remarried persons may face additional financial pressures and problems of new relationships with the spouse's children. Although their divorce rate is higher than that of individuals in their first marriage, those who remain remarried are usually very committed to making their new marriages work and achieve very rewarding and successful marriages.

CONSIDER THIS

Judge West looked up from his notes as he paused to review the facts. It was a complicated custody case, and he felt uneasy about the decision.

Stephen and Ellen Brock had divorced four years ago, and at that time, the custody of the two children—Amy, now aged eleven, and Roger, aged eight—had been awarded to their mother. Since that time, both the parents had remarried, and Stephen had been paying $400 a month in child support. The children also spent one weekend a month and part of their school vacations with him.

During the last year, Ellen had divorced again, and Stephen was petitioning the court for custody of Amy and Roger, claiming that the children would be better off living with him and his new wife. Ellen claimed that she had been the one responsible for the children over the past four years and that there was no reason that she could not continue to care for them as a single mother.

The court had assigned a family counselor to the case. After interviewing the children and the parents, she reported that the children would not be harmed by being raised by a single parent and, in fact, preferred to remain with the mother. But she noted that additional financial strain would be placed on the mother and the children because Ellen only worked part-time and would not be receiving any alimony from her second husband.

The counselor also noted that Stephen had a good job and could easily support the children. He could also offer them a stable and loving home.

It was obvious to Judge West that both parents loved and wanted the children very much, and he felt a great sense of responsibility in deciding their future home environment. Child custody cases were always difficult, but this was one of the hardest.

Questions
1. If you were Judge West, what consideration would you give to:
   a. the financial issue?
   b. the single-parent issue?
   c. the wishes of the children?
2. Would it make a difference if Stephen and his new wife were planning to have children of their own?
3. How might the children have been affected by experiencing two divorces in four years?
4. What are the advantages and disadvantages of joint custody? Is it a possibility in this case?

NOTES

1. Paul Bohannan, "The Six Stations of Divorce," in Paul Bohannan, ed., *Divorce and After*, Garden City, N.Y., Doubleday, 1970, p. 62.
2. U.S. Department of Health, Education and Welfare, *Divorces and Divorce Rates*, Series 21, No. 29, Washington, D.C., U.S. Government Printing Office, March 1978, pp. 2–3.
3. Ibid., p. 10.
4. Lloyd Saxton, *The Individual, Marriage, and the Family*, Belmont, Calif., Wadsworth, 1977, p. 353.
5. Hugh Carter and Paul C. Glick, *Marriage and Divorce: A Social and Economic Study*, Cambridge, Mass., Harvard University Press, 1976, pp. 436–437.
6. Ibid.
7. U.S. Department of Health, Education and Welfare, *Divorces and Divorce Rates*, p. 26.
8. Ibid., p. 11.
9. *The Book of the States: 1980–1981*, Vol. 23, Lexington, Ky., The Council of State Governments, 1980, p. 41.

10. Lenore J. Weitzman and Ruth B. Dixon, "The Transformation of Legal Marriage Through No-Fault," in Arlene and Jerome Skolnick, *Family in Transition*, Boston, Little, Brown, 1980, pp. 362–365.

11. Ruth B. Dixon and Lenore J. Weitzman, "Evaluating the Impact of No-Fault Divorce in California," *Family Relations*, 29 (July 1980): 299.

12. Ibid.

13. Paul Bohannan, "The Six Stations of Divorce," p. 34.

14. Ibid., pp. 36–37.

15. Kenneth Kressel, "Patterns of Coping in Divorce and Some Implications for Clinical Practice," *Family Relations*, 29 (1980): 238.

16. Robert Weiss, "The Emotional Impact on Marital Separation," *Journal of Social Issues*, 32, no. 1 (1976): 135–145.

17. Graham Spanier and Robert Casto, "Adjustment to Separation and Divorce: A Qualitative Analysis," in George Levinger and Oliver Moles, eds., *Separation and Divorce*, New York, Basic Books, 1979, p. 213.

18. Ibid.

19. Paul Bohannan, "The Six Stations of Divorce," p. 38.

20. Stan L. Albrecht, "Reactions and Adjustments to Divorce: Differences in the Experiences of Males and Females," *Family Relations*, 29 (1980): 67.

21. Mary Jo Bane, "Marital Disruption and the Lives of Children," *Journal of Social Issues*, 32 (1976): 112.

22. Gail Putney Fullerton, *Survival in Marriage*, Hinsdale, Ill., Dryden Press, 1977, p. 400.

23. Morton Yarmon, "Alimony Isn't What It Used to Be," *Philadelphia Bulletin*, April 8, 1979.

24. U.S. Bureau of the Census, "Divorce, Child Custody, and Child Support," *Current Population Reports: Special Studies*, Series P–23, No. 84, Washington, D.C., U.S. Government Printing Office, June 1979, p. 5.

25. Judith S. Wallerstein and Joan Berlin Kelly, *Surviving the Breakup: How Children and Parents Cope with Divorce*, New York, Basic Books, 1980, p. 10.

26. Ibid., p. 35.

27. Judith Brown Greif, "Fathers, Children, and Joint Custody," *American Journal of Orthopsychiatry*, 49 (April 1979): 318.

28. Elissa P. Benedek and Richard S. Benedek, "Joint Custody: Solution or Illusion?" *American Journal of Psychiatry*, 136 (December 1979): 1453.

29. O. J. Coogler, Ruth E. Weber, and Patrick C. McKenry, "Divorce Mediation: A Means of Facilitating Divorce and Adjustment," *Family Coordinator*, 28 (April 1979): 255–259.

30. Ibid., p. 256.

31. Lillian Snyder, "The Deserting, Nonsupporting Father: Scapegoat of Family Nonpolicy," *Family Coordinator*, 28 (October 1979): 595.

32. U.S. Bureau of the Census, *Current Population Reports*, Series P–20, No. 312, "Marriage, Divorce, Widowhood, and Remarriage by Family Characteristics: June 1975," Washington, D.C., U.S. Government Printing Office, August 1977, p. 3.
33. Ibid., p. 13.
34. Ibid., p. 3.
35. Hugh Carter and Paul C. Glick, *Marriage and Divorce: A Social and Economic Study*, p. 440.
36. Stan L. Albrecht, "Correlates of Marital Happiness Among the Remarried," *Journal of Marriage and the Family*, November 1979, pp. 857–868.
37. U.S. Bureau of the Census, "Marriage, Divorce, Widowhood, and Remarriage by Family Characteristics: June 1975," p. 7.

SUGGESTED READINGS

Benedek, Elissa, and Richard Benedek. "Joint Custody: Solution or Illusion?" *American Journal of Psychiatry*, December 1979, pp. 1540–1544. A clear description of the benefits and risks of joint custody arrangements.

Crosby, John F. "A Critique of Divorce Statistics and Their Interpretation." *Family Relations*, January 1980, pp. 51–58. A helpful explanation of divorce statistics and their validity.

Eisler, Diane. *Dissolution: No-Fault Divorce, Marriage, and the Future of Women*. New York, McGraw-Hill, 1977. A comprehensive analysis of marriage and divorce laws.

Krantzler, Mel. *Creative Divorce*. New York, New American Library, 1975. A sensitive account of the divorce process and suggestions for dealing with divorce and reconstructing one's life after divorce.

Wallerstein, Judith S., and Joan Berlin Kelly. *Surviving the Breakup: How Children and Parents Cope with Divorce*. New York, Basic Books, 1980. An informative study of how children and parents experience and respond to divorce.

THE CHANGING STATUS OF WOMEN AND MEN

Women are not better than men, but they are not lesser.

Judith M. Bardwick[1]

15

A great part of marriage and family life is structured according to the differing sex roles of men and women. The traditional stereotype of the family holds that the husband is better suited for work and issues outside the family, and the wife is better suited for home and family care.

There may be instances in which the division of family responsibilities based on traditional sex-role behavior works very well, but for the most part, American women have suffered from the rigid sex-role divisions of labor. Believing that "a woman's place is in the home" has led to discrimination against women and the denial of status and opportunity to those who, by choice or necessity, deviate from the expected norm.

There have always been some women who have challenged the consequences of the traditional female sex role, particularly as it affected them politically, economically, legally, and educationally. Although women today still have not gained equal social and economic status, much has changed. Women can vote and hold public office, many have jobs and careers, they have more equal protection under the law, and they have nearly equal educational opportunities.

The progressive change in the rigid sex-role stereotype of women has affected male-female relationships as well as marriage and family forms. When women are no longer expected to defer to men, they can relate to men as social and sexual equals. Like men, women can expect to seek personal fulfillment in many spheres of activity outside the family. Many women can now expect a fair distribution of power and decision making within their marriages, as well as the sharing of home-care and child-care duties. In short, changes in the traditional sex roles often give women more choices.

And because men's and women's traditional sex roles tend to be complementary, the increasing flexibility in women's sex roles has led to more choices and opportunities for men. A more flexible sex role frees men of the responsibility of being the sole economic provider for the family. Furthermore, the pressure that men feel to be dominant, competitive, aggressive, unemotional, and disinterested in family life is reduced.

Even though flexible sex roles can broaden the life options and satisfactions of many women and men, the change from traditional sex-role behavior can also create problems and conflicts. When sex roles are not rigidly defined, people may be uncertain of what is expected of them and how they should behave. Their beliefs and values may be questioned by others, and they may feel social pressures from family and friends to conform to traditional concepts of male and female roles. And those who are content with traditional roles may feel threatened by those who have adopted less traditional attitudes.

Social change occurs slowly, and no one today can predict what effects the trend toward changes in women's and men's sex roles will have on society and its many institutions, including the family. But nearly everyone is likely to be affected by these changes. In this chapter we examine the history of the women's rights movement; research findings on the actual behavioral differences between males and females; changes in employment, educational, and legal practices that affect women; and the changing male sex role.

THE HISTORY OF THE WOMEN'S RIGHTS MOVEMENT

Women's current position in society is a far cry from their status in the nineteenth century. At that time, American women were socially, legally, economically, and educationally "second-class citizens." As late as 1850, a married woman had no legal control over her own property, and in the event of a divorce, the husband retained custody of the children. Female wage earners and career women were regarded with suspicion and were sometimes excluded from social functions. Moreover, women were not permitted to vote, and their education was not taken very seriously.

The movement for women's rights arose in the pre–Civil War abolition, or antislavery, movement. Because women were generally forbidden to speak in public places, they were refused the right to denounce publicly discrimination against blacks.

Partly in response to this prohibition against free speech, some women organized the first women's rights convention at Seneca Falls, New York, in 1848. Its four basic objectives were (1) to establish legal rights for the married woman, freeing her and her property from the absolute control of her husband; (2) to open the doors of higher education to all women; (3) to demand the right to work; and (4) to procure full political rights for women.[2]

From the middle 1880s to the early 1900s, much of the traditional discrimination against women came to an end. The laws changed, and women were allowed to have control over their inherited property and earnings, to sue and be sued, and to obtain joint custody of their children.

But women's greatest gain came in 1920 with the enactment of the Nineteenth Amendment to the Constitution, which gave women the right to vote. Even so, after this and during the depression, the pursuit of equal rights for women lost its momentum. Some argue that the decline of the movement was due to the political climate of the 1920s or that because the right to vote was the movement's major goal, its support dwindled after the Nineteenth Amendment was passed. Sociologist Arlene Skolnick offers an additional suggestion:

But perhaps a more fundamental reason was that feminism was undone by the sexual revolution that began in the twenties. Most feminist women had been Victorians in their sexual attitudes, despite the presence of a few well-publicized advocates of free love in their midst. The majority had assumed that sex was unpleasant, that celibacy did not imply deprivation, and that being a spinster was an honorable role.[3]

Consequently, as Skolnick goes on to discuss, the flapper of the 1920s and the new sensuality she represented offended both Victorian conservatives and feminists, and thus the hopes of both feminists and traditional Victorian conservatives that "there could be a single standard of morals compelling men to be as chaste as women" were destroyed.[4]

When the Depression began, nearly everyone's attention turned to economic survival, as millions of men were unemployed or afraid they would lose their jobs. Although most employed women worked in "female" occupations—nursing, teaching, secretarial and office work—there was antagonism toward women who were taking jobs away from unemployed men. The general consensus was that a woman's place was in the home.

The Rise and Fall of Rosie the Riveter*

During World War II, record numbers of women came to the aid of a country at war and became welders, mechanics, machinists, taxi drivers, and streetcar operators; in fact, women could be found in virtually every branch of industry and business. By 1945, women accounted for 36 percent of the nation's labor force, up from 25 percent in 1940.[5]

But after the war, women were expected to leave the labor force and to return to being full-time homemakers. Although the war gave women more access to the work place and to higher-paying jobs, this did not change the public attitude toward working women. It also ignored the fact that the majority of women, like men, were working because of economic need.

A Department of Labor survey in 1945 found that 96 per cent of all single women, 98 per cent of the widowed and divorced women, and 57 per cent of the married women seriously needed to continue working after the war. Many women were laid off in the heavy industries. But for the most part, these women did not return to their kitchens. Instead, they found work in the traditional areas still available to them. These were the only options open to many women until the 1960s, when anti-discrimination legislation opened up new opportunities.[6]

The interest in obtaining women's equal rights and status was low during the period from 1930 to 1960, and the emphasis was on the family and the wife's contribution to a happy home. The women who did work continued to be employed in traditional female occupations, and those who wished to enter nontraditional jobs were regarded as deviant. A woman was supposed to be fulfilled by marriage and a family.

The Beginnings of Women's Liberation

By the 1960s, more and more working women came to feel that they were underpaid and underemployed. There was a growing feeling that although women had indeed made gains in the educational, political, and economic spheres, these gains were not only insufficient but in

---

*The popular phrase *Rosie the Riveter* symbolizes the millions of women who performed war-related industrial jobs between 1941 and 1945.

many ways amounted to little more than tokenism. Likewise, homemakers recognized and verbalized feelings of dissatisfaction. Women had been taught that their place was in the home, and they had been using their energy and talents to live through and for others.

The publication in 1963 of Betty Friedan's *The Feminine Mystique* was important to the rekindling of feminist thinking. In her interviews with American housewives, Friedan detected a sense of purposelessness and discontent. She emphasized that the importance of marriage and motherhood had been greatly exaggerated and that not all women should marry or have children. She encouraged women to press for specific social and economic changes that would make the female role more rewarding—a role with choices.

Who knows what women can be when they are finally free to become themselves? Who knows what women's intelligence will contribute when it can be nourished without denying love? Who knows of the possibilities of love when men and women share not only children, home, and garden, not only the fulfillment of their biological roles, but the responsibilities and passions of the work that creates the human future and the full human knowledge of who they are? It has barely begun, the search of women for themselves. But the time is at hand when the voices of the feminine mystique can no longer drown out the inner voice that is driving women on to become complete.[7]

Social and economic equality for women have not yet been obtained, although gains have been made. One reason for the slow change in the status and role of women is that people justify the traditional sex-role stereotypes by clinging to myths regarding the presumed "natural" differences between the sexes. Although there are obvious physical differences between men and women, innate differences in behavior and ability are more difficult to demonstrate. In fact, many of the commonly assumed differences between the sexes have been disproved. Women and men are innately alike in many ways. Most of the differences between them are due to socialization and are therefore arbitrary rather than absolute. There are some differences, however, which we now examine.

BEHAVIORAL DIFFERENCES BETWEEN MALES AND FEMALES

In 1974, psychologists Eleanor Maccoby and Carol Jacklin published an extensive analysis of research on sex differences. Their study found that some common beliefs regarding sex differences are supported by research evidence; others have not been adequately tested; and still others have no support and remain myths.[8] For example, generally there are no differences in the average IQs of males and females. In fact, the most frequently used intelligence tests counterbalance or eliminate questions that specifically differentiate between males and females. However, there are some differences in specific abilities.

It should be emphasized that the reported sex differences are average differences. Thus, the finding that girls excel on tasks involving verbal abilities does not mean that a particular boy's performance will not be equal to or even better than the average girl's performance. Likewise, many women are better than many men in areas in which males, on the average, usually excel. But there are four areas in which sex differences consistently occur: verbal ability, quantitative ability, spatial ability, and aggression.

Substantiated Sex Differences

Verbal Ability
During the period from preschool to adolescence, there are few sex differences in verbal skills, but after age eleven, girls tend to demonstrate, on the average, higher verbal abilities. Verbal abilities include articulation, spelling, punctuation, vocabulary size, use of language, and creative writing. This tendency for females to score higher than males do on verbal abilities increases through high school and probably extends beyond the high school years, even into old age.[9]

Quantitative Ability
Although there are few sex differences in quantitative ability in childhood, this changes by adolescence when boys begin doing mathematical tasks better than girls do. Although boys usually take more math courses, an analysis of high school boys and girls who had taken the same number of classes still showed this sex difference. Males tend to excel on mathematical tasks from age twelve or thirteen onward.

Spatial Ability
Spatial ability is the ability to visualize objects as three-dimensional and also to recognize their relationships to one another. For example, one test of spatial ability determines a person's ability to look at a three-dimensional pile of blocks and then estimate the number of surfaces that would be visible from another angle. Differences in spatial tests are not found in childhood, but males excel on them in adolescence and adulthood.

Aggressiveness Aggressiveness is the only other established behavioral difference between males and females. According to Maccoby and Jacklin, the term *aggression* refers to "a loose cluster of actions and motives that are not necessarily related to one another. The central theme is the intent of one individual to hurt another. But attempts to hurt may reflect either the desire to hurt for its own sake or the desire to control another person (for other ends) through arousing fear."[10]

In every society in which males and females differ in aggressiveness, the males tend to be the more aggressive. Maccoby's and Jacklin's research indicates that men are more aggressive in a variety of situations and that men are more often the objects, as well as the agents, of aggressive action.[11]

Sex Differences Needing More Proof

For the following commonly believed differences, Maccoby and Jacklin concluded that the findings were ambiguous or that not enough evidence was available to make any conclusions:

Are Males More Dominant than Females? Aggression and dominance are two different behaviors. Aggression may be a way of expressing dominance, but *dominance* is the act of influencing others—wanting to be the leader or boss.

Dominance appears to be more pervasive in boys' play groups than in girls' play groups. Boys are more likely to try to dominate one another, and they also attempt to dominate adults more than girls do. But when boys and girls are together in groups, it is difficult to determine which sex dominates the other. Dominant behavior in adults is partially determined by status, as Maccoby and Jacklin note:

In many interactions between adult men and women outside marriage, dominance relations are dictated by formal status, as in the case of the male employer and his female secretary. Judging from the work on leadership, it would be likely that, even when formal status requirements are not present, a man's generally higher status would lead him to adopt a dominant role, and a woman to accept or even encourage this.[12]

Males in our society are generally accorded higher status, and this in turn affects feelings and actions of dominance.

Are Females More Passive than Males? When individuals claim that females are passive, they are suggesting that females are less aggressive and more dependent and submissive.

Although this is a complex issue, the conclusion, for the most part, is that females do not exhibit more passive behavior than males do.

Both boys and girls explore a new situation with equal intent. Furthermore, both males and females are equally likely to be shy or to withdraw from social interaction if they feel uncomfortable.

Is One Sex More Active than the Other?

There are no sex differences in activity level at infancy. Some studies have indicated that during childhood, boys are more active than girls, but other studies have not found such sex differences. Although boys may be more encouraged to engage in physical activity, girls are not inactive. They may play more quietly, but they are just as involved in their activities. Maccoby and Jacklin concluded that there is a tendency for males to be more active but that this is not consistent for all age groups and experimental conditions.[13]

Is Competitive Behavior Typical of One Sex?

Although some studies have found that boys are more competitive than girls, others have shown no sex differences. Boys are much more likely to be involved in sports activities, but few would argue that female basketball teams are any less competitive than male basketball teams. More research is needed on the different age groups and the

Both males and females participate in competitive sports.

Jon Chase

effects of various situations and types of opponents on competitive behavior.

Are Females More Nurturing than Males? Girls are more often reared to be nurturing, and research shows that girls between six and ten are more likely to nurture younger children and animals. Yet if nurturing is defined as aiding and helping others, there is little evidence that the female sex is the more nurturing. Men, as well as women, are likely to come to the aid of a victim, and conclusions about the nurturing behavior of children are inadequate, since very little research has been done on how males respond to and care for infants and children. The myth of maternal instinct is discussed in Chapter 13, "Parenting."

Mythical Sex Differences

In their extensive analysis, Maccoby and Jacklin discovered that several beliefs regarding sex differences have not been supported by studies and are simply untrue. These myths are that females are more social than males; that females have lower self-esteem than males do; that females lack motivation to achieve; that males are more analytical than females; and that males are better at high-level learning tasks, whereas females are better at rote learning and simple repetitive tasks.

Maccoby's and Jacklin's work set a precedent for research on sex differences. Males and females are different, but the differences are far less dramatic than most people realize. In fact, there are probably more differences within each sex group than between the two groups. And yet, myths continue to exist. As Maccoby and Jacklin suggest, people remember only those behaviors that substantiate their beliefs regarding correct male and female behavior:

A more likely explanation for the perpetuation of "myths," we believe, is the fact that stereotypes are such powerful things. An ancient truth is worth restating here; if a generalization about a group of people is believed, whenever a member of that group behaves in the expected way the observer notes it and his belief is confirmed and strengthened; when a member of the group behaves in a way that is not consistent with the observer's expectations, the instance is likely to pass unnoticed, and the observer's generalized belief is protected from disconfirmation. We believe that this well-documented process occurs continually in relation to the expected and perceived behavior of males and females, and results in the perpetuation of myths that would otherwise die out under the impact of negative evidence.[14]

Stereotypes of male and female behavior differences influence sex-role socialization, as they greatly limit choices and freedom for both men and women. This limitation is probably the most pronounced in its influences on young women to become wives and mothers (see Chapter 9, "The Private Side of Marriage: Roles and Expectations").

THE EMPLOYMENT AND EDUCATION OF WOMEN

Employment

The first large-scale employment of women workers was in the factories and mills in the nineteenth century (see Box 15.1). Most of the workers were unmarried farm girls who worked in the textile mills to help support their families, spending long hours in noisy, dirty factories for very low wages:

> The typical factory working day lasted from sunup to sundown, and sometimes until . . . [well after dark]. The hours ran from 12½ to 15 or 16 a day. In Paterson, New Jersey, women and children had to be at work at 4:30 a.m. and work as long as they could see, with time off for breakfast and dinner, until a strike in 1835 cut the working day to twelve hours.
>
> Women's wages, always lower than those of men on similar work, ranged from $1.00 to $3.00 a week, out of which they had to pay $1.50 to $1.75 for board in company-owned or leased boarding houses.[15]

During the Civil War, an increasing number of occupations—office work, government service, and retailing—were opened to women, and this trend was repeated in World War I and World War II. After World War II, a large number of women continued to enter the labor force,* although they usually were employed in traditional "female" jobs.

Today women account for about 42 percent of the civilian labor force.[16] The percentages of all women who work are presented in Table 15.1. These statistics indicate that married women are less likely to work than are single, divorced, or separated women, and that large numbers of mothers with preschool (under age six) and school-age (six to seventeen years) children work.

*The *labor force* is defined as all persons sixteen years of age and over who are working for pay. Today men constitute 58 percent of the civilian labor force, and approximately 77 percent of all men work.

BOX 15.1 Women Workers Then and Now: 1880–1980

Then . . . 1880:

- 2,647,000 women, or 15 percent of all women ten years of age and over, were in the labor force, making up 15 percent of all workers.
- Less than 5 percent of all married women were wage earners, but over 40 percent of all single women and 30 percent of all divorced and widowed women were employed.
- The average woman worker was twenty-two years old.
- The average woman worker spent less than five years in the labor force.

- Occupational choice was extremely limited. Eighty-six percent of all women workers were employed in just ten occupations.

- Women's earnings, often as little as fifty cents a day for ten to twelve hours of work, were about one-fourth to one-third of men's earnings.

Now . . . 1980*:

- 43,391,000 women, or 51 percent of all women aged sixteen and over, are in the labor force, making up 42 percent of all workers.
- Almost 50 percent of all married women are in the labor force, and nearly 63 percent of all single women and 43 percent of divorced and widowed women are employed.
- The median age for women workers is thirty-four years.
- A woman entering the labor force at age sixteen can expect to work for an average of 27.7 years.
- Occupational choice is nearly unlimited, and some women are working in almost every type of job. However, about half of all women workers are in just twenty job categories.
- The average annual earnings for women workers are $9,350, 59 percent of men's earnings.

Source: Adapted from U.S. Department of Labor, Women's Bureau, *Women Workers Then and Now: 1880–1980*, (poster commemorating the one-hundredth anniversary of the birth of Frances Perkins, Secretary of Labor from 1933 to 1945). *The 1980 figures are based on 1977, 1978, and 1979 data from Bureau of Labor Statistics.

Today more and more women are employed in white-collar, managerial, and professional occupations. But despite the gains that have been made and the tremendous numbers of women who have joined the labor force, there still are many inequalities.

Most women workers are still in relatively low-paying occupations and lower status jobs. Women, for example, account for 63 percent of all retail sales workers and 80 percent of all clerical workers (see Figure 15.1). In higher status and higher paid jobs, such as managers and administrators, women represent only 25 percent of the workers. In fact, the Department of Labor reported that in the 1970s, more than 40

TABLE 15.1   Percentages of Women Who Work

Classification	Percent Who Work
All Women	51%
Never Married Women	63
Married Women	49
Separated Women	59
Divorced	74
Widowed Women	23
Mothers with Children 6 to 17 Years	62%
Never Married Mothers	63
Married Mothers	59
Separated Mothers	65
Divorced Mothers	83
Widowed Mothers	51
Mothers with Children Under 6 Years	45%
Never Married Mothers	49
Married Mothers	43
Separated Mothers	53
Divorced Mothers	70
Widowed Mothers	37

Source: U.S. Department of Labor, Bureau of Labor Statistics, *Marital and Family Characteristics of the Labor Force, March 1979*, Special Labor Force Report 237, January 1981, Table 4, p. 50.

percent of all women workers were employed in just ten job categories: secretary, retail sales worker, bookkeeper, private household worker, elementary school teacher, waitress, typist, cashier, sewer and stitcher, and registered nurse.[17]

Furthermore, women working full time in 1977 earned only fifty-nine cents for every dollar men earned—an earnings difference that has not changed substantially since 1961 (see Figure 15.2). These differences in pay are of vital concern to most women because they, like men, work because of economic need.

There are several reasons for the differences in men's and women's pay. As just mentioned, most women workers are in low-paying occupations that have little opportunity for advancement. Men generally have more work experience than women do, and because of the recent influx of women into the labor force, many women are still in or near their entry levels, and they generally do not belong to the highly paid unions—construction, longshoremen, plumbing, and electrical.

FIGURE 15.1
Women are
underrepresented as
managers and skilled
craft workers (data for
U.S. women).

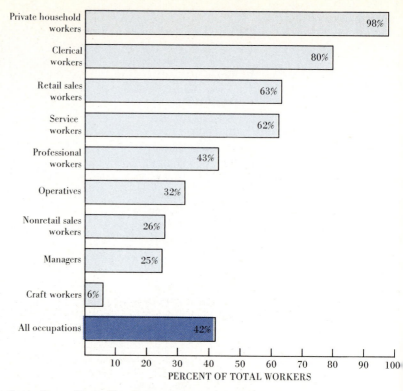

Source: Prepared by the Women's Bureau, Office of the Secretary, from 1979 annual averages data published by the Bureau of Labor Statistics, U.S. Department of Labor, October 1980.

Women also tend to work fewer overtime hours, and although women workers are as well educated as men workers, more men than women have received specific job training and education. Nevertheless, even when adjusted for differences of work experience and occupation, there still are differences between male and female earnings. For example, the median income for women college professors is 75 percent of that for men; the average salary for women elementary and high school teachers is 78 percent of that for men; female computer specialists earn 80 percent of what male computer specialists earn; and female engineers earn 78 percent of what male engineers earn.[18]

And although the likelihood that a woman will work increases with her educational level, there still are income differences between men and women with the same educational background. In fact, as Table 15.2 shows, women who have completed four years of college have lower median incomes than do men who have completed only the eighth grade.

Job opportunities for women are expanding.

Susan Lapides

Education

In the eighteenth century, young American women were not formally educated. It was thought that education would adversely affect a woman's health, make her nervous, or teach her to be dissatisfied, to run away from home, or to be treacherous. Perhaps the major objection

FIGURE 15.2
The earnings gap
between women and
men, 1955–1977

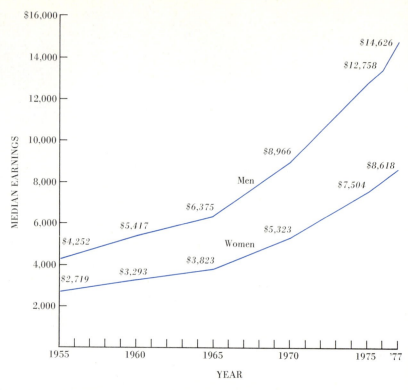

$16,000

$14,626

$12,758

14,000

12,000

MEDIAN EARNINGS

10,000

$8,966

$8,618

8,000

Men

$7,504

$6,375

6,000

$5,417

$5,323

$4,252

Women

$3,823

4,000

$2,719

$3,293

2,000

1955   1960   1965   1970   1975   '77

YEAR

Source: U.S. Department of labor, Women's Bureau, *The Earnings Gap Between Women and Men*, Washington, D.C., U.S. Government Printing Office, 1979, p. 6.

was the feeling that formal education would weaken the female's role as homemaker. But despite the varied protests, girls began to be admitted to elementary schools and eventually to secondary schools. In 1833, women's education scored a gain when Oberlin College in Ohio became the first college in the United States to admit both women and men. Today, most universities and colleges are coeducational. In addition, Title IX of the Education Amendments Act of 1972 prohibits any school—from preschool to graduate institutions—that receives federal funding from discriminating on the basis of sex.

At the present time, the average woman worker has completed the same number of years of education that her male counterpart has— 12.6 years.[19] There are more female high school graduates than male graduates, and women earn almost half the undergraduate degrees awarded. These statistics and the percentages for master's and doctorate degrees are presented in Table 15.3.

TABLE 15.2 Differences in Income Between Men and Women Twenty-five Years of Age and Over, by Educational Level, in 1977

Years of School Completed	Median Income Women (1)	Median Income Men (2)	Income Gap in Dollars (3)[a]	Women's Income as a Percent of Men's (4)[b]
Elementary School				
Less than 8 Years	$6,074	$9,419	$3,345	64.5%
8 Years	6,564	12,083	5,519	54.3
High School				
1 to 3 years	7,387	13,120	5,733	56.3
4 Years	8,894	15,434	6,540	57.6
College				
1 to 3 Years	10,157	16,235	6,078	62.6
4 Years	11,609	19,603	7,998	59.2
5 Years or More	14,338	21,941	7,603	65.3

Source: U.S. Department of Labor, Women's Bureau, *The Earnings Gap Between Women and Men*, Washington, D.C., U.S. Government Printing Office, 1979, p. 15.
[a]Column 3 = column 2 minus column 1.
[b]Column 4 = column 1 divided by column 2.

LEGAL EQUALITY

Since securing the right to vote, women have continued to campaign for equal legal rights. Since the 1960s, several laws have been enacted to eliminate sex discrimination in employment. The Equal Pay Act of 1963 prohibits sex discrimination in wages paid by both public and private employers. In addition, Title VII of the Civil Rights Act of 1964 contains a provision banning discrimination based on sex in hiring or firing, wages and salaries, promotions, and conditions or privileges of employment such as training and education. Although there have been many court decisions and out-of-court settlements, there is a backlog of discrimination cases (over 100,000), and widespread discrimination against women workers continues.[20]

To promote women's legal equality, Congress passed the Equal Rights Amendment (ERA) to the Constitution in 1972. Although equal rights amendments had been introduced in almost every Congress since 1923, it was not until 1972 that the House of Representatives and

TABLE 15.3 Educational Degrees Granted, by Sex, 1977–1978

	Total	Men	Women
High School	2,824,722	1,385,916 (49%)	1,438,806 (51%)
Bachelor's	921,204	487,347 (53%)	433,857 (47%)
Master's	311,620	161,212 (52%)	150,408 (48%)
Doctorate	32,131	23,658 (74%)	8,473 (26%)

Source: W. V. Grant and C. George Lind, *Digest of Education Statistics*, Washington, D.C., National Center for Education Statistics, 1980, pp. 65 and 100.

the Senate approved the Equal Rights Amendment and sent it to the state legislatures for ratification.

Section 1 of the amendment states that "equality of rights under the law shall not be denied or abridged by the United States or by any state on account of sex." The intent of the Equal Rights Amendment is to guarantee women full citizenship under the Constitution and to give them equal rights, responsibilities, opportunities, and treatment under the law.[21] In 1978 the United States Civil Rights Commission offered several reasons for ratifying the ERA:

Measured by any standard, women continue to be disadvantaged by gender-based laws and practices, despite the enactment of equal opportunity laws. As workers, they are victims of an earnings gap that is even wider today than it was in 1956. As wives, they are still subject to laws that deny them an equal partnership in marriage. As students, they are often steered away from both the education needed to break into the better paying jobs dominated by men and the sports programs that have been traditional grounds for leadership and the route to a college education through athletic scholarships. Further, women endure a criminal justice system that too often judges them by their sex and not by the acts they commit or by which they are victimized. This reality must dispel the myth that women have achieved equality under law.[22]

Opponents of the ERA argue that the amendment would destroy the family, degrade the roles of mother and housewife, erase men's obligations to support their families, and even result in the disappearance of separate women's and men's restrooms. However, proponents of the ERA point out that family support would depend on the needs and capabilities of each family member and that separate male and female public restrooms would not be affected, since privacy is a right protected by the Constitution. Furthermore, the amendment would not affect the private actions and social relationships of men and women.[23]

Women in traditional homemaker roles would benefit because the ERA would recognize the right of the wife to manage and control property and to obtain credit, and it would consider the homemaker's economic contribution to the marriage, a large step in securing legal and economic rights for the homemaker. Furthermore, the ERA would help reduce or eliminate sex discrimination in employment, education, housing, and criminal law.

As of this writing, thirty-five of the required thirty-eight states have approved the amendment, but in order to make it part of the U.S. Constitution, the amendment must be ratified by another three states by June 30, 1982.[24]

THE CHANGING ROLE OF MEN

Men, as well as women, have suffered from arbitrary sex roles. Throughout history, men have been burdened with the financial support of their families and have been expected to be dominant, fearless, logical, unemotional, strong, successful, and independent. While growing up, nearly all men receive strong messages from parents and peers regarding what is considered proper masculine behavior. A young boy who is unassertive or easily frightened or who gets upset and cries is told to "act like a man." Furthermore, a boy who is interested in anything regarded as sissy—for example, sewing, cooking, or ballet—is ridiculed by his peers and may alarm his parents. (Few consider that ballet dancers are among the best-coordinated and best-conditioned of all athletes.)

Social historian Peter Stearns believes that the male role of today reflects that of America's initial period of industrialization, roughly the years between 1840 and 1910. During this time, more men began working in factories than at home or in family-owned businesses. This intensified the value of work and transferred the determination of a man's success to his earning ability.[25] Now that over half of all married women work, the emphasis on the male as sole breadwinner has been outdated.

Nevertheless, four themes continue to characterize the modern American male role:

1. *Men should strive for success, achievement, and status.* The ultimate criterion for fulfilling this aspect of the male role is acquiring

great wealth or fame. Even a man who is not a successful businessman, political leader, film star, or athlete can still attain status and recognition by doing his job well, adequately supporting his wife and children, or being proficient at a particular skill or hobby.

2. *Men should be tough, hardened individuals who are emotionally restrained.* They should not cry, express tenderness and vulnerability, or do anything considered feminine or sissy.

3. *Men should be self-reliant, dependable, and confident.* Regardless of what he is doing, a male is expected to "act like a man," which usually means being strong when others are weak and providing loved ones with dependable leadership and protection.

4. *Men should be aggressive, competitive, daring, and, on occasion, violent.* These attributes are considered necessary for success in a highly competitive world.[26]

Today in the United States, some men are having difficulty meeting some of the expectations of the traditional male role. For example, because gender is not a criterion for performing most jobs, masculinity is not necessarily reinforced at work. Others want to shift from focusing all their energy on their jobs to achieving a better balance between work and home life. Also, because some men believe that the traditional male role has contributed to the social and economic inequality experienced by women, they are seeking changes in the male role that will encourage more egalitarian relationships between the sexes.[27] Furthermore, more and more women are voicing a preference for men who are tender and emotionally expressive. Another difficulty with the male role is that dominant, aggressive, and competitive behavior may possibly be unhealthy, leading to heart disease, ulcers, high blood pressure, and other chronic illnesses.[28]

Stearns suggests that American men who are having difficulty fulfilling the expectations of the male role are searching for "a new balance in life, different from that imposed by industrialization. . . . They seek meaning, some kind of manly identity, in a series of activities, leisure as well as work and family, now that the [importance] of work has been removed and [that the pattern of male dominance] has been disrupted."[29] Stearns does not foresee a complete discontinuance of the traditional male role but, rather, an attempt by men to become more family oriented, more emotionally expressive, and less concerned with achieving social status and wealth.

CONCLUSIONS

The emphasis on women's rights and equality between the sexes has often been labeled antifamily and antihomemaker. Many women fear that they will be forced to work outside the home and suddenly be placed in a world they are not trained for and may not understand. Likewise, men fear losing power and authority, since to them accepting egalitarian relationships means an increase in family work, which tends to be given low status. Few people like housework, and many men see such changes mainly in terms of costs.

But there are long-term benefits in equality between the sexes—more financial security; more feelings of usefulness, challenge, and fulfillment for both men and women in whatever roles they choose; less tension and unhappiness in their relationships; benefits for both in joint parenting, as well as consequent benefits for their children; and the freedom to choose a life style without being coerced into rigid sex roles which some individuals cannot follow without feeling stifled and incomplete.

Changes in attitudes toward and expectations of sex roles require changes in institutions. In a study of parents who share child-care functions and economic responsibilities, social researcher John De-Frain analyzed the difficulties these couples have in structuring their family life styles. These families indicated that the following social support systems would greatly aid those who are attempting to share work and family roles:

- more flexible work schedules—the employee having more control over work hours
- a four-day work week
- job sharing—two people sharing one full-time job
- better-paying part-time jobs
- more part-time jobs
- increased fringe benefits for part-time workers
- day-care programs in locations nearby or in building where parents work
- public school financing of day-care programs[30]

Without flexible job hours and day-care programs, parents have great difficulty in combining work and family life, as the responsibilities of two roles are too great without the help of other social institutions

Joint parenting is one of the benefits of flexible sex roles.

Owen Franken/Stock, Boston

and government support. In addition, our society must re-evaluate and change its current socializing practices. This is possible, as the following finds:

We suggest that societies have the option of minimizing, rather than maximizing, sex differences through their socialization practices. A society could, for example, devote its energies more toward moderating male aggression than toward preparing women to submit to male aggression, or toward encouraging rather than discouraging male nurturance activities. In our view, social institutions and social practices are not merely reflections of the biologically inevitable. A variety of social institutions are viable within the framework set by biology. It is up to human beings to select those that foster the life styles they most value.[31]

Sex differences have been overemphasized, and as Maccoby and Jacklin point out, a society can choose the behaviors it wishes to instill.

SUMMARY

The sex roles of men and women are important to the structure of marriage and the family. In the past, men were expected to focus on work and activities outside the family, and women were expected to concentrate on home and family life. This traditional division of labor is gradually changing.

Since the 1800s when women campaigned for equal economic, political, legal, and educational rights, they have made significant gains in all areas, although discrimination and inequality still exist, particularly in occupational and earnings differences between men and women.

Although there are only a few actual behavioral differences between men and women, myths regarding sex differences persist and contribute to the socialization process which instructs men to be dominant and competitive and women to be submissive and nurturing. People are now recognizing, however, that some of the justifications for traditional sex roles are arbitrary and, as a result, are now able to assume more flexible sex roles.

The changes in women's status and roles have also greatly affected men's roles. More and more couples are sharing the responsibilities of being economic provider and homemaker, and these changes in the traditional sex roles have required changes in other social institutions. Couples who share paid work and family work require more flexible work schedules, more opportunities for part-time work which also has adequate benefits, and affordable and accessible child-care facilities. In addition, the establishment of sexual equality necessitates socializing children into more flexible sex-role behavior.

CONSIDER THIS

Gary and Molly are second graders who often play together after school:

GARY: Let's play cowboys and Indians—we can pretend the wall around the patio is a wagon train.

MOLLY: O.K. I'll be the cowboy.

GARY: Girls can't be cowboys—you have to be the Indian.

MOLLY: Who says?

GARY: Because boys are bigger and stronger than girls.

MOLLY: I'm just as big as you!

GARY: Boys are better than girls so I get to say. Girls can't do anything!

MOLLY: That's not fair! That's not how it is at my house. Mom and Dad decide stuff together.

GARY: Oh yeah! Well at my house, Dad's the boss—so I get to be the cowboy.

MOLLY: My folks say girls are just as good as boys. So you can be the cowboy only sometimes, and I'll be the cowboy sometimes too.

Questions
1. What forces outside Molly's family may subvert her parents' efforts to teach her sexual equality?
2. Do you see any similarities between the status of certain minority races and the status of women?
3. What do you think the ideal of sexual equality will be ten years from now?
4. What are your views on the changing status of men and women?
5. How do your views regarding sex roles affect your relationships?

NOTES

1. Judith M. Bardwick, *In Transition: How Feminism, Sexual Liberation, and the Search for Self-Fulfillment Have Altered Our Lives*, New York, Holt, Rinehart, and Winston, 1979, p. 181.
2. For a discussion of the Seneca Falls Convention and other historical information about the women's rights movement, see Carol Hymowitz and Michaele Weissman, *A History of Women in America*, New York, Bantam, 1978.
3. Arlene Skolnick, *The Intimate Environment: Exploring Marriage and the Family*, Boston, Little, Brown, 1978, p. 33.
4. Ibid.
5. Sandra Stercel, "Women in the Work Force," in Editorial Research Reports, *Changing American Family*, Washington, D.C., Congressional Quarterly, Inc., 1979, p. 95.
6. Ibid.
7. Betty Friedan, *The Feminine Mystique* (10th anniversary ed.), New York, W. W. Norton & Co., Inc., 1974, p. 378.
8. The following information was reported in Eleanor Maccoby and Carol Jacklin, *The Psychology of Sex Differences*, Stanford, Calif., Stanford University Press, 1974.
9. Katharine Blick Hoyenga and Kermit T. Hoyenga, *The Question of Sex Differences*, Boston, Little, Brown, 1979, p. 237.
10. Eleanor Maccoby and Carol Jacklin, *The Psychology of Sex Differences*, p. 227.
11. Ibid., p. 239.

12. Ibid., p. 262.
13. Ibid., p. 177.
14. Ibid., p. 355.
15. Eleanor Flexner, *Century of Struggle: The Woman's Rights Movement in the United States* (2nd ed.), Cambridge, Mass., Belknap Press, 1975, p. 54.
16. U.S. Bureau of the Census, *Statistical Abstract of the United States: 1979* (100th ed.), Washington, D.C., U.S. Government Printing Office, 1979, p. 396.
17. U.S. Department of Labor, Employment Standards Administration, *1975 Handbook on Women Workers*, Bulletin 297, Washington, D.C., U.S. Government Printing Office, 1975, p. 91.
18. U.S. Department of Labor, Women's Bureau, *The Earnings Gap Between Women and Men*, Washington, D.C., U.S. Government Printing Office, 1979, pp. 8–10.
19. U.S. Department of Labor, Women's Bureau, *20 Facts on Women Workers*, Washington D.C., U.S. Government Printing Office, 1980, p. 1.
20. Sandra Stercel, "Women in the Labor Force," in Editorial Research Reports, *Changing American Family*, Washington, D.C., Congressional Quarterly, Inc., 1979, p. 82.
21. For an excellent discussion of the ERA and the effects it will have, see United States Commission on Civil Rights, *Statement on the Equal Rights Amendment*. Clearinghouse Publication 56, December 1978.
22. Ibid., p. 30.
23. Ibid., pp. 22–24.
24. *The Book of the States: 1980–1981*, Vol. 23, Lexington, Ky., Council of State Governments, 1980, pp. 36–37.
25. Peter N. Stearns, *Be a Man!: Males in Society*, New York, Holmes & Meier, 1979.
26. Deborah S. David and Robert Brannon, *The Forty-nine Percent Majority: The Male Sex Role*, Reading, Mass., Addison-Wesley, 1976, pp. 8–28.
27. See, for example, Joseph H. Pleck and Jack Sawyer, *Men and Masculinity*, Englewood Cliffs, N.J., Prentice-Hall, 1974; Marc Fasteau, *The Male Machine*, New York, McGraw-Hill, 1974.
28. Meyer Friedman and Ray Rosenman, *Type A Behavior and Your Heart*, New York, Knopf, 1973.
29. Peter N. Stearns, *Be a Man!: Males in Society*, p. 185.
30. John DeFrain, "Androgynous Parents Tell Who They Are and What They Need, *Family Coordinator* (April 1979): 242.
31. Eleanor Maccoby and Carol Jacklin, *The Psychology of Sex Differences*, pp. 373–374.

SUGGESTED READINGS

Hymowitz, Carol, and Michaele Weissman. *A History of Women in America*. New York, Bantam, 1978. One of many illuminating books on the history of the women's rights movement.

Maccoby, Eleanor, and Carol Jacklin. *The Psychology of Sex Differences*. Stanford, Calif., Stanford University Press, 1974. This book is unquestionably the most exhaustive study of sex differences.

Pleck, Jospeh H., and Jack Sawyer. *Men and Masculinity*. Englewood Cliffs, N.J., Prentice-Hall, 1974. A collection of essays covering all aspects of the changing male role.

Tavris, Carol, and Carole Offir. *The Longest War: Sex Differences in Perspective*. New York, Harcourt Brace Jovanovich, 1977. A stimulating overview of sex differences and sex-role socialization.

U.S. Bureau of the Census, *Current Population Reports*, Series P–23, No. 100, "A Statistical Portrait of Women in the United States: 1978." Washington, D.C., U.S. Government Printing Office, February 1980. A statistical overview of the changing status of American women during the 1970s.

MARRIAGE AND FAMILY LIFE IN THE LATER YEARS

Love makes those young whom age doth chill.

William Cartwright[1]

16

One of the most far-reaching social developments in our society in the twentieth century is the steady increase in the number of older people. Since the turn of the century, major improvements in medical care, public health, nutrition, and working conditions have almost doubled the expected life span of the average American. In 1900 the expected life span was forty-seven years; today it is seventy for men and seventy-eight for women. At the turn of the century, only about 40 percent of the population lived to age sixty-five. Today, approximately 80 percent of the population lives to that age. Currently, some 25 million people are sixty-five or older—approximately 11 percent of the population, or one in every nine persons. By the year 2000, the number of people over sixty-five will probably be around 30 million, and by the year 2030 it will probably be about 43 million—between 15 and 20 percent of the population (see Figure 16.1).

The aging of the American population is changing American family relationships. But because the number of older Americans did not begin to increase until about the middle of this century, the role of the family in the lives of older Americans has not yet been well defined. In some cultures, the old are revered and cared for by their adult children and other kin. In other cultures, the old are set aside to fend for themselves. Americans seem to be trying to steer a course between these two extremes. The high value that Americans place on individuality induces older people to try to live on their own, and it also makes adult children want to live in privacy away from their parents. But strong family ties do keep adult children and their parents close to each other, both emotionally and physically.

FIGURE 16.1
Percent of the total
U.S. population in the
older ages, 1900–2040[a]

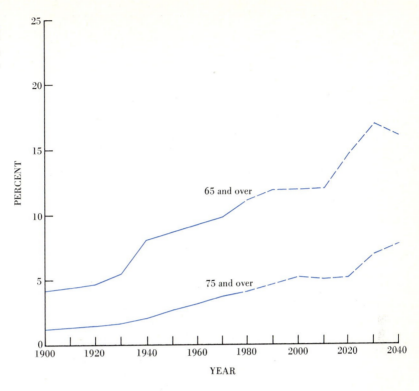

Source: U.S. Bureau of the Census, *Demographic Aspects of Aging and the Older Population of the United States, Current Population Reports*, Series P-23, No. 59, Washington, D.C., U.S. Government Printing Office, 1976, pp. 8–9.
[a]Projected data is shown by dashed lines.

As sociologist Ethel Shanas points out, today's older Americans and their families are pioneers, carving out new kinds of social and family relationships.[2] In this chapter we describe the characteristics of those patterns, some of which will surely influence the family life of many of today's young people when they are in their middle-adult and older years.

BEING OLD IN AMERICA

For many Americans, their later years are troublesome beyond the infirmities and frailties that may result from biological aging. In our society, old age is often characterized by loss: loss of income, loss of status, loss of social role, and loss of many social relationships. To be old in America means having to face *ageism*, which is defined as "a systematic stereotyping of and discrimination against old people because they are old, just as racism and sexism accomplish this in relation to skin color and gender."[3] Older Americans continually do battle with the stereotype that they are

white-haired, inactive, unemployed person(s), making no demands on anyone, least of all family; docile in putting up with loneliness, rip-offs of every kind, and boredom; and able to live on a pittance. [An older person], although not demented, which would be a nuisance to other people, is slightly deficient in intellect and tiresome to talk to, because folklore says that old people are weak in the head . . . and asexual, because old people are incapable of sexual activity, and it is unseemly if they are not. [Old people] are unemployable, because old age is second childhood and everyone knows that the old make a mess of simple work. . . . Their main occupations are religion, grumbling, reminiscing, and attending the funerals of friends.[4]

Given this negative stereotype, it is no wonder that many people fear growing old or fear acquiring the status of an "old person." With the passage of the Social Security Act in 1935, *old* became arbitrarily defined as being over sixty-five. But turning sixty-five does not signal automatic passage into decrepitude, and there is no reason why older people must disengage from an active life at any particular age. Older people are quick to point out that the cliché "You're only as old as you feel" is true. Nearly everyone knows vigorous, active older persons, and the ranks of world-renowned artists, musicians, statespeople, and humanitarians are filled with people over sixty-five (see Figure 16.2). As the famous statesman and financier Bernard Baruch once said, "To me, old age is always fifteen years older than I am."

More and more older people are asserting themselves and demanding that they be treated with respect and accorded the same opportunities as other people are. For example, an organization called the Gray Panthers was founded to fight for the rights of older people. Deploring the low status of the old in America, Maggie Kuhn, founder of the Gray Panthers, says:

To get from the airport to my home in Philadelphia, I have to pass a junkyard where old cars are thrown on a heap, left to rust and disintegrate, and finally smashed to smithereens by a society that wants everything shiny new. That junkyard haunts me because America does the same thing to old people. When we turn 65, we are trashed. Well, I don't want to be dumped on the scrap heap. I don't want to be isolated

Maggie Kuhn, founder and president of the Gray Panthers, with Ray Smith, a Boston member

Elizabeth Barry/The Picture Cube

from the mainstream of living or the companionship of people of all ages.[5]

Loss of Social Role

For many Americans, the transition to old age, whether signaled by retirement, loss of health, or widowhood, is usually an abrupt loss of one's functional social role, for which there is no ready substitute. In other life-cycle transitions—from child to adult, from single to married, and from childless to parent—the tasks of the new role replace those of the old. But as noted by gerontologist Irving Rosow, this is not the case for older people:

Aside from such general bromides as that [older] people should stay active, there is very little specification of what they should do and what standards to follow. In other words, there is no role *content*. Indeed, this is precisely why so many older people are consumed by inactivity and boredom. The culture does not provide them with meaningful norms as it does all previous life stages.

There are no clear expectations connected with the age role, so this becomes subject to personal preferences and private definitions which are intrinsically unshared. Thus, the role of the older person becomes *unstructured*, and there is little incentive to adopt with enthusiasm a basically empty role.[6]

FIGURE 16.2

Going strong in old age. Facing page: top left, Georgia O'Keefe, artist (b. 1887); top right, Arthur Rubinstein, concert pianist (b. 1886); bottom left, Eubie Blake, jazz musician and composer (b. 1883); bottom right, Katharine Hepburn, actress (b. 1909). Top left, Ronald Reagan, President of the United States (b. 1910); top right, Martha Graham, choreographer (b. 1894); bottom right, George Burns, actor (b. 1896).

Credits: Georgia O'Keefe, Wide World Photos; Arthur Rubinstein, United Press International Photo; Eubie Blake, Associated Press Photo; Katharine Hepburn, United Press International Photo; Ronald Reagan, United Press International Photo; Martha Graham, Wide World Photos; George Burns, United Press International Photo.

In addition, society emphasizes socializing people to function in all roles except the aged role:

In general, old people must learn from their own experience and adapt by themselves. The culture does little to help in their transition to old age or with the many problems they face for the first time: alienation from central roles, loss of status and respect, increasing marginality, and the withering of social participation . . . the transition to old age tends to be vague, amorphous and unregulated . . . with no prescriptions for such losses and no substitution of new norms, responsibilities and rights.[7]

THE SIGNIFICANCE OF THE FAMILY IN OLD AGE

The loss of economic function and status and the transition to an unstructured role force many older people to disengage from many parts of the larger social system. One major exception to this generality, however, is disengagement from the family. As relationships with others in society decrease, older people tend to turn to family members for social contact. About 80 percent of Americans over sixty-five have living children, and as people age, most expect and want to live close to their children and to visit them frequently. Research shows that more than half of the people over sixty-five who have children tend to see at least one child almost daily and that 75 percent of older parents see at least one child each week. Only about one older parent in ten sees a child less frequently than once a month. And approximately half of the persons over sixty-five who do not see their children often, or who do not have living children, tend to maintain weekly contact with siblings and other relatives[8] (see Table 16.1). If parents are not geographically close to their children or other family members, they usually keep in contact with them by telephoning and writing regularly.

The considerable frequency with which older Americans interact with family members suggests that family ties are important to adults in later life. One of the main family functions throughout the life cycle is emotional support and security. Since many of the traditional family functions—economic, educational, religious, and the like—now are carried out by nonfamily social institutions (see Chapter 1, "The Structures and Functions of the Modern Family"), the family has become the provider of feelings of belonging and intimacy.

The interaction between older persons and their family members includes giving and receiving help in times of crisis, sharing holidays and other traditional family occasions, and exchanging gifts and

Unlike other social roles, the role of the aged is unstructured.

Paul Conklin

services. Seventy percent of Americans over sixty-five report occasionally helping their children or grandchildren with such problems as home repairs, housework, and care during illness. A large percentage of older people help their children by taking care of grandchildren, and about 70 percent report receiving gifts, services, and care during illness from their adult children and other relatives. Older people often ask their adult children to help them deal with the governmental bureaucracy,[9] and they usually expect them to help in times of illness and economic hardship.[10]

Research surveys indicate that the quality of family relationships among the elderly tends to be positive; both older Americans and their adult children report generally positive feelings for each other. Relationships tend to be more harmonious when an elderly person's health and well-being are good, when the older person has a positive attitude toward aging, and when financial problems are minimal.[11] Consequently, family harmony is greatest when older family members are physically and psychologically able to contribute to the family, rather than needing care from their relatives.

Caring for Aging Parents

Despite Medicare, Social Security, and other benefits designed to help care for them, most older Americans turn to their families, particularly

TABLE 16.1   Percentage of Persons over Sixty-five Having Contact with Family Members

	Men (%)	Women (%)
Contact with Children		
See Child Almost Daily	50	54
See Child Almost Weekly	23	25
See Child Almost Monthly	13	12
See Child Infrequently	13	9
At Least Weekly Contact with Siblings and Other Relatives		
Parents Having Infrequent Contact with Children	35	43
Persons Without Children	44	63

Source: Ethel Shanas, "The Family as a Social Support System in Old Age," *Gerontologist*, 19, no. 2 (1979): 169–174.

to their children, for help in the later years. On their part, many adult children of older Americans accept some responsibility for "parent care." They do so for a variety of reasons: (1) love for the aging parents and the desire to see them happy and comfortable; (2) a sense of obligation for parental investment in the children's younger years; (3) a sense of obligation for the parents' help in times of need; (4) a sense of duty; (5) fear of social disapproval; and (6) guilt.

Regardless of the motivations, carrying out some of the responsibilities for parent care can create problems for both the adult child and his or her family. For example, if an individual is busy taking care of an aging parent, the spouse and children may feel neglected, resentful, and jealous. A person might not take a better job in order to remain close to an aging parent or may deny the family a vacation for fear that "something might happen" while he or she is away. These kinds of situations can cause marital and family turmoil.

Four-Generation Families

The demands of parent care seem to fall hardest on adult children who are themselves approaching retirement age. Because more people are living longer, many Americans in their early sixties have living parents, and most also have their own children and grandchildren. As a

Susan Lapides

result, about half of all people over sixty-five are members of four-generation families.

Usually, it is the second generation in a four-generation family that provides the economic, psychological, and social support for their parents. But this may come at a time when the second-generation family members are themselves struggling with the transition to old age:

Those middle aged persons who have perhaps looked forward to the time when their children would be grown as a time for freedom from major family responsibilities, now find themselves with new responsibilities, the care and often financial support of elderly parents. Many persons in the grandparent generation are experiencing some of the stresses associated with their own aging, retirement from work, lessened income, and perhaps health problems. Yet they are expected to be, and often are, the major social support of their own parents. The needs of their own children and grandchildren indeed may conflict with the needs of their elderly parents.[12]

In the four-generation family, the second-generation adult is often torn among offering help to elderly parents, being an available parent and grandparent, and taking care of his or her own needs and perhaps those of a spouse:

I've raised my family, I want to spend time with my husband. I want to enjoy my grandchildren. I never expected that when I was a grandparent I'd have to look after my parents.[13]

Family Ties in the Future

What will the family life of today's younger Americans be like when they are old? Optimistic prognosticators foresee more respect accorded to the aged and an increase in social programs to help with the transition to old age, especially with regard to economic support and health care. This would expand the social realm of older people beyond the family and also would free them from material dependence on their children.

If the status of the aged does improve in the future, then family ties may become more voluntary than obligatory, according to sociologists Beth B. Hess and Joan M. Waring:

The maintenance and sustenance of the parent/child bond will be increasingly based upon the willingness of both parties to engage in supportive behaviors. . . . While guilt and shame will remain powerful motivators of filial performance, and the injunction to "honor thy father and mother" continues to shape our socialization to obligations toward aged parents, the actual course of contacts and the satisfactions derived from them will be subject to the same type of role negotiation characterizing other interpersonal relationships. As a consequence, such variables as basic trust, respect, shared values and beliefs, and genuine affections will increasingly determine parent/child relations in later life.

Adult children will be spared the excruciating choices between the needs of their own children, themselves and their parents. And those bonds that do persist will do so because they have been willingly sought and nurtured by adults who are authentically concerned with the well-being of one another. . . . The future of parent/child relations in later life may be characterized by the strongest ties of all: mutual respect.[14]

Though not denying the importance of family ties in later life, some researchers speculate that a family's ability to support its older members adequately is limited and that age peers may provide a more effective support system in old age.[15]

Sociologist Russell Ward suggests that in a network of age peers, such as that in many age-segregated living arrangements, older people may be freer to engage in leisure "careers" following retirement (volunteer work, crafts, and the like), which the rest of society may consider unimportant. Age peers can also provide support and assistance in the form of retirement counseling, widow-to-widow programs, and telephone reassurance programs. In addition:

Involvement with age peers seems to facilitate discussion and legitimization of death, through role models of how to react to the death of others and how to face up to one's own death. The family rarely provides this, since older people tend to view death as a taboo topic for family discussions.[16]

Even if the social and economic status of the elderly improves, and even if age-peer relationships provide the aged with much of their meaningful social contact, it is unlikely that the family will cease to be an important focus of attachment for older Americans. Asking friends or neighbors for help may seem like intruding, and dealing with social agencies is often demeaning and suggests total dependency. Family relationships, however, have a history of reciprocity and emotional dependency.

For the rest of this century and well into the next, the family will probably continue to provide the principal social network that integrates older people into society, as well as the primary basis of security for adults in later life.

LIVING ARRANGEMENTS OF OLDER PEOPLE

Contrary to the pervasive myth, most old people do not live in old-age homes, hospitals, or other institutions. In fact, only about 5 percent of the elderly live in institutions (see Box 16.1); most older Americans live in their own households:

1. Seventy-five percent of American men over sixty-five are married and live with their spouse; 33 percent of American women over sixty-five are married and live with their spouse. (The percentage of older married men is greater than the percentage of older married women because women tend to outlive men.)
2. Two-thirds of the unmarried live alone.

BOX 16.1 Institutional Care for the Aged

The time may come when an elderly person becomes physically and mentally unable to care for himself or herself. When an older person's needs exceed a family's best efforts for care in a relative's home, the family might consider placing the elderly relative in a long-term care facility such as a home for the aged or a nursing home.

About 5 percent of the elderly in America live in extended-care institutions. Most are over eighty years old, and nearly 75 percent have a relatively severe degree of mental impairment. They may be confused or disoriented much of the time and have severe emotional problems. About 50 percent of the institutionalized population is unable to walk, and a large number have impaired body functions.*

Contrary to popular belief, families are not eager to put their older relatives into institutions. In fact, many families make heroic efforts to care for an enfeebled elderly relative at home long before they reluctantly agree to institutional care. These efforts, however, no matter how well intentioned, often exceed what is physically, financially, and emotionally possible, and the only alternative is full-time extended care.

Both the elderly and their families tend to resist institutional care. For years, institutions for the aged have had a reputation of being of poor quality. Many prospective residents and their relatives fear that care will be inadequate, and placing a relative in an institution may symbolize rejection of that person. The older person may become angry, resentful, and depressed, and the family may feel guilty and disillusioned. Many people oppose institutionalization because they believe it is a prelude to death.

Institutional care for an infirm older person need not be considered a banishment from the family or a prelude to death. In the best of circumstances, when care is ample, institutionalization can be viewed as a new experience in community living. Such quality care provides bed and board, social contacts, recreation and relaxation, basic medical care, and special medical services. It is important that the older person feel protected, as well as emotionally and psychologically secure. The goals of proper institutional care are to decrease fear or anger, to increase the sense of self-sufficiency, to increase pleasure and comfort, and to increase social integration while maintaining privacy and a sense of independence.

Families faced with the institutionalization of an elderly member may suffer considerable stress and may need to find ways to cope with guilt, anxiety, anger, frustration, and the difficulty of the decision. It often is helpful to talk to other families who have relatives in the same institution, to share feelings and to discover ways to cope with the institutionalization experience. Problems and negative feelings can also be discussed with a counselor or members of the institution's staff.

*Alvin I. Goldfarb, "Institutional Care of the Aged," in E. W. Busse and E. Pfeiffer, eds., *Behavior and Adaptation in Late Life* (2nd ed.), Boston, Little, Brown, 1977, pp. 264–292.

3. Twelve percent of all married older Americans live with their children.
4. Seventeen percent of all unmarried older Americans live with their children.

The fact that approximately 85 percent of the elderly do not live with their children is, in large measure, due to the American penchant for independence. Old people may want to live close to their children—half live within a ten-minute distance of a child[17]—but they also want to maintain their own households as long as possible:

I have absolutely no desire to live with any of my children. As long as I'm physically able, I want to stay in my own place. I love my children—and I'm sure they love me—but living with them is something else.

Here I can have my own life. I can come and go as I please. I can have my friends in whenever I want. I can cook whatever I like. I have my own bathroom. There are no youngsters underfoot. And I don't feel I'm intruding on anybody.

No, my children have their life; I have mine. That's the way it's going to stay. They've asked me a couple of times, but I'm not moving. Living with your children is for the birds.

From the authors' files

MARRIAGE IN THE LATER YEARS

Approximately 90 percent of Americans approach their later years as members of married couples. As the population ages, however, the percentage of married couples declines as the percentage of widows and widowers increases. Because wives tend to outlive their husbands, the percentage of older married men is much higher than the percentage of older married women (see Figure 16.3).

As we discuss in Chapter 10, "Marital Interaction," the typical American marriage develops through a series of stages. A marriage begins with a preparental stage, progresses through several child-rearing stages, and ends in the postparental period, which coincides with the approach of retirement and old age. Most married couples enter their sixties in the "launching stage" of marriage—with their last child preparing to leave home—or in the "empty nest" stage—with all their children grown and living in households other than their parents'. Because many older parents and at least one of their children remain socially and physically close, the parent-child separation can sometimes seem incomplete, as this woman describes:

I'm familiar with the term *empty nest*. But in our case, I'm not sure how much meaning it has. We have two grown children. One lives in

FIGURE 16.3
Percent of U.S.
population sixty-five
years and older, by
marital status and sex,
1978

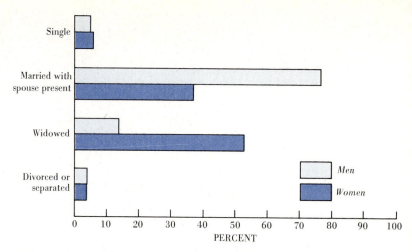

Source: U.S. Bureau of the Census, *Social and Economic Characteristics of the Older Population: 1978, Current Population Reports*, Series P–23, No. 85, Washington, D.C., U.S. Government Printing Office, 1979, p.3.

another state, and we see her infrequently. Our son Tom, on the other hand—it's like he never left home. He and his wife are always with us—they live only a few miles away. They eat with us once or twice every week. They sleep over whenever they feel like it. My husband's always giving them money and presents. All I can say is, some nests are emptier than others!

From the authors' files

Surveys report that both women and men in their postparental years enjoy greater individual and marital happiness than couples still in the parental stages do.[18] In general, couples find the parental stages of the family life cycle to be the most difficult, and therefore, marital happiness and satisfaction often increase once the children have departed.[19] The empty-nest stage is satisfying because individuals appreciate the time they can devote to themselves and their spouse. Some pursue hobbies and jobs that parental duties made impossible and others simply like having their privacy. As one woman said, "You can listen to Tchaikovsky instead of Chicago, and you can actually have a roast that will last more than one meal."

Marital interaction in later life is characterized by a sense of calmness and satisfaction in the companionship of the spouse. Older married people tend to value their marriages for the loyalty and

Companionship and satisfaction characterize marital life in the later years.

Pierre Boisclair/Black Star

emotional security they provide.[20] From their analysis of the research literature, Lillian E. Troll, Sheila Miller, and Robert C. Atchley conclude that

> For the happily married older couple, marriage is central to the "good life." It is a source of great comfort and support as well as the focal point of everyday life, and happily married couples can experience increasing closeness as the years go by. In addition, there can be a high degree of interdependence in such couples, particularly in caring for each other in times of illness.[21]

Coincidental with the loss of social and economic roles in the later years, there is often a weakening of traditional sex-role behavior in the marriages of older people. Men are more likely to do household chores, and women are more likely to be assertive. In many marriages, health is a major issue, and there may be a shift in the distribution of power from the male to the female if she is in better health than her partner is.

One of the most prevalent myths that older Americans have to contend with is that sex and old age are mutually exclusive. For a variety of reasons, many people think that older persons should stop being interested in and having sexual relations. They believe that sex is necessary only for procreation and therefore is improper for adults who are too old to have children. Or they may equate sex with youthful romance. Still others believe that aging bodies cannot perform sexually or that older bodies are incapable of being considered sexually attractive. Relatives are frequently upset with the idea of older family members being sexually active. Some children, even as adults, have difficulty accepting their parents as sexual. Also, because the elderly are often treated as children, their desire for sex may be considered wrong.

Although waning health and the biological aging process may diminish some of the body's sexual responses (that is, males and females may become physiologically aroused more slowly and male erectile capacity and female vaginal lubrication may be diminished),[22] there is no reason to expect sexual expression to be absent in everyone over sixty. Some older people do indeed lose interest in sex, but others are sexually active throughout their later years. Studies indicate that the best predictor of sexual activity in old age is the enjoyment of sex when a person is younger.[23] It is quite possible, therefore—since young people are now living in a more sexually permissive society—that sexual activity will increase in future generations of old people.

As we discuss in Chapter 7, "Sexual Interaction," sex need not be equated with genital intercourse, orgasm, and ejaculation. Sex is a way to communicate warmth, acceptance, and love; and those feelings and the desire to share them know no age limit. Indeed, sex in later life is often characterized by an emphasis on touching, caressing, holding each other, and the gentle expression of intimacy, rather than the physical act of sexual intercourse alone.

WIDOWHOOD

Nearly all of the marriages of older Americans end with the death of one spouse. Because women usually live longer than men and are younger than their spouses, widowed spouses in America are usually women. In the United States, there are approximately ten million widows and two million widowers over the age of fifty-five.

The loss of one's spouse is often the most traumatic event in a person's life.[24] The initial reaction to the death of a husband or wife can be shock, dismay, disbelief, and denial. Besides feeling emotionally upset, some newly widowed individuals experience physical symptoms such as loss of sleep or appetite, headaches, digestive trouble, and chest pains.

After the initial impact of the loss, a widowed person usually enters a period of bereavement that may last several months or even several years. During this time, the widowed person may feel empty, lonely, hopeless, and angry for being abandoned, and may experience uncontrollable episodes of crying. Eventually the widowed person works through her or his grief. This process may be facilitated by supportive and understanding children, other family members, and

Widowhood can be devastating.

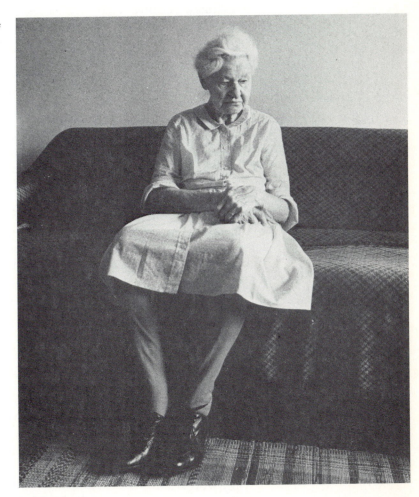

Paul Conklin

friends, as well as widow-to-widow peer counseling made available through various social agencies. The bereavement stage is followed by an adjustment period, or "recovery," during which the widowed person begins to establish a new life style.

The role of a widow can be very difficult for some women. One major problem is becoming used to being identified as an independent person, rather than as a part of a couple or an extension of the husband. Most women who are widows today had more traditional marriages and therefore usually derived their social status and identity from their roles as wives. With the husband gone, the role of wife evaporates, and many widows cannot easily adjust to having an independent identity.

Widows may also face economic hardships. Although many receive life insurance annuities and social security benefits, the amount of money is often insufficient to support an older woman who may have few marketable skills and who may face prejudice in the work place because of her age.

Widowers also may have difficulty adjusting to an independent existence. Having had their personal needs attended to by their wives, many older men lack the skills to care for themselves. For them, widowhood means having to learn to cook, clean house, do laundry, and see to their personal health needs. Widowers may also face economic hardships because they have retired from work. A widower often does not maintain close kinship and friendship ties when his spouse dies because either his wife used to maintain the couple's social relationships or the widower's retirement has disrupted work-related friendships. As a result widowers often do not have as large a supportive social network as widows do and hence may feel lonely much of the time. Some older men no longer have any living friends, for, as one man said, "At my age, all my friends have passed away."[25]

Remarriage Among the Widowed

Nearly 50 percent of all widowed men under the age of seventy remarry. Only 26 percent of all widowed women over the age of sixty-five remarry, however.[26] This discrepancy is due to several factors:

1. The number of unmarried women over the age of sixty is approximately three times larger than the number of unmarried men over sixty.

2. It is socially more acceptable for an older man to marry outside his age range than it is for an older woman. Therefore, widowers have a much larger pool of potential mates than widows do.

3. Men may be more motivated to remarry than women are. The tendency for widowers to have a weak social network may increase their desire for spousal companionship. Women may lose interest in remarrying because they know that the statistical odds of finding another spouse are high, and some do not want to remarry because they fear being made a widow a second time. Also, a few women do not wish to remarry because they find their independence as widows preferable to the role of wife.

The overwhelming majority of remarried older people report that they are satisfied with their marriages.[27] The new marital arrangement usually provides companionship and understanding, with little marital discord. There are no children, job pressures, or economic goals to argue about, and many older couples are content to adopt a "live and let live" attitude. Older couples are also happy to relieve their families of some of their "parent care" responsibilities.

Children of widowed people may object initially to their parent's plan to remarry. Some fear that they will lose their inheritance or that the new spouse is exploiting the parent. Children may also feel it is disrespectful to the memory of the dead spouse for a widowed parent to seek happiness in a new marriage. In general, however, once the marriage has taken place, most children accept their parent's marriage and are happy if the parent is satisfied.

A widowed person's friends tend to be the most negative about his or her remarriage. They may feel deserted or believe that the remarriage is not likely to make the friend happy. But, as with the family, friends usually come to approve of the marriage if the couple is happy.

THE NEVER MARRIED

At the present time, slightly less than 5 percent of all older Americans have never married. One might think, therefore, that because they lack a typical family life, these people would feel lonely and isolated. Several research studies have shown, however, that in general, the group of never-married people—the "independents"—adjust rather well. They learn early in life to look after themselves, and by the time they reach old age, they have acquired a fair measure of self-reliance and satisfaction.

SUMMARY

Throughout the twentieth century, the percentage of the U.S. population over sixty-five has been steadily increasing. At the present time, approximately 11 percent of the U.S. population is over sixty-five, and by the year 2030, the proportion of the population over sixty-five will approach 20 percent.

American society does not value its elderly, and it does little to prepare its members for the transition to old age. Old people are faced with the loss of social and economic roles, and they live in unstructured roles for which society provides little support. In addition, old people face destructive myths and stereotypes regarding their abilities and needs as people ("ageism").

Without social support and economic purpose, most aged Americans turn to their families to meet their social needs. Most of the elderly have adult children who live within a ten-minute distance and whom they see frequently. Adult children sometimes assume responsibility for the care of their parents, especially when their parents are infirm or economically needy. In four-generation families, the second generation often struggles with caring for aging parents at the same time they themselves are making the transition to old age.

As the percentage of older people increases, social programs and the status of the elderly may improve so that family relationships become more voluntary and less obligatory. The aged may also find more satisfaction from age-peer relationships.

Only 5 percent of all older Americans live in institutions, and about 15 percent live with their adult children. Most older Americans live in their own households. Three-fourths of the older men are married, but only one-third of the older women are married.

Marriage in the later years—the empty-nest stage of the life cycle—is often very satisfying and is characterized by close companionship and calmness. Many older people continue to be sexually active.

The death of a spouse is the major disruptor of marriage in the later years. Coping with the death of one's spouse and adjusting to a new, independent life style can often be difficult. Social attitudes and a large pool of eligible mates allow many widowed men to remarry, though widowed women tend to remain unmarried. Approximately 5 percent of all elderly people have never married but have adjusted well to single life.

CONSIDER THIS

Dear Penelope,

I was shocked at your answer to Flying South for the Winter, the widow who was moving to Florida to live with a widower without getting married.

I don't blame her children for being upset. She owes it to the memory of her late husband and to her children and grandchildren to stay home and behave like a mature woman and not like some rebellious teen-ager. I don't deny that old people need companionship, but it's shameful for two elderly people who should know better to live in sin. And you should be ashamed of yourself for encouraging them!

Offended at 67

Dear Offended,

After devoting a life to raising children and being a good spouse and citizen, I don't think any older person should be denied the chance for love and companionship in the later years, no matter how unconventional. My advice to Flying South goes for all seniors: Don't let your kids or anyone else clip your wings!

Questions
1. Who is right on this issue, Offended or Penelope?
2. Which of the two would most people agree with?
3. What are some probable reasons that Flying South's children oppose what she's doing?
4. What are some probable reasons that Flying South is choosing not to marry?
5. What life-style alternatives does Flying South have?
6. How would you feel if Flying South were your mother or grandmother?
7. When your generation is in its sixties, do you think that society's attitudes toward the aged will be different from what they are today?

NOTES

1. William Cartwright, *To Chloe*, 1651. (William Cartwright was an English poet, writer, and dramatist.)
2. Ethel Shanas, "Older People and Their Families: The New Pioneers," *Journal of Marriage and the Family*, 42 (1980): 9–15.
3. R. N. Butler and M. I. Lewis, *Aging and Mental Health*, St. Louis, C. V. Mosby, 1977, p. 3.
4. Alex Comfort, *A Good Age*, New York, Crown Publishers, 1976, p. 17.
5. Maggie Kuhn, quoted in Garson Kanin, "To Rest Is to Rust," *Quest Magazine*, June 1979, p. 66.
6. Irving Rosow, *Social Integration of the Aged*, New York, Free Press, 1967, p. 31.
7. Irving Rosow, *Socialization to Old Age*, Berkeley and Los Angeles, University of California Press, 1974, p. 27.
8. Ethel Shanas, "The Family as a Social Support System in Old Age," *Gerontologist*, 19 (1979): 169–174.
9. Ethel Shanas, "Older People."
10. Wayne C. Seelbach, "Correlates of Aged Parents' Filial Responsibility Expectations and Realizations," *Family Coordinator*, October 1978, pp. 341–350.
11. Lillian E. Troll, Sheila J. Miller, and Robert C. Atchley, *Families in Later Life*, Belmont, Calif., Wadsworth, 1979, pp. 94–95.
12. Ethel Shanas, "Older People," p. 14.
13. Ibid.
14. Beth B. Hess and Joan M. Waring, "Changing Patterns of Aging and Family Bonds in Later Life," *Family Coordinator*, October 1978, pp. 311–312.
15. Russell Ward, "Limitations of the Family as a Supportive Institution in the Lives of the Aged," *Family Coordinator*, October 1978, p. 368.
16. Ibid., p. 369.
17. Ethel Shanas, "Social Myth as Hypothesis: The Case of the Family Relations of Old People," *Gerontologist*, 19 (1979): 3–9.
18. Norval D. Glenn, "Psychological Well-Being in the Postparental Stage: Some Evidence from National Surveys," *Journal of Marriage and the Family*, February 1975, pp. 105–109.
19. Elinore E. Lurie, "Sex and Stage Differences in Perceptions of Marital and Family Relationships," *Journal of Marriage and the Family*, May 1974, pp. 260–269.
20. Margaret N. Reedy, "Age and Sex Differences in Personal Needs and the Nature of Love: A Study of Happily Married Young, Middle-Aged and Older Adult Couples," *Dissertation Abstracts International*, 38, no. 8 (February 1978): 3857B–3858B.

21. Lillian E. Troll, Sheila J. Miller, and Robert C. Atchley, *Families in Later Life*, p. 53.

22. Martha Cleveland, "Sex in Marriage: At 40 and Beyond," *Family Coordinator*, July 1976, pp. 233–240.

23. Eric Pfeiffer, "Sexual Behavior in Old Age," in E. W. Busse and E. Pfeiffer, eds., *Behavior and Adaptation in Later Life* (2nd ed.), Boston: Little, Brown, 1977, pp. 130–141.

24. Thomas H. Holmes and Richard H. Rahe, "The Social Readjustment Rating Scale," *Journal of Psychosomatic Research*, 11 (1967): 213–218.

25. Barbara Vinick, "Remarriage in Old Age," *Family Coordinator*, October 1978, p. 360.

26. Paul C. Glick, "The Future Marital Status and Living Arrangements of the Elderly," *Gerontologist*, 19 (1979): 301–309.

27. Barbara Vinick, "Remarriage in Old Age."

SUGGESTED READINGS

Glick, Paul C. "The Future Marital Status and Living Arrangements of the Elderly." *Gerontologist*, 19 (1979): 301–309. A prediction of the status of American elderly people in the next twenty-five years.

Shanas, Ethel. "Older People and Their Families: The New Pioneers." *Journal of Marriage and the Family*, 42 (1980): 9–15. Suggestions for the role of elderly people in family life.

Streib, Gordon F., and Rubye W. Beck, "Older Families: A Decade Review." *Journal of Marriage and the Family*, 42 (1980): 937–949. A review of research on the family life of the elderly in the United States.

Troll, Lillian E., Sheila J. Miller, and Robert C. Atchley. *Families in Later Life*. Belmont, Calif., Wadsworth, 1979. A thorough discussion of all dimensions of older Americans' family life.

ALTERNATIVE MARITAL AND FAMILY STRUCTURES

No one pattern of intimates and no one concept of marriage is appropriate for all people.

Roger W. Libby[1]

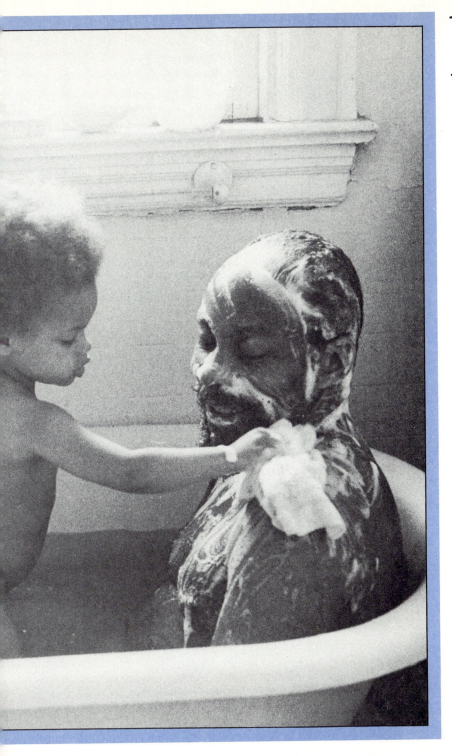

17

MULTIPLE-SPOUSE MARRIAGES
Polygyny
Polyandry
Group Marriage

POPULAR NONMARITAL ALTERNATIVES
Staying Single
One-Parent Families
Cohabitation
Communes

Various alternatives to traditional marital and family life have become increasingly common in our society. In the not-too-distant past, any life style other than heterosexual marriage, whether by choice or circumstance, was considered improper. Indeed, the term *alternative* was synonymous with *deviant*.

Although American society continues to favor marriage, there appears to be an increasing acceptance of nontraditional family life styles. For many, *alternative* no longer necessarily means deviant or immoral but simply refers to one of several acceptable possibilities. As if to certify this growing acceptance of alternative family life styles, a new journal, called *Alternative Lifestyles: Changing Patterns in Marriage, Family, and Intimacy*, was founded in 1978.

In recent years, many studies have examined a variety of alternative marital and family structures, including singlehood, single parenting, unmarried couples living together (cohabitation), open marriage, group marriage, communes, homosexual relationships (see Chapter 6, "Sexual Values and Behavior"), swinging (married individuals exchanging partners for sexual purposes), and childless marriage. Some of these, such as group marriage and swinging, have never involved a significant number of people. Others, such as staying single, single parenthood, and cohabitation, involve substantial numbers of people.

There are many reasons that people seek or find themselves in an alternative family life style. Some are disillusioned with the structure, and what they perceive to be the constraints, of our society's traditional forms of marriage and the family, and they explore various alternatives in search of more individual freedom. Others find themselves adjusting to a change in marital status because of separation, divorce, or the death of a spouse, and either choose to try a different life style or, in some cases, find that another life style is their only option. For example, a widowed person who would like to remarry may be forced to remain single because of ill health or a limited supply of prospective partners. Still other people want to experience nonmarital living arrangements before they marry or remarry.

Whatever the reasons, more and more people are living in alternative family structures. In fact, a very small proportion of American families are traditional nuclear families consisting of a working husband, housewife mother, and children. As we pointed out in Chapter 1, "The Structures and Functions of the Modern Family," this type of family structure did not increase in numbers during the 1970s.

Although most Americans marry—a fact of American life that is unlikely to change in the near future—some people will try one or more of the common alternative family life styles during their lifetimes. Often they will do so by choice, because the alternative seems to meet emotional needs and fulfill personal life goals better than a traditional marital and family arrangement can.

In this chapter we discuss the major alternative family life styles, including multiple-spouse marriages, which are viewed from a cross-cultural perspective because they are not common in the United States, as well as singlehood, single parenting, cohabitation (living together), and communal living, which are the more common and widely publicized nonmarital alternatives in our society. (It should be noted that many people fit into more than one of the alternative life styles that we examine. A single parent, for example, may also be a member of a commune.)

MULTIPLE-SPOUSE MARRIAGES

The dominant form of marriage in *all* cultures is *monogamy*—the marriage of one husband and one wife—sanctioned by religious or legal authority or both. Even when other forms of marriage are permitted, monogamy remains the most common marital practice, because in a monogamous system, (1) individuals have the best opportunity of finding a spouse; (2) the sexual gratification and emotional needs of both partners can be fulfilled; (3) sexual jealousies and quarrels, a possible problem in multiple-spouse marriages, are minimized; (4) inheritance, property rights, and lineage are fairly easy to determine; and (5) child-rearing practices can effectively be aimed at establishing close emotional ties between parents and children.

Three other types of marriage are found in other cultures: the two forms of polygamy—polygyny and polyandry—and group marriage. These are defined as follows:

1. *Polygyny*, the marriage of one husband and two or more wives.
2. *Polyandry*, the marriage of one wife and two or more husbands.
3. *Group marriage*, the marriage of two or more women to two or more men.

Of these three, only polygyny occurs with any frequency, and then only in non-Western societies, except among the Mormons of western America during the mid-nineteenth century. Polyandry and group marriage are exceedingly rare.

Polygyny

Polygyny has been practiced in many African tribes. It seems to be the most satisfactory marital form for societies in which women outnumber men. Yet most societies have no serious shortage of men (of the usual marrying ages), and consequently, for every man who has two wives, there is usually another who remains a bachelor.

Even in societies that permit having more than one wife, most marriages are monogamous. One of the main reasons is that polygyny is expensive, and most men cannot afford to support more than one wife. As a result, usually only economically or politically powerful males have several wives. Too, since it takes time to acquire wealth and power, it is likely that only older men have more than one wife. Consequently, having several wives is often a status symbol for the powerful leaders of a tribe.

This was true of the Mormon practice of polygyny in the nineteenth century in the United States. Initially, it was only the privileged leaders of the Church of Jesus Christ of Latter-day Saints who had many wives (see Box 17.1).

Polyandry

Although polyandry is a possible marital structure, it is exceedingly rare and has been practiced by only a small number of groups, including the Toda, Marquesans, Tibetans, and Jats. Anthropological data indicate that polyandry is often associated with difficult economic conditions and is often accompanied by the practice of *female infanticide*, the murder of female babies, a method of limiting population size. Polyandry thus provides a wife for the excess males

BOX 17.1 Mormon Polygyny*

The Mormons practiced polygyny for well over fifty years in the United States. But most of the explanations of why the Mormons first adopted polygyny are false or are mostly myth. The practice was not begun because there was an excess of Mormon females: census figures indicate that in the mid-nineteenth century, Utah, like most of the West, had an excess of males. Neither was polygyny an attempt to increase the Mormon birth rate or a "convenient method of satisfying the male sex urge."[†] Rather, Joseph Smith, the first leader of the church, claimed to have had a spiritual revelation that prescribed polygyny, and thus the Mormons openly practiced it because they believed that it had been ordained by God.

Although Smith's revelation was recorded in 1843, it is not known when the Mormons first began to practice polygyny. Apparently, before then, the leaders of the church practiced polygyny, but it was kept secret.

Estimates of the percentage of Mormon males who ever engaged in polygyny vary. The church reports that only 3 percent of all Mormon males had more than one wife. But researchers believe that approximately 10 percent of all Mormon males had more than one wife.[‡]

Mormon plural marriage ended because of external difficulties. Much of the United States population felt that Mormon polygyny was a threat to society. In 1862, President Abraham Lincoln signed a bill authorizing the federal government to punish and to prevent the practice in the western territories. But even though many Mormons were imprisoned for plural marriage, polygyny continued to be practiced in Utah. Finally in 1890, the president of the Mormon church issued a proclamation agreeing to abide by federal law. It is thought, however, that polygyny continued, and is continuing, among small groups of individuals who left the church or who were excommunicated because of polygynous practices.

Since the church banned polygyny, only a few Mormons have practiced it. Nevertheless, as sociologist William M. Kephart concluded: "For a period of almost fifty years the Latter-day Saints not only practiced polygamy but did so with a fair amount of success. It may well be that this exercise in marital pluralism was *the most unusual large-scale experiment in American social history*."[§]

---

*Although the term *polygamy* is often used, the correct term is *polygyny*.
[†]William M. Kephart, *Extraordinary Groups: The Sociology of Unconventional Life-Styles*, New York, St. Martin's Press, 1976, p. 206.
[‡]Ibid., p. 208.
[§]Ibid., p. 207.

and, in addition, raises the family's living standard by having several males serve as breadwinners instead of having only one. Since the husbands of one wife are often brothers, potential jealousy and conflict are minimized, but it is difficult to determine paternity, and unless males greatly outnumber females, many women in a polyandrous society do not have husbands.

Group Marriage

Early anthropologists wrote extensively about group marriage, but it seems unlikely that it has ever been the dominant marriage form in any society. Even its rare occurrences have seemed to be temporary phenomena or the result of changes in local conditions. The Toda of India, for example, practiced polyandry as a result of their custom of female infanticide. When British Colonial authorities forbade infanticide, the proportion of females increased, and occasionally a group of brothers would take wives in addition to the one they already shared. In this case, and also in other societies, group marriage and polyandry usually were practiced together. But group marriage creates lineage problems, complicates determination of inheritance and property rights, and often causes jealousy and interpersonal conflict.

Group marriage is illegal in the United States and thus there are no legal bonds tying a group marriage together. Nevertheless, a very small number of individuals do form group marriages, usually a marriage of four partners. In their study of group marriage, Larry and Joan Constantine found that persons form group marriages for several reasons. In order of decreasing importance, these include:

- personal fulfillment
- opportunity for personal growth
- new aspects of personality emerging in relating to more people
- richer environment for children
- sense of "community"
- multiple adult models for children
- variety of sexual partners
- greater intellectual variety[2]

There often are jealousies and other conflicts in group marriages, particularly if the partners enter a group marriage in order to resolve marital or personal problems. And like any other marriage, a group marriage has to deal with finances, communication, and emotional problems, as well as the distribution of housework and child care.

POPULAR NONMARITAL ALTERNATIVES

Staying Single

Today there are approximately fifty million unmarried adults in the United States.[3] This large number of single people, representing about one-third of the U.S. adult population, includes those who have never married, the widowed and divorced, and unmarried persons who are living together. Some singles are unmarried by choice and intend to remain single. Others are in a transitional stage before marrying or remarrying. The status and life goals of single people are so diverse that their only common feature may be their legal status as unmarried people.

To be single has been seen in relation to marriage and the family. Without "family," the concept of "single" has had no meaning. Single is a word used to categorize a vast and divergent group of persons in order to treat them on the basis of one common criterion—their non-marriage.[4]

Although single people differ considerably according to age, race, occupation, marital experience, and other sociological and personality factors, the term *singles* generally carries the stereotype of individuals in their twenties who are unmarried or divorced, who work, and who do not have children. There is a persistent myth that all young unmarried people live in "swinging singles" apartment complexes where casual sex and recreational activities are always available, that they frequent

Some singles confront their fear of loneliness by going to bars.

Ellis Herwig/Stock, Boston

single bars, and that they often have "one night stands." Another erroneous image is that older unmarried persons are unlovable and unable to give love, have emotional problems or personality shortcomings, and are always lonely. Because our society is marriage oriented, older unmarried people are seen by many as deviant and threatening to traditional marriage and family values. Being single, however, is no longer highly stigmatized, and often the life style of the single individual is envied.

Singlehood has both advantages and disadvantages. The advantages include having more money to spend on oneself, enjoying an independent life style with no other person to have to consider, being able to be totally absorbed in a career and not having to be concerned about family responsibilities or expectations, being free to travel, being flexible in the choice of a career and geographic location, and being able to explore a variety of interpersonal and sexual relationships.

In a study of singlehood, Peter Stein found that many single people emphasize the advantages of their individuality and independence:

The basis on which a successful single life style rests is economic independence, which, in turn, promotes a sense of dignity and self-esteem. While the importance of self-sustaining work applies to both sexes, it was dramatically evident in the cases of the women interviewed, since they had consciously rejected the traditional female role of dependence on a husband's income and status. . . . They cited advances in their career development, greater interest in work, and a gradual investment in a professional identity. . . .

The single men interviewed mentioned a heightened sense of choice about their work because they did not have to be as security-conscious as males with families. They were able to make professional commitments based on interest and mobility; they enjoyed the knowledge that they could explore other fields, if they wished, with relatively little risk. Both sexes, of course, derived satisfaction from having the freedom to choose how to spend their money, by not being tied down to joint financial decisions.[5]

On the negative side, single people are often at a disadvantage in regard to housing, loans and credit, and car insurance costs. They also may experience discrimination in their jobs. For example, the managers of some corporations believe that single executives tend to make hasty judgments and that single people are "less stable" than married people.[6]

Many single persons also are lonely, and most feel that they must cope with what Stein calls a "pro-marriage environment":

They are coping with the pressures of a pro-marriage environment—which confronts all singles. Single people described feeling uncomfortable or defensive in society-at-large—with their work associates, for instance, and in couple-dominated social situations. Their families often applied pressure to get married, implying that the single adults were not living up to their responsibilities or fearing that eventually they would find themselves all alone in the world. *Indeed, the fear of loneliness is the major problem single people confront.*[7]

Despite the disadvantages and the social pressure, staying single and living alone is becoming an increasingly popular life-style choice. The U.S. Bureau of the Census reported, for example, a 60 percent increase in the number of persons living alone during the 1970s (from 10.9 million in 1970 to 17.2 million in 1979). And today, individuals living alone represent approximately 23 percent of all American households.[8] Contributing to this figure are the increasingly large numbers of elderly widowed people who continue to maintain their own homes, the many young people who live apart from their families before marrying for the first time, and the increasing numbers of separated and divorced persons.

One-Parent Families

Currently, one-parent families make up over 19 percent of all American families with children living at home. This adds up to approximately fifteen million adults and children who are members of one-parent families.[9]

There are several situations creating one-parent families, including death of a spouse, divorce, separation, desertion, the adoption of a child by a single person, or the birth of a child by an unmarried woman. Although the number of single fathers is increasing, most one-parent families consist of a mother and her children (see Table 17.1).

Like unmarried people, many single parents are satisfied with being unmarried. They can have a relatively independent life style of their own choosing, and they have total freedom with regard to child-rearing practices. Today, there is also less social stigma attached to being an unmarried parent, as shown by the fact that one-parent families are no longer called "broken homes."

There is no question, however, that parenthood limits the single parent's life choices and increases the demands on his or her time and energies, often more than for married parents. The single parent is

TABLE 17.1 Total Number of Families with Children Living at Home

Type of Family	Percent	
	1970	1979
Two-Parent Families	89%	81%
One-Parent Families (total)	11	19
Maintained by Mother	10	17
Maintained by Father	1	2

Source: U.S. Bureau of the Census, *Current Population Reports*, Series P–20, No. 352, "Household and Family Characteristics: March 1979," Washington, D.C., U.S. Government Printing Office, 1980, Table C, p. 3.

solely responsible for his or her children and has no partner to help carry out household chores and child-care duties. Also, a single parent may have less money to live on than if he or she were married. Moreover, it may be exceedingly difficult to be socially active, to have enough time for work, to be with the children, and still to have any time left for personal needs.

Not only can parenthood restrict the individual life choices of a single parent, but it can also restrict a single parent's social activities (see Box 17.2). And if the single parent is interested in remarrying, the presence of children may restrict his or her choice of partners, since a prospective partner may be hesitant to assume responsibility for someone else's children.

Single Mothers According to data from the U.S. Bureau of the Census, there are substantially more single-mother families than there are single-father families.[10] And although only approximately 17 percent of all U.S. households are headed by women, 42 percent of the women maintaining one-parent families have incomes below the poverty line.[11]

The working single mother often finds herself responsible for child care during her nonworking hours, for the housework, and for the family's economic survival (including the costs of child care while she is at work). If there has been a divorce, there may be expensive legal bills, and even if she has been awarded alimony or child support or both, she may not receive it regularly or at all. A widowed woman may be faced with expensive medical bills or find that her small savings or pension is not enough to support herself and her family. Although she may never have worked, or may have not worked for many years, she may be forced to take an unskilled job, which often does not pay well. And because women are often discriminated against in the work place,

BOX 17.2 Sex and the Single Parent

Children often are an obstacle to their single parent's dating and sexual activities. The time and financial constraints placed on single parents often make it difficult for them to arrange extended periods of time to become acquainted with other people and to establish relationships. If child care is a problem, it may be difficult to leave the children for an evening, and many parents feel very uncomfortable having their sexual partners stay overnight. Or they may be afraid of setting a bad example for their children or believe that children should not be aware of their parent's sexual activities.

In one study, researcher Judith Greenberg reported that "the majority of the parents interviewed saw single-parenting as directly constraining their sexual activities because of location constraints (having to go away from home), reduced amount of sexual activity, and reduced quality as a result of tiredness or intrusion by children."*

Such interaction difficulties, coupled with family responsibilities and demands, can produce a very hectic and dissatisfying life style, as the following comments by a single father illustrate:

My children have to know a person very well before I will allow that person to sleep overnight. I have to be careful that I don't set a bad example for the kids. But it's a very lonely life for me. . . .

Actually, I should have gained freedom by being single, but that's true only to a certain limit. I am still not free to pick up and go when and where I want. In many respects it is as if I am still married without any of the benefits. . . . When they [children] are home, which is almost all the time, it limits my social life, because anyone I date will probably have children too. I feel like a square peg in a round hole.†

*Judith B. Greenberg, "Single-Parenting and Intimacy," *Alternative Lifestyles*, 2 (August 1979): 316.
†Jan Curran and Marcy Wetton, *The Statue of Liberty Is Cracking Up: A Guide to Loving, Leaving, and Living Again*, New York, Harcourt Brace Jovanovich, 1979, p. 43.

a single mother may be limited in her choice of work and have further difficulty making ends meet with a low-paying job.

Single Fathers Single fatherhood is not new in our society. In the past, when medical care was less effective, many men became single parents when their wives died in childbirth. But usually the man remarried, or the children were cared for by the man's family or neighbors. Today the increase in the number of single fathers is due largely to separation, divorce, and desertion. Because the courts no longer automatically give custody of the children to the mother, men are increasingly likely to receive sole custody of their children. And the adjustment of the single-father family, like that of the single-mother family, is dependent on many factors. Social researcher Arnold Katz lists several items that can affect the success of single-father families, which include the age of the children, the reason that the mother is gone, the size of the family, and so on:

> Equally important [to success] are the proximity of kin and their ability to help, the quality of relations with neighbors, the availability of social services, and the degree of understanding of employers. The father's income, the nature of his job, and the length and stability of the former marriage are also relevant. Motherlessness will unite some families; it will divide others. . . .
>
> Some fathers are able to continue their employment and the pattern of the family's life remains outwardly unaltered. Some find it a struggle to combine work and the care of children but manage to do so. Others find themselves compelled to give up work, thus suffering a drop in income, and often weakening their own self-respect and risking the good opinion of their friends and neighbors who fail to understand their problems.[12]

Initially, unmarried fathers may have difficulty combining parenting, housework, and a full-time job, and it may seem surprising that many single fathers cite money as their worst problem. Yet single fathers are often saddled with divorce costs and alimony, in addition to the costs of maintaining their family. The costs of quality day care and baby sitters alone can take up a large portion of a paycheck.[13]

Single fathers often report more acute feelings of loneliness than single mothers do, and men are much more likely to remarry than are women. It has been suggested that women receive and actively seek support from, and friendships with, other women but that single fathers have more difficulty establishing male friendships and sources of support.[14]

Because of these various problems, many single parents see their life style as a transitional stage. The financial and emotional stresses of raising a family alone are great, and many single parents would like eventually to live with a partner, marry, or remarry, share a home with other single parents or family members, or live in a communal setting.

Joint Custody Parents who have a joint custody arrangement with the former spouse may find that many of the frustrations of being a single parent are eliminated. Joint custody allows them to share the economic responsibilities and time demands of parenting. For some, this makes single parenting more manageable and may reduce the pressure to find an alternative life style.

Single parents may face financial and emotional stresses.

Paul Conklin/Monkmeyer

Cohabitation

To *cohabit*, according to the *American Heritage Dictionary*, is "to live together in a sexual relationship when not legally married." This definition carries none of the value judgment that our society once placed on what is now innocuously called living together or *cohabitation*. In the recent past, unmarried people who lived together *(cohabitants)* were said to be "living in sin" or "shacking up." As recently as 1968, an unmarried sophomore college woman was almost expelled from Barnard College in New York when it was discovered that she was living with a man. At the time, this incident created so much interest that it was reported on the front page of the *New York Times*. What was then considered to be shocking, immoral, and newsworthy, however, is now so commonplace on many college campuses that it is hardly even worth noting.

Many factors have contributed to the change in social attitudes toward unmarried persons openly living together and to the concomitant increase in the last two decades in the numbers of people doing so. Two factors greatly responsible for this are the increase in sexual permissiveness and the improved contraceptive methods now widely available. The women's liberation movement has strengthened the ideal of the egalitarian relationship and has stressed the possibility of women having life goals other than traditional marriage. And the stigma of deviance traditionally attached to alternative life styles has diminished, creating a more broad-minded environment in which people may live in nonmarital family structures.

Incidence of Cohabitation

The liberalization of social attitudes toward cohabitation is dramatically illustrated by the fact that during the 1970s the number of unmarried individuals living together more than doubled so that today there are approximately two million adults cohabiting in the United States. The growth in the incidence of unmarried cohabitation has been phenomenal, particularly in the late 1970s, as demographers Paul Glick and Graham Spanier point out:

From 1977 to 1978, there was a very substantial increase in the number of unmarried couples living together—19 percent. Rarely does social change occur with such rapidity. Indeed, there have been few developments relating to marriage and family life which have been as dramatic as the rapid increase in unmarried cohabitation.[15]

Glick and Spanier also point out that the increase in unmarried persons cohabiting is primarily among young couples without children. The number of unmarried couples living together with children, for example, has not varied significantly over the past twenty years (see Figure 17.1).

Most never-married individuals who are cohabiting are under the age thirty-five. But it is not only young people and college students who live together. In fact, the number of people living together who are over

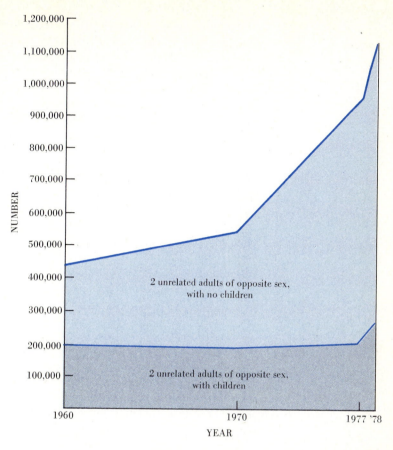

Source: Paul C. Glick and Graham B. Spanier, "Married and Unmarried Cohabitation in the United States," *Journal of Marriage and the Family*, 42 (February 1980): 20.

thirty-five is about two-thirds the number of people living together who are under thirty-five.[16] Also, the ages of people who are cohabiting differ according to whether or not they have been married previously, as we can see in the following table:[17]

Age	Not Previously Married	Previously Married
Under age 35	85%	38%
35–54	8	30
55 and older	7	32

This table shows that among never-married persons, most cohabitants are under age thirty-five but that among previously married persons, almost equal numbers of cohabiting persons are found at all ages.

Although the number of cohabiting persons has dramatically increased, this figure still represents only a small percentage of the total population. In fact, unmarried couples represent only 2 percent of the total number of couples living together.[18] But because this figure does not include those who lived together before marriage or those who are likely to cohabit in the future, it is obvious that this life-style alternative applies to a significant minority of the American population. According to Glick and Spanier:

Increased freedom in adult behavior, less pressure to marry at traditionally normative young ages, and greater acceptance of unmarried cohabitation as a life style are evidently providing a context in which this way of living is becoming increasingly accepted as an alternative to marriage or as a temporary arrangement preceding or following marriage.[19]

Reasons for Cohabiting

There are many reasons for living together, just as there are many reasons for marrying. Some people, disenchanted with the idea of marriage or disillusioned by previous marital experiences, may enter into a living-together situation instead of marrying. They may want a long-term relationship or simply the convenience of having a partner without the accompanying commitment that a marriage usually implies. For some, however, cohabitation is a prelude to marriage, and these couples consider living together as a way of testing their compatibility as marital partners. Even those who are not contemplating marriage with their current cohabitating partner almost always state that they are planning to marry in the future. In a study by Donald Bower and Victor Christopherson, for example, 96 percent of the cohabitants indicated that they would like to marry at some time.[20]

Many of those living together are very committed to each other and view their arrangement as a fairly permanent relationship. Initially, however, many of these relationships start slowly. Charles Cole explains:

Research . . . suggests that most couples do not make a conscious decision to live together but rather tend to gradually drift together as a result of spending increasing amounts of time together. The pattern usually starts with the partners spending one night a week together, moves on to their adding a second and then a third night a week, until one of them gradually finds it more convenient to move more clothes and personal items over to the other's room or apartment, and ends with their moving in and living together. . . . They must now redefine their social situation to account for the fact that they are cohabiting. This redefinition frequently is accompanied by a reassessment of their feelings toward their partner as well as their own self-concept. If the partners perceive that cohabiting provides them with a favorable reward-cost ratio, they will likely continue to live together.[21]

Characteristics of Cohabitants

Many studies indicate that cohabitants and noncohabitants are more similar than dissimilar.[22] Yet there are some interesting differences. As a group, cohabitants are less religious and have more liberal life styles; that is, they are more likely to have tried drugs, lived in a commune, and practiced other types of unconventional behavior.[23]

Demographic comparisons of married and unmarried couples living together have found that:

Couples living together without marriage are most likely to be residing in large metropolitan areas or large cities. They are characterized by relatively low income levels and high unemployment. Unmarried cohabiting women, however, are more likely to be employed than their married counterparts, many of whom are not in the labor force because of their primary activity as homemakers. Young never-married cohabitants tend to be better educated than either their married or previously-married counterparts. Blacks contribute a disproportionately large share to the number of couples living together outside marriage, although a large majority of all cohabiting couples are white.[24]

An interesting aside to the question of differences between cohabiting and noncohabiting couples is the issue of sex roles. Because cohabiting adults tend to be more liberal, one might assume that the division of labor would be less "traditional" in cohabiting couples, as compared with that for married couples. But research findings indicate that there are no significant differences between cohabitants and married people. Rebecca Stafford and her colleagues report that

although ultimate responsibility for many tasks is shared, generally wives and female partners do the women's work and husbands and male partners do the men's work. This division leaves the women most of the household duties whether or not they are also employed in the labor force.[25]

Thus, as in the case of traditional married couples, the female cohabitants tend to do the household chores, the cooking, and the washing, and the male cohabitants take care of household repairs, the car, and the lawn.

Advantages and Disadvantages of Cohabitation

Most cohabiting couples report a high level of overall satisfaction with their living arrangement. In Eleanor Macklin's study of cohabiting college students, for example, over 90 percent evaluated their cohabiting experience as "successful, pleasurable, and maturing."[26] Living together often gives individuals a better understanding of both themselves and others, and also gives them the experience of intimately relating to another person in the context of a continuing relationship. This provides an opportunity for intimacy, emotional support and security, personal growth, and economic savings. Younger never-married persons may prefer to marry after they have finished school or when they have a better job or more money. For them, living together does not entail the same financial responsibilities as marriage does, and also, if the relationship does not work out, they do not have to suffer the financial and emotional trauma of a divorce (although breaking up can still be a very emotionally upsetting experience).

Divorced and widowed persons may also find cohabitation rewarding for many of the same reasons. For those who have been unhappily married, cohabitation may offer a differently structured relationship, which if terminated, may not produce the same sense of failure that the ending of a traditional marriage would. Divorced or widowed parents who live together may not only benefit financially but they also may be able to share child care. Besides fulfilling emotional and intimacy needs, widowed and retired individuals may prefer living together for economic reasons, particularly since social security and other retirement benefits for two single persons are generally higher than those for a married couple. For the unmarried elderly, marriage sometimes means a loss of income.

In fact, both younger and older cohabitants cite similar benefits from this kind of relationship. Younger people generally report the advantages of companionship, sexual gratification, and economic gain, whereas older people report the advantages of the reinstatement of the spousal role, companionship, financial gain, and sexual gratification.[27]

But cohabiting couples also have certain problems. Noel Myricks and Roger Rubin remind us that "premarital cohabitation is still a criminal offense in approximately half of the states in this country."[28] And although criminal prosecution is extremely rare, other legal problems may arise. This is particularly true in the case of property rights. Marital laws attempt to secure the interests and rights of the individual, but these protections do not extend to cohabitants. But as we mentioned in Chapter 8, "The Public Side of Marriage: Legal and Social Issues," many possible legal problems can be avoided by writing personal living-together agreements.

Despite the growing social acceptance of cohabitation, many people

Cohabitation is a viable life-style alternative for single parents.

Richard Kalvar/Magnum

still do not approve of nonmarital unions. They believe that living together is wrong and that such people are simply avoiding responsibility. Opposition to cohabitation may be particularly strong in middle-aged and older individuals.

Among college students, parents are often a major source of problems. In Eleanor Macklin's study, nearly 80 percent of the college students who were cohabiting had attempted to hide their living arrangement from their parents.[29] Many students worry that their parents will discover that they are living with someone and either reject them or force them to move. Others feel guilty that they are deceiving their parents and sad that they are unable to share this important part of their lives with their families.

Cohabitants, like married people, also have communication, financial, emotional, and sexual problems. In addition, the partners may have different feelings of commitment which may create conflict if one person wants to have a long-term relationship or to marry, and the other is satisfied with a short-term living arrangement. These differences can often be resolved if the partners discuss their expectations, feelings of commitment, and reasons for cohabiting before they begin to live together.

Americans often look to Sweden as a predictor of American social trends. In Sweden, 99 percent of all couples say they lived together before they married, and over the years, the marriage rate has declined as cohabitation has increased. Also, fifteen out of every one hundred couples in Sweden are unmarried, as compared with approximately two out of one hundred couples in the United States.[30] But Sweden has had a long history of cohabitation, and that country's generous social welfare for children and adults decreases the economic incentive for marriage that motivates many Americans to marry. Like Americans, Swedes value marriage and usually get married once they begin having children, although more children are born out of wedlock in Sweden than in the United States. These factors make it difficult to compare the two countries, but if the United States follows Swedish trends, it is likely that more and more Americans will live together before they marry.

Although cohabitation will probably not weaken the institution of marriage, it is likely to change it. One effect may be an increase in the number of people marrying at an older age:

To the extent that cohabitation does delay marriage, however, it could produce significant secondary consequences for society such as a reduced birth rate and an increase in the quality of married life due to people entering marriage at a somewhat older age.[31]

Many proponents of cohabitation argue that it has positive effects on marriage, because people who have lived together have more realistic expectations for marital relationships. This and the experience of living with someone, they suggest, produce more satisfying marriages. The available studies, however, have consistently failed to find significant differences between married couples who have and who have not cohabited before marriage.[32]

Despite the increase in cohabitation during the 1970s, it should be remembered that the percentage of unmarried couples living together at any one time is quite small. Cohabitation has become an alternative to marriage for only a few people, and for most of those, living together is a temporary rather than a permanent living situation. Research studies indicate that most cohabiting couples believe in marriage, and it is very unlikely that cohabitation will ever pose a threat to the institution of marriage.

Communes

A *commune* is a "family" of several people, some or all of whom are unrelated, who live together. The term applies to many different types

Members of a commune share work and enjoy a sense of family.

of group-living arrangements whose members share responsibilities for work, pool their personal property and resources, establish and enjoy a sense of family and community, and may or may not share sexual partners.

Although there have been communes in the United States since the eighteenth century, only twice has this type of living arrangement emerged as a highly visible alternative family structure. The first time was from roughly 1800 to the Civil War and included such well-known groups as Brook Farm, Harmony, Oneida, Amana, Zoar, Bethel, and hundreds of others. Many of these early communes had utopian ideals. Their members sought a better, if not a perfect, social environment, and they structured their communities according to strict economic or religious doctrines. They completely discarded or radically revised some of the major social institutions, role behaviors, values, and norms that many in the outside society respected and followed. After the Civil War, however, the movement declined, and by 1900 only a few communes were left.

Then, in the late 1960s, there was a resurgence of communal living. Communes of all sizes and ideologies sprang up, and the variety seemed limitless. Most catered to younger people, and many were associated with the hippies in the Haight-Ashbury district of San Francisco. Exactly how many communes were formed in the sixties and seventies is unknown, but sociologist Ben Zablocki estimates that there were at least ten thousand separate communal experiments between 1965 and 1975. He also observes that "what was unique about this resurgence, besides its size, was that it centered around a search for alternatives to the family rather than around economic or utopian issues."[33] Unlike the people who joined communes in the mid-nineteenth century, those in the mid-twentieth century were mainly searching for alternative living arrangements; to them, making a political or religious statement was less important.

Reasons for Joining a Commune

People join communes for a number of reasons, but in most cases, dissatisfaction and disillusionment with society are high on the list. Some people join communal living groups so as to belong to and to have a "sense of family." They may be single persons who are unwilling to commit themselves to marriage or a living-together arrangement, but who want companionship and economic sharing; married persons who wish to enlarge their relationship or expand their sense of family and community; and single parents who find that the support and help from commune members ease the many difficulties and loneliness of raising a child alone.

One of the most comprehensive reports on communal living, compiled by the Urban Communes Project from data gathered from sixty American urban communes, listed the major reasons that the participants, who were mostly single, gave for joining an urban commune. In descending order of importance, these reasons were:

1. Economic
2. Order and regularity
3. Friendships and support from caring people in a non-caring world

4. As a way to leave home
5. To break with the past
6. In search of a viable alternative to things they had tried but did not like
7. Exploratory—a way of trying out a new lifestyle just for the sake of new experience
8. A way to live with a lover
9. A way to live in a single state in the company of others
10. A search for like-minded people
11. Companionship, or community[34]

Some people join religious communes because they are disillusioned with traditional religious institutions and want to experiment with new faiths. Others want to reduce the stress of living in a city and to try working and living in rural communes. For still others, living in a commune may be a political statement and an escape from society's regulations and demands. They may be tired of what they consider to be a materialistic and corrupt society over which they have no control, and for them communal living is a search for freedom in an alternative living structure. And there are those who view communal living as a way to learn more about themselves and to expose themselves to a nontraditional system of relationships and interactions.

Rewards of Communal Living

Many people are satisfied with communal living and often mention the personal growth and freedom they have experienced in a very open and supportive environment. Pooled resources decrease financial insecurity and allow for major purchases that an individual or a couple may not be able to afford on their own. For parents, communal living offers shared child care, and for the children, it provides additional parental figures and role models. All members have the opportunity of exploring a variety of relationships, and for many, the commune is a haven where they can interact with people who share the same outlook on life. Many, in fact, look upon their communal experience as being the happiest period in their lives. Gordon Yaswen's response is just one example:

At Sun Hill, in the fall of that year, I was undoubtedly the happiest that I had ever been in my entire life of, then, 29 years. For the first time in my existence I felt truly comfortable in my situation and surroundings. I wished to be where I was, and I was doing what I wanted to do; no place and no thing lured me elsewhere. . . .

It was a good life . . . and it helped me feel for the first time in my life that I BELONGED somewhere, and that the somewhere was on this Earth after all.[35]

Even though most people in communes do not expect to live there for the rest of their lives, they feel that their experience is very fulfilling and valuable.

Difficulties in Communal Living

Only a few communes last any longer than a few years. This is mainly due to limited financial resources, a lack of organization, and interpersonal conflict. Generally, communes are relatively easy to establish in an urban setting because housing is usually available and because it is fairly easy to gather a group of people. But the availability of people, as researcher Bennet Berger and his associates found, also means that urban communes have more turnover in their memberships. In addition, their members may be less committed because their new life style is not so very different from their old one, and an urban commune probably is not very isolated, either geographically or ideologically, from the rest of society. Furthermore, if the members do not work and contribute money, the group cannot survive. But, if they do work, they may feel entrapped by the very system they initially wished to avoid.[36]

Rural communes also have disadvantages. They may have financial problems, and many members may not have any agricultural skills. Land, equipment, and housing are often expensive to acquire and to maintain. And depending on where the commune is situated, its members may have difficulty finding outside employment.

The members' lack of commitment or a weak social organization can pose serious threats to any commune's success. Many groups seem to have no structure, and their goals are often poorly defined. These are extremely important problems, for as sociologist Rosabeth Kanter explains, commitment is crucial:

Since the commune represents an attempt to establish an ideal social order within the larger society, it must vie with the outside for the members' loyalties. It must ensure high member-involvement despite external competition without sacrificing its distinctiveness or ideals. It must often contravene the earlier socialization of its members in securing obedience to new demands. It must calm internal dissension in order to present a united front to the world. The problem of securing total and complete commitment is central.[37]

Many communes fail because their members are not committed, because they lack organization or effective leadership, or because there are too many internal conflicts.[38] Internal problems often are a result of disagreements over power and authority, commitment, or ideology.

Whatever societal hostility the communal movement faced in the 1960s and 1970s has largely subsided,[39] and charges that communes foster disrespect for authority, provide a haven for shiftless and irresponsible people, and encourage free sex and moral decay are no longer heard, perhaps because the enthusiasm for group living has subsided. Most of the communes that sprang up in the sixties and seventies are now defunct. The few that remain, however, demonstrate that it is unlikely that communes will ever cease to be a life-style alternative. As long as people continue to become disenchanted with society, the potential for communal living will remain.

SUMMARY

Although most people eventually marry and raise families, a small percentage of individuals experiment with alternative marital and family life styles. These alternatives include singlehood, single parenting, cohabitation, open marriage, group marriage, communal living, homosexual relationships, swinging, and childless marriage.

In all cultures, monogamy is the most common marital structure. Other marital structures include group marriage and the two forms of polygamy, polygyny and polyandry. Group marriage and polyandry have been seldom practiced, but polygyny has been practiced in many cultures, and was practiced in the United States by the Mormons.

There are currently over fifty million unmarried adults in the United States. These are young unmarried people, other never-married people, and those who are single because of divorce or death of a spouse. Single life includes such benefits as economic independence, an independent life style, the freedom to travel and to have geographic mobility, and the opportunity to try a variety of interpersonal and sexual relationships. Nonetheless, single persons may be discriminated against in regard to housing, loans and credit, and car insurance costs. Additionally, single people often feel lonely and are considered by some as deviant or less stable than married people.

The life style of single parents also has advantages and disadvantages. Although they enjoy independence and freedom, many single parents are solely responsible for their children and do not have a partner to help with household responsibilities or child care.

In the 1970s there was a dramatic increase in the number of unmarried couples living together. Most cohabitants have never been married and are under thirty-five, but many others have been previously married and are over thirty-five. Some cohabitants have short-term relationships based on companionship and convenience. Others, however, are deeply committed to each other and often see their living-together arrangement as a prelude to marriage.

Communal living is a family life-style alternative that has existed in the United States since the eighteenth century. Many people join communes because they are dissatisfied and disillusioned with the prevailing society. Communal living offers emotional support, a shared economic life style, and a sense of family and community. Although communes today are not as popular as they were in the 1960s and 1970s, some still exist, and communal living probably will become popular again in the future.

CONSIDER THIS

Mrs. Jackson had always considered her daughter Janice to be a bit of a maverick, but since Janice's divorce, Mrs. Jackson had become very concerned about how Janice and her nine-year-old daughter Karen were getting along. Although Janice assured her mother that she and Karen were fine, Mrs. Jackson felt it wasn't right that Janice and Karen had to manage all by themselves. But every time Mrs. Jackson voiced a new worry, Janice confidently countered it with a sound explanation.

Mrs. Jackson was particularly distressed that Karen no longer had a father at home, but, as Janice pointed out, Karen spent several weekends a month with her father and also talked with him on the phone regularly. Janice relieved her mother's concern that it was too difficult for her to work and to be a good mother at the same time by pointing out that her job had flexible working hours and that she started work after Karen left for school. After school, Karen went to a friend's house until her mother got home. Mrs. Jackson was sure that her daughter and granddaughter were lonely, but Janice and Karen belonged to a single-parent family group at their church, and they could be as busy as they wanted on the weekends with activities with their friends.

Still, Mrs. Jackson thought it just wasn't quite right. She wanted her daughter to remarry. But she was heartened by a conversation with her granddaughter: When she asked Karen if she would like to be part of a family again, Karen answered, "But Grandma, Mom and I are a family, and we take care of each other. Anyway, you and Granddad are our family, too!"

Questions
1. Is Karen right? Are she and her mother the only family she needs?
2. What are some reasons that Janice may not want to remarry?
3. Do you think Janice's and Karen's life together is typical of that of single-parent families?
4. What family life style is best for a recently divorced parent? Does it matter whether the parent is a man or a woman?

5. Are there any alternative living arrangements you would be willing to try? Are there any you definitely would not try? Why?

NOTES

1. Roger W. Libby, "Introduction," in Roger W. Libby and Robert N. Whitehurst (eds.), *Marriage and Alternatives: Exploring Intimate Relationships*, Glenview, Ill., Scott, Foresman, 1977, p. xxvi.
2. Larry L. Constantine and Joan M. Constantine, *Group Marriage: A Study of Contemporary Multilateral Marriage*, New York, Collier Books, 1973, p. 108.
3. U.S. Bureau of the Census, *Statistical Abstract of the United States: 1979* (10th ed.), Washington, D.C., U.S. Government Printing Office, 1979, p. 41.
4. Peter Stein, *Single*, Englewood Cliffs, N.J., Prentice-Hall, 1976, pp. 8–9.
5. Ibid., pp. 97–98.
6. Reported in Susan Jacoby, "49 Million Singles Can't Be All Right," *New York Times Magazine*, February 17, 1974, p. 48.
7. Peter Stein, *Single*, pp. 98–99.
8. U.S. Bureau of the Census, *Current Population Reports*, Series P–20, No. 349, "Marital Status and Living Arrangements: March 1979," Washington, D.C., U.S. Government Printing Office, 1980, p. 2; U.S. Bureau of the Census, *Current Population Reports*, Series P–20, No. 357, "Households and Families, by Type: March 1980 (Advance Report)," Washington, D.C., U.S. Government Printing Office, 1980, p. 1.
9. U.S. Bureau of the Census, *Current Population Reports*, Series P–20, No. 352, "Household and Family Characteristics: March 1979, Washington, D.C., U.S. Government Printing Office, 1980, p. 3.
10. U.S. Bureau of the Census, "Households and Families, by Type: March 1980 (Advance Report)," Table 3, p. 4.
11. U.S. Department of Labor, Women's Bureau, "Report for the World Conference on the United Nations Decade for Women," *Employment Goals of the World Plan of Action: Developments and Issues in the United States*, Washington, D.C., U.S. Government Printing Office, July 1980, p. 5.
12. Arnold J. Katz, "Lone Fathers: Perspectives and Implications for Family Policy," *Family Coordinator*, 28 (October 1979): 522.
13. Ibid., p. 526.
14. Judith B. Greenberg, "Single-Parenting and Intimacy," *Alternative Lifestyles*, 2 (August 1979): 308–329.

15. Paul C. Glick and Graham B. Spanier, "Married and Unmarried Cohabitation in the United States," *Journal of Marriage and the Family,* 42 (February 1980): 20.
16. Ibid., p. 22.
17. Ibid.
18. Ibid., p. 21.
19. Ibid., p. 30.
20. Donald W. Bower and Victor A. Christopherson, "University Student Cohabitation: A Regional Comparison of Selected Attitudes and Behavior," *Journal of Marriage and the Family,* 39 (August 1977): 451.
21. Charles Cole, "Cohabitation in Social Context," in Roger W. Libby and Robert N. Whitehurst (eds.), *Marriage and Alternatives: Exploring Intimate Relationships,* Glenview, Ill., Scott, Foresman, 1977, p. 70.
22. See Paul R. Newcomb, "Cohabitation in America: An Assessment of Consequences," *Journal of Marriage and the Family,* 41 (August 1979): 597–602; Eleanor D. Macklin, "Nontraditional Family Forms: A Decade of Research," *Journal of Marriage and the Family,* 42 (November 1980): 907–908.
23. Paul R. Newcomb, "Cohabitation in America"; Eleanor D. Macklin, "Nontraditional Family Forms"; Richard Clayton and Herwin Voss, "Shacking Up: Cohabitation in the 1970's," *Journal of Marriage and the Family,* 39 (May 1977): 273–283.
24. Paul C. Glick and Graham B. Spanier, "Married and Unmarried Cohabitation in the United States," pp. 29–30.
25. Rebecca Stafford, Elaine Backman, and Pamela DiBona, "The Division of Labor Among Cohabiting and Married Couples," *Journal of Marriage and the Family,* 39 (February 1977): 54.
26. Eleanor D. Macklin, "Cohabitation in College: Going Very Steady," *Psychology Today,* 8 (November 1974): 58.
27. Reported in Paul R. Newcomb, "Cohabitation in America," pp. 598, 601.
28. Noel Myricks and Roger Rubin, "Sex Laws and Alternative Life Styles," *Family Coordinator,* 26 (October 1977): 359.
29. Eleanor Macklin, "Cohabitation in College," p. 57.
30. Andrew Cherlin, "Cohabitation: How the French and Swedes Do It," *Psychology Today,* 13 (October 1979): 18.
31. Paul R. Newcomb, "Cohabitation in America," p. 600.
32. Eleanor Macklin, "Nontraditional Family Forms," p. 908; Jeffrey M. Jacques and Karen J. Chason, "Cohabitation: Its Impact on Marital Success," *Family Coordinator,* 28 (January 1979): 38.
33. Ben Zablocki, quoted in "Communes in Retrospect—A Search for Family Ties," *American Psychological Association Monitor,* 8 (1977): 6, 9.

34. Reported in James Ramey, "Experimental Family Forms—The Family of the Future," *Marriage and Family Review*, 1 (January/February 1978): 6.

35. Gordon Yaswen, "Sunrise Hill Community: Post Mortem," in Rosabeth Moss Kanter, *Communes: Creating and Managing the Collective Life*, New York, Harper & Row, Pub., 1973, pp. 465–466.

36. Bennett Berger, Bruce Hackett, and R. Mervyn Millar, "The Communal Family," in Marvin B. Sussman (ed.), *Sourcebook in Marriage and the Family*, Boston, Houghton Mifflin, 1974, p. 77.

37. Rosabeth Moss Kanter, *Commitment and Community: Communes and Utopias in Sociological Perspective*, Cambridge, Mass., Harvard University Press, 1972, p. 65.

38. See Thomas Shey, "Why Communes Fail: A Comparative Analysis of the Viability of Danish and American Communes," *Journal of Marriage and the Family*, 39 (August 1977): 605–613; William M. Kephart, *Extraordinary Groups: The Sociology of Unconventional Life-Styles*, New York, St. Martin's Press, 1976, pp. 283–304.

39. See Ruth Cavar, "Communes: Historical and Contemporary," *International Review of Modern Sociology*, Spring 1976, pp. 1–11.

SUGGESTED READINGS

Glick, Paul C., and Graham B. Spanier. "Married and Unmarried Cohabitation in the United States." *Journal of Marriage and the Family*, February 1980, pp. 19–30. A detailed discussion of the trends regarding unmarried cohabitation and the social and economic characteristics of cohabitants.

Libby, Roger W., and Robert N. Whitehurst (eds.). *Marriage and Alternatives: Exploring Intimate Relationships*. Glenview, Ill., Scott, Foresman, 1977. A collection of readings that examines both alternatives to marriage and the future of relationships.

Macklin, Eleanor D. "Nontraditional Family Forms: A Decade of Research." *Journal of Marriage and the Family*, November 1980, pp. 905–921. A review of the research on the major nontraditional family forms.

Newcomb, Paul R. "Cohabitation in America: An Assessment of Consequences." *Journal of Marriage and the Family*, August 1979, pp. 597–602. A survey of the consequences of cohabitation for never-married cohabiting couples, children of cohabitants, society, previously married cohabiting couples, and elderly cohabitants. Current legal trends are also discussed.

Ramey, James. "Experimental Family Forms—The Family of the Future." *Marriage and Family Review*, January/February 1978, pp. 1–9. An examination of the factors influencing alternative life styles and the types of experimental family forms.

APPENDIX: FAMILY ECONOMICS

CREATING A FAMILY BUDGET

A budget is a helpful means of analyzing where money is coming from and, more importantly, where it is going. In addition to allocating expenses on a regular basis, a budget can help an individual or a couple to assess their current financial position and to plan for a secure future.

Although there are guidelines to preparing any budget, each family must tailor its budget to its own income and life style. For example, the monthly budget of a childless couple who entertain a great deal will be very different from that of a couple who have young children and are saving to buy a house.

There are several steps involved in devising a spending plan. The five steps that follow are adapted from a guide prepared by the federal government.[1]

Step 1. Set Your Goals

Before setting up a budget, a couple must establish their short-term, intermediate, and long-term goals. Some examples include:

- *Short-term* (one month to one year): reduce debts; start saving for a better car; buy a new refrigerator.
- *Intermediate* (two to five years): begin a family; accumulate a down payment on a house; buy a new car.
- *Long-term* (five to ten years): save for children's college education and for retirement; pay off the house mortgage.

Financial goals usually change as a couple moves through the family life cycle. As goals set early in the marriage are accomplished, new ones arise. Also, goals may need to be redefined if a couple's financial circumstances change. For example, if one of the spouses loses a job or if a serious illness causes unanticipated medical expenses, some goals might need to be postponed.

Step 2. Estimate Your Income

The next step is to list the anticipated income for the planning period. (A planning period may be any length of time, but for most people it is practical to set up a budget on a monthly or yearly basis.) Monies counted as income include wages or salaries, commissions, interest from savings or dividends from stock, monetary gifts from family members, social security benefits, and pension payments. Because the budget subtracts expenses from spendable income, wage and salary income should be "take-home pay"—the amount you receive after taxes, social security payments, and medical and life insurance payments are deducted from your earnings.

Step 3. Estimate Your Expenses

Unless a family has kept financial records in the past, it may be necessary to keep track of actual expenditures for several months to determine expense categories. Most families can break down their expenses into three categories:

1. *Fixed Expenses* These are the unavoidable expenses that a couple has little or no ability to change. Fixed expenses include rent or mortgage payments, installment payments on automobiles, personal or educational loans, charge accounts, day-care expenses, and predictable household expenses such as gas, water, electricity, garbage collection, and telephone. Also included in this category are predictable expenses that occur only once or twice a year, such as premiums on home, life, medical, and automobile insurance; taxes on real estate and automobiles; personal taxes that have not been withheld; pledged contributions; physical and dental examinations; and membership dues.

2. *Flexible Expenses* These fluctuate from month to month and are subject to the greatest budgetary control. Flexible expenses include food, furnishings, housekeeping supplies, automobile maintenance, clothing, gifts, entertainment, unplanned medical bills and personal care products such as grooming aids. In addition, each member of the family should have a personal allowance, an allotted amount that each is free to spend as he or she chooses.

Initially, it is difficult to estimate flexible expenses. As a guideline, Table 1 illustrates selected household expenditures for families at three levels of income.

3. *Savings and Emergency Funds* Financial consultants suggest that a family include an expense category for medical and household

TABLE 1   Annual Family Budget of an Average Family[a] at Three Levels of Income (Autumn 1979)

Category	Lower Income		Intermediate Income		Higher Income	
Total Budget[b]	$12,585	100%	$20,517	100%	$30,317	100%
Total Family Consumption	10,234	81	15,353	75	21,069	69
Food	3,911	31	5,044	25	6,360	21
Housing	2,409	19	4,594	22	6,971	23
Transportation	1,004	8	1,851	9	2,411	8
Clothing	866	7	1,235	6	1,804	6
Personal Care	323	3	433	2	613	2
Medical Care	1,171	9	1,176	6	1,227	4
Other Family Consumption	550	4	1,021	5	1,684	6
Other Items	539	4	877	4	1,478	5
Social Security and Disability	781	6	1,256	6	1,413	5
Personal Income Taxes	1,032	8	3,031	15	6,357	21

Source: U.S. Department of Agriculture, *Family Economics Review*, Winter 1981, p.44.

[a]Average family is defined as an urban family of four consisting of a thirty-eight-year-old husband employed full time, a nonworking wife, a boy of thirteen, and a girl of eight.

[b]Because of rounding, sums of items may not equal totals.

emergencies. It is easy to fall into the trap of spending whatever income is available or saving only what happens to be left at the end of the month. Saving money should be a planned activity with specific financial goals rather than a haphazard occurrence.

Step 4. Set Up a Budget

The next step is to arrange income and expenses in a practical format. Table 2 shows a sample family budget. Families should add or delete categories according to their individual needs. Remember that a budget should be flexible and should be revised as family goals and income change.

Step 5. Balance Income and Expenses

The moment of truth comes when expenses are subtracted from income. If income matches expenses, there is no cause for alarm. If income exceeds expenses, the family can decide whether to purchase more goods or increase the amount it will plan to save. If expenses exceed income, the family must look carefully for ways to reduce expenditures.

TABLE 2 Sample Family Budget

Monthly Income

Take-home pay	$_____
Interest	_____
Dividends	_____
Social security benefits	_____
Other	_____
Total Income	$_____

Monthly Expenses

Fixed Expenses

Mortgage or rent	$_____
Loan payments	_____
Day care	_____
Utilities	
Gas	_____
Water	_____
Electricity	_____
Garbage	_____
Telephone	_____
Insurance premiums	
Home	_____
Life	_____
Medical	_____
Automobile	_____
Taxes	
Real estate	_____
Automobile	_____
Personal	_____
Savings	_____
Emergency fund	_____
Other	_____
	_____
Total Fixed Expenses	$_____

Total Income − Total Fixed Expenses =
Amount Available for Flexible Expenses $_____

Flexible expenses are the easiest to reduce. If cuts in entertainment and personal care items are not sufficient, the couple can consider ways to reduce automobile expenses. Many couples go into debt to meet their current expenses, but this only increases their fixed expenses when they begin making loan payments. The use of credit can escalate until all available income is going to pay debts and there is not enough

TABLE 2   (cont.)

Flexible Expenses

    Food $_____

    Household expenses   _____

    Clothing   _____

    Car maintenance   _____

    Medical expenses   _____

    Personal care   _____

    Entertainment   _____

    Personal allowances   _____

    Other   _____

                                                _____

Total Flexible Expenses $_____

Amount Available for Flexible Expenses
    − Total Flexible Expenses
        = *Balance** $_____

*If the balance is greater than zero, money is available for extra saving or spending. If the balance is less than zero, the family is spending more than their monthly income.

money to meet day-to-day expenses. The advantages and disadvantages of credit are discussed in Chapter 10, "Marital Interaction," and in the section that follows.

USING CREDIT WISELY

The use of credit—paying in the future in order to buy or borrow in the present—has become a way of life for most Americans. It makes sense to use credit to obtain things when it is inconvenient to pay cash, when a special sale is going on and cash is unavailable, or when an emergency arises that cannot be covered by savings or an emergency fund. Breaking down the cost of major purchases such as furniture, appliances, a car, or a house into manageable monthly installments is another sound reason for using credit. Financial problems may result, however, if a family uses credit impulsively, does not maintain cash reserves, or accumulates debt to the point where the family is borrowing money to meet current living expenses.

Because credit costs money in the form of interest charges, a family should carefully evaluate every credit purchase to determine if having the item now is worth paying additional money rather than waiting until cash can be paid. Using credit wisely means being an informed consumer and requires investigating various lending sources to compare credit terms.

Applying for Credit

Different lenders have different criteria for establishing whether an individual is a good credit risk. Being a good credit risk generally means having the ability to repay charges or loans, an ability summarized by the "three Cs" of credit—capacity, character, and collateral.

1. *Capacity*   Can the person repay the debt? Capacity is judged on employment information: occupation, length of employment, and earnings. Creditors are also interested in the person's expenses and the number of dependents he or she has.

2. *Character*   Will the person repay the debt? Creditors look at the credit history to see how much the person owes, how often he or she borrows money, whether bills are paid consistently and promptly, and whether the person lives within his or her means. They may also look for signs of stability—length of time lived at the current address and whether the person owns or rents.

3. *Collateral*   Is the creditor protected if the debt is not repaid? Creditors want to know what assets—savings, life insurance, stocks, or real estate—could cover the debt if it is not repaid.[2]

Creditors use various combinations of these factors to determine whether to grant credit, and different creditors may reach different conclusions based on the same information. If your request for credit is denied, you have the legal right to know the specific reasons why. Agencies that collect credit information sometimes make mistakes, and some lenders may illegally deny credit because of sex, race, or marital status.

Many people find that their initial applications for credit are refused, and at times it seems that an individual must already have credit in order to get credit. The Federal Reserve System offers several suggestions for building up a good credit record.

1. Open a checking account or a savings account, or both. These do not begin your credit file, but may be checked as evidence that you

have money and know how to manage it. Canceled checks can be used to show you pay utilities or rent bills regularly, a sign of stability.

2. Apply for a department store credit card. Repaying credit card bills on time is a plus in credit histories.

3. If you're new in town, write for a summary of any record kept by a credit bureau in your former town. (Ask the bank or department store in your old home town for the name of the agency it reports to.)

4. If you don't qualify on the basis of your own credit standing, suggest to the creditor that someone might co-sign your application.

5. If you're turned down, find out why and try to clear up any misunderstandings.[3]

Types of Credit

The three most common types of credit are credit cards, installment buying, and loans. Costs vary among the three, and each has advantages and disadvantages.

Credit Cards

Credit cards allow individuals to charge a wide variety of goods and services, and then (depending on the particular card) to pay the amount owed either once a month or over an extended period. If a partial payment is made at the end of each month, the remainder is treated as a loan and is subject to a finance charge (interest charged on the unpaid balance). There are three broad categories of credit cards.

1. Single-purpose cards are issued by a variety of businesses, including oil companies, motel chains, department stores, and car-rental agencies. Companies issue this type of card to encourage consumers to purchase their goods and services. There are no annual fees, the customer is billed once a month, and any unpaid balance is subject to a finance charge.

2. Travel and entertainment cards include American Express, Carte Blanche, and Diners Club cards, and are often used by business people to charge travel and entertainment expenses. Annual fees of $30–$40 are charged, there is generally no spending limit, and the total monthly bill is due on receipt. Interest is added if the account is delinquent, and credit privileges may be canceled if bills are not paid on time.

3. Bank credit cards are probably the most familiar type; Visa and MasterCard are the best known. Until recently bank cards, like single-purpose cards, were issued free. Now in many states annual fees

of $10–$20 are charged. These cards also have monthly billing cycles, and finance charges are applied to any unpaid balance.

Credit cards are a convenient way of purchasing goods and services, particularly by mail or phone, then paying a variety of expenses with one check at the end of the month. They also give the individual who purchases an item on the first of the month up to twenty-five interest-free days before payment is due. The convenience of credit cards, however, is probably their major disadvantage because they make spending so easy. They increase the possibility of impulse purchasing and overbuying.

Installment Buying Consumers are constantly assailed by the message "Buy now, pay later." Installment buying often is used when making major purchases such as furniture, appliances, or an automobile. After a down payment is made, the balance (which includes finance charges and possibly service and insurance charges) is paid in monthly installments on a contract ranging from a few months up to five years. The consumer gets possession of the item, but the seller retains legal ownership until the last payment is made. In addition, the seller often requires the consumer to sign a contract that gives the seller the right to repossess the item if payments are not made.

Finance charges vary considerably and, as with any type of credit, the contract should be read carefully. Because buying credit from the dealer selling the item is almost always higher than other sources of financing, it is usually cheaper to borrow the money elsewhere and pay cash for the purchase.

Loans Cash loans are usually obtained from lending institutions that compete on the basis of price, convenience, and service. The cost of borrowing money will vary with "the supply of money available to the lender, the size and purpose of your loan, your credit standing, the collateral you can offer as security, and the amount of risk taken by the lender."[4] Interest and service charges vary widely, so it pays to shop wisely for a loan. The most common sources of cash loans are discussed below.

1. *Borrow from Yourself* Probably the cheapest way to borrow money is from yourself. A savings account or life insurance policy can be used as collateral for a loan. The interest charges on a loan against a savings account will be offset by the interest on the account, making the loan very cheap. Interest rates on the cash-surrender value of a life

insurance policy (the dollar amount received if the policy is canceled) are also relatively inexpensive.

2. *Credit Unions*   Credit unions (organizations consisting of individuals who work at the same company or belong to the same union) are a very attractive source of money for their members. Because they have low operating costs, their interest rates are more favorable than those offered by banks.

3. *Bank Loans*   If you meet a bank's credit requirements, you may qualify for a personal bank loan. Banks generally offer both secured and unsecured loans. An unsecured loan—a loan based on your signature alone—may be more difficult to obtain and is more expensive than a secured loan, which requires the borrower to put up collateral.

4. *Credit Card Cash Advance*   A bank credit card is a quick and convenient means of obtaining cash. It is also relatively expensive. Because banks aggressively promote the use of their cards for cash advances and because it is so easy to borrow against an established line of credit, people often don't realize that the interest charges may be higher than the charges on a bank loan.

5. *Second Mortgage*   Taking out another mortgage (borrowing against the equity of your home) is another means of obtaining a cash loan. Repayment is made over a number of years, and it is a relatively quick way to borrow funds. As with any loan, the consumer should carefully consider the finance charges and, more importantly, the risk of having the mortgage foreclosed if payments are not made.

6. *Finance or Small Loan Companies*   These companies lend mainly to individuals who do not have established credit or who are bad credit risks. Consequently, small loan companies charge higher interest rates than many other lending sources.

7. *Pawnbrokers*   Pawnbrokers lend money against an item of value that is left with them as security. This is an extremely expensive way to borrow money, and an individual is able to borrow only a fraction of what the pawned item is worth. If payments are not made, the borrower risks losing an item of great financial or sentimental value. Pawnbrokers should be used only as a last resort.

8. *Loan Sharks*   Loan sharks are definitely at the bottom of any list of lenders. They are illegal lenders who charge whatever the market will bear and obviously cater to desperate people. Interest rates are exorbitant, and loan sharks threaten punishment if payments are not made promptly.

The Costs of Borrowing Money

The 1968 Truth-in-Lending Act requires lenders to give basic information about the cost of buying on credit. The creditor must tell the consumer the finance charge and the annual percentage rate, and both of these must be given in writing before any agreement is signed. The *finance charge* is the total dollar amount charged for credit. This includes interest costs and may include service or insurance premium charges. The *annual percentage rate (APR)* is the charge for credit stated as a percentage. This is the rate you should use to compare borrowing costs.

The lowest annual percentage rate is usually the best credit buy, but taking additional time to pay back a loan will increase the finance charge. Consider the following three credit arrangements for borrowing $4,000:[5]

	APR	Length of Loan	Monthly Payment	Total Finance Charge	Total Cost
Creditor 1	11%	3 years	$131	$ 716	$4,716
Creditor 2	11	4 years	103.50	968	4,968
Creditor 3	12	4 years	105.50	1,064	5,064

In these examples the lowest finance charge is available from Creditor 1. Extending the length of the loan by one year increases the finance charge by $252. But if lower monthly payments are more important than a higher total cost, Creditor 2's terms may be more attractive (a monthly payment of $103.50 instead of $131). If Creditor 3 were the only loan source, finance charges would be increased by $96 for the seemingly small addition of 1 percent in the annual percentage rate. Tables that calculate various interest rates can be found in government publications and books on personal finance or obtained from lending agencies.

Credit Rights of Women

The 1975 Equal Credit Opportunity Act prohibits financial discrimination on the basis of sex or marital status. Until this act was passed, women frequently were required to reapply for credit under their husband's name when they married. The credit history was reported in the husband's name, so if a woman became divorced or widowed, she had no credit history of her own and usually found it difficult, if not impossible, to establish credit.

The 1975 Act requires that reports to credit bureaus be made in both spouses' names if both are responsible for repaying the debt. In addition, a creditor cannot require a woman to reapply for credit if her marital status changes unless there is some indication that she is unwilling or unable to pay.

BUYING LIFE INSURANCE

The main purpose of life insurance is to provide financial protection for dependents in the event of a breadwinner's death. It creates an "instant estate" for the family, partially compensating for the loss of the breadwinner's earnings.

Many consumers find life insurance confusing, and because the life insurance industry is highly competitive, salespeople often push complex, highly expensive policies. As a result, instead of *buying* insurance most people are *sold* insurance, and many people do not have adequate life insurance protection or are paying more than is necessary for the amount of protection they have. Informed consumers should first determine the amount of protection they require, then shop around for the lowest cost. If both spouses work, they should both be insured.[6]

There are two basic kinds of life insurance policies, term and straight life.

Term insurance policies provide insurance protection only and are the least expensive. The buyer pays premiums (the monthly or yearly cost of a policy) for protection for a specific term (usually five years), and the insurance company pays the face value of the policy when the policyholder dies. When the term expires, the policy must be renewed with a higher premium to reflect the policyholder's greater probability of death. A term insurance policy has no cash or loan value, and no refund is given if the policy is canceled. However, for a young family with limited funds it is usually the best form of life insurance. Yet because the salesperson's commission on term insurance is much less than the commission on straight life, salespeople almost always try to persuade the consumer to buy straight life.

A disadvantage of term insurance is that policies are usually canceled at age sixty-five and then are nonrenewable. However, for most families, insurance is much more important during the breadwinner's working years than after retirement.

Straight life policies (also called ordinary, whole life, or cash-value) also pay a predetermined amount of money when the policyholder dies. Insurance protection exists for the holder's entire lifetime, and the premium generally remains the same because it is an average of the cost of the insurance over the lifetime. In addition, the policy accumulates a cash value that can be borrowed against or collected if the policy is terminated. Although this type of policy appears to be very attractive, its premiums are much more expensive than term insurance premiums, and the difference in cost between the two can be invested more profitably elsewhere. In fact, for people who have the discipline to save, purchasing a term policy and saving the difference in premium costs is an economic way to have adequate life insurance protection and cash savings. As cash savings accumulate the amount of term insurance can gradually be reduced, and in the long run this provides protection as great as or greater than straight life insurance.

NOTES

1. U.S. Department of Agriculture, *A Guide to Budgeting for the Young Couple*, Washington, D.C., U.S. Government Printing Office, Home and Garden Bulletin No. 98, July 1977, pp. 4–10.
2. Board of Governors of the Federal Reserve System, *Consumer Handbook to Credit Protection Laws*, Washington, D.C., U.S. Government Printing Office, June 1980, pp. 10–11.
3. Ibid., p. 18.
4. Mildred Novotny, *Use Credit Wisely*, Berkeley, Calif., University of California Agricultural Extension Service, Pamphlet No. 2844, September 1966, p. 6.
5. *Consumer Handbook to Credit Protection Laws*, p. 5.
6. For an excellent discussion on how to buy life insurance, see "Life Insurance: A Special Two-Part Report," *Consumer Reports*, Part 1, February 1980, pp. 79–106, and Part 2, March 1980, pp. 163–188.

SUGGESTED READINGS

Board of Governors of the Federal Reserve System. *Consumer Handbook to Credit Protection Laws*. Washington, D.C., U.S. Government Printing Office, June 1980. An excellent guide to shopping and applying for credit, maintaining a good credit standing, consumer rights, and correcting credit mistakes.

Consumer Reports. "Life Insurance: A Special Two-Part Report." Part 1, February 1980, pp. 79–106, and Part 2, March 1980, pp. 163–188. An extensive report on how to buy life insurance. It includes a worksheet that helps you calculate how much coverage you need.

Porter, Sylvia. *Sylvia Porter's New Money Book for the 80's*. New York, Doubleday, 1979. A comprehensive resource book on personal finance.

U.S. Department of Agriculture. *A Guide to Budgeting for the Young Couple*. Washington, D.C., U.S. Government Printing Office, Home and Garden Bulletin No. 98, July 1977, pp. 4–10. A helpful booklet on budgeting and money management.

GLOSSARY

Abortion. The medical termination of a pregnancy.

Adultery. Sexual relations between a married person and a partner other than his or her spouse.

Affinity. A relationship that exists through marriage. Approximately half of the United States have affinity restrictions, which prohibit marriage between stepparents and stepchildren, a woman and her husband's father or grandfather, and so on.

Afterbirth. The placenta, which is expelled from the uterus after a baby is born.

Ageism. Discrimination against older people solely because of their age.

Aggression. Forceful behavior with the intent to control another.

Alimony. Support money paid to a former spouse by the other spouse during legal proceedings or after a legal separation or a divorce.

Amenorrhea. The cessation of menstrual periods.

Amniocentesis. The examination of fetal cells to determine whether the fetus is normal or has a birth defect.

Androgynous role behavior. Role behavior that is a mixture of traditional male and female role expectations, rather than an expression of only one sex role.

Annulment. The legal decree that declares a marriage invalid.

Aphrodisiacs. Substances reputed to increase sexual desire.

Artificial insemination. The introduction by a doctor of a man's sperm into a woman's vagina or uterus in order for her to conceive a child.

Attachment-oriented dating. Dating with the intention of assessing another's suitability as a romantic partner.

Being love (B-love). Love given freely without expecting one's partner to fulfill all of one's basic needs.

Bigamy. The criminal offense of being married to two people at the same time.

Body language. The sending and receiving of interpersonal communication by means of gestures and body movements.

Bonding. The deep psychological attachment between a mother and her infant.

Braxton-Hicks contractions. Irregularly spaced uterine contractions that occur near the end of pregnancy.

Chancre. A painless sore that is the first sign of a syphilis infection.

Child abuse. The physical and emotional injury of a child by his or her parents, or by other adults.

Circumcision. The surgical removal of the foreskin of the penis.

Clitoral hood. The fold of skin covering the clitoris.

Clitoris. The sexually sensitive organ located just above a woman's vaginal opening.

Cohabitation. An unmarried couple living together in a sexual relationship.

Coitus interruptus. The withdrawal method of birth control, which requires that the man withdraw his penis from the vagina immediately before ejaculation.

Colostrum. The yellowish, nutrient-rich fluid expressed from a mother's breasts in the first few days after childbirth.

Commitment. The intent to devote time and energy to maintaining an intimate relationship.

Common-law marriage. A legal form of marriage based on mutual consent with no written documentation or license required.

Commune. A group of individuals (some or all of whom are unrelated) who live together and usually share resources, work, expenses, and ideology.

Communication. The exchange of meaningful information.

Companionate love. A deeply felt, calm, usually richly satisfying kind of adult love.

Complementary-needs theory. A theory of mate selection according to which persons choose partners who complement their personalities.

Condom. A contraceptive that covers the penis to prevent sperm from entering the vagina.

Conjugal. Referring to the husband-wife unit.

Consanguine. Related by blood; biologically related.

Consanguinity laws. Laws prohibiting marriage between close relatives.

Cunnilingus. Oral stimulation of the female genitals.

Dating anxiety. The fear of being rejected when asking for a date or going on a date.

Dating differential. The tendency to date persons of differing status, intelligence, or achievement.

Deficiency love (D-love). Love based on the desire to have a partner fulfill one's basic human needs.

Desertion. The physical abandonment of one's spouse.

Diaphragm. A contraceptive device that is placed in the vagina before intercourse.

Divorce mediation. The process of reaching a mutually agreeable divorce settlement using an impartial third party to help with negotiations.

Dual-career marriage. A marriage in which both spouses actively pursue careers.

Dyad. A two-person unit that has both its own qualities and those of the two persons.

Dyspareunia. Painful sexual intercourse.

Empathy. Feeling what another feels by placing oneself in the other's frame of reference.

Endogamy. Marrying within one's own race, religion, or nationality.

Endometrium. The inner lining of the uterus.

Episiotomy. The surgical procedure performed during childbirth to enlarge the vaginal opening.

Estrogen. A female hormone produced in the ovaries.

Exogamy. Marrying outside one's own race, religion, or nationality.

Extended family. The family unit consisting of a nuclear family and other kin relations. Also called a consanguine family.

Fallopian tubes. The pair of ducts in a woman's abdominal cavity that transport eggs from the ovaries to the uterus and that are usually where fertilization takes place.

Family of origin. The nuclear family into which one is born. Also called a family of orientation.

Family of procreation. The nuclear family formed by an individual when he or she marries and has children.

Family work. Household duties. Used instead of the term *housework* to emphasize that it is real work and that all family members can perform it.

Fellatio. Oral stimulation of the male genitals.

Fertilization. The fusion of a father's sperm and a mother's egg to form the first cell of their child's body.

Foreskin. The fold of skin covering the end of the penis.

Fornication. The legal term for premarital sexual intercourse.

Fraternal twins. Twins produced by the fertilization of two eggs by two sperm. Also called dizygotic (DZ) twins.

Gender identity. The awareness of being either a female or a male.

Genes. Hereditary factors that are passed from parents to their children.

Glans. The sensitive tip of either the penis or the clitoris.

Gonorrhea. A type of sexually transmitted disease.

Gretna Green. A term used to describe communities that do not require either blood tests or a waiting period between the application and issuance of a marriage license.

Group marriage. The marriage of two or more women to two or more men.

Herpes. The infection of the genitals caused by the virus *Herpes simplex*.

Heterogamy. The tendency to be attracted to and marry someone with differing social and personality traits.

Homogamy. The tendency to be attracted to and marry someone with similar social and personality characteristics.

Human chorionic gonadotropin. A hormone that appears in a pregnant woman's body.

Identical twins. Twins produced when, early in pregnancy, a fertilized egg splits in two. Also called monozygotic (MZ) twins.

Impotence. The inability of a man to get or maintain an erection.

Incest taboo. The prohibition against sex relations and marriage between close relatives.

Infatuation. A term describing intensely romantic feelings which, in hindsight, are considered less than "true love."

Infertility. The inability to have children.

Inhibited sexual desire. Loss of interest in sexual relations.

Interdependence. The intertwining of two people's lives and experiences.

Intimacy. Feelings of closeness, positive regard, warmth, and familiarity with another's innermost thoughts and feelings.

Intrauterine device (IUD). A small plastic contraceptive device that is placed inside the uterus.

Intrinsic marriage. A kind of marriage based on emotional intensity and close sharing. Two forms are vital marriage and total marriage.

In vitro **fertilization.** The fertilization of eggs in a laboratory dish.

Jealousy. Feelings of anger and anxiety arising from the fear that one may no longer receive love from an intimate partner.

Joint custody. The child custody arrangement that awards both parents equal legal rights and responsibilities for the care of their children.

Labia majora. The larger, outer pair of fleshy folds surrounding a woman's vagina.

Labia minora. The smaller, inner pair of fleshy folds surrounding the opening of a woman's vagina.

Labor. The process of childbirth.

Limited divorce. A type of divorce granted in the past by the Roman Catholic church that permitted partners to live apart, but not to remarry; a divorce from bed and board.

Literal communication. The actual, word-for-word meaning of a message.

Loneliness. Feelings of desperation and emptiness resulting from the absence of intimacy.

Marriage contract. A civil contract which is regulated by each state and which specifies the legal duties and responsibilities of marriage.

Menstrual cycle. A woman's near-monthly cycle of egg production and menstruation.

Menstruation. The periodic loss of tissue and a small amount of blood from a woman's uterus.

Metacommunication. A communication that conveys information about the quality of the relationship between those communicating.

Miscegenation. Marriage between members of different races; interracial marriage.

Monogamy. The marriage of one husband and one wife.

Mons. The small mound of soft tissue on which a woman's pubic hair grows.

Morning-after pill. A drug taken within one day after intercourse which interrupts the first stages of pregnancy.

No-fault divorce. A divorce granted on grounds of marital breakdown and irreconcilable differences.

Nuclear family. The unit consisting of a husband, wife, and their offspring. Also called a conjugal family.

Orgasm. The pleasurable release of sexual tensions.

Ovaries. The pair of female reproductive organs that produce eggs and sex hormones.

Ovulation. The release of an egg from a woman's ovary.

Passionate love. Emotionally intense, affectional feelings often accompanied by the desire for physical closeness and sexual contact.

Penis. The male organ of copulation.

Placenta. A special organ that forms in the uterus during pregnancy in order to transport nutrients and other materials from the mother to the developing child.

Polyandry. The marriage of one wife and two or more husbands.

Polygamy. Multiple-spouse marriage (see polygyny and polyandry).

Polygyny. The marriage of one husband and two or more wives.

Premarital sex. In general usage, sexual relations between unmarried individuals.

Progesterone. A female hormone produced by the ovaries.

Propinquity. Nearness in place, or proximity.

Puerperium. The period of recovery after childbirth.

Recreational dating. Dating to enjoy another's company with no implied romantic commitments.

Refractory period. The period of time after ejaculation or orgasm during which an individual cannot be sexually aroused.

Rhythm method. A method of birth control in which the couple has sexual intercourse only when an egg is unlikely to be available for fertilization.

Role. A set of social expectations that are appropriate for a given position or status.

Safe house. A residential facility for battered women and their children.

Scrotum. The flesh-covered sac containing the male testes.

Self-disclosure. The sharing of deeply held personal information.

Semen. The milky fluid emitted from the penis at ejaculation.

Serial polygamy. The practice of marrying, divorcing, and marrying again.

Sex typing. The labeling of a child as either a male or a female.

Sexually transmitted disease (STD). Infections or infestations transmitted from person to person primarily by sexual contact.

Sexual response cycle. A general description of the four-phase response to sexual stimulation.

Sperm ducts. A series of connected tubes that form the exit pathway for sperm cells produced in a man's testes.

Spermicidal cream. A sperm-killing contraceptive cream that can be used alone or with a diaphragm.

Statutory rape. Sexual relations with a person defined by state law as "under age."

Sterility. The condition of being permanently infertile.

Stimulus-value-role (SVR) theory. A mate-selection theory having three stages—stimulus stage (attraction), value-comparison stage, and role-comparison stage.

Testes. The pair of male reproductive organs producing sperm and sex hormones.

Tubal ligation. A method of birth control in which a woman's Fallopian tubes are cut and tied, causing the woman to be sterile.

Two-component theory of emotion. The hypothesis that emotions are the product of physiological arousal and that the aroused state can be labeled as a particular emotion.

Uterus. The pear-shaped organ in females in which a fetus develops.

Urethra. The tube through which urine is excreted from the body.

Urethritis. An irritation or infection of the urethra.

Utilitarian marriage. A kind of marriage based on similar interests and friendship rather than on deep emotional commitment. Three forms are conflict-habituated marriage, devitalized marriage, and passive-congenial marriage.

Vagina. The tube connecting a woman's uterus to the outside of her body.

Vas deferens. The male sperm duct.

Vasectomy. A method of male contraception in which each vas deferens is surgically severed, causing the man to be sterile.

Venereal disease. See "sexually transmitted disease."

Void marriage. A marriage that is never considered legally valid.

Voidable marriage. A marriage involving fraud or misrepresentation that can be canceled by a court decree.

Vulva. The lower part of a woman's pelvis where the external genitalia are located.

Wife battering. The psychological or physical abuse of a wife by her husband.

Withdrawal method. See "coitus interruptus."

Brotherly love, 35
Budget, 250–251, 475–479
Business travel, 220, 226
Calendar rhythm, 311
Capacity, 480
Capilano Canyon experiment, 41–42
Career responsibilities, 219–221
Catholics, 92–94, 137, 188, 367, 368
Cervix, 158, 278
Chancre, 179
Character, 480
Child abuse, 190, 254, 257–259
Childbirth, 178, 278–281, 292
  fetus during, 278–279
  postpartum depression, 285
  postpartum recovery, 284–285, 292
  preparation courses, 277–278
  see also Pregnancy
Child care
  and changing status of women, 393, 411–413
  in communes, 467
  division of, 214–218, 221–222, 339–342, 353
  by grandparents, 427
  marriage contract and, 190, 195–199, 205
  public day-care centers, 19, 219, 221–222, 411–413
  in single-parent families, 453–456, 469
  tasks of, 346–354
  in two-worker families, 220, 224–226, 339–342
Child-centered parenthood, 343–344, 353
Child labor, 11
Childless family, 8, 252, 291, 292, 345, 446
Children
  conflicts regarding, 252, 259
  cost of, 300–303, 328
  effect of environment on development of, 348–349, 352, 354

effect on parents, 344–346, 354
effects of divorce on, 378–381
effects of two-worker families on, 224–225, 339–342
family life cycle and, 240–243
legitimacy of, 190
older parents and, 426–440
out-of-wedlock, 5, 290, 464
reasons for wanting, 266–267, 335, 353
socialization of, 10, 13–14, 18–19, 22, 349–354
unwanted, 310
Child support, 377–378, 454
Christianity, 188, 368–369
Circumcision, 161–162
Civil Rights Act of 1964, 407, 408
Clap, *see* Gonorrhea
Climax, *see* Orgasm
Clitoral hood, 159
Clitoris, 159, 163, 164, 169, 180
Closed field, 111
"Code of the West," 16
Coeducation, 404
Cohabitation, 4–5, 8, 22, 446–448, 457–464
  and commitment, 463
  following divorce, 462
  legal rights, 198–200
Coitus
  frequency, 140, 150
  positions, 165
Coitus interruptus, 310–311
Colic, 283
Collateral, 480
Collusion, 370–371
Colostrum, 281–282
Commitment
  cohabitation and, 463
  establishment of, 57–59, 68–70, 73
  within marriage, 84, 188, 205

necessity of, for communes, 468
  within same-sex relationships, 147–148
  sex differences, 46
Common-law marriage, 202–203
Communes, 8, 19, 446, 464–470
  and religion, 465–467
Communication
  individual marriage contracts for, 197–200
  in intimate relationships, 59–62, 73, 84, 248–249, 253–254
  nonverbal, 60–62, 73, 169
  problems of, 243–247, 259
  sexual, 129, 156, 169–173, 180, 248–249, 328
Companionate love, 38–39, 47
Companionship
  family function, 10, 17–18, 22
  motivation for marriage, 84, 97, 205
  in utilitarian marriage, 237, 238
Competition, 116–118
Competitiveness, 399–400, 410
Complementary needs theory of mate selection, 105–107, 110–111, 122
Compulsive spending, 250
Computer dating service, 121
Condom, 318–319, 322–323, 325, 328–329
Condonation, 371–372
Conflict, 236–237, 243–254
Conflict-habituated marriage, 236
Conformity, 84, 97
Conjugal family, 6–7, 8
Connivance, 371
Consanguine family, 7–8
Consanguinity laws, 192–193
Contraception
  communications about, 170–171, 180, 328
  condom, 318–319, 322–323, 325, 328–329

Truth-in-Lending Act of 1968, 484
Tubal ligation, 319–320, 328
Twins, 287–289, 292
Two-component theory of emotion, 40–43
Two-worker families, 214–216, 218–226

Understanding, 57, 72–73
Unhappiness, within marriage, 233–235
Unmarried couples, 446–448, 457–464. *See also* Cohabitation
Unselfish love, 41
Urethra, 159–160
Urethritis, 160
Urination, 272
Uterus, 157–158, 180
    menstruation and, 267–268, 270–272
    nursing and, 284
    during pregnancy, 270–272, 274–276, 292
Utilitarian marriage, 235–238, 258

Vacuum curetage, 324
Vagina, 157–160, 169, 180
    lubrication of, 158, 164, 173, 174
    pregnancy and, 269
Vaginal foam and cream, 318–319, 322–329
Value(s)
    and acceptance of interfaith marriage, 93
    and acceptance of interracial marriage, 11, 90–91

and acceptance of premarital sex, 135
changes in, 4, 15, 19–22
definition, 108
Value comparison stage, 113, 122
Value consensus theory of mate selection, 108–109, 110–111, 122
Vas deferens, 320
Vasectomy, 287, 320–322, 326, 328
Venereal disease, 131, 175–180, 194. *See also* Disease, sexually transmitted
Verbal ability, 397
Videodating, 121
Violence, 254–259
Vital marriage, 239
Voidable marriages, 192
Void marriages, 192
Vomiting, during pregnancy, 272
Vulva, 159

Waiting period, 195
Weaning, 284
Wedding ceremony, 188, 195, 203–204, 206
Weight gain, 274–275
Widowhood, 131–132, 384, 423, 436–441, 453
    cohabitation following, 462
    credit and, 484–485
Wife battering, 190, 254–257, 259
Withdrawal, *see* Contraception
Women
    battered, 190, 254–257, 259
    credit rights, 484–485
    divorce, and status of, 4, 20, 368, 377, 384

    education, 393–394, 405–406
    employment, 394–395, 401–403, 407
    life choices, 305–307
    love behavior, 45–46
    name, 200–201, 212
    orgasmic experience, 166–167, 169
    property rights, 393–394
    role, 11, 195–196, 221, 337–339, 350–354
    self-disclosure, 68
    sexual anatomy, 157–160, 180
    status of, 20, 116, 247, 390–413
    working, 392–396, 401–407, 412–413, 452
Women's resource centers, 255
Women's rights movement, 119, 393–409, 411, 412
Work
    and single parenthood, 454–456
    by women, 392–396, 401–407, 412–413
Working wives, 214–216, 218–226, 245, 247
    and equal rights movement, 411, 413
    and family planning, 301, 305–307

X-rays, 275

You-messages, 245

Zoar, 465